Research and Practice in Applied Linguistics

General Editors: Christopher N. Candlin and David R. Hall, Linguistics Department, Macquarie University, Australia.

All books in this series are written by leading researchers and teachers in Applied Linguistics, with broad international experience. They are designed for the MA or PhD student in Applied Linguistics, TESOL or similar subject areas and for the language professional keen to extend their research experience.

Titles include:

Dick Allwright and Judith Hanks
THE DEVELOPING LANGUAGE LEARNER
An Introduction to Exploratory Practice

Francesca Bargiela-Chiappini, Catherine Nickerson and Brigitte Planken
BUSINESS DISCOURSE

Christopher N. Candlin and Stephen H. Moore
EXPLORING DISCOURSE IN CONTEXT AND ACTION

Francesca Bargiela-Chiappini, Catherine Nickerson and Brigitte Planken
BUSINESS DISCOURSE, SECOND EDITION

Alison Ferguson and Elizabeth Armstrong
RESEARCHING COMMUNICATION DISORDERS

Lynne Flowerdew
CORPORA AND LANGUAGE EDUCATION

Sandra Beatriz Hale
COMMUNITY INTERPRETING

Geoff Hall
LITERATURE IN LANGUAGE EDUCATION

Richard Kiely and Pauline Rea-Dickins
PROGRAM EVALUATION IN LANGUAGE EDUCATION

Marie-Noëlle Lamy and Regine Hampel
ONLINE COMMUNICATION IN LANGUAGE LEARNING AND TEACHING

Annamaria Pinter
CHILDREN LEARNING SECOND LANGUAGES

Virginia Samuda and Martin Bygate
TASKS IN SECOND LANGUAGE LEARNING

Norbert Schmitt
RESEARCHING VOCABULARY
A Vocabulary Research Manual

Helen Spencer-Oatey and Peter Franklin
INTERCULTURAL INTERACTION
A Multidisciplinary Approach to Intercultural Communication

Cyril J. Weir
LANGUAGE TESTING AND VALIDATION

Tony Wright
CLASSROOM MANAGEMENT IN LANGUAGE EDUCATION

Forthcoming titles:

Anne Burns and Helen de Silva Joyce
LITERACY

Sandra Gollin and David R. Hall
LANGUAGE FOR SPECIFIC PURPOSES

David Cassels Johnson
LANGUAGE POLICY

Marilyn Martin-Jones
BILINGUALISM

Martha Pennington
PRONUNCIATION

Research and Practice in Applied Linguistics
Series Standing Order ISBN 978–1–403–91184–1 hardcover
978–1–403–91185–8 paperback
(*outside North America only*)

You can receive future titles in this series as they are published by placing a standing order. Please contact your bookseller or, in case of difficulty, write to us at the address below with your name and address, the title of the series and the ISBN quoted above.

Customer Services Department, Macmillan Distribution Ltd, Houndmills, Basingstoke, Hampshire RG21 6XS, England

Also by Francesca Bargiela-Chiappini

ASIAN BUSINESS DISCOURSE(S) (*co-editor with Maurizio Gotti*)

FACE, COMMUNICATION AND SOCIAL INTERACTION (*co-editor with Michael Haugh*)

THE HANDBOOK OF BUSINESS DISCOURSE (*editor*)

LANGUAGES OF BUSINESS: AN INTERNATIONAL PERSPECTIVE
(*co-editor with Sandra Harris*)

MANAGING LANGUAGE: THE DISCOURSE OF CORPORATE MEETINGS
(*with Sandra Harris*)

POLITENESS ACROSS CULTURES (*co-editor with Dániel Z. Kádár*)

WRITING BUSINESS: GENRES, MEDIA AND DISCOURSES
(*co-editor with Catherine Nickerson*)

Business Discourse

2nd Edition

Francesca Bargiela-Chiappini
University of Warwick, UK

Catherine Nickerson
Zayed University, UAE

and

Brigitte Planken
Radboud University, Nijmegen, The Netherlands

First published 2007
Second edition published 2013 by
PALGRAVE MACMILLAN

Palgrave Macmillan in the UK is an imprint of Macmillan Publishers Limited, registered in England, company number 785998, of Houndmills, Basingstoke, Hampshire RG21 6XS.

Palgrave Macmillan in the US is a division of St Martin's Press LLC, 175 Fifth Avenue, New York, NY 10010.

Palgrave Macmillan is the global academic imprint of the above companies and has companies and representatives throughout the world.

Palgrave® and Macmillan® are registered trademarks in the United States, the United Kingdom, Europe and other countries.

ISBN 978–1–137–02491–6   hardback
ISBN 978–1–137–02492–3   paperback

This book is printed on paper suitable for recycling and made from fully managed and sustained forest sources. Logging, pulping and manufacturing processes are expected to conform to the environmental regulations of the country of origin.

A catalogue record for this book is available from the British Library.

A catalog record for this book is available from the Library of Congress.

Typeset by MPS Limited, Chennai, India.

Contents

List of Tables and Figure   xiv

General Editors' Preface   xv

Acknowledgements   xvi

Part I   The Field of Business Discourse
1   What is Business Discourse?   3
   1.1 What is business discourse?   3
   1.2 A short history of business discourse   5
     Profile: Mirjaliisa Charles   9
   1.3 The hallmarks of business discourse research   13
     Types of data   14
     The link between data and methodology:
       multimethod research   17
     Research purpose: description and prescription   18
     English versus other business languages   19
     The importance of the organizational context   21
   1.4 Different approaches to business discourse research   24
     Discourse and power   24
     Profile: Karen Lee Ashcraft   26
     Critical approaches and business discourse 27
     Intercultural business discourse   30
   1.5 Business discourse around the world   32
     Profile: Gina Poncini   34
     Profile: Janet Holmes   36
     Profile: Sharon Livesey   40
     Profile: Winnie Cheng   40
     Profile: Judith Baxter   42
   1.6 Summary   43
     Further reading   43
     Chapter 1 Tasks   44

2   Challenges in the Future   45
   2.1 Towards transculturality   45
     Rapport management   49
   2.2 Media, technology and business discourse   58
     Multimodality   59

Hypermodality   62
Multimodality for business discourse   68
2.3 From multimethod research to multidisciplinarity   69
Discursive strategies in multicultural business meetings   71
Identity and role construction: gender and discourse
in management   72
Discourse and the projection of corporate culture:
the mission statement   73
Discourse analysis and business meetings   74
Multidisciplinarity in the study of business discourse   77
Profile: Shanta Nair-Venugopal   79
Profile: Dalvir Samra-Fredericks   81
Profile: Rick Iedema   83
Profile: Lorenza Mondada   85
Further reading   86
Chapter 2 Tasks   87

Part II Applying Business Discourse Research
3 Research-based Business Discourse Teaching   **91**
3.1 Professionals and professors: substance or style?   91
Methodology   92
Findings and relationship with previous studies   93
How useful is survey research?   94
3.2 Teaching English to meet the needs of business education
in Hong Kong   96
Methodology   96
A survey of business professors: teacher perspective   98
The interface between the academy and the business world:
occupational perspective   99
The implications of the project: project recommendations   100
Research into practice?   101
3.3 A corpus-based study of Business English and Business
English teaching materials   102
The Business English Corpus   103
Findings of the BEC/BNC corpus analysis   105
What is Business English?   107
The BEC and the development of teaching materials   111
3.4 Promoting intercultural communicative competence
through foreign language courses   112
The business projects and tasks   113
The implications of the project   115

3.5 The CIBW and IBLC: a course in international business
    writing and the Indianapolis Business Learner Corpus   117
    The research project   118
    The CIBW teaching project   121
    The ILBC–CIBW project: research into practice   123
    Further reading   126
    Chapter 3 Tasks   126

4 **Research-based Consultancy Work**   **127**
    4.1 The REFLECT project   127
        Standardization versus adaptation?   129
    4.2 Horizontal corporate communication   131
        Methodology and findings   132
        Implications   134
        English as a corporate language: strategy or hegemony?   135
    4.3 The Language in the Workplace (LWP) Project   138
        Areas of interest   139
        Business discourse research in authentic settings   142
    4.4 An ESP programme for management in the
        horse-racing business   143
        Findings and implications   145
        ESBP or business discourse?   146
    4.5 Forms as a source of communication problems   147
        Methodology and findings   148
        Implications   149
        A way forward for business discourse research   151
        Further reading   152
        Chapter 4 Tasks   153

5 **Research-based Teaching Materials**   **154**
    Introduction   154
    5.1 A brief survey of published teaching materials   155
    5.2 Practice-driven approaches   160
    5.3 Theory-driven approaches   164
    5.4 Data-driven approaches   166
    5.5 Commentary   171
        Further reading   172
        Chapter 5 Tasks   172

Part III Researching Business Discourse
6 **Themes and Research Strategies**   **175**
    Introduction   175

6.1 Corporate communicative practices in Brazil 176
   Methodology 177
   Main findings 178
   Implications and relationship with similar studies 178
6.2 Email and English in an Anglo-Dutch multinational 181
   Methodology 181
   Main findings 183
   Implications and relationship with similar studies 184
6.3 Between text and context: the mission statement 185
   Methodology 186
   Main findings and relationship with similar studies 188
   Implications of Swales and Rogers' study 189
6.4 English in Dutch job ads: evaluation and
     comprehension 190
   Methodology 192
   Main findings and relationship with similar studies 194
   Studying the use and effects of foreign languages
     other than English in advertising discourse 196
   In conclusion 198
   Further reading 198
   Chapter 6 Tasks 199

7 **Research Methodologies, Frameworks and Project Ideas** **200**
7.1 Investigating the business environment: studies of
     business discourse in context 200
   Business discourse practices and communication
     needs in organizations: quantitative approaches 201
   Business discourse practices and business discourse
     in context: qualitative approaches 205
   Investigating context: the impact of ICT and
     new media on corporate practices 208
7.2 Researching written business communication 213
   Survey-based research into business writing:
     quantitative approaches 213
   Identifying text typology: genre-based studies of writing 217
7.3 Researching spoken business discourse 221
   Studying business talk: approaches inspired by CA
     (Conversation Analysis) 221
   Studying business talk: approaches inspired by
     pragmatics and speech act theory 227
   Studies of business negotiation 231
7.4 Investigating text quality and text production:
     studies in (business) document design 234

Text evaluation: testing a public document in a
   multilingual context 235
Text production: the collaborative construction
   of a new text form 239
Further reading 242

8 **Research Cases** **244**
8.1 Customer-friendly e-service? How Dutch and American
   companies deal with customers' email inquiries 244
Introduction and aims 245
Method 246
Data 246
Analysis 248
Main findings 248
Commentary 251
8.2 Standardize or adapt? Audience reaction to localized
   product advertisements 252
Introduction and aims 252
Method 254
Main findings 256
Commentary 257
8.3 Tailor-made teaching: the English workplace needs
   of textile merchandisers in Hong Kong 258
Introduction and aims 258
Method 259
Main findings 260
Commentary 263
8.4 English as a lingua franca in corporate mergers 264
Introduction and aims 264
Method 266
Main findings 267
Commentary 271
8.5 The use of metadiscourse in the CEO's letter 272
Introduction and aims 272
Method 274
Main findings 275
Commentary 277
8.6 A multimodal analysis of text and photographic
   themes in annual general reports 278
Introduction and aims 278
Method 279
Main findings 281
Commentary 282

8.7   Investigating international audience reaction to the annual
       report in English: UK-based financial analysts' response to
       Dutch-English and British letters to stakeholders   283
       Introduction and aims   284
       Method   286
       Main findings   288
       Commentary   289
8.8   Social media in corporate communications: an analysis
       of the corporate blog as a relationship-building tool   290
       Introduction and aims   291
       Method   293
       Main findings   294
       Commentary   295
8.9   The storytelling organization: a narrative analysis
       of change accounts   297
       Introduction and aims   297
       Method   298
       Main findings   300
       Commentary   300
8.10 What's your style? Does adapting communication style to
       local audiences make business newsletters more effective? 302
       Introduction and aims   302
       Method   304
       Main findings   306
       Commentary   306

Part IV   Resources
9   A Guide to Resources for Business Discourse Research   **311**
   9.1 Books, edited collections and special issues   311
         Book-length studies   311
         Edited collections   312
         Recent journal special issues (from 2002)   314
   9.2 Journals   314
         Business and corporate communication journals   314
         Other relevant journals which publish papers on Business
            Discourse and its sub-fields   316
   9.3 Professional associations   318
         Specially devoted to business discourse   318
         With an interest in business discourse and
            business-related language teaching   318
         With an interest in culture, communication and
            management in international business   319

9.4 Principal conferences and workshops   319
    Other relevant conferences and workshops   319
9.5 Email lists and bulletin boards   320
9.6 Databases and abstracting journals   320
9.7 Corpora   321
9.8 Postgraduate courses at Masters and PhD level   321

References   323

Index   357

List of Tables and Figure

Tables

3.1   BEC positive key words (top 50) that occur with unusual
      frequency in the BEC   106
3.2   A comparison of keywords in the BEC and the BNC   108
4.1   The LWP Project: main datasets   138
8.1   Overview of methods used by Louhiala-Salminen et al. (2005)   267

Figure

4.1   Language choice factors (adapted from Bäck, 2004)   130

General Editors' Preface

Research and Practice in Applied Linguistics is an international book series from Palgrave Macmillan which brings together leading researchers and teachers in Applied Linguistics to provide readers with the knowledge and tools they need to undertake their own practice-related research. Books in the series are designed for students and researchers in Applied Linguistics, TESOL, Language Education and related subject areas, and for language professionals keen to extend their research experience.

Every book in this innovative series is designed to be user-friendly, with clear illustrations and accessible style. The quotations and definitions of key concepts that punctuate the main text are intended to ensure that many, often competing, voices are heard. Each book presents a concise historical and conceptual overview of its chosen field, identifying many lines of enquiry and findings, but also gaps and disagreements. It provides readers with an overall framework for further examination of how research and practice inform each other, and how practitioners can develop their own problem-based research.

The focus throughout is on exploring the relationship between research and practice in Applied Linguistics. How far can research provide answers to the questions and issues that arise in practice? Can research questions that arise and are examined in very specific circumstances be informed by, and inform, the global body of research and practice? What different kinds of information can be obtained from different research methodologies? How should we make a selection between the options available, and how far are different methods compatible with each other? How can the results of research be turned into practical action?

The books in this series identify some of the key researchable areas in the field and provide workable examples of research projects, backed up by details of appropriate research tools and resources. Case studies and exemplars of research and practice are drawn on throughout the books. References to key institutions, individual research lists, journals and professional organizations provide starting points for gathering information and embarking on research. The books also include annotated lists of key works in the field for further study.

The overall objective of the series is to illustrate the message that in Applied Linguistics there can be no good professional practice that isn't based on good research, and there can be no good research that isn't informed by practice.

CHRISTOPHER N. CANDLIN and DAVID R. HALL
Macquarie University, Sydney

Acknowledgements

Our thanks go to the editors of this series, Chris Candlin and David Hall, and in particular to Chris, whose encouraging remarks in the margins, gentle editorial nudges in relevant directions, and encyclopedic knowledge of all things linguistic and applied played an essential role in making our writing truly collaborative and multidisciplinary. Not only the first time, but now also the second time around. We are grateful too to the publisher: to Olivia Middleton, Commissioning Editor at Palgrave Macmillan and to Christine Ranft, Editorial Services Consultant, whose sharp eye for detail made light of the latter stages of the production process. A special thank you is reserved for our own 'editor', Tammy Costa Mallo, who painstakingly worked through the original manuscript at very short notice before we sent it off to the publisher, successfully juggling coursework and exam revision at the same time.

We are indebted to a great number of colleagues from a variety of disciplines for supplying us with references, research data or other materials for this book, or for reading passages 'under construction' and subsequently providing constructive comments that stimulated us to consider issues from multiple perspectives. In this light we would like to thank Bernhard Bäck, the late Margaret Baker Graham, Mary Barrett, Carmela Briguglio, Marinel Gerritsen, Julio Gimenez, Elisabeth de Groot, Sandra Harris, Anne-Wil Harzing, Andreu van Hooft, Carel Jansen, Jennifer Jenkins, Alan Jones, Almut Koester, Sharon Livesey, Meredith Marra, Frank van Meurs, Louise Mullany, Mike Nelson, Jennifer Peck, Priscilla Rogers, Helen Spencer Oatey and Lorrita Yeung. Other colleagues agreed to tell us about their professional lives in the profiles that give the book a personal quality: many thanks to Karen Lee Ashcraft, Judith Baxter, Mirjaliisa Charles, Winnie Cheng, Janet Holmes, Rick Iedema, Eva Lavric, Sharon Livesey, Lorenza Mondada, Gina Poncini, Dalvir Samra-Fredericks and Shanta Nair-Venugopal.

This undertaking lends much of its inspiration from our colleagues in Warwick, Nijmegen and Dubai, many of whom appear in the pages of this book; we thank them for their encouragement and support on both a personal and professional level. And our Bachelors and Masters students, around the world, have provided perhaps the greatest input and incentive for this book. Their contributions to our courses and seminars over the years have greatly clarified our own understanding of the field and helped highlight a gap in provision that we hope the volume will fill.

Finally, we thank our families for accommodating our blatantly non-collaborative behaviour during revision work. This book is for you.

Part I
The Field of Business Discourse

1
What is Business Discourse?

This chapter will:

- Define *business discourse* as it will be referred to in the rest of this book;
- Provide a brief overview of the *historical development* of business discourse with a number of landmark studies;
- Discuss the *hallmarks* of business discourse research including the types of data investigated;
- Provide details of the most important *approaches* that have been taken in business discourse research;
- Give a *geographical and disciplinary overview* of how business discourse has evolved around the world together with profiles of a number of prominent researchers.

1.1 What is business discourse?

Business discourse is all about how people communicate using talk or writing in commercial organizations in order to get their work done. In this book we will view business discourse as social action in business contexts. We will discuss the work of researchers (and practitioners) primarily interested in the investigation of spoken and written communication in general and language in particular in business settings, most often in corporate settings. We will be looking at (a) what business discourse research has told us about how people in business organizations achieve their organizational and personal goals using language, (b) how the findings of that research have been applied in teaching and training materials, and (c) how to go about doing business discourse research.

Business organizations and the types of communication used within them are complex entities. Many different factors can contribute to the ways in which business people use language in order to carry out their work. As we will see in the next section in this chapter, researchers interested in business discourse have referred to a number of approaches and disciplines in their investigation of language at work, such as genre theory, discourse analysis, organizational communication and applied linguistics. This cross-disciplinarity has led to a number of different ways of thinking about business language and the different contextual variables that can be of influence in how people talk and write at work. We will discuss many of these ideas in this chapter and the next, and then go on to look at their applications in Parts 2 and 3 of this book.

The variety of definitions, approaches and methodologies that make business discourse an 'interdisciplinary space' is illustrated in the *Handbook of Business Discourse* (Bargiela-Chiappini, 2009). The contributions represent two current debates in the social sciences that are relevant in understanding the identity of business discourse: that of discourse versus communication, as well as specifically, what constitutes business discourse versus business communication (see Concept Box 1.1). The popularity of discourse (analysis) in the social sciences is undisputed. Scholars studying institutions and organizations, including business organizations, claim that 'discourse is very popular because it is somewhat better than other approaches for understanding organizations' (Alvesson and Kärreman, 2011: 1123). These are some of the reasons given for this focus on discourse and discourse analysis: (1) the emphasis on the communicative character of human interaction; (2) the analytical focus on mundane, observable communicative activities; (3) the empirical nature of the analysis; (4) the view of organization as emergent from the performance of (power-ful) acts. In other words, discourse analysis allows the researcher to understand the relationship between human beings and the organizations they create. And in addition, bringing the two traditions of business discourse and organizational discourse together affords access to an extensive range of epistemological and methodological choices, resulting in a deeper understanding of a wider range of organizational phenomena (Aritz and Walker, 2011).

As we will see in the chapters that follow, discourse analysis, in all its diverse forms, has been successful at engaging with multiple aspects of business discourse.

Concept 1.1   Business discourse and business communication

Business discourse (BD) and business communication (BC) are complementary disciplines which often overlap. Louhiala-Salminen (2009), for instance, concludes that it is largely a question of degree rather than of actual difference; whereas BD may be more textual in approach, BC may be more contextual. As a result, where a project falls on the BD/BC cline 'is often a matter for the researchers to decide' (2009: 305).

(Adapted from Nickerson, 2013)

1.2 A short history of business discourse

Business discourse has been influenced by a number of different approaches and disciplines including discourse analysis, conversation analysis, the pragmatics of interaction, ethnography, genre theory and organizational communication. We will return to many of these and the way that they have been used in Part 3, when we talk about doing business discourse research. An additional characteristic of business discourse research is that many of those researchers involved in the investigation of business discourse are also active in teaching. This has meant that applied linguistics in general, and LSP (Language for Specific Purposes) and ESP (English for Specific Purposes) in particular, have also been influential, especially outside of the North American context where many of those involved with business discourse research are teachers of English or other languages for specific business purposes (for overviews, see: Candlin and Crichton, 2011a and Swales, 2000; see also the volume on LSP by Gollin and Hall, 2006). The evolution of professional communication as a field that 'straddles two domains of study: applied linguistics and studies in professional and organizational communication' (Sarangi & Candlin, 2011: 3) is well-documented in the *Handbook of Communication in Organisations and Professions* (Candlin & Sarangi, 2011), which includes numerous empirical studies carried out in legal, health and corporate settings.

In addition, business discourse research shares some of the same concerns as the North American business communication tradition, although unlike business communication, business discourse research does not generally claim a vocational focus. A number of the researchers we will profile later in this volume have been influenced by and influential on both business discourse and business communication through their involvement with the Association for Business Communication and the *Business Communication Quarterly* (e.g. Gina Poncini, Priscilla Rogers, Linda Beamer). The conversation between the two fields is clearly likely to continue; as Mirjaliisa Charles (see Profile 1.1) concludes: 'Increasingly, business discourse is being referred to as business communication. How does that affect our disciplinary status? However named, I hope that business discourse researchers will continue to be the practically oriented, applied scholars that we, to date, take pride in being' (Charles, 2009: 461–2)

In this section, we will present a short historical overview of the development of the field of business discourse from the late 1980s onwards, referring to a number of landmark studies to do so.

Concept 1.2 Applied linguistics, LSP, ESP and business discourse

Applied linguistics is concerned with how people learn languages, what it means to speak or write a language effectively, and how people might learn to speak or write languages more easily. One important branch that developed within applied linguistics in the 1980s is the investigation of Language for Specific Purposes or often more narrowly, English for Specific Purposes, where researchers are particularly interested in how language is used in a specific social context, such as in an academic setting, in the doctor's surgery or in a business organization. Many of the methodologies associated initially with LSP/ESP research, such as needs analysis surveys, genre analysis and close text analysis, have also been used in investigating business discourse. Unlike LSP/ESP research, however, business discourse is less motivated by pedagogical concerns and more with a concern with understanding how people communicate strategically in an organizational context.

There is now also an established cadre of organizational and professional communication scholars who do not have much to do with either LSP or ESP directly, e.g. Britt-Louise Gunnarsson, Srikant Sarangi, Celia Roberts, Rick Iedema (see Profile 2.3), etc. Their work has, and will continue to be of influence on business discourse research. One scholar, however, who has made a sustained and distinctive contribution to both LSP and discourse scholarship in the last four decades, is Christopher Candlin (e.g. Candlin & Crichton, 2011a). In collaboration with Srikant Sarangi he has proposed a cross-disciplinary understanding of 'communication' in organizational and professional settings, which blends insights from applied linguistics (specifically LSP) and communications studies, (cf. Candlin & Sarangi, 2011; Sarangi & Candlin, 2011). With Jonathan Crichton, he has also introduced and applied a multiperspectival model of discursive practices that combines textual and semiotic analyses with interpretive and ethnographic approaches (Candlin, 1997, 2006; Candlin and Crichton, 2011b, in press, in press; see also: Crichton, 2003, 2010).

The late 1980s did not seem to have much to offer to the linguist in search of an understanding of the role of language in corporations, other than in research with a prescriptive motivation. At that time, the *Journal of Business Communication, Business Communication Quarterly*, the *Journal of Business and Technical Communication* and, to a lesser extent, the *Management Communication Quarterly*, reflected the strong vocational and applied intent of much research in North America, as did work in LSP and applied linguistics, where journals such as *English for Specific Purposes* also tended towards a pedagogical focus. Researchers interested in business discourse in the 1990s were faced with the task of defining the field and also with identifying those approaches and methodologies that could be useful in understanding how business people use language to achieve their goals (e.g. Bargiela-Chiappini & Harris, 1997a, 1997b; Bargiela-Chiappini & Nickerson, 1999).

Quote 1.1   Business discourse

Business discourse as contextual and intertextual, self-reflexive and self-critical, although not necessarily political, is founded on the twin notions of discourse as *situated action* and of *language at work*. This perspective seems now quite remote from early discussion on the nature of *professional language* that originated from within LSP, or Language for Specific Purposes (Johns, 1986). In its attempt to recontextualize discourse within the current dialogues between related disciplines and combined approaches, and between praxis and social theory, business discourse also remains distinct from recent developments in LSP (Swales, 1999) and ESP (Louhiala-Salminen, 2002).

(Bargiela-Chiappini & Nickerson, 2002: 277, original emphasis)

Bargiela-Chiappini (2004a) provides a historical overview of the evolution of the field of spoken business discourse beyond the boundaries of a primarily peda-gogical focus. She describes the lack of interest in language by authors of books on business negotiation in the 1970s and 1980s and their reliance on quantitative analysis. Attention to the role of communication in bargaining (Putnam & Jones, 1982) and the strategic use of language in negotiation (Donohue & Diez, 1985) continued to be relatively unexplored topics in the literature on negotiation until quite recently (e.g. Candlin, Maley & Sutch, 1999). The positivist influence of cognitive and behavioural approaches to the study of language in business settings remained dominant and language was treated as one of the dependent variables. It was not until 1986 when Lampi's seminal monograph on the discourse of negotiation was published, that studies of negotiation became language-based and began to proliferate. The numerous publications that date from that time, as evidenced by the following list, are an indication of how influential this shift to language-based analysis was (e.g. Ehlich & Wagner, 1995; Firth, 1995; Ulijn & Li, 1995; Trosborg, 1995; Jaworski, 1994; Graham, 1993; Holden & Ulijn, 1992; Mulholland, 1991; Neumann, 1991; 1994). The most representative of these, including a variety of different languages and settings, are the two collections both published in 1995, edited by Alan Firth, and Konrad Ehlich and Johannes Wagner, respectively. Although authored by scholars from a variety of disciplines, the research in these collections marks the establishment of a growing body of discourse analytic and pragmatic studies of real-life language in the workplace. Unlike earlier research in nego-tiation, Firth's (1995) collection of fourteen articles approaches negotiation as discourse, i.e. as language in use (p. vi). In his introduction, he reviews the theoretical approaches to negotiation research, ending with what had until that time been referred to as the 'discourse approach'. Firth's discussion makes clear that this is a potentially misleading label as this approach in fact tended to describe studies that used (decontextualized) transcripts of negotiations but analysed them by means of preset coding systems, or through conversation analysis. In contrast, Firth's volume illustrates a range of discourse-based (contextualized) methodologies applied to negotiation talk, such that the chapters approach negotiation not as an isolated activity, but as an activity embedded in a variety of workplace interactions (e.g. meetings, intercultural negotiations, technical problem solving, general practice consultations, travel agency calls, etc.).

In a similar way, Konrad Ehlich and Johannes Wagner's collection (1995) echoes Firth's discussion on negotiation through the micro-analyses of authentic or simulated business interactions in Dutch, French, German, Spanish, Danish, Japanese, British English, American English and Australian English. In their introduction, the editors note the growing interest in business negotiation among practitioners, novices and researchers. They also recognize that observation of the interactions and audio-recordings are essential to sound research but that issues of access, data sensitivity and transcription detail often complicate the job of the discourse analyst. Now almost two decades later, business discourse researchers are still grappling with the same problems, but have however acquired much more experience in ethnographic research in corporate and institutional environments. As we will discuss in the next chapter, we are now more often able to work alongside 'the research' as our peers in co-constructed collaborative projects.

A pioneering work on negotiation for its time, Mirjaliisa Lampi's multilevel, micro-analytical discourse analysis of British business negotiations (Lampi, 1986); see Profile 1.1 Mirjaliisa Charles), firmly established the credentials of language-focused research in business and international relations. The discourse features that contribute to perceived strategy in negotiation are the focus of Lampi's study, hence her approach concentrates on 'levels of discoursality': acts, moves, exchanges and phases, all converging to form a negotiation 'encounter'. This terminology will have been familiar to discourse analysts in the 1980s but the originality of the study lies in the application of these analytical categories to the study of strategy in real business interactions. In a later paper, Lampi (1990) moves the field on again by discussing the influence of company agendas on negotiation talk. In this way, she points towards a systematic analysis of the contextual components of verbal interaction in business settings; six years on from there (now writing as Charles, see Profile 1.1) she definitively makes the connection between the business context and language in a self-proclaimed attempt 'to partly fill the gap between a contextual, business approach and a linguistic text-based approach' (Charles, 1996: 20). In this 1996 study, she draws both on discourse analysis and business studies of negotiation, and demonstrates how the linguistic choices made in negotiation situations are a direct reflection of whether the business relationship between the participants involved is established or new.

Profile 1.1   Mirjaliisa Charles

Professor Emerita in Business Communication, the first scholar to hold this title.

Born: in Finland
Educated: in Finland (MA, University of Helsinki; Phil. Lic., University of Jyväskylä) and UK (PhD, University of Birmingham, UK)
            Divides her life between Finland and the UK

Mirjaliisa Charles is identified in Europe and beyond as a founding figure in the history of business communication as a new academic subject. Now Professor Emerita, her career spans four decades and at least three academic fields, Applied linguistics – in particular English for Specific Purposes (ESP); English Business Communication; and International Business Communication. Her involvement with business dates back to English language training for business managers in Finnish companies in the seventies, followed by consultancy work through her own company. As a result of this experience, her academic work links up linguistics with business and management studies.

Mirjaliisa's current title belies years of change and transformation within the then Helsinki School of Economics (HSE), now part of the new Aalto University. The evolution of her academic profile from English language for business to international business communication via applied linguistics will resonate as a story with the often complex trajectories that seem to characterize business communication as a higher education subject within Europe.

Her academic career has interesting parallels with the development of the field of business communication in Europe, which, crucially, depends on a combination of visionary curriculum policies and the energy of flexible and inspiring academics.

Quotations:
- The biggest challenges for 21st century business discourse and communication research come from the globalization of businesses and their communication processes, the impact of technology on discourse creation and communication, and the implications of networking for knowledge creation and sharing.
- Discourse is a basic, formative process which shapes and develops organizations, making them what they are, and what they are perceived to be.
- Analysing organizational discourse and communication means describing and explaining the very essence, the very being, of organizations.

- Business discourse research should not be merely 'reactive' – seeing an organization as a 'locus', or a 'context' for discourse – 'describing', 'following', and 'reflecting' developments in business. Research should be proactive – showing businesses the way forward – the way communication leads the way toward corporate goals.
- A big research question for our field is: 'How do communicative and discoursal processes create, impact, change or consolidate the enterprise?'
- The ultimate aim of business discourse research must be to produce a discourse and communication based theory of organizations.
- The term Business English Lingua Franca (BELF) refers to English used as a 'neutral and shared communication code'. BELF is neutral in the sense that none of the speakers can claim it as her/his mother tongue; it is shared in the sense that it is used for conducting business within the global business discourse community, whose members are BELF users and communicators in their own right – not 'non-native speakers' or 'learners'.
- Making the NS >< NNS dichotomy seems, in many respects, to be common sense, but it is inherently dangerous if used as a basis for communication studies: It divides the world of communication into 'us' and 'them,' resulting in 'linguistic ethnocentricity'.
- The global business community is the 'culture' that has created BELF, and within which BELF evolves. As with all cultures, the global business culture is diverse and dynamic, and has groups who see themselves as its 'owners', with certain shared values (e.g. that of doing profitable business).
- For businesses, heightening awareness of communicative and cultural diversity, and working on ways to increase mutual understanding of the Englishes (or other shared languages) used globally – whether NS or NNS – is of vital importance. We need research that helps us to better understand the complex process of how people relate to each other across language barriers. Whether native or non-native, communicators need to learn (be taught!) to listen, make situational adjustments, and use sociopragmatic, situational potential to jointly create meanings and operational cultures.
- The best international negotiators are not necessarily those who have the best command of the English language.

In meeting discourse, Haru Yamada's work on the differences between Japanese and US meetings (1990; 1992; 2002), is another pioneering work in business discourse studies. It provides a detailed account of the crucial difference between the two cultures involved and the rhetorical action that each group is trying to achieve in a meeting situation. The Japanese, for instance, use the meeting in order to exchange opinions, whereas the Americans use a meeting to come to a decision. Yamada's studies include both cross- and intercultural analysis and are among the first full-length studies of the interaction between two different cultures in a business setting.

The publication of Deidre Boden's *The Business of Talk: Organizations in Action* in 1994 originally combines distinctive intellectual and methodological traditions such as conversation analysis, organizational theory and social theory. It provides a detailed and singular account of how organizations bring about action through the business of talk, in an analysis of talk in organizations such as the health sector, academia and business. Drawing on the work of the sociologist Anthony Giddens (1984; 1987), Boden discusses how the organizations she studied generate talk, and are themselves simultaneously constructed through that talk, in a process that Giddens has referred to as *structuration*. Using ethnomethodology and conversation analysis (CA) as an analytical framework, Boden shows how the talk is influenced or shaped by the organization, i.e. the social context, and that an organization is in turn, influenced or shaped by the talk that takes place within it. Boden's choice of meetings as an object of study is significant. As the substance of management, meetings are central to organizing structure and action, time and space. No other researcher has yet been able to deconstruct this process in quite such a convincing (and readable) way, in unpacking the complex nature of the role played by language as a fundamental contributor to organizational communication.

Quote 1.2 Talk and organizations

Talk, I shall propose, is the lifeblood of all organizations and, as such, it both shapes and is shaped by the structure of the organization itself.

(Boden, 1994: 8)

Three years after the publication of Boden's study of meetings in the United States, Bargiela-Chiappini and Harris' investigation of British and Italian business meetings includes both a crosscultural analysis of the structural and pragmatic properties of British and Italian business meetings respectively, as well as an intercultural study of the specific meetings that took place in an Anglo-Italian joint venture (Bargiela-Chiappini & Harris, 1997a). This study therefore re-emphasizes an important hallmark of business discourse that we will refer to in many places in this book, i.e. that business often involves communication across national borders between people who do not share the same culture. Business discourse research therefore needs to account not only for organizational cultures, but also for ethnolinguistic cultures (see Sarangi & Roberts (1999) for an important discussion on the distinction between ethnolinguistic cultures on the one hand, and organizational and institutional cultures on the other). We will return to this issue later in this chapter and look at it in detail in the next. Like Charles' studies of negotiations, Bargiela-Chiappini and Harris' work has also been of considerable influence on later work on the discourse of business meetings. The 1997 study remains of interest as a ground-breaking attempt to understand real communication involving real business people, and it provides countless examples of the mismatch between the language taught for meetings and the language used in meetings that Williams so eloquently described at the end of the 1980s (Williams, 1988).

Marian Williams (1988): The relationship between reality and teaching materials

In 1988 Marian Williams published an article reporting on the relationship between the language used by native speakers of English in business meetings and the language taught by business English textbooks at that time for use in meetings. She analysed the language used in three meetings by a total of twelve native speakers of English and then compared this with the language taught for meetings in thirty English textbooks. She found that there was almost no correspondence between the meetings and the textbooks and that the speakers' use of language was far more complex than the way in which it was represented for the student. Although now over two decades old, the study remains a landmark study of the mismatch that continues to exist between teaching materials and real language (see Part 2 for further discussion on this point).

For written discourse, the work of the genre analyst Vijay Bhatia has shaped the work of a generation of applied linguists specializing in writing in organizational contexts. Published in 1993, Bhatia's book-length study extends the ESP approach to genre analysis that was pioneered by John Swales for academic writing (e.g. Swales, 1990a), and re-applies it to professional discourse, including sales letters and application letters. Now a classic within the ESP literature, the 1993 volume remains an influential account not only of how context and text are intertwined, but also of how writers use a genre creatively to achieve their own ends. Bhatia's 2004 volume *Worlds of Written Discourse* moves even further away from the ESP tradition and continues to explore the way in which context and text are related. We will discuss Bhatia's work and the usefulness of a genre approach to the analysis of discourse, in Parts 2 and 3 of this volume in relation to the work of researchers such as Ulla Connor, Catherine Nickerson and Leena Louhiala-Salminen.

Work on written business discourse in the 1980s and early 1990s was characterized by the analysis of the business letter, as an important genre of communication in business setting at that time. From the study by Ann Johns of cohesion in different types of business discourse (Johns, 1980) through the contrastive study of business letter writing in English, French and Japanese by Susan Jenkins and John Hinds (1987) to the book length study of requests in British, American and Finnish business correspondence by Hilkka Yli-Jokipii (1994), the field was dominated by the business letter. The 1999 edited collection on the genres of written business discourse (Bargiela-Chiappini & Nickerson, 1999), for instance, includes two important types of business letter, i.e. sales letters and mass-produced correspondence with customers (but also showcases a number of other written genres used in business, such as email, business faxes and business magazines). The characteristics and influence of the business letter have continued to be of interest, particularly the way in which the genre has been subsumed into other genres such as the annual general report and email correspondence, as exemplified by the collection edited by Paul Gillaerts and Maurizio Gotti (2005). The role played by the communicative purpose in the letter was generally of more interest in this type of research than the interpersonal relationship between the writer and reader (although see Maier, 1992; for a study of politeness strategies in business letters, and James, Scholfield & Ypsiladis, 1994; for a study of the effects of using different strategies in application letters).

Over the course of the last two decades working at the Helsinki School of Economics (now part of Aalto University) the Finnish researcher Leena Louhiala-Salminen has made an extensive contribution to the development of business discourse, particularly in her study of the use of electronic media in business contexts. In a series of publications dating from the mid 1990s onwards she has used a variety of different methodologies, such as survey-based research, corpus-based genre analysis, text analysis and informant studies, to investigate the role played by fax communication in English in Finland, its discourse characteristics and the response of readers to those characteristics (Louhiala-Salminen, 1995; 1996; 1997). Furthermore, in collaboration with Didar Akar at Bogaziçi University in Turkey, she has investigated the similarities and differences in fax communication in English as it is used for international business in Turkey and Finland, and most recently, she has worked with her colleagues Mirjaliisa Charles and Anna Kankaanranta also at the Helsinki School of Economics to investigate how English is used in two Swedish–Finnish cross border mergers, involving the integrated analysis of meetings and email, as well as a series of in-depth interviews with Finnish and Swedish business people (Akar & Louhiala-Salminen, 1999; Louhiala-Salminen, Charles & Kankaanranta, 2005).

1.3   The hallmarks of business discourse research

In this section, we will discuss the hallmarks of business discourse research. We will look at the type of data that has been analysed and the relationship that has developed between certain types of data and different methodologies. We will also examine the role played by context in business discourse research, the research aims behind business discourse research and the dominance of English in international business, as well as the work that has been done on business discourse involving languages other than English.

Types of data

Business discourse research draws on a variety of different kinds of data, depending on the research aims in each case. These could be as diverse as the results of a survey, the analysis of a real business discussion or the findings of an experiment. In Part 3 of this book we will look in detail at the increasing body of research which has focused on *authentic* data, and we will also consider business discourse research where it has been most appropriate either to use *simulated* data, or to use *manipulated* data in an experimental setting. Sometimes business discourse researchers will also use a combination of different kinds of data in one investigation. Findings based on a corpus of authentic data, for instance, can be used to inform the collection of simulated data to tell a researcher more about what students do as opposed to what business people with experience. Likewise, a corpus of authentic data can be used to inform an experimental investigation into readers' response to a particular textual characteristic, e.g. the use of 'I' rather than 'we' in business writing.

Many business discourse researchers prefer to work with authentic data, despite the difficulties associated with gaining access to business organizations and the confidentiality agreements that are necessary to work on the data and publish the findings. Authentic examples of business discourse provide invaluable insights into how people actually communicate in organizations. As many of the studies we profile in Chapter 8 show, increasing numbers of researchers are managing to persuade corporations to let them in to investigate their communication first hand. Authentic data tends to be messy, however, and one of the challenges that business discourse researchers have to meet initially is how to organize the data so that it can be analysed.

The extracts below are examples of authentic data, the first taken from a meeting at a Finnish–Swedish multinational (Data 1.1) and the second from a set of internal email correspondence collected at a Dutch multinational corporation (Data 1.2). In both cases, the researchers involved have taken a set of raw data, i.e. audio recordings of meetings and a set of electronic files respectively, and transformed them into a set of data to be analysed. The recordings have been transcribed into a written form and the electronic files have been separated and then merged into one consistent corpus. In both cases, the researchers have then made the extracts anonymous in order to be able to publish their findings, as well as gaining written permission from the corporations involved that they could do so.

Studies of writing may have more pervasive results in that they can reveal the degree to which competency in writing is used as a mark of expertise and also as a means of sanction. We will look at an example of this in detail in Chapter 4 when we review the work by Baxter, Boswood and Peirson-Smith at the Hong Kong Jockey Club (Baxter, Boswood & Peirson-Smith, 2002).

Data 1.1   An example of authentic spoken data

1	C	since this is in Swedish Bob why don't you er comment on it first please
2	S1	Yes I think er we got the status and I think you Chris has also made
3		comments on it
4	F	Yupp I have yes
5	S1	Er so I think most of us have seen this text or (.) is it new for anyone (.) er (.)
6		that they say in (.) er from Company D side that they say that what you have
7		said from the Finnish side er it's about 'tycke och smak' what's what is it in
8		English I don't know and er . . . you agree
9	F	yeah
10	S1	in that
11	F	yeah
12	S1	maybe you can continue I think

(Taken from Louhiala-Salminen, Charles & Kankaanranta, 2005)

Data 1.2   An example of authentic written data

ÞMSG FROM: INASM2 – INTRAVM01 TO: INAHA3 – INTRAVM01
24-05-96 10:01:05
To: INAHA3 – INTRAVM01 A. van Edel
From: J.L.C.Smal SIC-INTRO/1 'Separations'
Introduct, Rotterdam
Internal address: NL 32-14tel.3185
Subject: werINanvrSUSen
Anton
Hierbij de reactie op min ELFjes en Klokken
Over de klokken is een dikke file aanwezig incl. TKF en VVF.
Hans B. heeft daarin gesuggereerd dat er geen TKF maar een ELF dient

te worden ingestuurd. En dan krijg je deze reactie . . .
Ook bij een recente opknapbeurt van NL 32–13 is de klok niet weggehaald.
Bij het opknappen van NL33 is er niets aan de isolatie vanleidingen gedaan.
Klantgericht??
Ik stel voor dat we 4 juni samen lunchen. Accoord?
With kind regards, Jos Smal
Introduct, Rotterdam
tel. +31 20 630 3185, fax. 4037; e-mail: SMAL9@sic.introduct.nl

(Adapted from Nickerson, 2000)

In some situations, it may be necessary to work with *simulated* rather than *authentic* data, in order to investigate a particular aspect of business discourse. This may be because it has proved impossible to gain access to an appropriate set of authentic data, or because the researcher is interested in a specific aspect of language use and therefore needs to control as many variables as possible. Simulated data is collected on the basis of a set of instructions for the writers or speakers involved in which they are asked to play a particular role intended to elicit the aspect of language the researcher is interested in. The data collected as a result will then be treated much like authentic data, as can be seen in the transcribed example of simulated spoken data in the extract below (Data 1.3). Simulated data like this has been used by business discourse researchers, for instance, to compare the language produced by students with no experience of work with that produced by experienced business people. We will discuss this in more detail in Part 3.

Data 1.3   An example of simulated spoken data

S: Uhuh. *Do you have to sell your marketing erm sales policy? Because before you were selling to wholesalers I suppose?*
B: No, we were always a chain of stores.
S: Uhuh.
B: Highly specialized and quite known I think from erm all the consumers erm the young people
S: Uhuh.
B: that travel and go camping.
S = Seller, B = Buyer

(Adapted from Planken, 2005)

Quote 1.3   On the use of simulated data

> . . . there are considerable advantages to using simulation as a method of data collection. The use of simulation as opposed to observation in an authentic setting, for example, allows for greater control of stimulus conditions, as well as comparisons and generalizations across data produced in any number of interactions elicited by a particular simulation game. Also, simulation serves as the best alternative, in terms of data collection, in situations where access to authentic data in an authentic setting – for example, access to authentic negotiation discourse, produced in an authentic organizational environment – is difficult, because participants are protective of potentially sensitive corporate information, or because they are reluctant about being observed and recorded on the job.
>
> (Planken, 2002: 51)

In addition to authentic and simulated types of data, a more recent type of business discourse research has made reference to manipulated forms of data in order to investigate the response of a particular target readership to a specific aspect of language. This could be, for instance, the use of English in advertising texts rather than the national language of a particular country, the use of one type of argumentation strategy in a fund-raising letter rather than another, or the use of a particular type of pronoun in an email message. In this type of investigation, reference is usually made initially to a set of authentic data and a series of test items are then developed on the basis of that authentic data representing the target variable. The 2005 study by Nickerson, Gerritsen and van Meurs, for instance, refers both to the texts used in original advertising campaigns, as part of an authentic corpus of advertising texts containing English, together with a set of manipulated test items, used with different target readers to investigate the effects of including English in advertising in glossy magazines (Nickerson, Gerritsen & van Meurs, 2005). As we will discuss in Parts 2 and 3, this type of investigation has been a hallmark of the type of research generally referred to as *document design*, which has developed largely in Belgium and the Netherlands to investigate and improve the effectiveness of technical, professional and, more recently, business documents.

The link between data and methodology: multimethod research

One of the defining features of business discourse research is that it has not relied on any one approach or methodology. In the analysis of authentic data in particular, researchers have allowed themselves to be data rather than theory-driven, and have selected the most appropriate type of analysis on the basis of the data set they have been interested in. In this respect, business discourse researchers have taken a similar stance to that of the genre analysts John Swales and Vijay Bhatia. They have been more interested in saying something useful about a set of data through reference to an appropriate theoretical approach and associated methodology (data-driven research), rather than the other way around (theory-related research). In the process, they may also have been able to make a contribution to the development of theory. As we will discuss in Part 3, however, similar types of data have often been analysed using the same approach, such that conversational analysis or discourse analysis, for instance, have often been considered the most appropriate methods of analysing spoken interaction in business meetings; genre analysis (which itself allows for a combination of different methodologies) has been widely used in the analysis of written business discourse. It has also been characteristic of business discourse to combine one or more approaches in order to say something useful about a set of data. We will return to this combinability or multimethod approach, and the multidisciplinarity it has led to, as a central theme in the next chapter and in Chapters 6, 7 and 8 in Part 3.

Research purpose: description and prescription

Business discourse research has been both descriptive and prescriptive in its research aims. With its roots partly in the business communication tradition in North America and the applied linguistics tradition elsewhere, much of the early research that was carried out at the end of the twentieth century was pedagogically motivated. Business language was investigated not as an end to itself, but largely to inform teaching or training programmes, for pre- or post-experience business people respectively. As we will see in Part 2, when we look at the ways in which business discourse research has been applied, some business discourse research involving needs analysis or linguistic surveys remains prescriptive in its aims in that it seeks to improve language training provision for the business people of the future.

Other studies, such as those in document design that we look at in Part 3 are also unashamedly prescriptive in their aims, since the main research aim is to improve the effectiveness of specific types of business writing on the basis of text analysis combined with experimental investigation. In contrast, although the pedagogical or wider prescriptive implications are often clear, there is now a large body of work in business discourse where the primary aim is to describe and interpret, and therefore understand better, how people communicate using talk or writing as social action in commercial organizations in order to get their work done. As we will discuss in Part 3 this may be through reference to a variety of different types of information collected using a variety of different methods, including a written survey or interviews with business people, a corpus of written documents or spoken events, or a case-study approach focusing on one particular organization.

English versus other business languages

There has been an undeniable bias towards English in the research carried out in business language over the past two decades. This is partly due to the status that English holds as an international business language and also as a consequence of the ESP/applied linguistics background that many business discourse researchers share. As we will see in Parts 2 and 3, many researchers have focused on English, or they have included English in their investigations together with other languages (see Data 1.4 for a rare example of work on business texts comparing English and Arabic, by Mohammed Al-Ali, 2004). The exceptions to this have been the small group of European researchers such as those included in section 1.5 below, as exemplified by the Austrian researcher Eva Lavric (as profiled below), and Asian researchers such as Lorrita Yeung, Li Wei, Zhu Hua, Li Yue, Margie Li, Yuling Pan, and Keiko Emmett. The latter group, for instance, have given (intracultural) accounts of Cantonese (Yeung, 1997; 1998), Putonghua (Pan, 1994; Li Wei, Zhu Hua & Li Yue, 2001; Li, 1999) and Japanese (Emmett, 2003). The work of Lorrita Yeung is especially relevant here and also unique in that it includes both contrastive studies of Chinese/ Australian management discourse (Yeung, 2000; 2003; 2004a; 2004b) and intracultural studies of Chinese management discourse (Yeung 1997; 1998). Three collections published in the 2000s under the 'Asian business discourses' banner include further intracultural studies from India, China, Vietnam, Japan, Malaysia and Thailand (Bargiela-Chiappini & Gotti, 2005; Bargiela-Chiappini, 2005a; Bargiela-Chiappini, 2006; see section 1.5 for details). Finally, there is a growing body of research on business communication (e.g. Barbara, Celani, Collins & Scott, 1996; Thatcher 2000a; dos Santos Pinto, 2002; Conaway & Wardrope, 2004; Pacheco de Oliveira, 2009) and organizational communication (do Carmo Leite de Oliveira & Gomes Silva, 2009; Cortes Gago & Sonia Bittencourt Silveira, 2009) in Latin America, which also includes contrastive studies such as Thatcher (1999; 2000b; 2000c) and de Moraes Garcez (1993).

In the next chapter we will talk more about the dominance of English and Anglo-Saxon perspectives in business discourse research, and the problems that this may pose in reporting on the findings of investigations into intercultural business communication.

Eva Lavric: Code choice / code switching in business and professional contexts

As a specialist in Romance languages and linguistics with twenty years of teaching practice in a business university, Professor Eva Lavric has conducted and instigated a number of major projects over the past decade looking at code choice in various different types of business and professional settings in Austria and beyond. Her 1991 study, for instance, is an early (quantitative) language needs review among the alumni of the Vienna University of Economics and Business, which looks in detail at the relationship between levels of language proficiency and professional activities. This study is particularly interesting as it centres on the language needs of Austrian professionals in communication with their Eastern European neighbours in the late 1980s, just as the political map of Europe was about to change. Other studies have also looked at the use of and need for languages other than English, notably French, Italian and Spanish, within the Austrian business context (e.g. Bäck, 2004; Daublebsky, 2000; Kubista-Nugent, 1996; Mrázová, 2005; Rheindt, 1997; Seeböck, 1999). In more recent work from 2003 onwards, Lavric and her colleagues have continued to look at a variety of different languages, e.g. German, Italian, French, Russian and Spanish, and to investigate a wide range of different sectors, including tourism, banking, fruit import and transport (e.g. Lavric, 2009; Lechner, 2010), as well as in the less familiar areas of language use in the wine-making industry (through the EU project Vinolingua with Maria Gnilsen) and in professional football (e.g. Steiner, 2011). These, and the many other projects that Lavric has been associated with, provide a picture of language use that belies the assumed dominance of English as a lingua franca in business communication and the corresponding attention that it has received in previous studies.

Data 1.4   A comparative corpus-based analysis of English and Arabic job application letters

Mohammed Al-Ali (2004) used genre analysis to identify and describe the main components and rhetorical strategies used by Arabic and English writers to articulate the same communicative purpose, i.e. to elicit a call for a job interview. The data for the study consisted of 60 application letters, written by 30 English and 30 Arabic university teachers based in Jordan. Applicants had responded to either of two simulated, but roughly identical job advertisements, one in English and one in Arabic, for a teaching assistant position at a Jordanian University. The advertisements were both advertised by the researcher in Jordanian daily newspapers. To investigate similarities and differences between the writer groups in terms of their preferences for organizing the genre, across cultures and across languages, Al-Ali used a *moves* analysis in which he compared the relative occurrence of genre components, and the types and average length of these strategic moves, across cultures. Overall, the two groups of writers used different frequencies and different moves sequences to achieve the same communicative purpose. Also, the Arabic letters contained moves that none of the English letters did, such as 'glorifying the prospective employer', and 'invoking compassion'. By the same token, the English letters included moves that were not found in the Arabic letters, such as supportive discussions to promote the candidate and explicit requests for a job interview. Al-Ali's findings suggest that different rhetorical strategies are regarded as effective in different cultures and, at a higher level, that culture is a determinant factor of genre and poses constraints on writers' rhetorical options. More specifically, the findings suggest that an awareness of the cultural specificity of generic patterns employed in the genre of application letter in the two languages under study deserves special attention in Arabic and English (business) writing curricula for FL learners. This observation is also likely to be relevant for other genres and other national cultures.

The importance of the organizational context

The final hallmark of business discourse research that we will discuss here is that it has become increasingly concerned with the role played by the organizational context in shaping the spoken and written genres that evolve within business organizations and the language that is used to realize them. Business discourse researchers do not consider language in isolation as their object of study, but they seek to establish how written texts and spoken events reflect the social and organizational contexts in which they are used. All of the studies that we refer to in Part 3 when we talk about doing business discourse research are examples of contextualized language analysis or its experimental investigation. To conclude this section we will discuss the landmark study carried out during the 1990s, by the Belgian researcher Sonja Vandermeeren, that makes a definitive link between language use on the one hand, and the business context on the other, as well as the work by Naoki Kameda (2005; 2008; 2012) which looks at the impact of context on Japanese business communication.

Vandermeeren's large-scale project completed at the end of the 1990s (e.g. Vandermeeren, 1998; 1999) surveyed foreign language use in European business, focusing on companies in Germany, France, the Netherlands, Portugal and Hungary. The project aimed not only to identify patterns of language use within the target corporations, but also to establish why these patterns existed, whether there was a link between foreign language use and export performance, the attitudes held by employees towards the use of foreign languages, foreign language needs in general – including unmet needs, and the strategies that could be employed to improve foreign language proficiency. In 1993 and 1994, corporations representing the car components sector and the electrical and electronics industry were surveyed in the five countries, resulting in a response from 415 corporations. For Germany, France and the Netherlands, for instance, this accounted for 143, 83 and 81 corporations respectively. The study provides a great deal of detailed information on the use of foreign languages within the responding corporations, but its most interesting aspect is the relationship it establishes between the need for languages and the corporations' business activities.

As in the studies within the framework of the European Union co-ordinated by Stephen Hagen that we profile in Chapter 4, although English was in widespread use in Vandermeeren's study, other languages were also used and were also considered necessary by her specialist informants. For instance, 42 per cent of the French companies reported that they used German almost always in correspondence with German companies, compared to only 30 per cent who almost always used English, and likewise, although just over 30 per cent of the German companies reported that they almost always used English in correspondence with French companies, almost 25 per cent reported that they almost always used French. As Vandermeeren observes, at least for German–French written business interaction in 1993 and 1994, English did not dominate as a lingua franca and a considerable number of the corporations chose to use the first language of their business partner.

In his research on Japanese business communication (reviewed in Bargiela-Chiappini and Zhang, 2013), Naoki Kameda, former CEO of his own company and with over twenty five years' experience in international trade, looks at the interaction between technology and language in the virtual context of e-commerce. Business English as a Lingua Franca (BELF) is the language of choice for websites aimed at the international market. However, focusing on Japan, Kameda (2012) observes that Japanese corporate websites in English tend to be literal translations from Japanese, with little or no attention paid to the semantic complexity of understatement, indirectness and idiomatic language. Moreover, he argues that we cannot assume that English (and Japanese) are accessible to 'important and powerful customers and investors' (Kameda, 2012: 76) such as the Chinese. A further important issue concerns the type of knowledge accessible on corporate websites. According to Kameda, Japanese company websites tend to concentrate on 'explicit knowledge' (Polanyi, 1966) whilst there is a level of knowledge that often remains inaccessible to the majority of non-native speakers worldwide, i.e. 'tacit knowledge' (Polanyi, 1966), 'the implied or intuitive knowledge which native speakers can easily pick up but which is difficult for non-native speakers to comprehend' (Kameda, 2012: 75).

Kameda attributes the information gap due to 'tacit knowledge' in Japanese websites to native/local attitudes towards verbal communication. The reader or listener is expected to fill the gaps in the knowledge provided; 'hearing one, and understanding ten' captures the essence of Japanese communication (Kameda, 2005; 2008). Kameda considers this a source of potential misunderstanding and miscommunication when operating on the international arena. 'Quantity' of information is only one of the challenges posed by the Japanese communication style; the other is the structure of argument in Japanese, which differs from the dominant 'western' logic that is taken for granted in international business communication.

The importance of contextual knowledge in business discourse research has also been highlighted in relation to the study of two processes that are central to organizational life: decision-making and problem-solving. Decision-making has been analysed as happening mainly within meetings, thus ignoring the fact that decisions are often made during informal talk, back stage talk and talk 'on the move' (Halvorsen, 2010). Similarly, understanding the dynamics of problem-solving (Angouri & Bargiela-Chiappini, 2011) requires appreciation of organizational structures, local history and employees' shared perceptions of professional practices.

Data 1.5   Hanford (2010) The Language of Business Meetings

The **Language of Business Meetings (LBM)** is a corpus-informed study of the language and practices interlocutors employ in business meetings. CANBEC (The Cambridge and Nottingham Business English Corpus) contains one million words of authentic spoken discourse, mainly business meetings from a wide variety of companies in different industries in the UK and elsewhere.

The data is important because:

1. it is a large corpus of authentic business interactions
2. it is fully transcribed and therefore allows for fine-grained linguistic analysis
3. over a quarter of the meetings are from inter-organization meetings, and therefore very rare
4. several meetings are supported with ethnographic data.

LBM analyses the meetings in CANBEC at several levels. Statistically significant lexicogrammatical items (e.g. 'we', 'if' and 'problem'), and lists of the most frequent clusters (such as 'we need to') are produced, and several of these items are categorized according to discursive practice. They are then explored in longer extracts. For instance, one chapter analyses decision-making in meetings, specifically the use of 'problem' and 'issue' to raise an issue, the keyword 'if' to hypothesize solutions, and metaphors and idioms to evaluate them.

The methodology developed in LBM shows how corpus data can be interpreted in terms of discursive, professional and social practices: it therefore links the local text level to much broader layers of context. The book is also of note from a theoretical perspective because it explores what is meant by 'practice' and how it applies to the context of meetings as genre. The notion of power is dealt with throughout, as is the way relationships are negotiated. As such, it is highly interdisciplinary, combining methods and insights from corpus linguistics, (critical) discourse analysis, management studies, intercultural communication studies and linguistic anthropology, and adds to the growing number of interdisciplinary studies of institutional discourse.

(See: Handford, 2010a, 2012; McCarthy & Handford, 2004; Handford & Koester, 2010; Koester & Handford, 2011)

1.4   Different approaches to business discourse research

In addition to choosing between descriptive and prescriptive approaches within business discourse research, researchers in the field have also studied the influence of power and status in language use in business settings, or the communication that takes place between different cultures, or they have taken a critical approach to business discourse on ideological and political grounds. We will look at each of these aspects in turn, as important areas of concern within the wider field of business discourse research.

Discourse and power

The workings of power and status in business organizations have been the focus of interest of a number of business discourse researchers who view language as 'powerful action' (e.g. Yeung, 2004a; 2004b, for a series of publications looking at interlingual and intercultural banking discourses in Australia and Hong Kong). In Chapter 4, we will look in detail at a large-scale project centred on power and language called the 'Language in the Workplace Project', involving a team of linguists under the direction of Janet Holmes (e.g. Holmes, 2000a; Holmes et al., 2011) based at the University of Wellington, in New Zealand. One of their studies, for instance, analyses the relevance of status and the exercise of power through the use of directives in a New Zealand workplace, using speech act theory as a theoretical framework (Vine, 2004). In this study, the power differences observed tend to be minimized through the use of mitigation and the gender of the (female) managers observed seems to contribute to the preference for a participative style of management, which in turn tends to empower lower level staff. The studies that fall within the LWP project all provide examples of how important the role of language is in creating and/or maintaining power relationships in business organizations.

Researchers examining power relations at work have also tended to be sympathetic to a critical approach that seeks to account for inequality and unfairness: 'collectively, critical researchers share a concern for understanding power relationships and language use within complex social practices with the hope of emancipating the disenfranchised and marginalized' (Deetz and McClellan, 2009).

Feminist approaches to the analysis of business discourse, for instance, partly attribute power inequalities to persisting, if subtle, gender discrimination that forces women managers to choose between family or career. Until recently, studies in language and gender in the workplace have followed the traditional view that men and women, understood as monolithic categories, speak differently, helping to reaffirm stereotypical ideas such as 'men are direct and competitive, while women are more tentative and collaborative', that most western societies hold (e.g. as exemplified by the work of the American sociolinguist Deborah Tannen in publications such as the 1995 volume *Talking from 9 to 5: Women and Men at Work – Language, Sex and Power*). The emphasis on the distinguishing features of men's talk as opposed to women's talk is, however, gradually changing and studies in language and gender in the workplace are now moving away from differences in gender and are concentrating on the effects that contextual features can have on the communication of men and women at the workplace. Some workplace studies have, for example, demonstrated that men's and women's styles of communication show considerable variation not only between groups (men–women) but also, and more importantly, within gender groups (men–men and women–women) (Holmes & Marra, 2004). Another interesting perspective on language and gender in the workplace has resulted from considering how power roles, real or perceived, operate in workplace communication. Recent studies have revealed a complex situation, sometimes helping to debunk long-standing gender myths (e.g. Gimenez, 2006b; Holmes & Stubbe, 2003; Holmes, 2005; Mullany, 2003; 2007; Peck, 2000; 2005; Baxter, 2006; 2010). In one of these, for instance, Holmes and Stubbe (2003), demonstrate that at a meeting the chair tends to talk longer than any other participant, regardless of their gender, and also that women managers use imperatives to get things done and are as good as men at using humour (see also Chapter 2 for a discussion of the multidisciplinary nature of Mullany's work). And most recently in work carried out in business organizations in the United Kingdom, Baxter (2010) discusses the way in which successful female leaders use a variety of different discourse strategies, including double-voiced discourse (being able to adjust to the 'hidden' agenda) and using gender counter-talk (being able to deal with male subordinates without threatening their 'face') (see also Profile 1.7). The performance of leadership has also been examined in the context of meetings and 'away-days' where the chair is found to influence decision-making through the strategic use of distinctive discursive strategies (Wodak *et al.* 2011)

Other researchers who take a similar approach are the North American scholar Karen Lee Ashcraft (profiled below), the Austrian researcher Marlene Miglbauer who is investigating gender and power in banking contexts in Austria and Croatia, and the British feminist sociolinguist Deborah Cameron who has focused on power and women's discourse in business settings (Cameron, 2007; see Chapter 4 for details on one of her studies that reveals the (inappropriate) nature of the language strategies provided in communication training targeted at women). Finally, from within organization studies the issues of race and decolonization of management discourse have been raised. Patricia Parker and Diane Grimes, both based in the United States, note that the construction of 'race' in organizations is complex and requires critiquing taken for granted assumptions as well the self-representations of dominant groups. Thus, 'decolonising management practice . . . involves unmasking racialised arrangements that reproduce subordinate "Others" in everyday rituals such as recruitment, hiring and workplace interactions' (Parker and Grimes, 2009: 300). In the UK, members of the Linguistic Ethnography Forum (http://www.ling-ethnog.org.uk/) Celia Roberts (2010; 2011) and Jan Blommaert (2004; 2009) have authored influential work on language, ethnicity and discrimination in institutional settings such as job interviews and the treatment of asylum seekers.

Profile 1.2   Karen Lee Ashcraft

Professor, Department of Communication, University of Colorado Boulder, Boulder, CO, USA.
http://comm.colorado.edu/people/4-faculty/209-ashcrak

Trained as: A student of organizational communication and an ethnographer
Inspired by: Cultural, critical studies of organization and feminist scholarship
Speciality: Organizational and occupational cultures and identities
Life: Born, educated and living in the USA

For:

- 'Articulating the distinctive contribution of communications studies to scholarship of work.'
- 'Blending the more typical attention of organization scholars to today's workplace settings with a historically conscious interest in how public discourse organizes gendered labour relations.'
- 'A fuller account of "intersectionality", or the ways in which gender interacts with race, class, sexuality, age, and other systems of identity and power.'
- 'Gendered organizational communication scholars articulating their distinctive contributions and relevance to wider audiences of scholars and practitioners.'

- The development of complex, candid perspectives on sexuality – however taboo and politically contentious – that could usefully disrupt the foundations of any "science" of work and organization.'

Against:

- 'Culture as a unified phenomenon' or as a concept used to 'capture aspects of race, ethnicity, gender, class, and so forth . . . yet to obscure the complex intersections across these varied aspects of identity.'
- 'Extended discussions of ethnographic positionality for its own sake; to me, these often sound like self-absorbed scholarly confessionals.'
- 'The current trend among critical and postmodern organization scholars to focus analyses of resistance on discourse and micro-practice, often to the exclusion of broader temporal and material frames.'

Quotations:

- 'I study the relationship between organization, power, and identity. I investigate how communication theory and practice creates, sustains, obscures, and transforms their complex connection.'
- 'A common purpose guides my work: to promote productive dialogue between organization theory and practice in an effort to generate feasible forms of organizational justice.'
- 'In many ways, the discipline of communication studies is interdisciplinary in nature and the sub-field of organizational communication is no exception.'
- 'I would place myself on that part of the social constructionist continuum that acknowledges material realities beyond text, even some basic realities independent of language.'
- 'For me "language" usually refers to actual talk or vocabularies-in-use, and in that sense, might be almost synonymous with – or, at least, practically interchangeable with – "communication". I generally use "discourse" to refer to more crystallized, meso- or macro-narratives about something, or to what might be seen as a collection or distillation of talk/texts.'
- 'I believe that all organizational scholarship carries political implications, whether these are admitted or not. The absence of a visible political agenda should not be mistaken for neutrality, for knowledge is always situated, and a view from nowhere is not possible.'

Critical approaches and business discourse

The label 'critical' has become something of an attitude, an attempt to provide a new perspective on traditional ways of seeing the world and engaging with it. The literature is full of 'critical' studies in a variety of disciplines with an equally varied set of ideas and motivations. It is perhaps possible, however, to generalize that researchers in the critical tradition embrace a reflexive and self-reflexive stance on the subject of the study, the way they study it and in their role as researchers. The website on Critical Thinking (http://www.criticalthinking.org) provides the following definition of 'critical':

> Critical thinking is the intellectually disciplined process of actively and skillfully conceptualizing, applying, analysing, synthesizing, and/or evaluating information gathered from, or generated by, observation, experience, reflection, reasoning, or communication, as a guide to belief and action. In its exemplary form, it is based on universal intellectual values that transcend subject matter divisions: clarity, accuracy, precision, consistency, relevance, sound evidence, good reasons, depth, breadth, and fairness. (http://www.criticalthinking.org/about)

In the last two decades critical approaches have proliferated, not least in the study of the language of management and other types of professional discourse, and political engagement with the inequalities generated by dominant discourses has come to be seen as an important research motivation. Critical discourse analysts are purposively engaged with the inequalities and asymmetries in social practices and with a commitment to changing it. They have looked, for instance, at the ideology of the language of marketization of higher education (Fairclough, 1993), at the ideology of clinical practice (Iedema, Degeling, Braithwaite & White, 2003) and that of the Internet (Berry, 2004). It is worth remembering that 'critical' does not only refer to research practices that question social injustice and inequality; 'critical' is a definition for researchers who apply self-reflexivity in their work and remain open to continuous change, inspired by their findings and by practitioners' needs and feedback.

Text-based or field-based research with a 'critical' label remains in its infancy in business discourse, however, since many linguists involved in the analysis of business language have shied away from a critical positioning that espouses a political agenda for social change and have preferred to maintain a more neutral stance. The exceptions to this are the gender and feminist researchers on both sides of the Atlantic that we have introduced above (e.g. Baxter, 2010; Peck, 2005; Mullany, 2003; Ashcraft & Mumby, 2003; Gherardi, 1995), and the pioneering studies by Sharon Livesey in the *Journal of Business Communication* and the *Management Communication Quarterly* (e.g. Livesey, 1999; 2001; 2002a; 2002b; 2002c; Livesey & Graham, 2007; Livesey, Hartman, Stafford & Shearer, 2009) that have provided a critical analysis of the corporate discourse realized by corporations such as Shell, McDonalds and ExxonMobil (see Data 1.6 below for an overview). As we will discuss in the next chapter, this type of qualitative, multi-approach analysis may provide a fruitful line of enquiry for business discourse researchers in the future.

Data 1.6 An overview of Sharon Livesey's work in the *Journal of Business Communication*

1. *McDonalds*: in her award-winning 1999 case study, Livesey examines the public discourse of an alliance between McDonalds and the Environmental Defense Fund in the US which drew both on the (then) emerging discourse of market environmentalism, and on issues of command and control. She comments that 'the McDonald's–EDF partnership was at once constrained by this discursive struggle over the environment and a constitutive element in the struggle itself' (1999: 5).
2. *Royal Dutch/Shell Group*: the 2001 study of Shell's public discourse in response to criticisms of its plans to de-commission the Brent Spar and its (controversial) operations in Ogoniland, Nigeria, extends Mauws and Phillips' (1995) use of Wittgenstein's term 'language games' together with Foucauldian discourse theory, to deconstruct Shell's engagement with, and 'cautious embrace of the language of sustainable development'. Livesey argues that 'such local conflicts over meaning-making around the natural environment must be understood in terms of discursive struggle at the socio-political level where they both reflect and influence the dynamics of cultural and institutional change' (2001: 58).
3. *ExxonMobil*: the 2002 study of advertorials produced by ExxonMobil draws both on rhetorical analysis and (Foucauldian) discourse analysis 'to illuminate the role of corporate public discourse in maintaining organizational legitimacy and influencing social and institutional stability and change' (2002c: 117). Livesey's analysis shows that 'the ExxonMobil texts reactualize other texts, specifically; discourses of environment and economic development articulated in *Brundtland** and entailed in contemporaneous climate negotiations under the umbrella of the UN' (2002c: 139).

*The *Brundtland Report (Our Common Future)* was a highly influential document produced in 1987 by the UN World Commission for Environment and Development.

In his chapter on critical applied linguistics for the Blackwell *Handbook of Applied Linguistics*, Alastair Pennycook (2004) remarks that the notion of critical is as contentious as the role and scope of applied linguistics and argues for a critical turn in applied linguistics with reference to Christopher Candlin's insightful observations on the topic over a decade earlier (see Quote 1.4). Much of what both Candlin and Pennycook suggest can also be seen to apply to business discourse research if we pose the question '*What happens when business discourse research goes critical?*'

Quote 1.4   Critical applied linguistics

One of the central goals of applied linguistics has been to place questions of language in their social context. . . . It is in this orientation to the socially relevant, the contextualized, the real, that we can find another version of the critical. In his plenary address to the 8th World Congress of Applied Linguistics in Sydney (AILA. 1987), Candlin (1990) asked 'What happens when Applied Linguistics goes critical?' Candlin argued for a critical dimension to applied linguistics for two main reasons: First, because applied linguistics had started to lose touch with the problems and issues around language faced by ordinary language users. Applied linguistics, he argued, was becoming an arcane, sectarian and theory-oriented discipline that was increasingly distanced from the everyday concerns of language use. Second, he suggested, a critical dimension was needed to reveal 'hidden connections . . . between language structure and social structure, between meaning-making and the economy of the social situation, but also connections between different branches of the study of language and their relationship to our central objective, the amelioration of individual and group existences through a focus on problems of human communication. A study of the socially-constituted nature of language practice' (1990: 461–2). In this view, then, critical applied linguistics can be seen as an attempt to make applied linguistics matter, to remake the connections between discourse, language learning, language use and the social and political contexts in which these occur.

(Pennycook 2004: 789)

Intercultural business discourse

One very fruitful area of research in business discourse has been the investigation of the communication that takes place when different cultures come into contact with each other in order to do business. In a review of the issues and challenges of intercultural business discourse research, Bargiela-Chiappini, Bülow-Møller, Nickerson, Poncini and Zhu (2003) discuss the priorities and concerns that informed and motivated the methodological choices of the five authors involved in the discussion. A synopsis of some of the most salient findings of their work appears in Quote 1.5 and serves as an introduction to ways in which business discourse researchers have viewed intercultural communication. Chapter 2 will look at recent and future developments in intercultural business discourse research in some detail; the purpose of this section is to introduce the field and some of the issues that have been brought to the fore in recent research.

Quote 1.5   Intercultural business communication: the challenges facing researchers

1. The presence of 'fluid roles and flexible relationships' observed in inter-cultural business meetings (Poncini: 78), which forces the analyst to move beyond using limiting national stereotypes as interpretative cate-gories. Further on this point, Bülow-Møller speaks of 'multiple identities' (84) as reflected in 'transactional discourse' (85). This is characterized by the suspension of fixed expectations and judgement, the tolerance of ambiguity and the willingness to engage in building new discursive frames (85).
2. The importance of professional experience as an attribute in intercul-tural negotiations, the importance of which stands well above cultural differences and individual linguistic competence: '[s]easoned business people . . . pay much less attention to culture and more to terms of agreement' (Bülow-Møller: 82); and 'students demonstrated time and again that an extensive knowledge of English grammar . . . could never compete with twenty years of experience as an international negotiator in successfully closing a deal' (Nickerson: 82).
3. The ethnocentrism of extant analytical categories and theories of cross-cultural communication and the mono-disciplinary nature of much comparative and contrastive intercultural business research.

(Adapted from Bargiela-Chiappini et al., 2003)

One of the most comprehensive (and comprehensible) theories of intercultural communication with a focus on the use of language in a business setting is provided by the British researcher Helen Spencer-Oatey. Working within the specific context of intercultural negotiations, Spencer-Oatey distinguishes five interrelated domains all of which contribute to building a working relation-ship. In a series of landmark publications on its theory and application, she has referred to her framework as 'rapport management' (Spencer-Oatey, 2000a; 2000b; see also the volume co-authored by Helen Spencer-Oatey and Peter Franklin (2006) on Intercultural Communication). As in Gina Poncini's work on multilingual business meetings discussed in Chapter 2 and in Mirjaliisa Charles' work on negotiations that we have introduced above, the emphasis is therefore on how participants work together to find a solution, rather than on defining the communication breakdowns that may occur (see also Ken Willing's pioneering work on white collar multicultural workplaces in Australia as profiled in Chapter 4). As a theory of interaction, Spencer-Oatey's framework (see also Chapter 2) pinpoints a number of key dimensions that may play a role in the success or failure of intercultural communication in business contexts, including content, the organization of talk, politeness, style and deference, and body language. Applications of Spencer-Oatey's theoretical framework that we will discuss later in this book (in Part 3), include Spencer-Oatey and Xing (2003) in their account of two business meetings between Chinese and British native speakers, and Planken (2005) in her investigation of how rapport is managed differently by professional and aspiring negotiators.

Concept 1.3   Iris Varner on intercultural business communication

Varner (2000) provides a conceptual model for intercultural business communication that combines business strategy, intercultural strategy and communication strategy. In doing so, she makes the crucial link between the business context on the one hand and the discourse that realizes that context on the other. Her work is a rare example of a US-based researcher acknowledging the role played by discourse in a macro-theory, perhaps as a result of her European background. We will look at her co-authored teaching materials (with Linda Beamer) in Chapter 5. Varner observes: 'It is amazing how often we refer to research by Hofstede, Trompenaars, Hall to justify our discussion of German culture, French culture, American culture, or Japanese culture. However, we do not do business with "the" Germans or Italians, or Chinese; we do business with specific people in specific industries who come from specific cultures. Our understanding of culture requires a solid grasp of the history of the culture and how this history has shaped cultural priorities. We also need to understand how rhetorical patterns come out of these cultural priorities and specific world views' (Victor, 2012: 14).

1.5   Business discourse around the world

In the final section of this chapter we will look at business discourse research around the world as well as profiling a number of researchers that represent each geographical area and cultural tradition. Turning first to North America, we can see that disciplinary boundaries and questions of identity have been common concerns for researchers involved with the field of business communication in particular, the field in which some researchers interested in business discourse are active. Business communication is characterized by researchers such as Priscilla Rogers (e.g. Rogers, 2000) and Jane Thomas (e.g. Thomas, 1997) who have specifically focused on language in their research work, while at the same time making a contribution to innovative teaching practice. Rogers' work on mission statements with the applied linguist John Swales appears in Part 3.

Concept 1.4 'Business Discourse' as a space for dialogue

The inspiration for *The Handbook of Business Discourse* (Bargiela-Chiappini, 2009) came from the realization that 'business discourse' as an eclectic scholarly enterprise emerges from and thrives on the dialogue between diverse disciplines, approaches and methodologies. Based on an understanding of 'discourse' as dialogue, – between fields, worldviews and schools of thought, – *The Handbook* includes contributions from linguistic anthropology, gender studies, sociology, organizational and business communication, etc. The methodological approaches are equally varied, including corpus linguistics, ethnomethodology, negotiation studies, multimodal analysis, etc. Finally, the section on 'Localised Perspectives' brings together for the first time 'non-western' researchers whose voices still remain somewhat marginalized in the international arena.

Business communication is a well-established component in North American academic programmes, and as Bargiela-Chiappini (2004: 25) has recently written, it tends to struggle with a competition between theory on the one hand and application on the other 'i.e. the conflict of interest arising between research and teaching/training priorities'. Outside of the business communication community, scholars working within disciplines such as rhetoric, speech communication and organizational communication, have also sought to understand the role played by language in the construction of (business) organizations. The work of Linda Putnam is an example of this being both multidisciplinary and multimethod in nature, for instance, in her work in the 1990s on communication and negotiation (e.g. Putnam & Roloff, 1992), and her co-edited collection of papers focusing on organizational communication from a (US) perspective over the course of two decades (e.g. Putnam & Pacanowsky, 1983; Jablin & Putnam, 2001; Putnam & Krone, 2006).

Other notable work of relevance for business discourse research includes a collection of papers on the rhetoric of international professional communication edited by Lovitt & Goswami (1999) in which a group of (largely) US-based researchers consider the role played by (national) culture in different forms of professional communication. Although the North American tradition has not tended to prioritize the type of close text analysis that is a hallmark of many of the (European-based) studies that we will talk about later in this book, it has been of enormous influence in terms of the macro-theories that it has produced, such as the media richness theory proposed by Daft & Lengel (1984) and the concept of organizational genres proposed by Yates & Orlikowski (1992) working in the new rhetoric tradition.

Quote 1.6   On the nature of business communication from a US perspective

> . . . we do appear to share an interest in providing practical knowledge that can enhance the communication effectiveness of all kinds of organizational stakeholders, particularly related to business.
>
> (Rogers, 2001: 21)

As Bargiela-Chiappini and Nickerson point out, 'disciplinary boundaries have not traditionally been an area of such concern on the European side of the Atlantic' (2002: 275). Researchers have come primarily out of the applied linguistics field, and have been more likely to be involved with a close text analysis of the written texts or spoken events that they have investigated than their North American counterparts. Their work has focused on intercultural negotiations, business meetings and corporate communication (e.g. emails, annual reports, letters to shareholders, etc.). Despite the dominance of English, an increasing variety of other European languages used in business discourse have been investigated, including French (van der Wijst, 1996; Christian, 1998), Dutch (van der Wijst, 1996), German (Zilles, 2004), Spanish (Villemoes, 2003; Tebeaux, 1999; Candia, 2001; Charteris-Black & Ennis, 2001; Ulijn & Verweij, 2000; Conaway & Wardrope, 2004), Danish (Grindsted, 1997), Norwegian (Neumann, 1997) and Portuguese (Silvestre, 2003; 2004; Pereira, 2004). The 2003 compendium of Spanish for Specific Purposes from 1985 to 2002, for instance, compiled by Myriam Bueno Lajusticia (Bueno Lajusticia, 2003), provides an extensive illustration of the work that has been carried out outside of the English speaking world. The construct of 'context' has been of concern to European researchers and specifically how to bridge the gap between the different contextual dimensions that are of relevance in business discourse, such as the wider social context, the organizations investigated and the individuals who work within them, and on the whole, the European business discourse tradition has tended to be neutral in its stance and has been largely uncritical in its approach. The work of Gina Poncini, profiled below, which we will also refer to in Chapter 2, is an example of a Europe-based business discourse researcher who has investigated the use of as many as eight different (European) languages used in multilingual meetings.

Profile 1.3   Gina Poncini

Associate Professor in the Department of Economics, Management and Quantitative Methods, Faculty of Political, Economic and Social Sciences, University of Milan, http://www.economia.unimi.it

Trained as: An applied linguist (undergraduate degree in marketing)

Specialty:	Intercultural business communication, management communication, issues concerning expertise and the role of discourse and communication when members of different professional communities come together
Inspired by:	Business and management, interactional sociolinguistics and ethnography
Life:	Born in the US, educated in the US (including Master's) and the UK (PhD). Has lived in Italy since 1978, near the border with Switzerland, working first in international banking in Milan before starting to teach in Switzerland in 1988 and then in Italy.

For:

• More 'going into the company' to do research on actual communicative practices in business.
• More interdisciplinary dialogue and collaborative work with scholars from other disciplines.

Quotations:

• 'Looking at things differently – whether the interactional context, other situational factors, or the wider social, historical or economic context – makes for a more innovative approach during the research process. In a sense, "looking at things differently" can be seen as a research-oriented application of design thinking – a creative approach leading to richer results and the potential for a greater impact.'
• 'In approaching multicultural settings, there would clearly be limits to viewing each participant as a representative of a homogenous national culture without recognizing that a range of other factors may come to bear on the interaction – from individual differences to the business context, from professional roles to relationships, from level of expertise to shared knowledge.'
• 'Communication is interdisciplinary, and with business representing such a complex environment, the use of multimethods is especially able to provide a richer picture. An understanding of the wider business context and the way language can be used strategically is key.'
• 'Focusing on miscommunication in intercultural settings is limiting because this approach assumes intercultural interactions are problematic and consequently tends to ignore factors possibly contributing to successful intercultural communication.'
• 'One important ability for a leader's performance in multicultural, multiparty settings is that of shifting in and out of frames.'

- 'Training needs to give attention to context in intercultural business settings, especially business issues, goals, roles and relationships. This encompasses leader behaviour and the range of roles that may be enacted in business encounters.'
- 'Intercultural meetings seem to have their own culture, or at least their own character and sense of "groupness", not necessarily linked to national cultures.' Similarly, research connected to industry events has brought to light shared practices across professional communities and the notion of an event-related community.
- 'If conflict is observed [in the intercultural meetings examined] it involves factors not necessarily related to the different national cultures of participants.'

Quote 1.7   The nature of business communication from a European perspective

There seems to be a general understanding of the identification of the utilitarian goal of developing and disseminating knowledge that increases the effectiveness and efficiency of business operations.

(Louhiala-Salminen, 1999: 26)

Elsewhere in the world other aspects of business discourse research have been a focus of attention. As we will discuss in detail in Chapter 4, the issues of power investigated in the Language in the Workplace project co-ordinated by Janet Holmes (see profile below) and her colleagues in New Zealand are a reflection of the multicultural nature of contemporary New Zealand society, as well as a concern with inequality that has characterized Australasian discourse research for a number of years.

Profile 1.4   Janet Holmes

Professor of Linguistics, Victoria University of Wellington, New Zealand
http://www.vuw.ac.nz/lals/staff/janet-holmes/holmes.aspx

Trained as: A linguist
Inspired by: Sociolinguistics, John Pride, Dell Hymes, Robin Lakoff
Speciality: Language and gender, workplace discourse
Life: Born in Liverpool, England, university at Leeds, moved to New Zealand for work and have been there ever since . . . but travel a lot now.

For:

- Working with researchers from different disciplines
- Data-based interpretation
- Integrating quantitative and qualitative research approaches
- Valuing the background information that traditional sociolinguistic approaches supply
- Recognizing the contributions of earlier scholars

Against:

- Extreme positions in any form
- Treating reported data as evidence of what people do

Quotations:

- Approach to multidisciplinary research: 'getting in there and doing it is the answer from our perspective, not worrying too much in advance but trying with good will to make sure that you understand what the other persons' concerns are'.
- 'We tend to define culture as shared values and beliefs and ways of doing things that characterize a particular group or community of practice.'
- 'Access to the sites usually depends on knowing somebody who will vouch for you.'
- 'Sociolinguistics and pragmatics are the areas of linguistics that I would see as making the most obvious contribution to research on workplace discourse.'
- 'What is most important is to get people who want to work together; one of the ways of doing this would be to indicate what goals you are going to have for a project and then invite people perhaps for an initial discussion on how they would contribute.'
- 'I tend be a bit sceptical of the idea that there are no sociological categories and that they have to be constructed anew every time somebody speaks; every time we speak we either re-enforce or challenge the patterns but the speakers are making use of what they assume are the norms; part of our jobs as sociolinguists is to capture those norms where we can and to describe them so that we can interpret what is going on at the micro-level.'
- 'I tend to use interactional sociolinguistics as a broad framework within which to describe context. Within that, you tend pragmatically to describe as much of the context that is needed to understand what is going on.'

- 'Social constructionism has a lot to offer but there are insights to be gained from realizing that people bring to the interaction assumptions and preconceptions and stereotypes about gender, status, ethnicity, etc.'
- 'I do think we are not totally constrained agents, we *can* contest and challenge, but a lot of the time we do not, we go along with things and we follow the patterns that people expect. We tend only to notice when people break the rules.'

Finally, outside of Europe and the English-speaking world, there has been a proliferation of work on languages and, significantly, cultures other than English and the Anglo-Saxon cultures in business contexts, resulting in a wealth of information on business cultures as diverse as Argentina (Gimenez, 2002), Turkey (Akar, 2002), and China (Zhu, 2005). The 1990s in particular were characterized by intercultural business analyses of interactions involving Asian languages (together with English), mainly Japanese (e.g. Miller, 1994; Marriott, 1997; Yamada, 1997) but also Chinese (Bilbow, 1995; 1997; Rogerson-Revell, 1998; see also Yeung, 1998 for a crosscultural study of Hong Kong and Australian bank meetings). In Hong Kong, research on professional discourse and intercultural communication investigating the needs of practitioners and students and led by Winnie Cheng (see Profile 1.7) and colleagues has generated a distinctive body of publications (e.g. Cheng and Mok, 2006; Cheng and Warren, 2005; Cheng and Warren, 2006; Cheng and Kong, 2009; Cheng 2009). The interest in business discourse in Asian contexts has grown to include field studies of the Malaysian workplace (Nair-Venugopal, 2000; 2001) and the Indian workplace (Kaul, 2003; Kaul, Ansari & Rai, 2005; Kaul, 2012), of Chinese and Chinese–British interactions (Bilbow, 2002; Spencer-Oatey & Xing, 2003; Spencer-Oatey & Xing, 2005), and of the role of English vis-à-vis other Asian languages (Kameda, 2001; Miller, 2000; Li So-mui & Mead, 2000). Finally, at the end of 2005 and the beginning of 2006, three landmark collections on Asian business discourse appeared in the *Linguistics Insights Series* and the *Journal of Asian Pacific Communication* (Bargiela-Chiappini & Gotti, 2005; Bargiela-Chiappini, 2005a; Bargiela-Chiappini, 2006), including the work of researchers such as Yeonkwon Jung (2005) for Korean business correspondence, Habil Hadina and Shameem Rafik-Galea (2005) for Malaysian electronic business discourse, Kusum Dhanania and Sandhya Gopakumaran (2005) for Marwari business discourse in India and Grace Chye Lay Chew (2005) for Vietnamese business communication. We will discuss many studies of business discourse from around the world in Part 3 of this book.

Concept 1.5   Inter-Asian business discourse(s)

Most Asian business discourse research focusing on intercultural communication has concentrated on differences between the East and West based on essentialist or neo-essentialist views. In such studies, Asia has been treated as a monolithic 'periphery'. The application of conventional dichotomies such as collectivist – individualist fails to capture the complexities of differences among Asians. Recent studies have sought to redefine intercultural business discourse from an Asian perspective by examining interaction between individuals of Asian backgrounds. This new approach reveals the plurality of Asian business discourse(s). The investigation of intra-Asian business interaction has highlighted that the role of language chosen for communication is critical, where this is usually English as a lingua franca (ELF). ELF acts as more than a tool for intercultural communication. Examples of intra-Asian business discourse research:

Paramasivam's study of negotiation between Malaysian and Japanese business practitioners (2007). Paramasivam examines how power and politeness work on the business site where both parties negotiate for knowledge exchange. Du-Babcock and Tanaka (2010) investigate intercultural and intra-cultural decision making meetings between and among Hong Kong Chinese and Japanese business professionals. While each cultural group strives to achieve group harmony, the data show that Hong Kong Chinese and Japanese use silence and negotiate disagreement differently. Tanaka (2011) analyses Indian-Japanese business meetings recorded in India and maps the emergent patterns of ELF communication from the two (different) perspectives. The linguistic analysis of spoken data shows frequent use of restructuring and lexical repetition for confirmation. Furthermore, the interview data suggest solidarity as the speakers monitored each other's language proficiency, which enabled the interactants to determine the appropriateness of a setting-specific strategy such as multi-modal confirmation. Finally, Tanaka (under review) concentrates on asymmetry in Indian and Japanese business discourse by analysing lying behaviour. The conflicting interpretation of lying behaviour shows that discrepancy among Asian business discourse(s) is as great as the discrepancies between East and West discussed in earlier research.

We conclude this brief overview with the profiles of Sharon Livesey, Winnie Cheng and Judith Baxter, three of the scholars we have referred to in this chapter. In Chapter 2 we will discuss the challenges to be met in the future of business discourse research.

Profile 1.5 Sharon Livesey

Associate Professor of Management, Fordham University Schools of Business, New York, NY

Trained as: Literary critic, lawyer
Inspired by: Julie Graham, Kath Gibson, Judith Butler, Michel Callon, Bruno LaTour, John Law, William Connolly
Specialty: Business environmental & CSR discourse
Life: Born in the US, worked for civil rights & labour law attorneys in London & Boston, critical teacher/ theorist at Harvard Business School & Fordham Schools of Business with focus on social and environmental responsibilities of business & (in)capacities of business to have positive impacts on society

For:

- Increasing understanding of the performative effects of language and storytelling
- Research that takes integrates socio-political and cultural contexts with micro-level analysis
- Enhancing institutional theory by adding discursive methods and approaches
- Acknowledging and valuing the contributions of feminist scholarship
- The amazing experiments in dialogue and democracy and knowledge creation that are Occupy Wall Street, the Occupy's everywhere, and the precedents that inspired them including Tahrir Square, the Spanish *Indignados*, Wisconsin, Greece, and France

Against:

- Attempts to make social science fit the straight-jacket of natural science norms
- Failures to take into account the rhetoricity of numbers

Profile 1.6 Winnie Cheng

Professor, Department of English, The Hong Kong Polytechnic University, Hong Kong SAR, China
Director, Research Centre for Professional Communication in English, Department of English, The Hong Kong Polytechnic University, Hong Kong SAR, China http://www.engl.polyu.edu.hk/People_staff.php?recid=151

Trained as: A researcher of conversation analysis in intercultural communication

Inspired by: The notion of 'trust the text' (Sinclair, 2004)
Specialty: Critical discourse and pragmatic studies of professional communication
Life: Born, educated, living and working in Hong Kong SAR, China

For:

- 'In the studies of professional communication, the importance of capturing all the discourses in the discourse flow, studying the ways in which language use evolves within the discourse flow, and eliciting different parties' input to fully understand the discourses and their inter-relationships.'
- 'Adopting a multidisciplinary approach to the study of linguistic, cognitive, technological, and social aspects of human communication in the context of modern society with all the technological advancement in new media and tools.'
- 'Studying the communicative value of intonation by focusing on meaning making by speakers in the moment-by-moment real-time interaction.'

Against:

- 'Inaccurately transcribed spoken data due to negligence.'
- 'Having collected data from the workplace but failed to examine them and disseminate research findings.'

Quotations:

- 'The division between form and meaning has been steadily eroded by the plentiful evidence of corpus linguistics to the point where the two aspects are better conceived as one.'
- 'Those who fail to communicate using the conventional phraseology may be less effective in both meaning making and making themselves understood.'
- 'Contact between people is an essential element of our lives and conversing is a basic medium for performing this extremely vital function and achieving this universal end.'
- 'Professionals and academia alike need to be culturally sensitive and approach intercultural communication with a positive attitude. Explicit instruction in intercultural pragmatics that draws on empirical studies can help students and professionals take steps towards interculturality.'
- 'Studying the patterns of co-selection of lexical items in business texts and discourse reveals complex textual and intertextual relationships which together are part of the mechanism that creates surface lexical cohesion, but more fundamentally textual and intertextual meanings and coherence.'

Profile 1.7   Judith Baxter

Reader in Applied Linguistics, Aston University, UK
http://www1.aston.ac.uk/lss/staff/baxterj

Trained as: An English teacher; then a sociolinguist
Inspired by: Janet Holmes; Sara Mills; Deborah Cameron
Speciality: Language and gender
Life: Born in Belfast, N. Ireland, moved to Bath then to Winchester, UK; now live in Porlock, Somerset on the top of a very steep hill

For:

- Imaginative theorizing that takes us beyond the obvious
- Crossing disciplinary and professional boundaries
- Self-reflexivity in research: always questioning our assumptions, values and positions, recognizing that in every research act we have made a discursively informed choice.
- Demystifying post-structuralism so that it makes sense to scholars and lay people alike
- The notion that we are agentic beings who can do more than just 'resist' discursive positions: we can make a difference. This means being prepared to break the rules!

Against:

- The critical agenda which polarizes people into heroes, villains and victims often based on spurious judgements about class, gender and ethnicity.
- The feminist agenda which tends to characterize women (and some men) as victims without realizing how subject positioning involves shifts of power from one context to the next.
- Self-serving, elitist, academic research which never reaches beyond one's own community of fellow scholars.

Quotations:

- 'Women need to become linguistically aware and expert if they are to survive and to thrive in their organizations. In short, they need to outwit men.'
- 'Leadership is almost literally constructed through the step-by-step choices speakers make as they enact leadership in the course of decision-making forums such as business meetings.'
- 'An exclusively female voice may become a limitation if it suppresses vital differences between women, thus precluding a belief in the plurality of human identity.'

- 'I worry that very senior women aren't doing enough to help talented, less senior women move up their organizations. I see this in academia as much as in the business world.'
- 'Post-structuralism isn't just high theory; it can offer issue-orientated, pragmatic, contextualized, and outcome-based approaches to research.'
- 'No perspective is producing disinterested knowledge and each one represents particular positions within power relations.'

1.6 Summary

This first chapter has surveyed the field of business discourse starting with a definition of 'business discourse' and of the scope of the research activities clustered under this label. Following on from this introduction, a historical perspective of business discourse was offered with a brief discussion of landmark studies in a range of geographical and cultural contexts, together with examples of spoken and written types of data and an overview of the approaches adopted by analysts within varying methodological traditions. The concluding section focused on the cultural spread of business discourse around the world as illustrated by the diverse profiles of a number of researchers who also represent distinct disciplinary approaches.

Further reading

Bargiela-Chiappini, F. (Ed.) (2009). *The handbook of business discourse*. Edinburgh: Edinburgh University Press. In 36 chapters, this volume surveys the origins, features and advances in business discourse, as well as offering an overview of the disciplinary, methodological and localized approaches to the field.

Bargiela-Chiappini, F., & Gotti, M. (Eds.) (2005). *Asian business discourse(s)*. Bern: Peter Lang. This volume showcases linguistic and cultural studies of aspects of communication in Asian business contexts.

Bhatia, V. K. (2004). *Worlds of written discourse: A genre-based view*. London: Continuum. This book moves genre theory away from educational contexts and into the 'real world'; the texts analysed represent the worlds of advertising, business, academia, economics, law, the media and fundraising.

Gouveia, C., Silvestre, C., & Azuaga, L. (Eds.) (2004). *Discourse, communication and the enterprise: Linguistic perspectives*. Lisbon, Portugal: Centre for English Studies, University of Lisbon. The twenty-seven essays in this collection explore discursive strategies in written and spoken communication in a variety of countries and business settings.

Trosborg, A., & Flyvhom Jørgensen, P. E. (Eds.) (2005). *Business discourse: Texts and contexts*. Bern: Peter Lang. A collection of essays on aspects of written and spoken business communication in intra and intercultural settings, including mission statements, international contracts and decision-making meetings.

Chapter 1 Tasks

Task 1: Terminology and its consequences

Jian, Schmisseur and Fairhurst (2008) discuss how scholars within the social sciences have come to different conceptualizations of 'discourse' and 'communication'. The authors focus on articles published in journals of communication studies, organization studies and interdisciplinary research. Read the article and decide whether you agree with the approach the authors take and the arguments they present. What is the article's contribution towards advancing a multidisciplinary understanding of business discourse?

Task 2: Prescription vs. description and interpretation

Choose a popular textbook on business communication, for example one widely used in your country or in your institution, and find the chapter on Meetings. Compare the authors' treatment of the topic with approach(es) adopted in the empirical studies of meetings referenced in this chapter. Discuss the relevance and usefulness of each for different types of users, e.g. researchers, students, teachers, business practitioners, corporate trainers, etc. If you were asked to produce a set of materials on business meetings, describe how you would go about this.

Task 3: The interview

You have been asked to approach a well-known scholar in the field of business discourse with a view to interviewing him or her: decide what you would ask in a semi-structured interview to be conducted face to face or by telephone.

References

Jian, G., G. T. Fairhurst, A. M., Schmisseur, (2008). Organizational discourse and communication: the progeny of Proteus. *Discourse & Communication*, 2, (3), 299–320.

2
Challenges in the Future

This chapter will:

- Discuss the future of *intercultural business discourse* research with particular reference to *rapport management*;
- Provide a discussion of *multimodality* and how this might change business discourse in the future;
- Discuss *multimethod, multidisciplinary* research as a way forward for business discourse research.

This chapter discusses some of the issues around the formation of a research agenda for business discourse in the future. It begins by looking at the implications of increasing globalization and the multilingual workplace on intercultural business discourse research and continues with a discussion of multimodality theory. In the third part of the chapter we then go on to look at a number of studies that have used a multimethod, multidisciplinary approach as examples of one way forward for business discourse research in the future.

2.1 Towards transculturality

In Chapter 1, we discussed intercultural business discourse as one of the most fruitful areas of research in business settings. Harris and Bargiela-Chiappini (2003) identify a pressing need to study the language of the multilingual workplace and the multinational organization. It is against the background of increasing globalization that business discourse researchers will need to identify the most appropriate methods and approaches that will allow them to say something meaningful about the communication that takes place in such environments.

The literature on intercultural business discourse thus far has tended to build on the micro-analytical research of monographic works such as Willing

(1992) (see Chapter 4), Clyne (1994; 2003), Goldstein (1997), Yamada (1997), Rogerson-Revell (1998), Li (1999), Nickerson (2000) and Nair-Venugopal (2000) which consider multilingual and bilingual work environments in Australia, Canada, Japan, Hong Kong, the Netherlands and Malaysia, or on edited collections of academic studies like those by Ehlich and Wagner (1995) and Bargiela-Chiappini and Harris (1997a; 1997b) on the discourse of negotiations and meetings respectively.

A later collection of essays concentrates on intercultural aspects of institutional and professional communication conducted in English (Candlin & Gotti, 2004). Specifically, the authors 'explore to what extent intercultural pressure leads to particular discourse patternings and lexico-grammatical/ phonological realisations, and also the extent to which textual re-encoding and recontextualisation serve to obscure or emphasise particular locally-relevant aspects of the communication' (Gotti, 2004: 14). The dominance of English as a lingua franca in business professional and organizational contexts continues to be in evidence in both (multicultural) European and Asian contexts (Salvi & Tanaka, 2011a). Even though English is confirmed as the principal medium of intercultural communication, business practices do not necessarily conform to the Anglo-Saxon, neoliberal model of business. Discursive adaptation that is sympathetic to local historical and socio-cultural patterns is detectable in both spoken and written intercultural communication. Furthermore, technology is blurring the boundaries between written and spoken genres (see also Chapter 7) in a business world that has become extremely reliant on mediated communication (Salvi & Tanaka, 2011b).

Within these studies, the concept of culture has often been approached uncritically, although scholars have acknowledged the existence of cultural differences especially in the case of multinational companies. Instead, such studies have concentrated on description and application (e.g. Feely & Harzing, 2003; Marschan-Piekkari et al., 1999; Charles & Marschan-Piekkari, 2002; see Part 2 for further discussion).

Concept 2.1   Three developments in intercultural analysis

Interculturality: Bargiela-Chiappini (2004b) defines this construct as 'the process and the condition of cultures-in-contact' (2004: 29). It is therefore seen as contextualized experience within which processes of negotiation and accommodation dialogically realize three overlapping interactional dimensions: the social, the linguistic and the cognitive. Interculturality is viewed as language as social action and seeks to capture culture in the making in intercultural encounters. As a theoretical construct, it challenges some of the Western assumptions embedded in much inter- and crosscultural research: ethnocentrism, the individualistic perspectives on self that has characterized some Western research, the exclusively cognitive explanations for interpersonal relations, and the limits of Hofstede's (1984) 'national culture' as an all-encompassing analytical category.

SIPs: Spencer-Oatey and Jiang (Spencer-Oatey & Jiang, 2003) have suggested that politeness maxims in crosscultural pragmatics can be replaced by a new notion, that of sociopragmatic interactional principles (SIPs). SIPs are 'socioculturally-based principles, scalar in nature, that guide or influence people's productive and interpretive use of language. The principles are typically value-linked, so that in a given culture and/or situational context, there are norms or preferences regarding the implementation of these principles, and any failure to implement them as expected may result in mild to strong evaluative judgements' (Spencer-Oatey & Jiang, 2003: 1635). The authors' comparative study of SIPs in China and England shows similarities across cultures in the type of SIPs that people use but also that there is variation at a more detailed level; for example, situational factors may explain variation across cultures in the overall importance that people attach to a given SIP in a given interaction or a given encounter (1644).

Asian Intercultural Communication: In her critique of the Western paradigm that dominates intercultural communication scholarship, Kim (2010: 176) surmises that we need to become 'self-conscious about what is being taken for granted in the formulation of the problem and about the labels that are used'. This applies to both Western and Asian scholars. Firstly, the homogenizing effect of the 'Asian' label has meant that distinctive regional variations have coalesced in the widely accepted description of Asians as collectivists, and their communicative style as reserved and indirect. Secondly, the characterization of the Asian 'other' in ICC research has helped perpetuate power relations between the West and Asia. Thirdly, she perceives that the hegemony of US communication studies in intercultural communication has stifled the development of alternative, indigenous perspectives, which have only recently begun to emerge and which remain confined to select journals (*Asian Journal of Communication, Asian Communication research, Keio Communication Review* and *Chinese Journal of Communication*), a view which is widely held by Asian communication scholars. Change in intercultural communication studies calls for an awareness of the complexity and heterogeneity of Asian communication styles (see, for example, Du-Babcock & Tanaka, 2011; Tanaka, 2011, and for openness to a new paradigm based on 'cross-indigenization', which taps into local 'knowledges' (see also Concept 2.2. Asiacentricity).

Elsewhere, for instance in management studies, crosscultural investigations focusing on organizations have largely ignored language and communicative practices in intercultural contact. They have also tended to take an *etic* approach, which is one based on comparative analyses between two or more countries, where *culture* is deemed to be equivalent to national culture. Crosscultural management (CCM) research and education are notoriously ethnocentric. Curricula are often modelled on prescriptive sets of 'cultural patterns and skills', and broad-brush ethnocentric, analytical categories are often applied unreflexively and uncritically to define both contexts and people.

Zhu and Bargiela-Chiappini (2013) draw on situated learning and ethnography of communication to reconceptualize CCM learning and research as a cumulative process of acquiring knowledge through active engagement with emic practices in specific cultural workplace contexts. Both students and teachers are invited to become 'ethnographers', i.e. to adopt a reflexive attitude towards learning from/as doing, within their context of practice, whether this is the classroom or the workplace. Group work on extensive, fine-grained and situated analysis of authentic data from the field that reconstructs workplace practices in the classroom is the first step in ethnographic appreciation. The analytical tools and insight acquired in the classroom are intended to prepare students for work placements or project organization in the community where they will be able to engage more reflexively and therefore more deeply with the emic, situated nature of practices. In recent work, attention has been drawn to the *etic/emic* dimensions (e.g. Jack & Zhu et al., in press; Sinkovics et al. 2008; Zhu, 2009), and the importance of developing understanding from the perspective of the culture or cultures under investigation before attempting comparisons across cultures. The linguist Kenneth L. Pike (1967) is credited with first proposing the etic/emic distinction, which was later introduced to crosscultural psychology by John W. Berry (1989) who sought to integrate in-depth insights from intra-cultural analysis with broad patterns of relationships across cultures. Berry (1989) elaborated a set of research steps rooted in the emic–etic conceptualization which enable psychologists to pursue both the indigenous and comparative goals. In spite of this development, the use of stereotypical, universalistic dimensions remains a prevalent approach in international management textbooks (e.g., Deresky & Christopher, 2012; Luthans & Doh, 2010; Thomas, 2008).

In the section below, we will look in detail at rapport management, as a potentially emic perspective on communication in intercultural settings, and we will explore its potential for the investigation of spoken business discourse. We will illustrate the wider applicability of the framework to the study of (intercultural) business discourse by considering two investigations that have used the rapport management framework as a theoretical and analytical starting point.

Rapport management

It has been suggested that the appreciation of cultural diversity requires new ways of knowing, more reliance on intuition than on rationalization, and even a 'radical consciousness shift' (Subbiondo, 2005). As we suggested in Chapter 1, one approach to the analysis of interaction that is sensitive to issues of face, interpersonal perceptions and assumptions, and how these may determine and impact on (intercultural) communication is offered within the framework of rapport management (Spencer-Oatey, 2000a; Spencer-Oatey & Franklin, 2009). Using the broader term 'rapport' rather than politeness, Spencer-Oatey argues that, in addition to face concerns, there is another motivation underlying the management of relations, namely 'sociality rights', or the personal and social entitlements that individuals claim as part of their – professional – role or status in interactions with others (see Quote 2.1 below). The rapport management framework, which draws on social pragmatics, politeness theory and face theory, essentially seeks to explain how language is used to manage relationships. According to Spencer-Oatey, rapport, or 'the management of harmony–disharmony' needs to be managed not only at the level of (face-threatening) speech acts, but across five interrelated domains of interaction: the illocutionary domain (the performance of speech acts), the discourse domain (the choice of topic, structure and sequencing, etc.), the participation domain (including turn-taking, the inclusion or exclusion of participants, and back-channelling), the stylistic domain (incorporating choice of tone, formality level, register), and the non-verbal domain (including eye contact and hand gestures, etc.). The model offers a way to account not only for the (non)verbal politic behaviour that speakers may use strategically to create and maintain a pleasant atmosphere and good relations, but also the defensive, challenging or even rude behaviour that is manifested in potentially conflictive communication settings (e.g. business negotiations). In this way, it is of potential interest to business discourse researchers interested in accounting for aspects of relational talk in business interactions, ranging from politeness forms and accommodation strategies to contentious and conflictive strategies, as well as the linguistic manifestations of power, and the motivations that might underlie such behaviours.

Quote 2.1   Rapport management defined

[R]apport management (the management of harmony–disharmony among people) involves two main components: the management of face and the management of sociality rights. Face management, as the term indicates, involves the management of face needs . . . . I define face needs as 'the positive social value a person effectively claims for himself by the line others assume he has taken during a particular contact'. The management of sociality rights, on the other hand, involves the management of social expectancies, which I define as 'fundamental personal/social entitlements that individuals effectively claim for themselves in their interactions with others'. In other words, face is associated with personal/social value, and is concerned with people's sense of worth, dignity, honour, reputation, competence and so on. Sociality rights, on the other hand, are concerned with personal/social expectancies, and reflect people's concerns over fairness, consideration, social inclusion/exclusion and so on.

(Spencer-Oatey, 2000a: 13–14)

Below we discuss two studies that have used the framework to identify and analyse different aspects of rapport management in spoken business discourse: Spencer-Oatey and Xing's study of a problematic British–Chinese business encounter (2003) and Planken's investigation of professional and novice negotiators' discourse (Planken, 2005). The underlying concern in both studies is the relational work that informs (business) interactions (e.g. Miller, 1994).

Differing assumptions and expectations: relational communication in intercultural business contexts (Spencer-Oatey & Xing, 2003)

This multimethod, data-driven study, conducted as part of a larger investigation of relational management in Chinese–British business encounters, investigated how business professionals establish an initial relationship in intercultural business encounters. Through video observation, fieldwork and interviews in a British company, the researchers identified similarities and differences in the communication behaviour of participants in two Chinese–British welcome meetings that preceded company visits by two Chinese delegations. Despite many similarities between the two encounters, they were evaluated very differently by the parties involved: while both were satisfied with the first meeting, the Chinese were extremely unhappy about the second. In considering the two parties' perceptions of, and reasons for, communication behaviour in the two welcome meetings, this study provides insight into the reasons why the British hosts and the Chinese visitors evaluated these encounters, and the subsequent visits, so differently.

Quote 2.2   Some comments from the postmeeting interviews with participants

'it shouldn't have been that he was the chair and we were seated along the sides of tables. With equal status, they should sit along this side and we should sit along that side' (Chinese delegation leader)

'According to our home customs and protocol, speech is delivered on the basis of reciprocity. He has made his speech and I am expected to say something . . . Condescension was implied. In fact I was reluctant to speak, and I had nothing to say. But I had to, to say a few words. Right for the occasion, right? But he had finished his speech, and he didn't give me the opportunity, and they each introduced themselves, wasn't this clearly implied that they do look down upon us Chinese.' (Chinese delegation leader)

'It is understandable for them to praise their own products, but by doing so in fact they made a great mistake. Why? Because, you see, because for a company when they haven't got new orders for their products for several years it is a serious problem, to them, but they didn't talk about it . . . He didn't mention our orders. So in fact this is a very important matter. It is not just a matter of receiving us.' (Chinese Marketing Manager, Delegation Two)

'That's interesting, so it goes back to the point of our concern for interpretation, because if the interpreter had said to me that they are just making a return speech, then it would have been fine.' (British Chairman, Visit Two)

(Spencer-Oatey & Xing, 2003: 39–41)

Using triangulation of three types of data (observational, interview and fieldwork data), Spencer-Oatey and Xing provide a detailed, 'thick' analysis (Geertz, 1973) of how contextual and cultural factors – in combination – seem to have played an important role in influencing meeting outcomes. Although a structural and content analysis of the meetings showed that they were similar in terms of seating arrangements (in both, the British chair was seated at the head of the table), discourse content (the content of the chairman's welcome speech was similar in both encounters), and discourse structure (neither Chinese delegation leader was asked to give a return speech), meeting two was still evaluated far less positively by both parties than meeting one. There seemed to have been what the researchers term a 'compounding effect' in meeting two, where contextual factors, and the assumptions of the two parties regarding each other's behaviour, status and expectations combined in a negative way. The second Chinese delegation's conception of their higher status and importance relative to the hosts (they mistakenly assumed that the British had nearly been bankrupted and had only survived because of their dealings with the Chinese) heightened their sensitivity to face issues. Hence, the seating arrangement (the Chinese leader had expected to sit directly opposite the British chair) and the delegation leader's lack of opportunity to give a return speech became face-threatening acts. Similarly, the British chairman's welcome speech was seen as offensive in meeting two because it did not sufficiently praise the visitors – in accordance with their higher status – and because the

British hosts' behaviour was not humble or complimentary enough to enhance the visitors' face. Indeed, it emerged from the post-meeting interviews that the British hosts had decided recently to adopt a more informal attitude and communication style during Chinese visits, given that Chinese delegation members had become younger over the years. The British had mistakenly assumed that the Chinese had therefore become less concerned about protocol and formalities, such as giving a return speech.

In addition to emphasizing the need to examine the macro-context of business interaction and the importance of gathering perception data to do so (see: also Sarangi 2005; Roberts & Sarangi, 2003; Sarangi & Candlin, 2010 on the concept of 'thick' participation, discussed alongside 'partnership research', Quote 2.5), this study offers support for Spencer-Oatey's rapport management framework. The contextualizing approach the researchers use in their analysis provides convincing evidence that rapport is indeed managed through multiple domains, including the non-verbal.

Managing rapport in lingua franca sales negotiations: a comparison of professional and aspiring negotiators (Planken, 2005)

This study looks at how facework was used in intercultural sales negotiations, most especially in the achievement of interpersonal goals. The researcher compared two contrastive English lingua franca corpora comprised of simulated negotiation discourse, one produced by eighteen professional negotiators and the other by ten students of international business communication, i.e. aspiring negotiators, all of whom participated as buyers or sellers in the same negotiation game (Kelley, 1966), and focused on the following aspects of verbal rapport management:

1. The initiation of interactional (safe) talk (facework in the discourse content domain): (categories of) safe topic, and frequency and locus of occurrence.
2. The use of personal pronouns as indicators of the negotiator relationship (facework in the participation domain): use of pronouns 'you' (indicator of other-orientedness) and inclusive 'we' (indicator of cooperativeness) versus use of exclusive, institutional 'we' (indicator of professional distance) and use of 'I' (indicator of self-orientedness) (Planken, 2005: 383–4).

The study revealed considerable differences between the pre- and post-experience negotiators, not only in the categories of safe talk selected and their frequency of use, but also in their use of pronouns, particularly the institutional 'we'. It therefore provides an insight into the way in which professionals build rapport in a negotiation situation, as well as suggesting areas of concern for the (ESP) business communication classroom. Data Box 2.1 shows the findings for the categories of safe talk, including a description of each category.

Data 2.1 Findings for safe talk in the corpora: categories and topics

Professional corpus Categories:	
1. initiator	greeting; enquiry after well-being; introduction; business card exchange; personal work history
2. business relationship	prenegotiation contact; history of corporate relationship
3. future business	future cooperation; future dealings
4. business environment	markets; target groups; competitors; the economy; EU
5. product information	product characteristics; manufacturing information; product range; delivery
6. corporate information	management; company history; core activities; distribution, promotion, personnel, or pricing policy
7. invitation	lunch; drinks; coffee; company/factory visit (business); private visit
8. non-business	travel; sports; news; culture; language; hobby; holiday; family
Student corpus categories:	
1. initiator	greeting; enquiry after well-being
2. business relationship	prenegotiation contact
3. future business	future cooperation
4. business environment	——
5. product information	——
6. corporate information	——
7. invitation	lunch; drinks
8. non-business	hobby
(Planken, 2005: 386)	

Planken's analysis reveals that categories 4, 5 and 6, business environment, product information, and corporate information, were used only by the professional negotiators and not by the students. In addition, there were considerable differences in how often the two different groups introduced a safe talk topic into the negotiation, and at what stage, i.e. in the Opening Phase, Bargaining Phase or Closing. The professional negotiators used a total number of 192 instances of safe talk, whereas the aspiring negotiators used only 12, and the professionals used safe talk in all three phases of the negotiation, whereas the students used safe talk only in the Opening and Closing phases. A final interesting characteristic in both corpora, was that the negotiators made little use of the 8th Category of safe talk, non-business, such that Planken concludes 'the safe talk topics initiated in both corpora, and by the professionals in particular, largely constituted business-related content in the sense that they could be seen as further instances of professional talk' (2005: 389).

Data 2.2   Examples of safe talk categories in Planken (2005)

Category 2, business relationship, incorporated longer sequences about prenegotiation contact between participants' companies or the history between companies. Excerpt 1 is an example from the professional corpus (in italics):

Excerpt 1

PS: *You have been a good customer of ours for many years and we would like to continue that. You are our entry into France and the French market.*
PB: Uhuh. Well, we would be happy to assist you of course.

Category 7, invitation, usually occurred in the closing stages of a negotiation. Excerpt 2 provides an example from the student corpus:

Excerpt 2

IS: It was nice doing business with you.
IB: Yes.
IS: We will draw up a contract later on but now, *are we going to have a drink?*
IB: Yes. OK. Good idea.

(Planken, 2005: 387–8, slightly adapted)

When Planken investigated the 'degree of solidarity and involvement' (392), as reflected in the negotiators' use of first and second person pronouns ('I' and 'you') and third person plural pronoun (inclusive vs. exclusive or institutional) 'we', she found both similarities and differences between the two different groups (see Quote 2.3 for a summary of the findings). The most interesting findings were that the student negotiators underused the institutional 'we' in comparison to their experienced counterparts and that, unlike the experienced negotiators, they also used non-inclusive pronouns ('I' and 'you') in particular in the Bargaining phase of the negotiation, therefore producing 'highly subjective discourse in potentially the most conflictual and face-threatening negotiation phase' (2005: 396).

Quote 2.3   Pronoun use in negotiations

The analysis of pronoun use in the corpora pointed out a number of similarities and differences between the aspiring negotiators and professionals. Inclusive 'we', regarded an indicator of involvement and co-operativeness, was used by both groups, but the majority of professionals used higher proportions than the aspiring negotiators. With regard to the use of 'you' (indicating other-orientedness), the professionals were found to have used significantly higher proportions than the aspiring negotiators. In addition, the aspiring negotiators seem to have used this pronoun in other, potentially face-threatening, discourse contexts than the professionals, suggesting hostility rather than reflecting the no-nonsense, businesslike approach that they might have been aiming for.

(Planken, 2005: 397)

Planken's study shows how Spencer-Oatey's framework may be usefully applied to uncover the different ways in which the relational aspect of the discourse is managed – or indeed, not managed, in the case of the student negotiators. The findings, at least for the discourse content (e.g. safe talk) and participation (e.g. personal pronouns) domains, are a clear indication of how rapport management can be used to underpin the development of research-based teaching materials.

Researching intercultural business discourse in the future

Rapport management offers a comprehensive emic framework that can be usefully applied to the analysis of intercultural spoken business discourse. The studies we have profiled above show that it is equally effective in the analysis of different types of spoken discourse (e.g. meetings and negotiations), in encounters involving native speakers of different languages (e.g. English and Chinese), in interactions with non-native speakers of a language (e.g. speakers of English as a lingua franca), and in distinguishing between pre-experience and post-experience interlocutors (e.g. professional and student negotiators). As such, it can be used to account for all the different aspects of intercultural discourse that have recently been of interest to business discourse researchers, while at the same time avoiding the ethnocentric pitfalls that have been associated with cross-cultural contrastive etic approaches. As the world continues to globalize, and multilingual, intercultural encounters increase as a result, we believe that nowhere will the analysis of intercultural discourse be more pertinent than in the business arena. Rapport management represents one inherently positive way of viewing business not just as a competitive transactional activity, but also as a collaborative, and ultimately relational, human endeavour.

Developments in the social sciences suggest that the way we look at intercultural communication in general, and at 'culture' as an analytical category, in particular, may have fundamentally changed. The ethnocentrism of communication studies has been the object of critical debate among non-western scholars, 'Africans', 'Asians' and 'Latin Americans' alike (e.g. Matsumoto & Yoo, 2006; Levine et al., 2007). Homogenizing labels such as 'Asian', 'African' and 'Latin American' are in themselves problematic and raise again the issue of ethnocentric categorization from which also discourse studies are not immune, hence the precautionary use of quotation marks. After discussing cultural differences in social relationships in China, Japan and Korea, Lee et al. (2012) conclude that each culture places a different emphasis on the nature and function of social ties; the blanket attribution of high-contextuality and collectivism frequently associated with these countries is therefore at least misleading.

In a critical discussion of the new field of 'Asian' business discourse(s), Bargiela-Chiappini (2011b) admonishes that labelling is 'constructing'; cultural labels are ways of defining others for our own purposes and in terms that they do not necessarily share or agree with. History teaches us that in their meeting with non-Western cultures, the West did not seek dialogue but the imposition of religious, economic, behavioural values alien to indigenous populations. It is necessary to question the premises and presuppositions of a politically-loaded 'cultural paradigm' that has largely exhausted its interpretative potential.

Perhaps the best-known Afro-American critique to have inspired intercultural communication to date is associated with Molete Kefi Asante (1998; 2006; 2008; http://www.asante.net/) whose concept of Afrocentricity eventually influenced the work of other non-Western scholars, such as the Japanese scholar Yoshitaka Miike (see Concept 2.2.).

Asante's philosophy is based on the idea of recognizing the agency of 'African' peoples after five centuries of existence on the historical, cultural and intellectual periphery of Europe. The process of decentring knowledge production away from Eurocentric hegemony and allowing alternative worldviews to emerge can also be seen in the field of 'Latin American' discourse studies, where commonalities with other peripheral research communities is beginning to be treated as a resource. As Argentinian scholar Laura Pardo writes (2010: 188), speaking on behalf of Latin American communication scholars: 'Unlike Asian intellectuals, we do not have alternative philosophies such as Confucianism, Buddhism, Taoism, Hinduism or Shinto. Little has remained of Mayan, Aztec, Inca, Mapuche, Toba and other worldviews . . . Looking towards Asia and Africa now, however, we are beginning to perceive common experiences where we used to see only differences. This shared background might lead to new paradigms of dialogue that would enhance both our mutual understanding and our discursive studies, provided that we learn the lessons from our colonial past and reach a balanced judgement about it.' A Brazilian researcher, Viviane de Melo Resende (2010), who conducted participant research with the National Street Children's Movement in the 2000s argues that the emergence and validation of indigenous perspectives depends on both daring and legitimacy: daring not to apply Western theories and methodologies uncritically to the analysis of local phenomena, but rather engaging in sustained critical dialogue with existing knowledge and powerful discourses. De Melo Resende believes that it is only through exploring their own untapped potential and distinctiveness that indigenous voices can gain legitimacy and begin to be heard in their own right and on their own strength.

It is interesting to note, however, how the intellectual mission of the 'West' to refashion the 'East', more recently through the imposition of a certain type of modernization, has led to a cultural refashioning of western practices, as illustrated in Nair-Venugopal (2012). This suggests that the interconnections belying the 'East–West' are much deeper that the enduring dyadic categorization would have us believe, to the extent that it is possible to reframe the discourse of cultural opposites in terms of connecting as well as destabilizing mutuality (cf. Bargiela-Chiappini & Tanaka, 2012).

Concept 2.2   Asiacentricity: the idea of being deep and open

Yoshitaka Miike offers these reflections on the potential of an Asiacentric perspective in the social sciences:

'How can we see the Asian world from the perspective of Asians? How can we view Asians as subjects and agents of their experiences rather than as objects of analysis and critique? How can we have better understanding and deeper appreciation of Asian worldviews and ways of communication? The idea of Asiacentricity suggests that we place Asian cultural traditions as theoretical resources at the center of inquiry.

In other words, when we discern the psychology of Asian communicators and the dynamics of Asian communication, we should actively use (1) Asian words as key concepts, (2) Asian religious philosophical teachings as behavioral principles and codes of ethics, (3) Asian histories as rich contextualization, and (4) Asian aesthetics as analytical frameworks for space–time arrangement, nonverbal performance, and emotional pleasure.

Asiacentricity (not Asiacentrism) is not ethnocentrism because it does not impose the Asian worldview as the only and best frame of reference on non-Asians. It does not insist that we look at non-Asian cultures and communication from the Asian-centered standpoint. Being Asiacentric in theory and practice has nothing to do with going against other cultures. We can be rooted in our own culture and also open to other cultures by reciprocating the principle of centricity.

Asiacentricity is about drawing on Asian cultural traditions for describing, interpreting, and evaluating Asian premises and practices of communication. The Japanese Zen Buddhist scholar, Daisetzu Suzuki's philosophy of intercultural communication aptly captures the spirit of Asiacentricity: "Outwardly, be open; Inwardly, be deep".' (See also: Miike 2006; 2010; 2011)

2.2   Media, technology and business discourse

The advent of new media such as electronic mail and the web has revolutionized interpersonal communication in the business world, and has opened up a series of new research areas for business discourse research to explore. Some applied linguists, for instance, have been intrigued by the effect of technology on the evolution of the email genre (e.g. Gains, 1999; Mulholland, 1999; Louhiala-Salminen & Kankaanranta, 2005; Gimenez, 2005; 2006a) and others have investigated the interplay of organizational context and linguistic choices (Yates, Orlikowski & Okamura, 1999: Nickerson, 1999; 2000; Gimenez, 2002); more recently, earning calls have been subjected to scrutiny (Crawford-Camiciottoli, 2009a; 2010). Other work has also begun to use established approaches to the analysis of business discourse, in the analysis of multimodal texts, as in Askehave and Nielsen's 2005 study of a homepage, which applies genre analysis from a multimodal perspective (Askehave & Nielsen, 2005). The web has opened up new vistas on marketing and advertising that exploit the potential of multimedial communication to secure an increasingly multicultural share of the international market. More importantly perhaps, the digitization age has been responsible for a shift from monomodality, expressed in static generic types such as the traditional, printed business letter, to increasingly complex and dynamic examples of 'multimodality' (e.g. online commercial websites). In turn, the use of such new, and particularly web-based, media has cultivated an interest in the multimodal signification of meaning inherent in such media (computers, email, chat rooms, cell phones, palmtop computers, etc.), involving as they do not only text, but also visual and sound-based modalities. According to Kress (2003) a de-emphasis on writing in exchange for an emphasis on other representational modes (i.e. pictures, sounds, films, etc.) provides researchers with an opportunity to broaden their approach to how 'text' is viewed.

In his overview of research on mediated communication in business (MCB), Julio Gimenez (2009) identifies two phases: an earlier phase in the Eighties and Nineties, the 'medium turn', which concentrated on the capabilities of the medium itself (e.g. email, facsimile); and a later phase, the 'discourse turn', during which the communicative context is also included in the analysis. This latter development, in evidence since the 2000s, looks at the complex relationship between mediated communication and global and local cultures, and individual and organizational identities. Issues of power, presence and evaluation have emerged as relevant, thus requiring a more critical approach to the study of media, context and discourse.

The book that marked the beginning of multimodality research is very probably *Reading Images*, by Gunther Kress and Theo van Leeuwen, published in 1996, followed by a second edition in 2006, and now in its third edition, *Reading Images: the Grammar of Visual Design* (1996, 2006, 2013). Finally, in 2001, Kress and van Leeuwen published *Multimodal Discourse*, providing a comprehensive multimodal framework which we will discuss in more detail below. In the 2000s, there have been numerous monographic contributions to multimodality theory, for example van Leeuwen (2005), Baldry & Thibault (2006), Machin (2007), Bateman (2008); as well as collections of essays on various aspects of multimodal semiotics (Unsworth, 2008), text-image relations (Ventola & Moya Guijjaro, 2009), mediated discourse analysis (Norris & Jones, 2005), work in the 'Sydney School' tradition of social semiotics (Bednarek & Martin, 2010), and a survey of the field (Jewitt, 2009).

The related hypermodality theory, as developed by Jay Lemke (2002), provides business discourse analysts with a way of looking beyond the textual aspects of e-communication through hypertexts. These theories allow for the investigation of linguistic as well as non-linguistic aspects of the new, multimedial communication environments that characterize the business world today. In other words, they potentially afford business discourse researchers the means to explore the interplay between the various modalities (including language) that constitute 'situated practice' as a whole (Knox, 2009a; 2009b). As Garzone (2009: 162) observes, the most salient feature of (corporate) websites is 'the constant presence of a dialogic dimension, the traces of which are perceptible in linguistic and discursive choices, as well as in the contents and in the overall organisation, where an interpersonal component is always at work'. In the remainder of this section we will expand on the notions of multimodality and hypermodality (and related concepts) and explore how these have been influential on the analysis of business discourse.

Multimodality (Kress & van Leeuwen, 2001)

Multimodality is the foundational construct that underpins the theory of communication proposed by Kress and van Leeuwen in *Multimodal Discourse* (2001; see also van Leeuwen, 2005; Kress and van Leeuwen, 2013). The authors define multimodality as 'the use of several semiotic modes in the design of a semiotic product or event, together with the particular way in which the modes are combined'. Kress and van Leeuwen envisage two strata, Content and Expression, which encompass four domains of practice: Discourse and Design (substrata of Content), and Production and Distribution (substrata of

Expression). A Discourse is essentially a 'resource' or a 'semiotic mode', that is a socially constructed body of knowledge, developed in a specific context (e.g. institutional, geographical, social, etc.) by a particular community of social actors (e.g. business practitioners, experts, family members, etc.) to suit that community's specific needs (e.g. to work, act, bond, etc.). Discourses can be realized in different materialities: marketing discourse, for instance, can be realized in writing or speech and each of these in turn, or in combination, can be realized in various media (e.g. a product brochure, a product demo speech, etc.). Discourses are thus independent of genre and design. The second stratum, Design, is defined as '(uses of) semiotic resources, in all semiotic modes and combinations of semiotic modes', to realize a given Discourse in the context of a specific communication situation. Essentially, Design creates the communication situation in which socially constructed knowledge evolves into 'social (inter-)action' (Kress & van Leeuwen, 2001: 5). Consider a product demo given by a sales representative at a trade show; at the same time as the sales rep realizes marketing discourse, she uses a mode of interaction whose purposes are to inform and persuade an audience of a particular kind. To achieve these purposes, the way semiotic resources are used and combined (the Design) may either be traditional and predictable, or it may be innovative or groundbreaking, for instance, to capture the audience's attention. It is important to realize that the semiotic modes on which Design draws can be realized in different materialities; for example, the presenter of the product demo, apart from using language, may also use resources of the mode of argumentation to design a demo speech that is persuasive.

The second stratum, Expression, is sub-stratified into two domains: Production and Distribution. Production relates to the material forms that realize semiotic products or events. Production can give more than perceivable form to designs; it can create additional meanings that follow from the 'physical process of articulation and the physical qualities of the materials used' (21). For example, gesturing and facial expression will add meanings in speech production, just as the colours and textures used in a painting will contribute to the significance of the picture as a whole. Production thus involves a distinct set of skills, including 'technical skills, skills of the hand and the eye, skills not related to semiotic modes, but to semiotic *media*' (6). Media are distinct from modes, which are semiotic resources through which designs simultaneously realize discourses to create distinct types of (inter)action (21). Media are the *material* resources, including tools and materials used, involved in producing semiotic events and products. The second domain of Expression, Distribution, refers to the technologies involved in the 'technical re-coding' of semiotic products and events, for the purposes of analogue or digital recording or for distribution (e.g. via radio, tv, telephony, etc.). With the advent of digital communication media, the functions of Production and Distribution have started to merge to a certain extent.

Quote 2.4 The multimodality project

The project of multimodality is an attempt to make the point overtly and decisively that an interest in representation modes other than speech or writing is essential and not merely incidentally interesting; that it is central to actual forms of communication everywhere, and not simply a kind of tangential or marginal concern which could be taken up or not, but which leaves language at the centre of communication. The proposal rests on the hypothesis that all [practices] are always multimodal, and that a theory has to be developed in which that fact is central, and a methodology produced for forms of description in which all modes are described and describable together. From an occasional interest in other semiotic modes this project moves to a norm where all texts are seen as multimodal and are described in that way. Language is likely to be a part of these semiotic objects – though it might not – and often it might not be a dominant or most significant mode (Kress and Ogborn, 1998, quoted in Lemke, 2002: 39).

Kaye O'Halloran (2004; 2005), director of the Multimodal Analysis Lab based at the National University of Singapore, has led The *Multimodal Knowledge* research project, which involves the development and use prototype interactive digital media software *MDA-Knowledge* to analyse the multimodal construction of knowledge in mathematics, science and English in print and digital textbooks, CD-ROMs and on-line materials for primary, secondary and university students. *Multimodal Knowledge* adopts a revolutionary research approach where page-based methodologies are replaced with dynamic interactive digital tools and platforms. Later developments will include *MDA-Classroom* software for the analysis of classroom activities, which may be used for educational research (adapted from: http://courses. nus.edu.sg/Course/ellkoh/index.html).

Multimodality is all about multiplicative meanings and *Multimodal Discourse*, building on Hallidayan linguistics and structuralist semiotics, is a landmark in the exploration of meaning-making through the exploration of modes of signifying other than through the language code (e.g. van Leeuwen, 1999; Hodge & Kress, 1988; Kress & van Leeuwen, 1996). In more recent years, social semiotics – the field that considers human signifying practices in particular cultural and social contexts – has further increased its scope by focusing on 'semiotic resources' and their situated interpretations and uses, rather than on 'static' signs and sign systems (Kress & van Leeuwen, 2001; van Leeuwen, 2005). According to van Leeuwen (2005), semiotic resources are integrated to form multimodal texts and communicative events in four ways: rhythm, composition, information linkage and dialogue. The particular attractiveness of multimodality (and social semiotics) for Business Discourse is its inherent multidisciplinary nature (see section 2.3 below). Van Leeuwen (2005), for example, provides some illustrative examples of how social semiotics operates in interdisciplinary conjunction with other fields of enquiry. In this view, language still informs a variety of modes or resources of meaning making (e.g. narrative, poetry etc.) but is displaced as a privileged meaning-making mode in favour of image, sound, film, and even everyday objects and office space, etc.; the tensions between different semiotic modes thus become an important topic of research (e.g. Iedema, 2003). For example, Cross's (2010) extensive analysis of multimodal teamwork at an advertising agency shows the role of concepts in the production of common texts by graphic artists and writers, the role of the visual in individuals' composing, and the verbal-visual rhetorical elements in processes and products. Within this multimodal landscape, technological advances, new media, economic globalization and multiculturalism are responsible for the dissolution of traditional, linear and hierarchical representational practices and genres (Iedema, 2003: 38; see also Chapter 7).

Hypermodality (Lemke, 2002)

Jay Lemke has also made a distinctive and important contribution to the research on multimodality. In his detailed analysis of two scientific web pages from the NASA (National Aeronautics and Space Administration) domain, he combines hypertextuality with multimodality in a further expansion of meaning creation: hypermodality. Through hypermodality 'not only do we have linkages among text units of various scales, but we have linkages among text units, visual elements, and sound units' (Lemke, 2002: 301). Lemke suggests that, in order for different modalities (e.g. language, image, sound, film) to be combined into multiplicative and meaningful associations they need to share a common source of meaning-making. Lemke suggests that there are three sets of interdependent meanings: presentational, orientational and organizational (see Concept 2.3).

Concept 2.3   The three interdependent meanings in hypermodal discourse

Presentational meanings: are those which present some state of affairs. We construe a state of affairs principally from the ideational content of texts, what they say about processes, relations, events, participants and circumstances.

Orientational meanings: are more deeply presupposed. They are those which indicate to us what is happening in the communicative relationship and what stance its participants may have to each other and to the presentational content. These are the meanings by which we orient to each other in action and feeling and to our community in terms of point of view, attitudes and values.

Organizational meanings: are largely instrumental and backgrounded. They enable the other two kinds of meaning to achieve greater degrees of complexity and precision. Most fundamentally, organizational resources for meaning enable us to make and tell which other signs go together into larger units.

(Adapted from Lemke, 2002: 304)

Lemke remarks that meaning-making potential is increased in specificity and precision when different modalities (for instance, text and image) are combined, compared to the meaning potential of the individual modalities taken separately. Furthermore, he emphasizes that all modalities in a multimodal genre need to be taken into account for the recovery of all three sets of meanings. Below we will consider Bargiela-Chiappini's (2005b) investigation of new meaning creation on a website with reference to Lemke's work, which illustrates how the traditional promotional letter genre is re-interpreted as a hypermodal discourse on a UK banking website.

The multimodal investigation of business discourse: three studies

Garzone (2002) explores whether 'traditional models and categories of analysis can be used effectively in the description of hypermedia computer-mediated text' (2002: 279). She employs text linguistics categories to demonstrate how the various components of a website, linguistic and iconic, interact in the construction of multiple meanings at three overlapping levels: the level of inherent textuality of the alphabetic text; the level of textuality of the page realized by the interplay of linguistic and iconic elements, and the overarching third level of hypertextuality. Garzone observes that the website is an unstable and unfinished hypertextual configuration. The multiplication of meaning is generated by customers' subsequent or repeated visits to the site, or created by routine updating of the web pages' content. In addition, new meanings are created from the integration into the website, and their ensuing transformation, of traditional business genres. She concludes as follows, 'The traditional models and categories of linguistic and textual analysis are not in themselves inadequate, but need to be adapted and oriented towards a more generally semiotic, rather than strictly linguistic, approach' (Garzone, 2002: 295).

De Groot, Korzilius, Nickerson & Gerritsen (2006; see Chapter 8 for a detailed description) analyse the visual themes employed in a corpus of Dutch–English and British managerial forewords to annual reports. They use the multimodal discourse approach of Kress and van Leeuwen (2001) and look at modes and their constitutive signs which articulate what the picture is about. The authors define 'photographic themes' by associating the objects (rather than colours, patterns, etc.) displayed in the picture with a view to obtaining a set of thematically related signs. Their treatment of objects-as-mode was intended to yield concrete themes that would allow a relatively unambiguous interpretation of the visual image. The overall findings show that the main photographic and textual themes focused on performance and policy overviews and on illustrations of objects that were representative of group or company. There was a significant difference between the photographic content of the British statements and the Dutch–English statements: in the former, images related to both management and employees, in the latter to employees only. Interestingly, visual images were used not to illustrate the textual themes but rather to identify the author of the statement.

Gatti's (2011a) approach to the study of corporate websites illustrates the benefits of combining cognitive linguistics with discourse analysis and multimodal analysis. It is based on two main assumptions. First, the lack of principled distinction between semantics and pragmatics, whereby meaning is a function of the activation of conceptual knowledge structures as guided by context. Second, and this is crucial for hypertext analysis, that language, as the outcome of general properties of cognition, is closely related to visual perception (Gatti, 2011c). Gatti observes that our understanding of how co-patterns of meanings deployed on the multimodal page are perceived acts at the intersection between discourse and cognition. Moreover, it requires the comprehension of how we perceive and make sense of the world around us. For example, our perception of reality is based on the apprehension of structures and events through the temporal and spatial domains. Gatti demonstrates that the application of theoretical frameworks with a focus on basic conceptual notions such as space and time , i.e. space–time schemas and spatiotemporal causal structures, can be particularly effective in shedding light on the culturally-filtered discursive strategies that are deployed in the representation of action and change in corporate web-site discourse, both in the language and semiosis that is used (Gatti, 2011b). The study of time–space processes as represented on websites enables the reading of culture-specific constructions of events encoding corporate action as 'progress' (Gatti, 2013).

A hypermodal analysis of a banking website (Bargiela-Chiappini, 2005b)

Bargiela-Chiappini (2005b) begins her account of a banking website by detailing how in recent years, consumers have become familiar with business organizations that rely entirely on their websites for interaction with their customers, e.g. Amazon, the online bookshop. These organizations, she observes, were conceived to operate as *virtual* organizations, with the website as a 'shopfront', that is the only or main interface with customers. A forerunner in the banking sector is the object of her study, the *smile.co.uk* website, 'the Internet bank from the Co-operative Bank plc', a UK-based high street bank. She goes on to say that information accessibility and operational user-friendliness are strong selling points in a cyberspace that is crowded with corporate sites competing for attention, and all high street banks now have dedicated websites. Moreover, in the UK, the reduction of face-to-face service through the planned closure of branches, especially in rural areas, means that Internet banking is likely to become the most economic and, possibly the only, alternative to traditional banking. The fast rate of spread of Internet access in the western world means that in the future banks and other corporate concerns are likely to experience an increase in Internet-based customer activities. She then continues with an in-depth analysis of the website, as we will describe below.

After logging in on the *smile* homepage, customers can manage their accounts remotely in the same way as they would do (face to face) at a local branch. *smile* generally communicates with its customers by email; the bank uses 'secure messages' that can only be read by logging on to a personal account, or it sends circular letters about non-sensitive matters directly to its customers' email accounts. When *smile* first established a web presence in 1999, the website was cluttered and difficult to navigate. The textual layout was confused and confusing and the bank's visual identity was in danger of becoming associated with the disturbing icon of the 'Cheshire cat', the large feline with an eerie grin found in Alice in Wonderland which *smile* adopted as a distinctive graphical icon. Five years later, the bank's homepage carried black text and fuchsia pink banners and hyperlinks against a white background. The iconic smile remained but evolved into the bank's powerfully unique brand: ☺©. Overall, the site adopted a simpler and much more effective design; in fact, according to the website's content manager, the *smile* house style which he defines as 'colloquial, chatty and informal', was later copied by other online banking sites (Simon Jamieson, 2004, personal communication).

The *smile* discourse is hypermodal in that it promotes financial services and actions through various modalities. In its textual and graphic modes, the *smile* website deals not only with customers' personal or business accounts; its homepage (smile.co.uk) also invites visitors to 'invest' and to 'shop'. The triple identity captured in the top banner ('bank/invest/shop') is unpacked in the hyperlink options listed on the left side of the homepage. The main body of the page is devoted to the latest product offer and the right hand column proposes 'fun' activities like casting e-votes in a 'Who should smile more?' competition and 'Stop Press' hyperlinks that expand into various promotional and instruction texts.

Following Lemke's (2002) three semiotic functions (presentational, orientational and organizational meaning) Bargiela-Chiappini examines how these 'make meaning' on the home page of *smile*. From a *presentational* perspective (Lemke's first type of meaning), the linguistic ties between the top navigation bar and the left-hand links are those of header-list, while the semantic relationship is one of exemplification (bank – apply/demo/application tracker, etc.). An expansion of this semantic relationship is established between the page title, which is illustrated by a graphic, and the contents provided in the textual unit, which contains a verbal explanation of the graphic. Textual and visual modalities are therefore doubly interrelated through the effective use of the unique and consistent visual signifier of the smile-logo, repeated horizontally and vertically in the two corporate colors. Then, at the level of *orientational* meaning stance to the user and stance towards the thematic content are all achieved linguistically and appear to be three-directional: other–us ('9 out of 10 smile customers would recommend us to a friend'), you–us and you–other (for instance, in the textual directives and in the fuchsia-coded action link anchors 'tell me more'; 'tell a friend'; 'send and view'). Finally, at the level of *organizational* principles (or organizational meanings), which can be structural or cohesive, the *smile* page relies mainly on vertically ordered lists (links) at either side of the main vertical text, which usually consists of a graphic combined with a textual unit. Colour coordination provides a cohesive tie and orients the user to the action links. Vertical and horizontal links are cohesively tied by repetition; in the same way the use of 'smile' in the right-hand list of link anchors serves as a cohesive device.

Like many other Internet sites, *smile.co.uk* is designed to stimulate proactive, explorative use rather than to provide a virtual replacement for face-to-face service, over the counter. The response to the appearance of *smile* in the UK online banking sector has earned them credit for creating a new multimodal, multigenre online discourse, characterized by a dominant 'conversational' register. Indeed, a cursory visit to other UK high street banks' websites confirms the remarkable degree of similarity between their designs and the *smile* design, varying only in the balance between graphic/pictorial and textual components.

Given the importance attached by business organizations to their web-based presence, there is no shortage of data available for analysis and, as a result, linguists have been prolific in their research output on various aspects of website discourse (e.g. Garzone, 2009; Turnbull, 2011; Cesiri, 2011; Gatti, 2001). However, multidisciplinary approaches to the analysis of websites that combine insights from organizational communication, cognitive studies and linguistics are still rare, if very much necessary to show how language and cognition are skillfully exploited by corporate designers to create memorable multimodal experiences for the web user.

Cristina Gatti (2011a) proposes a multiperspective analytical model of corporate websites based on a theoretical framework that conflates methodological perspectives derived from Discourse Analysis, Multimodality and Cognitive Linguistics. The originality of this approach resides in the deployment of tools that not only consider crossmodal integration and inter-semiotic interaction, but which also provide a series of ways to understand the *cognitive constructs* underlying the formatting of the message in terms of conceptually integrated artifacts constructed through multiple modalities. This cognitive-multimodal approach to corporate discourse allows for the study of multidimensional notions such as organizational memory and the modes of its conceptualization, through literal and nonliteral meanings, and across different modalities (Gatti, 2013).

Further studies of e-communication: design preferences across cultures

Cyr, Bonanni, Bowes & Ilsever's (2005) study analyses *within* culture preferences for design features of a local versus a foreign website, and looks at participants' subsequent perceptions of trust, satisfaction and e-loyalty. The aim of the study, conducted in Canada, the US, Germany and Japan, was to determine whether some cultures are more sensitive than others to culturally biased Web design. The researchers found no indications that respondents in any of these countries trusted the local website (Samsung) more than its foreign, Hong Kong counterpart. However, whereas Canadian and German participants reported similar levels of satisfaction, trust and loyalty for the foreign and local websites, American respondents were more loyal to the local website despite reporting equivalent levels of trust and satisfaction for both websites. Japanese respondents put equal trust in the foreign and local websites, but were more satisfied with the foreign website and would be more likely to revisit or purchase from it (21).

Hu, Shima, Oehlmann, Zhao, Takemura & Matsumoto (2004) compare first impressions of Business to Customer (B2C) static webpages in three countries: Japan, China and the UK. The pages involved a combination of eight design elements: title format, title position, menu size, clipart size, main colour, background colour, colour brightness and colour harmonization. A self-report questionnaire was used to identify the relations between users' first impressions and webpage design aspects. The general findings were that most design factors elicited similar impressions on the part of the three groups (Japanese, Chinese and UK) but that a number of design aspects, such as use of colours and spatial effect, seemed to reflect cultural preferences. The authors advise designers of B2C websites to 'localize' the visual design of international pages to avoid negative first impressions on the part of potential Internet customers (from various different cultures).

Multimodality for business discourse

The concept of multimodal communication that has been developed by people like Kress, van Leeuwen and Lemke is a stimulating new development for business discourse research. It represents a disciplinary crossover that lends further support for the argument for crossdisciplinary dialogue and collaboration that we will discuss in the final section in this chapter. For business discourse researchers, adopting a multimodal analytical approach would require a wider analytical focus that accounts not only for the language in use in business contexts, but also for the nonverbal, visual and sound components of the interaction. Notions such as organization and organizing, or context and contextualization, acquire new meanings and significance in a multimodal perspective. As François Cooren and colleagues of the 'Montreal School' of organizational communication have demonstrated in their research (e.g. Cooren et al., 2010; Brummas et al., 2009, Castor & Cooren, 2006), charting the role played by material artifacts in the constitution of an organization in interaction with human agents, requires us to consider meaning making beyond text and discourse. Similarly, Lorenza Mondada (see: Profile 2.4), in her research on workplace practices, focuses on the emergence of interaction from the sequential deployment of multimodal resources (Mondada, 2011a; 2011b; 2012). For this researcher, practices can only be understood as embodied, and her fine-grained analyses of video-recordings are exemplary illustrations of the nuances of situated meaning creation in organizational time–spaces.

As the multimodality of social practices increases, business discourse researchers will have to take into account the role of multimodal (and multimedia) textuality in the reproduction and transformation of the artefacts they choose to study. The (written and verbal) texts that have formed the mainstay of much of the work we look at in this book would then come to be analysed as only one mode among many others that contribute to the making of meaning. Whether (other) applied linguists will be prepared to embrace the 'multimodal turn' in business discourse research, inspired by the work of colleagues like François Cooren and Lorenza Mondada, will remain to be seen.

2.3   From multimethod research to multidisciplinarity

Multidisciplinarity in research and teaching continues to be of interest to researchers in a number of the social sciences that are relevant to business discourse, despite the practical difficulties of achieving it. Language and gender, for instance, could not be imagined as anything but a multidisciplinary field encompassing linguistics, sociolinguistics, social psychology and anthropology (Acuña-Ferreira & Álvarez-López, 2003), and the combination of insights from management studies, organization studies and ethnography has further enhanced the recent multiperspectival approach to gender and managerial discourse (Mullany, 2003). Equally, within management studies, Barbara Czarniawska, a specialist in cultural studies of management, proposes 'creole researchers' operating across 'hybrid disciplines' and authoring 'pidgin writing'. Within the business discourse community specifically, researchers such as Priscilla Rogers and the late Margaret Baker Graham in the US, and Francesca Bargiela-Chiappini and Catherine Nickerson in Europe, have all called for the development of an multidisciplinary agenda and have suggested ways in which this could be achieved.

Rogers (2001), for instance, in a plenary address to the members of the Association for Business Communication, proposes an agenda for business communication research comprised of convergence on the one hand and commonality on the other. She sees that convergence 'challenges us to get inside the head of other disciplines, to adopt them as our own. It challenges us to use methods that are foreign to us and to study research areas investigated by colleagues whose conference sessions we would not be inclined to attend' (Rogers, 2001: 17). She further sees convergence as 'multidisciplinary, multimethod, and multifaceted' (2001: 18). In this way, convergence, she observes, 'challenges the viability of disciplinary distinctions and methodological specializations' (2001: 21). Commonality relates to the common purpose shared by members of the Association for Business Communication (ABC) who 'share an interest in providing practical knowledge that can enhance the communication effectiveness of all kinds of organizational stakeholders, particularly related to business' (2001: 21).

In response to Rogers' agenda, Bargiela-Chiappini and Nickerson (2001) put forward the concept of *partnership research,* which is comprised of researchers representing different disciplines and therefore a combination of different insights, methods and tools, since, as they point out, 'an individual cannot be easily expected to acquire multidisciplinary expertise' (2001: 248). Bargiela-Chiappini and Nickerson single out Priscilla Rogers' collaborative work with the applied linguist John Swales as 'an excellent example of how effective such a research partnership can be' (2001: 249). We will feature their work later in this chapter.

Quote 2.5 On partnership research

> . . . the convergence challenge does not stop at multidisciplinarity. In complex research environments, such as those presented by business organizations, a mono-method approach is at best narrow, and at worst inadequate. Of course, the choice of methods can affect findings, but it is often possible, indeed desirable, to bridge the apparent incomparability of findings from distant methods, such as experimentation and in-depth interviews, in a multimethod approach. The translation of aims, objectives and findings is another benefit of partnership research, and it can be seen as a natural stage in the design of multiparty projects where the participants come to share a working language, as well as tools and insights. In fact, the identification of shared research questions in the initial stages of project design is a necessary first step towards the harmonization of foci and strengths from separate disciplinary domains.
>
> (Adapted from Bargiela-Chiappini & Nickerson, 2001: 249; see also Candlin & Crichton, 2011a)

Some of the epistemological and methodological implications of 'partnership research' become operational in the realization of 'thick participation' (Sarangi, 2005; Roberts & Sarangi, 2003; Sarangi & Candlin, 2006). Sarangi (2005: 376–7) argues that the 'thick participation' is the premise of Geertzian 'thick description'; the notion of participation being inclusive of 'continuity of involvement in a research setting', and 'maintenance of relationships with participants in temporal and spatial terms', both of which require long term immersion (376). The socialization process involved in 'thick participation' should not aim at the acquisition of professional expertise: rather, the researcher should seek to acquire what Sarangi calls 'professional/organisational literacy' (377), which facilitates interpretive understanding.

In the previous chapter, we suggested that multimethod approaches have been one of the enduring hallmarks of business discourse research in recent years, and we will discuss many examples of multimethod research in this book that have been carried out by (applied) linguists, discourse analysts and sociolinguists alike within the community of business discourse scholars (see Part 3 in particular). In the rest of this section, we look at four studies in which a purposeful multimethod and multidisciplinary approach is taken, which we believe will characterize business discourse research in the future.

Concept 2.4 Disciplines of relevance for a multidisciplinary approach to business discourse

> *Anthropology*: empirical research in the anthropological tradition affords a glimpse of the macro through its manifestations in the micro, thus bringing

the larger context within reach of the researcher. Christina Wasson, a linguistic anthropologist who practices within American corporations, has this to say about her research: 'When I talk about language I always talk about linguistic practices and linguistic ideologies, where practices are resources for the individual on the ground whereas ideologies are resources for the larger, organizational structures that tend to help promote their goals' (personal communication). In her approach, the micro and macro dimensions of analysis are conflated in the interrelated concepts of 'linguistic practices' and 'linguistic ideologies'.

Conversation analysis: claims a distinctive understanding of organizing through language which has been and will no doubt continue to be of influence on business discourse analysis. Deirdre Boden combined CA and social theory in her seminal study of organizational practices (see Chapter 1). Emanuel Schegloff (2003: 163) argues that the mode of enquiry of conversational analysis gave researchers 'access to the terms of human practice in interaction itself and in so doing it proved philosophy wrong on what empirical research could not do'. The interventionist agenda of CA is documented in a collection of empirical studies conducted in a range of institutional settings and encounters, e.g. medical, government, voluntary sector (Antaki, 2011).

Sociolinguistics: has traditionally favoured a realist approach to research that seeks to account for the interplay between culture, structure and agency. To this effect, it employs analytical social categories such as gender, race and ethnicity. According to this perspective, language becomes one element within the cultural system, alongside social actors and structural properties (Sealy & Carter, 2001: 13). Recent sociolinguistic studies of company meetings have engaged critically with notions of gender and culture and have shown how both phenomena resist ready-made, narrow and static definitions (cf. Mullany, 2003; Poncini, 2004). Instead, their interactional and dynamic nature emerges from observation and interpretation of authentic multiparty encounters. This is a useful tension between apparently unproblematic sociolinguistic categories and their construction in language as action is one that will stimulate further cross-disciplinary debate among business discourse analysts.

Discursive strategies in multicultural business meetings (Poncini, 2004)

In her longitudinal study of an Italian company, Gina Poncini concentrates on three areas of concern to business discourse analysts: intercultural communication in corporations, business discourse in multilingual settings, and the management of cross-company communication in large multiparty interactions.

She deliberately avoids the 'problem approach' to intercultural communication, focusing instead on three salient linguistic aspects of multiparty interaction: personal pronouns, lexis and evaluation.

Poncini's approach to the Italian company that is the subject of her study has several advantages over prescriptive knowledge administered to business students through texts that are not based on real-life practices:

1. it privileges situational factors over presumed cultural differences;
2. it focuses on the group and on what actually happens when business people from various cultures have to work together;
3. it illustrates how English as a common language is used to establish and maintain business relationships;
4. it avoids the pitfalls of the one speaker-one culture perspective and the limitations of concepts such as national culture and organizational culture.

Gina Poncini draws the notion of 'business relationship' (44) from the business marketing literature, a useful heuristic that she applies to her longitudinal analysis of the company–distributors relationship, as expressed during multiparty meetings. This analysis is combined with a pragmatic approach to the issue of how to define 'culture' in corporate, multinational contexts: Poncini introduces the perspective of meetings having their own culture or *groupness*. What emerges from the study overall is that 'groupness' helps overcome potentially 'disruptive behaviour' such as monologues or side conversations among meeting participants, and overrides difficulties generated by variations in information level among participants and their varying degrees of competence in (lingua franca) English. The 'groupness' in multiparty meetings is maintained through the hard work of those participants (main company speakers) who facilitate, coax, moderate, interpret and summarize for the benefit of all the parties at the meeting table.

Poncini also investigates the role of lexis and evaluation in the meetings. Specialized lexis works to reflect and construct the social roles that the participants play in the company and at the meetings, to frame the business activities and to support 'groupness'. Evaluation is used strategically in meetings to accomplish a variety of tasks including: (1) image-building; (2) preempting criticism; (3) building positive connotations; (4) managing participation and (5) construing roles.

Identity and role construction: gender and discourse in management (Mullany, 2003)

Louise Mullany's work is an original study of the interplay of gender and discourse at management level. It is based on ethnographic case studies of two UK-based companies, one from the manufacturing sector and one from retailing. Mullany managed to gain full access to these companies and, once inside, managed to record a number of authentic meetings. Furthermore, she also conducted one-to-one interviews with selected managers. Through her work, Mullany develops a multidisciplinary approach that she terms 'critical feminist sociolinguistics', a multimethod approach drawing from disciplines such as discourse analysis, gender studies, organizational ethnography and management studies. The analytical framework that Mullany proposes is heavily influenced by language and gender studies, from which it derives the conceptualization of gender as a performative social construct and the construct of community of practice (CofP). Moreover, Mullany's twofold (micro and macro) perspective on discourse affords a potentially fine-grained basis for analysing gender bias in management: she complements an analysis of the (interactional) discourse of meetings where gender is 'performed' with an understanding of gender in the workplace as it emerges from her interviews with managers.

Based on her analyses Mullany concludes that several factors influence the linguistic strategies that participants use to perform their identities at meetings. In contrast with the sparse research that exists in language and gender studies in the workplace, Mullany observes that female managers in her study used speech norms normally associated with a stereotypical notion of 'masculine speech style'. She also observed numerous examples of male managers using speech patterns commonly associated with a stereotypical 'feminine speech style'. Interestingly, Mullany also identified similarities in female and male managers' speech, particularly when participants held the same status and role. At least in the meetings analysed by Mullany then, there would seem to be consistent evidence that counters the perception of male managers being dominant and using competitive, direct strategies.

If gender differences were minimal at the interactional level, the interviews revealed that dominant gender discourses continue to place women in management positions at a disadvantage compared to their male counterparts, thus keeping alive the best-known representation of the insurmountable obstacle to female career progression: the 'glass ceiling'.

Discourse and the projection of corporate culture: the mission statement (Swales & Rogers, 1995)

John Swales and Priscilla Rogers' study of the genesis and construction of the mission statement as an organizational text type is an example of a genre-based investigation of business discourse that combines corpus analysis, case study research and ethnographic methodologies (desk research and interviews). Its primary aims were to characterize the mission statement and to determine whether it constitutes a genre, and to trace the creation and development of a specific set of mission statements within their wider corporate context.

The study employed a multimethod approach that combined a text-based analysis of a corpus of 100 mission statements with a detailed contextual analysis of the organizational 'framing' of three such texts. The contextual analysis considered the history, authorship and institutional function of the texts within the corporation in which they originated. The researchers interviewed employees involved in creating the mission statements, in order to establish the reasons for writing such documents, and to determine what role they play in organizations. They consulted other corporate policy documents to gain insight into the corporations' histories and corporate processes and philosophies. Their study thus incorporates many methodologies that could be considered ethnographic in their approach.

In general, the mission statements were seen to be extensions of the goals, values and purposes of the corporations that published them, and originated at the level of the CEO and senior management. All the mission statements shared the aim of encouraging and fostering identification with the corporation, and can thus be regarded as a management tool for promoting corporate culture and values and for effectively encouraging employees to buy in to that culture and those values.

The final stage of the study centered on the case histories of three mission statements from two large US corporations. Interviews with relevant informants within the corporations (e.g. policy committee members and senior management) were held to determine the motives and strategic corporate goals underlying the statements and to gain an overview of the development of, and textual changes in, the text over time in relation to the corporations' recent histories and their performance. In addition, to gain greater insight into the 'framing' of these mission statements within the corporations' histories and their environment, the researchers consulted a large number of other corporate policy documents.

The 1995 study extends an earlier study of corporate codes published five years previously in 1990 (Rogers & Swales, 1990). The 1990 and 1995 studies are interesting from a multidisciplinary perspective, as they combine the work of a corporate communication specialist (Rogers) and an applied linguist (Swales) who have a shared interest in genre. The studies therefore combine a variety of insights from different disciplines, including applied linguistics, critical discourse analysis and management communication (see also Chapter 6 for a more detailed discussion of the methodology used in the 1995 study, together with a recent study in which Rogers traces the changes that had taken place in the corporate mission statement she looked at with Swales in 1990 (Rogers, Gunesekera & Yang, 2011)).

Discourse analysis and business meetings (Stubbe, Lane, Hilder, Vine, Vine, Marra, Holmes, & Weatherall, 2003)

Perhaps the most concise comparative study of *discourse analytical approaches* has been accomplished by Maria Stubbe and her colleagues in New Zealand

(Stubbe et al., 2003). In the space of a journal article, they deal with five different (discourse analytic) approaches, using a single extract from a business meeting recorded for the Language in the Workplace Project (LWP) (see Chapter 4). Firstly, they highlight the different theoretical assumptions underpinning the five different approaches: conversation analysis (CA), interactional analysis (IA), discursive psychology (DP), politeness theory (PT) and critical discourse analysis (CDA). Secondly, they move on to the commonalities, which are equally substantive and include the analytical angle (micro/macro), the relevance of context, the range of linguistic and discursive features selected by participants and the jointly constructed nature of the interaction. So for example, they conclude that CA, IA and PT apply an internal understanding of interaction that looks at micro-patterns; this contrasts with DP and CD, which seek to link the local interaction to macro-discursive formations. CA is unique in not taking into account the effects of the situational context and of socio-cultural factors, although it has recently made some concession on this position (see: Antaki, 2011). With the exception of PT, which implies a transmission model of communication, the other approaches occupy various positions within social constructionism, with CA embracing a strong form of social constructionism and IA a weak one. Work such as Stubbe et al.'s are particularly useful to business discourse analysts because through a comparative analytical mode they offer an update of the ongoing debates on methods and perspectives and a healthy reminder of the continuing challenges facing practitioners of multimethod research.

Concept 2.5   Beyond 'discourse' and discourse analysis in business discourse research?

'It is useful to recall the disciplinary diversity mooted by the "discourse' analysis" label: linguistics, pragmatics, psychology, sociology, anthropology, semiotics, communication, social theory, all have developed and applied often distinctive methods, if not methodologies, for the analysis of the diversely defined phenomenon of "discourse". . . . in organization studies in general, and organizational discourse in particular, widespread adhesion to "strong" social constructionist or constructivist ontologies has generally translated in the characterization of "discourse" as constitutive of social reality. This stance has promoted unprecedented attention to the details and potentialities of situated talk in the workplace while often relegating to obscurity non-discourse facts of organizational life.' (Bargiela-Chiappini, 2011: 1185)

Most research in business discourse thus far has not moved beyond discursivity (but see Mondada, 2011a; 2011b; 2012; Profile 2.4) One possible way of reconnecting language and discourse with the material context in which they are situated, thus acknowledging the embodied nature of communication, is through 'sensory pragmatics'. Sensory pragmatics explores 'the possibilities and consequences of the body as the primary locus of communicative acts that are at once linguistic, sensual, affective and material. "Embodiment" then does not stop at meaningful gesturing, posturing, and coupling with the material world. The incarnation of communication opens up new horizons on the dimensions of conscious and unconscious sensory perception and affective "perceptuality" in which communicative bodies are immersed.' (Bargiela-Chiappini, 2013)

The overview below shows some of the main qualitative methods that have been used in articles in the *Journal of Business Communication*, together with other studies that we refer to elsewhere in this volume.

- *Action research*: refers to a number of different qualitative methodologies (e.g. participatory research, collaborative inquiry, emancipatory research, action learning and contextual action research). Action research is attractive to researchers operating in institutional and organizational settings as it affords closeness to subjective human experience, i.e. it allows for 'understanding unique individuals and their meaning and interactions with others and the environment' (Lopez & Willis, 2004: 728). In Chapter 4 we will discuss a consultancy project based on action research principles by Baxter, Boswood & Peirson-Smith (2002).
- *Phenomenology*: focuses on understanding experience from the first-person point of view and offers a range of descriptive and interpretative options that can be viewed as both theoretical and methodological. The 1997 *JBC* study by Krider and Ross uses a phenomenological approach to give an account of the experiences of women working in a US public relations firm (Krider & Ross, 1997).
- *Critical hermeneutics*: has an emphasis on understanding how interactants come to develop a common language, and is known for its transformative ethos, similar to that of action research (Lopez & Willis, 2004). The 2002 publication by Prasad and Mir in the Special Issue of the *JBC* on qualitative research is a critical hermeneutic analysis of CEO letters to shareholders in the oil industry (Prasad & Mir, 2002).
- *Interpretive (or reflexive) ethnography*: is based on the work of the anthropologist Clifford Geertz (1973; 1983) and 'aims to chart the network of shared meanings that constitute reality within a community' (Smart, 1998: 113). It allows for interaction with a social group to 'gain a quasi-insider's

understanding of a locally constructed reality' (1998: 124). A more radical interpretation of this approach, *participative ethnography*, demands that the researcher is engaged on two, or sometimes even three, fronts. First-person research is characterized by reflexivity, or 'critical subjectivity'. Second-person research entails cooperative inquiry where a group of co-researchers (and co-subjects) engage in cycles of action and reflection. Third-person research focuses on anonymous constituencies, i.e. people who have become engaged in the inquiry who are not personally known to the researchers but which the researchers are seeking to empower. The work of Geoffrey Cross on collaborative writing processes, and Graham Smart on the interface between the communication at a central bank and the economic model it refers to, in the *JBC*, are both examples of an ethnographic approach applied to the analysis of workplace discourse (e.g. Cross, 2000; Smart, 1998).

- *Foucauldian Discourse Analysis*: seeks to expose 'discursive formations' that is stabilized discourse within which meanings, subjects and objects are fixed (Mills, 1993). Foucauldian DA shares an emancipatory political agenda with critical discourse analysis (CDA), but unlike CDA it does not examine samples of texts retrieved from the institutional context but looks at the contextualized practices. As we discussed in Chapter 1, the US researcher Sharon Livesey has published several articles in the *JBC* in which she uses Foucauldian DA to investigate the public discourse produced by a number of major corporations (e.g. Livesey, 2001; 2002c).
- *Business anthropology*: operates in the borderlands of practicing and scholarly purposes and is conducted by those engaged to address inquiries of direct interest to the corporation. A participant in corporate settings in such roles as researcher, consultant, manager, and designer, the anthropologist operates as a mutual corporate actor with other members of the corporation. Anthropology is identified as an acceptable and often desired area of expertise in job descriptions for positions as diverse as product designer to learning consultant (Cefkin, 2012: 95; see also: Baba, 2012; Czarniawska, 2012).

Multidisciplinarity in the study of business discourse

In their inaugural editorial for the new *Journal of Applied Linguistics*, Candlin and Sarangi (2004: 2) move decisively beyond the debate on the nature and identity of applied linguistics when they write:

> we see applied linguistics as a many centred and interdisciplinary endeavour whose coherence is achieved in purposeful, mediate action by its practitioners . . . [t]he issue addressed is not then what is the matter with applied linguistics, but what is applied linguistics' matter.

Later in the same piece they outline some maxims for what they call 'a good applied linguistic ethos'. These include:

- 'Methodological eclecticism'. Applied linguistics has a tradition of borrowing constructs and methodologies from other disciplines and deploying them in 'mixtures' that have proved variably effective. The issues of deregulated eclecticism and selective borrowing from other disciplines should be given more attention.
- 'Crossdisciplinary dialogue'. For historical reasons, applied linguistics has come to be associated with language education, leaving the potential of collaboration with other disciplines still largely untapped.
- 'Evidence-based practice'. Forensic linguistics leads the field: its evidence-based claims have been regularly subjected to severe scrutiny. The same standard will be expected of other branches of applied linguistics research.
- 'Differential voicing'. Applied linguists must make their research understandable to their professional audiences outside academia, as well as to other disciplines within it.
- 'Collaboration in action'. Applied linguists are invited to submit critical accounts of their experience of collaborative research and publication. This is a process that raised numerous, important issues of access, of co-responsibility, of professional boundaries and professional integrity.

This is a comprehensive programme, many aspects of which are documented in the twenty-six chapters of the *Handbook of Communication in Organisations and Professions* (Candlin & Sarangi, 2011). It is also a programmatic statement not only for applied linguistics in general, but one that could apply equally well to business discourse in particular. Within business discourse, for instance, research has already moved from description to interpretation, most valuably so where the process has involved practitioners and professionals. From this vantage point and in collaboration with colleagues in other relevant disciplines, business discourse is now in a position to pursue methodological eclecticism and engage in a crossdisciplinary dialogue. Although interdisciplinarity still remains an aim rather than a reality for business discourse as we write this volume, the active participation of business discourse researchers who themselves come from different disciplinary backgrounds in current methodological debates, will continue to create more opportunities for dialogue and joint collaboration across disciplines as the field continues to develop.

We end this chapter with four profiles of researchers representing different perspectives that will shape the future of business discourse research: Shanta Nair-Venugopal, whose pioneering work in intercultural communication in the Malaysia workplace sits within the tradition of critical studies; Dalvir Samra Fredericks, who has blended ethnography and ethnomethodology in her analyses of organizational practice; Rick Iedema, a linguist conducting multidisciplinary research in clinical settings alongside professional practitioners and users; and Lorenza Mondada, a linguist whose work focuses on the embodied nature of workplace interaction.

Profile 2.1   Shanta Nair-Venugopal

Professor and Principal Fellow in Language and Intercultural Communication at IKON:
http://www.ikon.ukm.my/

Trained as: Applied/sociolinguist but working currently in interdisciplinary studies

Inspired by: Dell Hymes, Noam Chomsky (as public intellectual), and Edward Said

Speciality: Language, intercultural discourse and communication with specific reference to the workplace; English language/Occidental studies

Life: Born in Malaysia (of South Asian/Indian descent); educated in Malaysia and the UK (Edinburgh and Cardiff); Malaysian citizen

For:

- Revisionary views of difference; a greater understanding and appreciation of the significance of the concept of the 'stranger' in intercultural encounters as opposed to the more facile construct of the cultural 'other'. As the former foregrounds the individual as a social actor in ICC, it helps to dismantle the view that ICC is predicated wholly and irreparably on culture.

- Rethinking culture as the most salient construct in ICC by moving away from essentialist views to reconceptualize it as 'approximations of social reality' in order to explain interactional fracture and communication breakdown. This incorporates the notion of personal and social identity and 'voice' (as a metaphor for self-expression) since individuals are firstly human and social beings.

- Localized models of English that expose the gap between contextualized language use and prescribed usage in localized business contexts which are preeminently sites of intercultural contact and contestation.

Against:

- Differences predicated as 'problems' rather than recognized as 'creative practices', and denying difference based on perceived similarities and

commonalities which conversely marginalizes the legitimacy and mini-
mizes the significance of otherness.
- Intercultural communication defined by Anglo-American speakers of
English and within sites of aggressive assimilative immigration marked
by the ideology of cross-cultural adaptation and hegemonically enforced
borderlands.
- The lucrative commodification of English for business communication
worldwide – which I see as the 'global terrorist' (after Piyush Pandy,
executive director of *Ogilvy Mather India*, 2002) of an idea; that of the
ideology of linguistic normativity.

Quotations:

- 'To start with, when you are in the academe, your *raison d'être* is to be
critical which is not to endorse deconstruction carte blanche. Good intercultural research should not only avoid the pitfalls of both essentialism
and homogenization, it should also be "mindful" and judiciously apply
the criterion of "realistic cultural empathy".'
- 'I find that the most compelling studies of workplace interactions are on-
the-ground fine grained linguistic analyses that include multidisciplinary
perspectives such as input from speech/communication theories and
cultural studies, besides social theory, which explicate more fully both
the social motivations and the meanings that underlie code and style
choices. In this way emic realities emerge from etic frameworks as sociopragmatic realizations.'
- 'The language of local team work interactions and negotiations on the
shop floor tends to be the dominant local language (which may well
be English as a localized community norm or lingua franca) especially
in sites of outsourced operations (perhaps with the exclusion of call
centres). However, many business organizations in postcolonial sites
continue to expect their middle and top management to be proficient if
not fluent in English and aspire towards the use of idealized norms which
continue to remain abstractions.'
- 'Thus almost all English language communication skills training conducted for business and industry worldwide are based on prescribed
patterns of English usage. Presented as the normative language for such
purposes these are invariably available in commercially reproduced texts/
materials that are the basis of a lucrative industry.'
- 'But it is data obtained from local business contexts in real time that
can provide the contextual basis for developing appropriate indigenous
approaches to training for business purposes in localized workplaces.
For instance, it doesn't make much sense to teach native speaker norms

of social interaction in communication and negotiation skills for non-native English speaking contexts that do not share the same "cultural" frames of reference.'

- 'The point is that while language teachers or trainers may be seen as the custodians of usage, usage cannot be prescribed in contexts of use.'
- 'Commercially produced texts display a surprising lack of sociocultural awareness of the fact that in different areal sites, contexts and business settings there are different ways of speaking and communicating that are a reflection of "differences" (and idiosyncrasies) in business practices, linguistic norms and social values, organizational priorities, and cultural attitudes to the use of English itself.'
- 'Globalization, or rather glocalization is a phenomenon that has to be captured in the final things one says about the workplace. The global is not resistant to the local as workplace culture demonstrates in many parts of the world. Globalization threatens homogeneity too.'

Profile 2.2   Dalvir Samra-Fredericks

Professor of Organization Studies, Nottingham Business School, Nottingham, UK
http://www.ntu.ac.uk/research/nottinghambusinessschool/academic%20profiles/ 8987.html

Trained as: Worked in Sales/Marketing first, then undergraduate exposure to 'Communication Studies'

Inspired by: Garfinkel, Goffman and Sacks alongside the general 'frame' forwarded by Berger and Luckmann; recently, Boden too who is exemplary in terms of adopting a multidisciplinary stance

Speciality: 'Talk-in-interaction' blending the ethnographic and ethnomethodological 'stance'; strategic/management practices

Life: Born, educated and still living in the UK

For:

- Fine-grained talk-based ethnographic studies of practitioners at their everyday work across time and space realizing self/other, tasks and 'organization' – also aiming to displace misunderstandings that, for example, ethnomethodological studies ignore 'big' issues and questions *or* a belief that it focuses upon 'local social phenomena' when instead it focuses upon the 'localization and embodiment of phenomena' (the documentary relationship with 'other-than-local' matters).

- Illuminating, where possible and relevant, power-as-exercised, gender as 'done'/accomplished and to integrally acknowledge the emotional and moral aspects. For some, incorporating these elements may be seen as challenging or extending the scope of ethno-studies as traditionally conceptualized.
- Taking what this overall research orientation yields back into a 'classroom' context and to engage management/organizational studies' students *and* practitioners and critically reflect on what is taken-for-granted and *how* our world is made to happen (Boden) and, perhaps idealistically, hope that future change is made present.

Against:

- Monodisciplinary research – our world just does not happen according to the boundaries drawn between disciplines and hence, it cannot be easily understood along such lines.
- Abstractions and generalizations which leave us searching for meaningfulness and connections to the world as lived.
- The unreflexive use of categories/concepts drawn from the field by researchers and then, 'fed' back to the 'field'/practitioners who then pass them back onto us! (Giddens)

Quotations:

- 'I don't use the term "discourse" in my work; I use talk or talk-in-interaction (Schegloff, Psathas, Boden). Discourse has broader theoretical and conceptual coverage and retaining distinctions allows some precision in our thinking and research activities and subsequent offerings.'
- 'I would like to see the "linguistic turn" taken more seriously in management studies; at the moment there is still much "jumping-over" actual language use in context.'
- 'My engagement with "culture" is implicit I suppose: it is not an "out-there" measurable entity or easily discernible phenomena. It is something enacted by human beings as they observe and fine-tune historically established notions of what is appropriate, expected and so on and so forth.'
- 'I see myself as drawing on a number disciplines: linguistics and pragmatics, business/management/organization studies, sociology and anthropology; we cannot box off research into human interaction just as we cannot box off the world into neat categories.'
- 'Disciplines are ways of creating centres of expertise through which we are also potentially creating centres of ignorance. What is crucial is the willingness to instigate conversations across disciplines.'

- 'Linguistics can make us more aware of the fine-grained nature of inter-action, of what we take for granted – aspects of applied linguistics may even open up possibilities for change especially through teasing out (in my case) managers/strategists' routine, unreflective ways of talking/being and hence, maybe, just, other ways of talking/being.'
- 'Social theory, as any other theory, offers us a sensitizing frame and some theoretical and conceptual leverage for understanding "what is going on" – I have employed a range of "theories" as "resources" as I search for ways of making sense of the dynamic, complex and intricate forms of talk-based human interaction.'
- 'What is the macro? If we took away human beings and their everyday "doings" (ostensibly, the "micro"), then what would be left? Boden is excellent on this.'
- 'I am very aware that whenever I am writing, the analytical story is limited – the biggest problem for me has been (and continues to be), how do you get it down into seven thousand words or so [the "average" size article]? Just writing the broad ethnographic story could take seven thousand words!'
- 'As social scientists we have to retain certain protocols otherwise any-thing goes and we need to be careful about the sorts of analytical claims that we can make given the methodology/empirical data.'

Profile 2.3   Rick Iedema

Professor, Director, Centre for Health Communication, University of Technology, Sydney, Australia
http://www.centreforhealthcom.org/members/rick-iedema

Trained as: A linguist
Speciality: Organizational communication; health services research; patient safety; consumer involvement in health care decision making
Inspired by: Organizational discourse studies/analysis; Affect Theory; Participatory Enquiry; Video Reflexive Research Methods
Life: Born in the Netherlands, was educated in the UK and Australia, lived in Indonesia and a few other places, and is now an expatriate in Australia

For:

- Social researchers immersing themselves in practitioners' priorities and problems, in the policy and organizational reform agendas bearing on

the practice chosen for study, and in the political tensions permeating the interface between practice and policy;
- Social researchers deploying and adapting social science in ways that enhance its social relevance, ignoring the costs that may incur to the 'purity' of any one particular disciplinary endeavour.
- Social researchers realizing that the modality of the relationship they institute between themselves and their subjects of research (their 'researchees') will be reflected in the relationship between their researches and the findings of the research: distance begets distance; objectification begets objectification.

Against:
- Monodisciplinary research which, using a particular theory or method as its taken-as-given point of departure, and in spite of its best intentions, inscribes itself into a rigid stance towards what it researches and what it produces, and makes itself unresponsive and unaccountable to those whom it researches.
- Research being deployed to produce academic findings at the expense of practitioner-relevant changes and innovations;
- Research approaches and methods objectifying organization and organizing, as these erase fragmentation, complexity and dynamics, each of which I believe are central to understanding and intervening in organizing.

Quotations:
- 'Talk is never one-dimensional and is always multiscalar and multimodal: talk is not only shot through with other talk (Bakhtin, Volosinov) but also with intentionalities embedded in and derived from affective (pre-discursive), technological, architectural and social contexts and materialities.'
- 'Technology is a recursive, semiotizing and exo-somatic materialization of effort that seeks to render affect amenable and subject to discursive practice'.
- 'Context is the space that facilitates rather than acts as target of our resemiotizing and productive efforts: it is *the space of the taken-as-given,* or *where affect need not kick in.*'
- 'Monodisciplinary research is concerned to confirm the importance of the discipline's own origin, of its own boundaries and "truths" (and its "experts"), and it eschews "risking" a more dynamic, open and experimental stance – that is, a more *degenerate* stance – on what research is and can be about.'

- 'Discourse is multimodal and dynamic: it is the 'mangle of meaning-making' that intertwines affect, gesture, gaze, kinesics, but also resemiotized phenomena including "exo-somatic" technologies and architecture.'
- 'I see the field of organizational discourse studies developing on from representation towards affect as the dimension of human agency that is opened up (or closed off) by the dynamics of social relations.'
- 'Affect is what regulates, first and foremost, our relationships and meaning making. Affect both precedes and drives discourse.'
- 'Organizations are peculiar phenomena in that they are sites that people often experience as routinized and repetitive, but that are in fact sites where people are confronted with and can experiment with unfamiliar social configurations and innovative ways of being, doing and saying; that is, new affects.'

Profile 2.4   Lorenza Mondada

Professor, University of Basel, Basel (CH)
http://franz.unibas.ch/seminar/mitarbeitende/profil/portrait/person/mondada/

Trained as: a linguist with many interdisciplinary connections
Inspired by: Ethnomethodology, conversation analysis, video analysis, studies of embodied interaction, workplace studies, interactional linguistics, emergent grammar (Garfinkel, Sacks, Schegloff, Goodwin, Heath, Hakulinen, Thompson, Hopper)
Speciality: The study of social interaction in a variety of settings (ordinary conversation, institutional contexts, professional activities) considering the multimodal resources that participants mobilize to organize and make intelligible their action
Life: Born and educated in Switzerland, living and working in Europe

For:

- Considering all embodied resources participants mobilize for organizing their action: this encompasses not only gesture, gaze, facial expressions, body postures, but also object manipulations and movements within space.
- Taking into account the emic, endogenous perspective of the participants in interaction as they accountably orient to, display, publicly exhibit the local relevancies of the ongoing activities.
- Grounding conceptual and theoretical insights about language in action and the organization of human action in in-depth and detailed analyses of naturally occurring social interactions.

- Taking fieldwork as not only a way of gathering naturalistic data, but also a way of anchoring research practice in relations of trust and engagement in the field, which are necessary for securing the quality of the data and for giving a fair and empowering feedback to the participants.

Against:

- Treating language as autonomous: language is irremediably situated, dynamically changing in context, intertwined with other embodied resources.
- Research confined within the institutional borders of the disciplines: interactional phenomena constantly cross borders without asking for permission . . .
- Imposing etic, exogenous categories on the observed phenomena and then treating participants as 'judgmental dopes' who do not know what they do.

Quotations:

- 'The focus on the detailed embodied organization of talk and action as they are locally organized does not exclude a focus on their systematicity. Complex multimodal actions are "methodically" organized and it is the task of the analyst to unpack the orderly ways in which they are achieved.'
- 'Language is irremediably situated within emergent courses of action: therefore it cannot be studied in isolation as an abstract system of rules. The natural home of language is social interaction, and that's where its order comes from.'
- 'Multimodal resources are temporally organized: they unfold step by step, moment by moment, in an emergent and incremental way, in multiple simultaneous flows, achieving recognizable and accountable actions that are sequentially organized.'
- 'The study of language in social interaction in professional settings reveals the way in which complex workplace configures specific language use and in turn is reflexively structured by linguistic, embodied and interactional opportunities.'

Further reading

Kotthoff, H., & Spencer-Oatey, H. (Eds.) (2007). *Handbook of intercultural communication* (Handbooks of Applied Linguistics Vol. 7). Berlin: Mouton de Gruyter. This is probably the most comprehensive and wide-ranging reference volume on intercultural communication for the years to come.

Marschan-Piekkari, R., & Welch, C. (Eds.) (2004). *Handbook of qualitative research methods for international business.* Cheltenham: Edward Elgar. The book examines the use of qualitative methods in international business research in terms of contextualizing the research process; designing and managing crossnational collaborative research; rethinking current and alternative research methods; and publishing qualitative research.

Nakayama, T. K. and Halualani, R. T. (Eds.) (2010). *The handbook of critical intercultural communication*. Chichester: Wiley-Blackwell. A state of the art collection on advances in critical intercultural communication studies, with special, though not exclusive, emphasis on the US context.

Piller, I. (2011). *Intercultural communication: a critical introduction*. Edinburgh: Edinburgh University Press. An accessible introduction to intercultural communication from a discourse analytic and sociolinguistic perspective. A companion volume to Nakayama & Halualani (Eds.).

Spencer-Oatey, H., & Franklin, P. (2007). *Intercultural communication*. Basingstoke: Palgrave Macmillan. This book takes a multidisciplinary and contextualized approach to intercultural communication which bridges the gap between current research and real-life intercultural communication issues and professional training demands.

Chapter 2 Tasks

Task 1: What is 'Culture'?

Starting with the word 'culture', draw a web consisting of words that you associate with culture. Extend the web by adding more words. Do not use any scholarly sources to complete this first stage of the task.

Look up the website (http://geert-hofstede.com/) and compare it with the 2007 article by Daphne Jameson in the *Journal of Business Communication* on culture and cultural identity. How are the views expressed by Hofstede and Jameson similar, and how are they different? How do they compare to your web of associations? Finally, make a case contrasting both sets of definitions, highlighting advantages and limitations, and bearing in mind that your reader is new to the topic.

Task 2: A new commercial website

Draw up a plan for the elaboration of design and contents of a multimodal website promoting wine as a new product in a country classified as a 'developing economy' where half of the population are Muslim. Include in your plan a note on the kind of information you need to acquire – historical, cultural, economic, religious, geo-political, etc. before formulating the concept design.

Propose a simple concept design for the home page, i.e. an idea for a design specifying colours, themes, patterns, etc. Follow it up with a design mockup, integrating the textual component as you go along. Refer to existing corporate websites for inspiration. Describe the process – and the challenges encountered – in designing such a document and discuss your findings with colleagues.

Task 3: Partnership research and 'thick' participation

You have been offered the opportunity to conduct a project for a financial organization with headquarters in Frankfurt and an existing network of branches in 17 countries worldwide. Due to the international financial crisis, the organization is planning to reduce its branches to about half the current number over a period of two to three years, with a loss of hundreds of jobs. Senior management are seeking to gauge the perceptions of a sample of the local staff in the offices which are rumoured to have been selected for 'streamlining'. As an external researcher, you have been asked to collaborate with individual managers responsible for the local offices over a period of six to nine months. You will have unrestricted access to the organization's premises. Given the sensitive nature of the issues under investigation, decide how best to negotiate your relationship with senior management, local managers and their staff; what data collection and analytical methods are best suited for the objectives that you will negotiate with management, and what project schedule you are going to suggest bearing in mind that findings should be reported formally to the Human Resources directorate within nine months from the official start of the project.

References

Jameson, D. (2007). Reconceptualizing cultural identity and its role in intercultural business communication. *Journal of Business Communication, 44* (3), 199–235.

Part II
Applying Business Discourse Research

3
Research-based Business Discourse Teaching

This chapter will:

- profile five examples of projects related to *research-based business discourse teaching* from around the world;
- discuss the *methodologies* used and *implications* for teaching or training;
- show how the profiled teaching projects critically reflect the *developments* in business discourse research we have discussed in Part 1.

This chapter will profile a number of examples of projects related to research-based business discourse teaching from around the world. Three of the projects were intended to generate research-based information gathered in the real world of business to underpin teaching or training in a specific academic context (Seshadri & Theye, The Hong Kong Project, Nelson) and two are accounts of research-based teaching applications (Planken et al., the CIBW/IBLC project). The studies have used various methodologies and approaches to collect the information needed and apply it in a classroom setting, from interviews with specialist informants within and beyond the business community through extensive needs analyses within business organizations in the form of a questionnaire survey or set of interviews, to corpus-based analysis and genre analysis, and an investigation of real versus textbook language. We will show how studies like these have drawn on the knowledge held by the business community as a communicative (discourse) community, together with their communicative practices, to contribute to the design of appropriate teaching or training materials.

3.1   Professionals and professors: substance or style?

The study of reader response by Seshadri and Theye (2000) compares the views of business professors with those of business executives in the US, in order to investigate not only what business people consider as effective writing, but also to determine whether these views are the same as those held by the teaching community. It is grounded in the US-based tradition of respondent surveys exemplified by the needs analysis survey by Casady and Wasson (1994), the respondent survey evaluating different direct and indirect organizational plans in job refusal letters by Smith, Nolan and Dai (1996) and the survey of business executives' reactions to a series of written examples that are generally considered as writing errors, by Gilsdorf and Leonard (2001). Seshadri and Theye provide an empirical example of the mismatch that may exist between the content and process of the business communication classroom on the one hand and what we focus on in our teaching, and the perceptions of the real business world on the other.

Methodology

Fifty business professionals and fifty business faculty in the United States were asked to evaluate a set of three reports written by students in an introductory marketing class, using a set of criteria reported in previous studies as contributing to effective writing, for instance, sentence structure and syntax, and content and conciseness. The students had been asked to think of a persuasive message and a strategy related to a topic given to them by their instructor, and to provide a summary of this in a short report. Reports on the three topics most frequently chosen by the students were then randomly selected for the study; the importance of global marketing, the ethics of cigarette advertising and the marketing challenges of nonprofit organizations. Each of the respondents were asked to evaluate three reports by completing an evaluation sheet or rating form consisting of eight bipolar adjectives and a Likert-type scale (see Concept 3.1) – in this case a five-point scale. The evaluation sheet was pretested three times and the final instrument consisted of eight evaluative criteria: purpose/theme, content, organization/focus, sentence structure/syntax, spelling/grammar, conciseness, wording/style, and appearance. As with many studies in the positivistic research tradition, i.e. in research that attempts to describe actual, observable, human behaviour, Seshadri and Theye constructed a set of eight hypotheses which they then considered on the basis of their research findings.

Data 3.1   Seshadri and Theye: hypotheses and results

H1	Business professionals are more lenient than business faculty in the global evaluation of reports – SUPPORTED
H2	Business professionals are less critical of violations of rules of business writing style than are business faculty – NOT SUPPORTED
H3	Business professionals evaluate reports on fewer criteria than do business faculty – SUPPORTED
H4	Business professionals emphasize substance more than do business faculty – SUPPORTED

H5   Business professionals, on the average, spend less time evaluating a report than do business faculty – SUPPORTED

H6   Business faculty emphasize mechanics more than do business professionals – SUPPORTED

H7   Business professionals give higher grades to reports which are less demanding of their time – NOT SUPPORTED

H8   Business faculty give lower grades to reports which require more time to grade – SUPPORTED

(Seshadri and Theye, 2000: 17)

Concept 3.1   Scales

An important aspect of research involving a respondent survey is the scales used in the evaluation instrument. A common type of scale is a *Likert scale* combined with a set of *semantic differentials* which allow respondents to rate a text, of one aspect of a text, on a set of different criteria. A Likert scale is a gradually increasing or decreasing scale of equally spaced steps, usually five or seven, connecting two opposite (and absolute) rating values, e.g. appropriate versus inappropriate, which in turn are related to the set of criteria under investigation, e.g. content. A set of semantic differentials are the adjectival opposites that can be used at either end of a Likert scale on a respondent survey, e.g. strong versus weak, succinct versus wordy and professional versus unprofessional. They are chosen by the researcher as an appropriate way of describing or rating each individual criterion, e.g. the adjectives *professional* and *unprofessional* are used by Seshadri and Theye to rate the criterion *appearance* in business writing (as reproduced below).

An Example of a Likert Scale
CRITERIA   RATING
Appearance   (Professional)   5   4   3   2   1   (Unprofessional)

(Adapted from Seshadri & Theye, 2000: 23)

Further information on the design and use of Likert scales in applied linguistics, which is also relevant for business discourse research, can be found in Paltridge and Phakiti (2010).

Findings and relationship with previous studies

Seshadri and Theye revisit several similar previous surveys in the discussion of their findings, e.g. Waner (1995), Epstein (1999) and Casady and Wasson (1994), and show how their findings agree with both Epstein (1999) and Casady and

Wasson (1994) in the factors that were reported as important by business professors and business people respectively, but are different than Waner (1995) who found no significant differences between the views expressed by business faculty and business professionals. Their study suggests several differences between the business executives and business faculty in their (reported) evaluation of the students' writing, the most notable being that whereas business professionals reported that they emphasized substance (i.e. content) and wording (i.e. style), business faculty reported that they emphasized the mechanics of writing, such as spelling, grammar and appearance. In addition, both groups reported that they emphasized organization or focus. The conclusions of the study are presented in Quote 3.1.

Quote 3.1   Executives versus business professors

We may also conclude that business professors emphasize the *process* of writing while business professionals focus more on the *product*. This is not surprising given the role of an instructor, who must concentrate on the process of writing in order to deliver a good product for the business professional. Business communication professors, to better prepare business students to succeed in the business world, should focus more on developing skills that lead to improved content, organization and style. Taking advantage of software that can flag errors in spelling and provide guidelines to improve grammar and punctuation, business communication classes can now concentrate on the core of effective communication, namely the thought processes, rather than the mechanics of writing.

(Seshadri and Theye, 2000: 21)

How useful is survey research?

Seshadri and Theye conclude that the views held by business professors on what constitutes good or effective business writing may not be universally shared by the business community. What is not clear, however, is whether all the respondents either within or across the two types of respondent groups were, in fact, interpreting the criteria presented to them in the same way, e.g. *conciseness*, ranging from *succinct* to *wordy*, or *content*, ranging from *strong* to *weak*. This illustrates the problem of reliability that is inherent in research that relies on a survey only, in order to collect a set of data, i.e. the findings are based on what the respondents *report* they are doing, and not on what they may actually *be doing*. In the Seshadri and Theye study, for instance, it would have been useful to check the interpretation that the respondents gave of the evaluation criteria they were presented with, rather than just assuming that they were all interpreting them in the same way. Some researchers address this issue by working with an *interrater-reliability analysis*, such that more than one researcher (in the case of text analysis) is presented with the same set of data and their interpretation of that data is then compared. The study by Hyland (1998) that we profile in Chapter 8 in Part 3 uses this approach in the analysis of metadiscourse in annual general reports, where a team of three researchers investigated the same set of data. This is also the case in the 2008 multimodal study of textual and visual metadiscourse in annual reports by de Groot (2008), which involved five different analysts. Some of the other studies we discuss in Part 3 have provided specific examples of why the findings of survey research need to be interpreted carefully in business discourse research in particular. In a pioneering study of the Brazilian business context, for instance, Barbara et al. (1996) comment on the problem associated with the nomenclature of business documents as texts with the same purpose that are referred to using different names across different companies (e.g. memo, report and project), and Nickerson (2000) confirms this by combining a survey of the use of written English by corporations in the Netherlands with the collection of a corpus of real data, which showed a diversity of text types within the corpus that was not apparent from the reports given by the respondents in the initial survey. Other studies that have used one or more surveys to collect their data, such as the 2000 study by Li-Somui and Mead of the use of English in the Hong Kong textile industry, the 2005 study by Louhiala-Salminen et al. of the use of English in two Nordic corporations (both profiled in Chapter 8 in Part 3) and the *Teaching English to meet the needs of business education in Hong Kong* project that we will discuss next in this chapter, all draw on survey data as useful background information, but then combine this method with one or more other research methodologies such as in-depth interviews, observation, the collection of corpora and text analysis. In more recent research, although stand alone surveys do still inform research-based business discourse teaching, as is the case in the extensive survey of the use of English in professional communication in Hong Kong provided by Evans (2010), most studies have continued to combine several methods of data collection in their analysis of teaching or training needs in a given context. Evans (2012) for instance, combines interviews, ethnographic case-studies of a professional's week, and the analysis of authentic emails in the design of email tasks for the teaching of Business English, and Wozniak (2010) uses interviews, a questionnaire and an analysis of the foreign language certification process in her needs analysis survey on the language needs of French mountain guides. Similarly, in her study of the use of English at a German multinational corporation, Ehrenreich (2010) draws on 24 qualitative interviews, the observation of internal meetings, external meetings and dinners, two days of shadowing and a further nine recordings of phone conferences and meetings. As she observes in discussing the reasons for taking this approach, 'To capture the multidimensional realities of language and communication as experienced by mid- to top-level business managers as comprehensively as possible – ultimately aiming to gain access to their conceptual worlds – an ethnographic, multimethod approach was adopted' (Ehrenreich, 2010; 413, slightly adapted).

3.2   Teaching English to meet the needs of business education in Hong Kong

The *Teaching English to meet the needs of business education in Hong Kong* (Bhatia & Candlin, 2001) project was a large scale multimethod needs analysis project designed to inform tertiary level business English teaching and post vocational training. It involved the collaborative efforts of nineteen different researchers, five different tertiary institutions and a range of different methodologies and specialist informants. Against a fluctuating linguistic background in Hong Kong at the end of the 1980s (as summarized by Jackson, 2005, in Quote 3.2), and the resulting need to evaluate needs and existing levels of communication skills, the project drew on the views of the business students themselves, on business faculty, on ESBP practitioners and on the views of business people working in Hong Kong at that time. The main purpose of the project was 'to investigate the nature of requirements imposed by the multidisciplinary academic programmes and teaching staff in five tertiary institutions in Hong Kong on their undergraduate BBA (Bachelor of Business Administration) students in the use of English and to evaluate the extent to which their requirements are met by the English Language support courses' (Bhatia & Candlin, 2001: 3).

Quote 3.2   English in Hong Kong in the 1990s and beyond

Before the Handover of Hong Kong to China in 1997, the official language of instruction in most schools was English, although Cantonese or mixed-code (Cantonese with some English) was used in many classrooms. This policy was changed in 1998 and the language of instruction in approximately 70 per cent of the secondary schools is now Chinese (Cantonese) with English and Putonghua (Mandarin) taught as subjects. Only a small percentage of schools are now designated as English-medium (EMI) schools with courses taught in this language. By contrast, English is the official language at most tertiary institutions although the Chinese University has a bilingual (Chinese–English) policy and classes are offered in both languages. In the wider community, officials of the Hong Kong government advocate the importance of a trilingual (Cantonese–English–Putonghua) community to maintain the region's competitive position in Asia.

(Jackson, 2005: 294–5)

Methodology

Between April 1998 and October 2000 a series of investigations were completed using a variety of different methodologies to collect the data: 2684 business students and twelve English department staff received *questionnaires*, focus group *interviews* were held with 115 students and 45 business professors, current *teaching materials* were collected from both business professors and ESBP practitioners, *writing samples* were collected from 220 students and a *questionnaire* was submitted to a sample of new entrants to the banking sector in Hong Kong. As Bhatia and Candlin comment, the project was therefore 'a comprehensive multifaceted needs analysis aimed at a large representative sample' of the target population (2001: 7). The project also focused on six different research perspectives, each one designed to collect different – although complementary – information, and each using different methodologies (see also our discussion on multiperspectival approaches in Chapter 1 as exemplified by Candlin and Crichton, 2011a). These six perspectives were as follows:

- Student Perspective
- Teacher Perspective
- Curriculum Perspective
- Writing Performance Perspective
- Textual Perspective
- Occupational Perspective.

In the remainder of this section we will focus on two investigations from project members which highlight – although not exclusively – two of these perspectives: the survey of business professors as detailed in Jackson (2005) centred on the Teacher Perspective, and the interface between the academy and the business world as discussed by Chew (2005), which is centred on the Occupational Perspective.

Data 3.2   The main objectives of the Hong Kong English for Business Education Project

1. To describe the nature of English language demands placed on business students by their subject teachers, by the nature and complexity of the subject discipline(s) they study, and also by the nature and variety of academic tasks they are required to accomplish as part of their business education.
2. In the context of (1) above, to evaluate the efficacy of currently taught English and communication skills courses to cope with these demands.
3. To suggest measures to improve the nature and scope of English and communication skills teaching (whether English for Academic Purposes, or English for Specific Purposes) for business studies.

(Bhatia & Candlin, 2001: 3)

A survey of business professors: teacher perspective

Jackson (2005) gives an account of a series of twenty interviews held with forty-five business professors at five of the Hong Kong tertiary institutions. These included local as well as expatriate professors, with an average of seven years of teaching experience in Hong Kong. They also represented a range of specializations that business students are likely to encounter in the course of their studies, including management, marketing, accountancy, law and international business. Five key areas were investigated:

- the status of the students' English, including their background and entry level,
- the specific demands of the sub-discipline,
- their progress through the degree programme,
- the assessment procedures followed, and,
- the role of the English support teacher.

Jackson reports that despite the fact that the business professors held a wide range of views, there was a general consensus that disciplinary variation within the range of specializations offered in undergraduate degree programmes was the most difficult aspect of their studies for many students particularly in the first year of study. This was because it required them to complete a variety of different speaking and writing tasks in English for which they did not have sufficient skills. The interviews made clear that there was a need for a business communications course for first year undergraduates to equip them with the English language skills they needed in the initial stages of the degree, followed by a set of discipline-specific ESP courses, in the second and third years of study, when the students were specializing in one or more of the sub-disciplines of business. Jackson's study reveals, therefore, a complex situation in which to provide appropriate teaching materials, not only in the use of Cantonese alongside English in the contexts she investigated, but also in the range of sub-disciplines that students were required to deal with during the course of their studies, each with their own discipline-specific tasks and discourse.

Quote 3.3   The advantages of multifaceted needs analysis

A thorough, multifaceted needs analysis can help ensure that ESP/EAP practitioner/course coordinators have the information necessary to develop courses that are more attuned to the needs of students and lecturers. It can help maximize the potential of ESP/EAP courses and play a significant role in helping students acquire the requisite language and communicative skills for success in the academic arena. Collaboration among institutions, such as in the Hong Kong SCOLAR* project, can foster a closer linage between ESP practitioners/researchers and content specialists and encourage the sharing of resources and ideas among institutions.

(Jackson 2005: 304–05)

*SCOLAR refers to the Hong Kong Standing Committee on Language Education and Research – the funding body for the Hong Kong Project.

The interface between the academy and the business world: occupational perspective

Like Jackson's study, the study by Chew (2005) also reveals a complex situation in relation to the English language needs required by new entrants in banks in Hong Kong, a potential employer for many of the students graduating with a BBA degree. The study investigates the English language skills used by entrants in the banking sector and seeks to identify the communicative tasks that were required in a variety of departments at four Hong Kong banks. Using a combination of an interview and a follow-up questionnaire with 16 new bank employees, Chew focuses on issues such as the amount of time spent on a daily basis communicating in English and the tasks completed, which English language skills were used most, and the difficulties that the bank employees reported in using English. The interviews and survey also asked the informants for information on the type of English language courses they felt would best improve their language skills. The study reveals a communication setting in which 'almost all written communicative tasks are carried out in English while most oral communicative tasks are carried out in Cantonese, the language of the majority of people in Hong Kong' (2005: 430). The only exceptions to this were those occasions where there was a non-Chinese speaker present, a rare event for most of the informants. As a result of the language choice most usually associated with the medium of the task, i.e. written tasks in English and oral tasks in Cantonese, there was also a considerable amount of Chinese-to-English translation that took place in order to produce a written English version of information collected from (mostly) Chinese sources. Ten out of the 16 informants reported that they had difficulties with the language demands posed by the communicative tasks required of them, and this was most especially the case for those employees working in environments alongside colleagues who spoke English as a first language. The study provides an insight into the interface between English as an international written language and Cantonese as a local spoken language. As part of the wider Hong Kong project to evaluate English language needs for BBA undergraduates, Chew's study provides compelling evidence that those needs were not being sufficiently met – at least in 1999.

Quote 3.4   Use of written sources in the Hong Kong banking sector

Some amount of Chinese-to-English translation work goes on so that much of the gathering of information is carried out in Chinese whether it is talking to colleagues, clients, the media and other professionals in the industry. This information is then translated into English for the written product in the form of memos, minutes of meetings, reports, rules and regulations for bank customers, opinion and complaint letters from customers. The extent of synthesizing and selecting information and leaving out other information depends on the final product so that if the final product is a memo or minutes of a meeting, there is probably more synthesis of the information, and more room for judgement as to what part of the information may be omitted. On the other hand, if the final product is converting data about Chinese companies into an English report, or a complaint letter from a customer, it is likely that the translation has to remain as close to the original as possible in terms of content and meaning . . . The importance of English in gathering information from written sources such as research reports, brokers' reports, Bloomberg Financial Services and other such sources needs to be underscored. If the research content is international in nature or deals with international companies, the reading materials are in English. Technical and computer manuals are also read in English. However, if the research content is locally based or about Hong Kong companies or from Chinese newspapers, the reading materials are in Chinese. To sum up, much of the reading and almost all of the writing are done in English while the oral activities and tasks are conducted in Cantonese unless the oral communication is with non-Chinese participants.

(Chew, 2005: 430–1)

The implications of the project: project recommendations

As Bhatia and Candlin observe in their project report, the findings of the Hong Kong project as a whole raise a number of important questions of relevance for the design and implementation of appropriate ESP programmes. These include (i) accounting for the dynamic complexity in academic and professional genres in ESP programmes (ii) exploiting the overlap in academic discourses across disciplines, but at the same time addressing any disciplinary tensions or conflicts, and (iii) integrating the potentially conflicting perspectives of interdisciplinary academic discourse and the discourse required by the post-academic workplace professions (Bhatia & Candlin, 2001: 105). The box below shows some of the immediate recommendations, and recommendations for the future, that conclude the report.

Data 3.3   The Hong Kong English for Business Education
Project: recommendations

The incorporation of:

1. A well-designed English for Academic Purpose programme for all first year business education students aimed at developing a common core of academic discourse while at the same time highlighting disciplinary and cross disciplinary variations.
2. A modular genre-based ESP course with each module introducing students to a set of academic business genres, and sensitizing them to some of the typical lexico-grammatical realizations and rhetorical features of such genres as well as making them aware of generic conflicts across disciplinary boundaries.
3. A modular genre-based set of English for Occupational Purpose electives focusing specifically on individual genres and linked to professionally oriented tasks, introducing students to some of the demands of key post academic professional workplaces.

The further investigation of:

1. Some of the main professional genres and sub-genres to be used as input to curriculum design.
2. How best to convert the insights from needs analysis into the design of specific curricular packages keeping in mind the institutional demands and constraints.
3. The development of ESP (EAP/EOP) teaching materials for use in specific modules suggested in the recommendations.
4. The feasibility of self-access and/or web-mediated ESP modular materials for use in ESP (EOP) courses.

(Adapted from Bhatia & Candlin, 2001:106)

Research into practice?

The Hong Kong Project provided a wealth of information on the ESP needs for business education in Hong Kong at the end of the 1990s, the most notable of which were the cross-disciplinary variations that existed in the way in which different genres had evolved across the different specializations within the broad umbrella of business education, and the apparent mismatch that there was between the English language skills that were provided in the tertiary education setting and those that were required in the workplace. The challenge for large scale, multimethod, projects like this, however, is to build on the findings and move beyond the project recommendations to translate them into usable teaching materials while the findings of the project still obtain. In the next chapter, we will profile a second Hong Kong-based project, in which a complex needs analysis survey combining a survey, corpus and genre analysis, was used to great effect to develop and then successfully carry out a training course for executives at the Jockey Club in Hong Kong (Baxter, Boswood & Peirson-Smith, 2002). Finally, to illustrate how quickly the need for research-based teaching materials may change, we conclude this section with a quotation taken from recent work by Bargiela-Chiappini and Zang (2012) on the integrated approach which is currently being taken by the 32 different institutions across Mainland China that have received government approval in the past few years to teach Bachelors programmes in Business English. It includes information on the particular role played by business discourse in facilitating this process and highlights, as in the Hong Kong English for Business Education project, the need for students to differentiate both generically and discursively between the different business disciplines.

Quote 3.5   Business English in Mainland China

The University of International Business and Economics (UIBE) in Beijing was one of the first three universities to run a BA in Business English; the first cohort of their four-year Business English undergraduate programme graduated in 2011. Their Business English multidisciplinary curriculum is a composite of subjects organized in three core components of equal status: knowledge of business disciplines, business discourse, and professional practices where business discourse acts as a bridge between the other two components. While elements of 'business knowledge' have been present since its inception in Business English teaching in China, the integrated curriculum of the current Business English programme gives ample room to subjects such as economics, management, international business law, international trade, etc. and relies on highly qualified academics in the individual disciplines to deliver courses of comparable level to those found in business degrees normally available in business schools.

(Adapted from Bargiela-Chiappini & Zhang, 2012)

3.3   A corpus-based study of Business English and Business English teaching materials

The PhD corpus-based study of Business English and Business English teaching materials by Mike Nelson (2000) (available at: http://users.utu.fi/micnel/

BEC/downloadable_materials.htm), is concerned with two main research questions:

1. Is the lexis of Business English different from everyday general English? and;
2. Is the lexis found in Business English published materials different from that found in real life business?

Nelson created two corpora in order to investigate these questions; a Published Materials Corpus (PMC) consisting of 33 published Business English course and resource books comprised of 590,000 running words and a Business English Corpus (BEC), with 1,023,000 running words divided between spoken (44 per cent) and written (56 per cent) texts, representing British and US native speaker business discourse. The British National Corpus (BNC) was used as a reference corpus, together with *WordSmith Tools 3* (Scott, 1999), which allowed him to examine how Business English differed from general English and likewise, how the Business English presented in published materials differed from 'real' Business English. A breakdown of the BEC is shown below. It contains spoken and written genres that are used to talk and speak about business, e.g. business newspapers and radio reports, as well as spoken and written genres that are used to actually do business, e.g. emails and meetings. In Chapter 1 of this volume we discussed Handford's (2010a) study of the language of business meetings, based on the CANBEC corpus, and in Part 3, we will discuss the usefulness of corpus-based approaches in general to researching business discourse.

The Business English Corpus

A Breakdown of the Business English Corpus (reproduced by kind permission of Mike Nelson).

Writing about business

Part of Corpus	Tokens	Contents
Business books	53,470	5 extracts from different books (approx. 10,000 words each)
Business newspapers	64,291	121 articles
Business journals & magazines	78,846	52 articles
Total	**196,607**	

Writing to do business

Part of Corpus	Tokens	Contents
Annual reports	34,537	3 annual reports
Business press releases	21,656	29 business press releases
Business contracts	29,602	13 contracts/agreements

Business faxes	23,105	114 faxes
Business letters	26,793	94 letters
Business reports	62,908	17 reports
Company brochures	23,239	13 company brochures
Emails	28,857	202 emails
Job advertisements	22,293	87 job advertisements
Manuals	21,160	5 manuals
Memos	12,542	47 memos
Minutes	34,805	15 sets of minutes
Product brochures	26,175	19 product brochures
Quotations	8,997	21 quotations
Miscellaneous	2,427	OHT, job description & agendas
Total	**379,096**	

Talking about business

Part of corpus	Tokens	Contents
Interviews	70,894	24 interviews
Business on radio & TV	148,983	72 broadcasts
Total	**219,877**	

Speaking to do business

Part of Corpus	Tokens	Contents
Job interviews	17,447	6 interviews
Meetings	126,243	15 meetings
Negotiation	16,450	4 negotiation sessions
Telephone calls	30,414	89 phone conversations
Speeches/presentations	19,020	5 speeches
Training sessions	17,867	1 session
Total	**227,441**	

Methodology: Wordsmith Tools (http://www.lexically.net/wordsmith/index.html)

Wordsmith Tools is a concordancing programme developed by Mike Smith, now in its sixth version, which has been published since 1996. It allows researchers to analyse specific linguistic features in a set of texts and to compare the features of different sets of texts, e.g. a set of business texts versus a set of general texts. It can identify which words occur together – or the *concordances* – it can make lists of the most frequently occurring words in a set of texts – the *keywords* – and it can compare the concordances and keywords in two different corpora. Wordsmith Tools has been used by several researchers looking at business texts, including Nickerson (2000), who used it to isolate and compare some of the interpersonal discourse features that occurred in a corpus of 200 corporate email messages, 100 written by Dutch writers in English and 100 written by British writers, all working at the same corporation, with just over 15,000 words in each set of data, and Upton and Connor (2001) who used Wordsmith to analyse a number of the linguistic features used to realize the politeness strategies that occurred within the rhetorical moves found in a corpus of 153 application letters in English; 70 from Belgium, 26 from Finland and 57 from the US. Most recently, Crawford Camiciottoli (2009b; 2009c) has used Wordsmith Tools to investigate the discourses of business education.

Findings of the BEC/BNC corpus analysis

Nelson used the *key words* facility in *Wordsmith Tools* to identify those words in the BEC that occurred unusually frequently, compared to the general corpus (the BNC). He found that the BEC lexis, i.e. vocabulary, represented a limited number of semantic, i.e. meaning, categories related to the following things; business people, companies, institutions, money, business events, places of business, time, modes of communication and lexis concerned with technology. He also found that the key lexis of Business English was positive in nature, and that very few negative words occurred. Most of the adjectives referred to things such as products and companies, therefore emphasizing action rather than emotion. In addition, in his later study of semantic associations in the BEC compared to the BNC, he provides three further ways in which (the BEC) Business English differs from general English in the BNC as follows:

1. The *collocates*, i.e. the words that occurred together, in the BEC were more fixed than in the BNC. In other words, there were fewer combinations of words that occurred together in the BEC than in the BNC.
2. Some collocates were the same in the BEC as in the BNC, e.g. *send & documents*, *big & people*, *big & companies/institutions*, etc. although there were variations in both the frequency with which these occurred and in their content. For instance, the *documents* referred to in the BEC were business related, whereas in the BNC they were more varied and general, and while *big & people* and *big & companies/institutions* occurred together in both corpora, there were many more instances of *big & companies/institutions* in the BEC than in BNC, and many more instances of *big & people* in the BNC than in the BEC.
3. Some collocates were characteristic of the BEC, but hardly occurred at all in the BNC, e.g. the word *package* occurred much more often in the BEC than in the BNC together with financially related lexis (e.g. *financial package*) and

the BEC collocates, *competitive package, excellent package,* and *effective package,* did not occur et all in the BNC.
(Adapted from Nelson, 2006).

Table 3.1 shows the top 50 Key Words that occurred in the BEC, i.e. words that occurred with unusual frequency. The frequency of each word in the BEC is presented and then compared to its frequency in the BNC. The final column then shows how *key,* i.e. how important, it could be considered as an item of lexis within business discourse. Table 3.2 shows a comparison of keywords in the BEC and how they occurred in the BNC, for a number of different categories such as People, Places and Things. They show the areas of lexis that can be considered as important in Business English on the basis of the BEC/BNC corpus analysis.

Quote 3.6   On the nature of Business English

The world of business found in real-life language is a limited one made up of business people, companies, institutions, money, business events, places of business, time, modes of communication and vocabulary concerned with technology. The language found was surprisingly positive, with very few negative words featuring at all. It was also found to be dynamic and action-orientated and non-emotive.

(Mike Nelson, Thursday 20 March 2003, *Guardian Weekly*)

In summary it can be said that, to a large extent, there actually is something called 'Business English' that can be seen as semantically distinct from 'general' English though at the same time is still quite clearly attached to it.

(Nelson, 2000, http://users.utu.fi/micnel/BEC/downloadable_materials.htm)

Table 3.1   BEC positive key words (top 50) that occur with unusual frequency in the BEC

N	Word	BEC Freq.	BEC %	BNC Freq.	BNC %	Keyness Log L.
1	BUSINESS	2837	0.28	542	0.03	3557.7
2	COMPANY	2934	0.29	782	0.04	3118.6
3	MARKET	2336	0.23	831	0.04	2056.1
4	CUSTOMER	1199	0.12	147		1763.0
5	OK	897	0.09	38		1635.1
6	PRODUCT	1385	0.14	412	0.02	1377.2
7	SALE	1210	0.12	343	0.02	1239.4
8	FAX	613	0.06	32		1085.0
9	MANAGEMENT	973	0.10	279	0.01	989.6
10	PRICE	1302	0.13	586	0.03	941.5
11	FINANCIAL	780	0.08	237	0.01	765.0
12	BANK	940	0.09	379	0.02	749.0

(continued)

Table 3.1 Continued

N	Word	BEC Freq.	BEC %	BNC Freq.	BNC %	Keyness Log L.
13	BILLION	515	0.05	67		743.4
14	SERVICE	1461	0.14	916	0.05	728.7
15	STOCK	889	0.09	350	0.02	722.5
16	ORDER	1224	0.12	681	0.03	709.0
17	EXECUTIVE	529	0.05	86		707.3
18	CONTRACT	656	0.06	183		678.3
19	CLIENT	535	0.05	126		607.4
20	MAIL	380	0.04	34		607.2
21	CONTRACTOR	326	0.03	16		582.3
22	WILL	4335	0.42	5038	0.26	572.4
23	MANAGER	742	0.07	317	0.02	562.4
24	PER	1014	0.10	585	0.03	562.4
25	SELLER	298	0.03	12		546.6
26	INVESTMENT	577	0.06	185		546.2
27	SHARE	1148	0.11	762	0.04	528.8
28	INTERNET	249	0.02	1		521.0
29	COST	1127	0.11	747	0.04	520.2
30	TO	29495	2.88	47851	2.44	514.5
31	DATE	782	0.08	389	0.02	512.3
32	GLOBAL	324	0.03	34		497.6
33	PROFIT	799	0.08	429	0.02	482.0
34	SELL	789	0.08	419	0.02	481.8
35	REGISTER	399	0.04	86		473.3
36	PROJECT	642	0.06	283	0.01	473.1
37	PERFORMANCE	507	0.05	175		455.8
38	YEAR	2874	0.28	3184	0.16	445.4
39	INTERNATIONAL	606	0.06	269	0.01	443.7
40	ITS	2077	0.20	2085	0.11	428.5
41	MILLION	789	0.08	473	0.02	417.1
42	CORPORATE	277	0.03	33		410.6
43	RATE	803	0.08	496	0.03	408.4
44	BUYER	292	0.03	42		407.9
45	CREDIT	392	0.04	110		403.8
46	INDUSTRY	712	0.07	404	0.02	402.8
47	SUPPLIER	288	0.03	44		393.9
48	TECHNOLOGY	445	0.04	157		393.7
49	BUDGET	437	0.04	152		390.7
50	SHALL	803	0.08	515	0.03	388.2

What is Business English?

As we have described above, the first area of investigation in Nelson's study was a comparison of the difference between Business English – as represented in the BEC – with general English – as represented in the BNC. This raises the interesting issue of what we actually consider to be Business English. In

Table 3.2 A comparison of keywords in the BEC and the BNC

Business Lexis (positive keywords)	Non-Business Lexis (negative keywords)
1. **People from the business world:** *Customer, contractor, manager, seller, buyer*	1. **People:** family, royalty, domestic relations: *man, mum, wife, dad, baby, Queen*
2. **Institutions:** Companies and business institutions *company, industry, airline, telecom*	2. **Institutions:** Societal *church, army, hospital, council*
3. **Things:** business-related, concrete: *product, property, equipment*	3. **Things:** diverse: *horse, cat, diamond, glass, river* abstract: *expression, intelligence, preference*
4. **Places:** Business-related: *Office, department, boardroom*	4. **Places:** House and home: *Curtain, bedroom, bathroom, kitchen* Countryside: *bay, hill, sea, forest*
5. **Days of the week:** Not key	5. **Days of the week:** Saturday, Sunday
6. **States and qualities:** Business-related and positive: *Growth, stability, leadership, competence*	6. **States and qualities:** Ethical questions/meaning of life: *Death, life, war, peace, truth, age, peace*
7. **Dynamic *public* verbs:** *Sell, manage, manufacture, deliver, confirm*	7. **Positive and interpersonal *private* verbs:** *Know, see, pray, feel, die, lie, marry*
8. **Positive impersonal adjectives:** *new, best, successful, available, relevant*	8. **Positive and negative personal adjectives:** *nice, lovely, beautiful, bloody, dead, dark*
9. **Money:** focus on money/finance *cash flow, VAT, GDP, capital, earnings*	9. **Money:** No/little mention of money/ finance only mentions: *quid* and *pound*
10. **Activities:** business-related: *investment, payment, development, production*	10. **Activities:** personal, family related: *birthday, Christmas, marriage, prayer*

the BEC, for instance, the texts surveyed were all collected from two types of native speaker sources, i.e. Britain and the United States (see Nelson, 2006, for details), whereas as we (and many others) have observed, English is used as an international business language by native, second and foreign language speakers in a wide variety of interactions, and, of course, not only by British and American native speakers. Much of the research that we discuss in this volume involves the (Business) English produced (and interpreted) by people who are speakers of languages other than English, (e.g. Poncini, 2004; Nickerson, 2000; Louhiala-Salminen et al., 2005; Planken, 2005, etc.), and, as the 2002 study of the communication in multinational settings by Charles and Marschan-Piekkari shows, native speaker English can be a source of communication problems (see next chapter for details).

For business contexts specifically, a large scale corpus-based investigation of the language used in BELF (Business English as a Lingua Franca) interactions would be a useful complement to work like Nelson's based on native speaker sources, in that it would help to pinpoint those areas where native and non-native varieties of Business English are different (and therefore potentially problematic). In addition, contrastive (micro) studies of BELF speakers from different backgrounds are also useful, in that like Seidlhofer and Jenkins' work for general ELF interactions, they help not only in identifying problem areas, but also in identifying those characteristics which do not necessarily need to be a teaching or training focus since they are 'non-essential for mutual intelligibility' (Seidlhofer & Jenkins, 2003: 151, see also below for recent developments in ELF research, together with the review provided by Jenkins, Cogo & Dewey, 2011). The Research Cases we profile for Planken (2005) in Chapter 2 and for Louhiala-Salminen et al. (2005) in Chapter 8 in Part 3, for instance, provide examples of investigations into BELF which reveal the influence of business experience (Planken) and of national culture (Louhiala-Salminen et al.) as determining factors in the inclusion of certain discourse strategies in a business interaction. Likewise, the CIBW/IBLC project – a collaborative international business writing project between institutions in the US, Belgium and Finland – that we profile later in this chapter, confirms the useful information that can be incorporated into teaching materials by collating crosscultural lingua franca data and offsetting that against native speaker data.

Recent developments in English as a lingua franca

The Vienna–Oxford International Corpus of English (VOICE) project, directed by Barbara Seidlhofer, is focused on ELF communication specifically related to interactions between non-native speakers of English. The VOICE corpus comprises more than 1 million words of ELF transactions, mostly involving European ELF speakers, and includes meetings, interviews, service encounters and seminar discussions (http://www.univie.ac.at/voice/ page/corpus_description). The publications that have resulted from the project thus far (e.g. Jensen, 2009; Seidlhofer, 2010; Facchinetti, Crystal & Seidlhofer, 2010) discuss the nature of ELF discourse in general and how this operates in some forms of business discourse.

In other work, David Graddol's 2006 report for the British Council looks at the use of global English and the English as a Foreign Language (EFL) industry. He reviews developments in the global demography and economy, changes in the use of technology and the structure of society, and finally how English can be compared now and in the future with other important world languages. The report contains a large amount of background information for scholars interested in ELF, including the numbers of speakers currently estimated to be learning English around the world (mostly business English), and the impact that this is likely to have on native speakers of English who are rapidly losing their traditional linguistic advantage. He also makes two important points that are relevant for teaching business English; i) that the rise in the importance of global English will lead to a corresponding fall in the relevance of native speaker models both for the teaching of English and for how speakers (of global English) are evaluated, and ii) that English is now considered by many as a basic component of a person's general education, alongside other skills such as general literacy and computer literacy, and that this attitude towards English will continue to gain ground in the future.

(Adapted from Nickerson, 2012a)

Additional information on the relationship between ELF in general, and Business English as a Lingua Franca (BELF) in particular, with reference to the teaching of English for Business Communication, is provided by Bhatia and Bremner (2012) in their state of the art review of the field. Bhatia and Bremner discuss the need to integrate English for Business Purposes and Business Communication in the design of English for Business Communication programmes.

The Centre for Global Englishes

In May 2012, the University of Southampton in the United Kingdom launched the Centre for Global Englishes (CGE).

CGE (Centre for Global Englishes) produces and disseminates research on the linguistic and sociocultural dimensions of global uses and users of English (Global Englishes), and on English as a Lingua Franca in particular. The centre provides a forum for knowledge-sharing and collaboration with other interested researchers and centres around the world.

The main aims and focus of CGE are:

1. To produce, support and disseminate research on the linguistic and sociocultural dimensions of global uses, usages and users of English (i.e. Global Englishes), and on English as a Lingua Franca in particular.
2. To explore the implications of such research and develop new conceptualizations of (English) language and communication.

3. To investigate, evaluate, promote, and influence conceptions and applications of English in academic settings, including a strong focus on internationalization in Higher Education.
4. To provide a forum for knowledge-sharing and collaboration with other interested researchers and research centres around the world, as well as with those not directly involved in researching the field, but interested in learning more about it.
(http://www.southampton.ac.uk/cge/about)

Writing in the *Financial Times* to mark the launch of the CGE, Skapinker (2012) discusses the impact of the rise of Global Englishes on business and industry, and observes 'many international business conversations in English proceed swimmingly until a British or American speaker's use of colloquial language leaves everyone stumped'. As Charles and Marschan-Piekkari (2002) have observed, non-native speakers of English often find other non-native speakers of English easier to understand than native speakers of English, as the native speakers are less able to adapt their English to take the communicative conventions of others into account (see Chapter 4 for a detailed discussion on Charles and Marschan-Piekkari, 2002).

The BEC and the development of teaching materials

In the second part of the project, when Nelson compared the Published Materials Corpus (PMC) to the BEC, he found that a problem solving approach was often used in the PMC, together with an emphasis on a set of lexis that was different than the real-life texts in the BEC corpus. The PMC, for instance, focused on meetings, presentations, travel, entertaining and food, and presented positive and negative lexis in equal proportions, and unlike the BEC, there was an emphasis on personal and interpersonal lexis, and on politeness. The project website (http://users.utu.fi/micnel/BEC/downloadable_materials. htm) provides several examples of how Nelson has referred to the findings of the BEC corpus analysis to develop relevant teaching materials that represent real-life business language for learners of Business English.

Nelson's study shows the usefulness of a corpus-based approach contrasting a general and a specialized corpus first to investigate the nature of the lexis used in a specific context and then using that to generate teaching materials. The analysis of the PMC in particular confirms the findings of other studies into published EFL materials (e.g. St John, 1996; Nickerson, 2005), suggesting that with very few exceptions, little has in fact changed since Marion Williams concluded in 1988 that there was a disconnect between the language actually used in business (meetings) and the language taught for business (meetings) (see Part 1, Chapter 1). In Chapter 5, we will profile the teaching materials developed by Willa Hogarth and Linda Burnett (Hogarth & Burnett, 1995), based on Ken Willing's 1992 investigation of white collar immigrant interactions (Willing, 1992), together with the 2004 volume by Almut Koester on the *Language of Work* (Koester, 2004) as well as her subsequent volumes (Koester, 2006; 2010). These provide an interesting complement to Nelson's study, in that they are examples of published teaching materials based on the collection and analysis of real-life interactional data. They therefore move one step closer to the presentation of contextualized language use in a teaching situation that we identified in Chapter 1 of this volume as a hallmark of business discourse research.

Quote 3.7   Mike Nelson on teaching materials for Business English

So how can materials be improved in the future? The most important task is to change the basic premise on which they are usually written. It is not enough for materials writers to sit down and write what they think happens in business. They need to look at the actual language being used. Publishers will say that they now include many authentic texts in their books, but these authentic documents tend to be related to 'talking about' business (interviews with a CEO are a common example). They do not include the language used at the 'hard end' – the kind of language actually used to 'do business' in real meetings, real emails and real negotiations. The main reason for this is the difficulty of access to them, but without it we are just scrambling about in the dark.

The language and vocabulary used in materials should aim at reflecting those used in real life. The materials writers' job, then, would simply be to lead the students through this real world, rather than make up the world as they go along. Next time someone tries to sell you a BE book, you are entitled to ask them, 'How do you know it is business English?'

(Thursday 20 March 2003, *Guardian Weekly*)

3.4   Promoting intercultural communicative competence through foreign language courses

Planken, van Hooft and Korzilius (2004) describe the development and execution of a set of learning projects (the 'business projects') and associated tasks ('the communication tasks') for first-year BA students studying intercultural business communication (IBC) at the Radboud University Nijmegen, in the Netherlands. The projects were developed as part of the curriculum for the teaching of English, Spanish, French or German to Dutch students and their aim was to contribute to 'the development of (a degree of) intercultural communicative competence' (309). The project-based courses in general use a student-centred approach and the 'learners are required to become actively involved in recurring communicative action in the FL in various (intercultural) business communication settings' (309). As we will illustrate below, the teaching materials used in the projects draw on published teaching materials focusing on common business genres, such as negotiations, meetings and business letters, but they do so in an innovative way by referring to the findings of business discourse research when these genres are discussed in class.

The business projects and tasks

The first year IBC students in Nijmegen follow four business projects as part of their foreign language (FL) studies. Each project lasts seven weeks and the focus is on the completion of a series of tasks that are relevant for international business, e.g. meetings, negotiations, emails, reports, etc. An additional language skills workshop focusing on issues such as vocabulary, grammar, and pronunciation, etc. is given alongside the business projects, and the students are also encouraged to draw on their non-FL courses within the IBC programme, such as marketing, management and intercultural communication. Data 3.4 shows the project description (for English) for the third business project *A first step on the road to cooperation*, together with the associated communication tasks.

Data 3.4   The Nijmegen business language projects: a first step on the road to cooperation

Project description

In this project you will simulate the first phase ('getting acquainted') in the cooperation between a Dutch and an English company. You and your team will choose a medium-sized Dutch company (between 100 and 500 employees). You could decide to choose the company that you studied in term 2, but you are also free to choose a new company.

This Dutch company would like to extend its network abroad, and would like to contact a comparable company in Great Britain (comparable, that is, in terms of activities and size). It is still to be determined how intensive the potential relationship with the foreign partner can or should be. The partnership may be restricted to exchanging information and experiences, but it could eventually also result in a joint venture. What is essential is that both parties in some way *benefit* from the relationship.

The ultimate goal of Project 3 is that you and your team, in a role play, conduct exploratory talks as representatives of the Dutch company and the British partner that you have selected. In this role play (the final task in the project), two members of your team will act as representatives of the British company, and two other members of your team will represent the Dutch company. During the talks the two parties are supposed to compare each other's organizations (in terms of goals, strategies, business culture, etc.) to find out whether the two companies 'click' and whether future cooperation is desirable and feasible.

During the project you and your team will first have to find a suitable British business partner for the Dutch company that you have chosen to represent. You will have to find out as much as possible about this British company (but also about the Dutch company, of course!) to be able to play your roles convincingly in the role-play at the end of the project. The first three tasks in the project will help you collect and organize your information and will consequently enable you to make a comparison between the two companies.

Tasks

To improve your skills and extend your knowledge in the area of formal communication in an organizational context you will be required to carry out four tasks, all of which are related to the overall project.

- An oral presentation in groups about a real-life joint venture;
- Writing a formal letter in reply to a request for information;
- Writing a management summary of a report in which you compare the Dutch and the British company;
- Conducting exploratory talks between the prospective partners.

(Class Reader Business English 1, Business Communication, Radboud University Nijmegen)

As Planken et al. (2004) discuss, the communication tasks can be divided into two main types; awareness raising and production tasks (see below). In the awareness raising tasks, the students 'observe and analyse' the target genre as it is produced in the target FL by native and non-native speakers, and they are then asked to identify certain aspects of that communication, e.g. direct versus indirect strategies in a negotiation situation, contrasting these with their own (L1) language. For Task 4 (Conducting exploratory talks between the prospective partners) in the project described above, for instance, the students were shown a series of video recordings taken from the 1998 course published by OUP by Jeremy Comfort on *Effective Negotiating*. These consisted of a number of business negotiations conducted in English as a lingua franca between native and non-native speakers of English about an international joint venture, during which the students were asked not only to identify certain key linguistic realizations, such as formulating an *offer*, a *rejection* or an *interruption*, but also to reflect on what Planken et al. refer to as 'broader discourse aspects', such as turn taking, back channelling and direct and indirect styles of communication, and in particular how these may vary across cultures. It is this second part of the analysis that allows the teacher to draw on existing business discourse research to illustrate the target discourse characteristic, in doing so making the link for students between their theoretical course content in other courses in their BA, and the way in which business people from around the world actually communicate.

Quote 3.8   The Nijmegen Business Language Projects

Awareness-raising activities are initially presented as open tasks. Students are first asked to discover regularities in the communication they are presented with on their own or in small peer groups. In some instances, however, more guidance is provided. For example, students may be asked to look at certain aspects in greater detail or to focus specifically on what is relevant in another part of the (*BA*) programme at a particular moment in time. To help students consider a feature more systematically, checklists may be provided.

Production tasks involve assignments in which students practice FL and business pragmatic ability by participating in business communication activities. These tasks involve student-centred interaction in which the participants take on professionally relevant speaker or addressee perspectives. The tasks incorporate various business genres within which students co-create different types of communicative action in the FL. For example, longer role-play simulations provide practice in a wide range of linguistic and business pragmatic abilities.

(Planken et al., 2004: 313 emphasis added)

The implications of the project

Planken et al.'s project is a useful illustration of research-based (teaching) practice for two reasons. First, it makes use of established published teaching materials in which authentic business language is presented, but then links these specifically with research findings that illustrate how these linguistic realizations contribute to the achievement of (business) discourse. Students look, for instance, not only at the *language* used in meetings, but also at how turn taking contributes to the overall realization of the meeting event, through reference to conversational analysis theory. They therefore combine a micro analysis of the language used in the written business genre or spoken event, together with the application of a relevant macro theory that they are (or at least should be) familiar with from another part of their degree programme. Second, the project specifically explores the intercultural variations that are relevant in 'lingua franca' situations where native and non-native speakers, and/or non-native speakers from different cultural backgrounds, are involved in the interaction, and it encourages students to evaluate their own culture and language use in contrast to that of others. In doing so, it de-emphasizes the traditional role that the native speaker of English (or Spanish, French or German) has played in language teaching, and focuses instead on the more likely business scenario that a language is used as a means of communication by speakers or writers of various different (national) cultures, i.e. they use it as a tool to get their work done. Much of the research we discuss in this book confirms that this is the case (e.g. Nickerson, 2000, in her investigation of internal corporate email; Poncini, 2004, in her discussion of multilingual, multicultural meetings; Louhiala-Salminen et al., 2005, in their study of the use of English in Finnish–Swedish joint ventures; Briguglio, 2005b, on the use of English at multinational companies in Malaysia and Hong Kong; and Kankaanranta & Louhiala-Salminen, 2010 and Kankaanranta & Planken, 2010, on perceptions of English as a lingua franca in European multinationals) but it is relatively rare to find this systematically incorporated as Planken et al. do, into teaching materials that make an explicit link between national culture on the one hand and discourse realizations on the other.

Pre-experience versus post-experience: English in corporate settings in Hong Kong and Malaysia

Carmela Briguglio's project involved a comparative study of intercultural communication in the workplace and intercultural communication in student teams, highlighting the differences between the use of English as a lingua franca in multilingual companies and among groups of students. The multilingual companies were based in Hong Kong and Malaysia, and the students at Curtin University of Technology in Australia.

Briguglio aimed:

1. to determine the aspects of English for global competence that are required in an international workplace; and
2. to ascertain if the skills identified as necessary in multinational companies are being developed in business courses in Australian universities.

Briguglio's findings confirm earlier research in Hong Kong and Malaysia, such that in Hong Kong, English is used mainly for written communication whereas in Malaysia spoken and written communication is mainly conducted in Malaysian English. She also found that English for email communication and for informal internal reports was in high demand, as was the ability to work collaboratively across cultures and languages. In the student case study, which involved students working collaboratively in a culturally mixed team, she found that when the tutors intervened to lead students in the process of probing, understanding and questioning cultural differences, then the students were better disposed towards other cultures and tensions were minimized or controlled. Briguglio concludes that it is important to utilize more fully the cultural diversity already present in Australian universities and that both L1 and L2 speakers of English are responsible for successful communication.

(Briguglio, 2005b)

3.5   The CIBW and IBLC: a course in international business writing and the Indianapolis Business Learner Corpus

The CIBW teaching project and the IBLC research initiative were part of a large scale collaborative project between institutions in the US (Indiana University–Purdue University), Belgium (Handelshogeschool Antwerp) and Finland (Åbo Akademi Finland) that took place during the 1990s, involving a series of simultaneous research and teaching projects (see Connor, Davis & De Rycker, 1995; Connor, Davis, De Rycker, Phillips & Verckens, 1997; Verckens, De Rycker & Davis, 1998; Upton & Connor, 2001). The project as a whole draws on the genre analysis of application letters written in English by American, Belgian (Flemish) and Finnish writers, and uses this as the basis for the CIBW. The application letter was selected as an appropriate genre, as an accessible form of communication that is used across several different cultures to interface with the business world, and the series of publications that were generated as a result, provide useful information about the analysis of the application letter, the research findings and then how these findings were applied in a teaching situation. Connor et al. (1995), for instance, present a crosscultural genre and move analysis focusing on the rhetorical strategies that Flemish and US writers use. Connor et al. (1997) and Verckens et al. (1998) show how the research findings were used to inform the course in international business writing, and the most recent publication to come out of the project by Upton and Connor (2001) reports on the linguistic features that realized the politeness strategies that writers selected in their letters. In the discussion below, we will look first at the two research accounts (Connor et al., 1995; Upton and Connor, 2001) to show how these were used to generate research findings and the input for teaching materials, and we will then look at how the team specifically drew on these sources in the business writing course (Connor et al., 1997; Verckens et al., 1998).

The research project

Connor et al. (1995) discuss how the project looked first for crosscultural similarities and differences between US and Flemish letters of application. University students in Indianapolis and Antwerp were presented with a simulated job advertisement (tailor made by the research team) for a summer internship. This resulted in a data base of about 200 letters written in English, and a random selection was made of 74 application letters (written by 37 US applicants and 37 Flemish applicants) to use for further analysis. The letters were analysed in terms of their correctness and clarity, where correctness referred to four features: '*mechanics* (absence of mistakes in punctuation and spelling); *words* (absence of mistakes at the lexical level like word choice); *sentences* (defined basically as sentence-level syntax); and *paragraph* structure' (Connor et al., 1995; 462–3, original emphasis), and clarity to 'textual message properties which demonstrate the writer's overall sense of the writing situation (writer, reader, subject, and purpose), the content and the organization of his or her message' (1995: 463). Drawing on Bhatia (1993), Connor et al. placed the primary focus in the clarity analysis on the organization of the text, i.e. they looked at the 'rhetorical moves which give a textual genre its distinctive cognitive structure' (463, see also Part 3 of this volume for further details on the application of Bhatia's approach to genre analysis to written business texts). Data 3.5 shows the six moves (or categories) they identified in the application letters in the project. As Connor et al. observe, these 'describe the generic profile of the text, or its prototypical sequence of functional meanings, specific to the subgenre', and for application letters specifically, they are 'the functions (or communicative intentions) which a particular portion of the text realizes in relationship to the overall tasks of applying for . . . an overseas student internship' (463–4).

Data 3.5   Meaning components of a letter of application: a coding scheme

Identify the source of the information (Explain how and where you learned of the position.)
Apply for the position (State desire for consideration, either as a direct strategy; '*I apply for this position . . .* ' or as an indirect strategy; '*I would be a good candidate . . .* '
Provide supporting arguments for the job application (Describe your qualifications, personal and professional. Describe reasons for application. Describe benefits to you and/or prospective employer.)

Indicate desire for interview
Specify means of further communication (Indicate how you can be contacted or when you will contact the prospective employer.)
Express politeness (pleasantries) or appreciation

(Connor et al., 1995: 464)

The findings of the research project point to a number of crosscultural variations across the US and Belgian letters (see Quote 3.9 for a summary). The US letters were longer (197 words compared to the Flemish average of 105 words) and, as could be expected from the non-native writers, the Flemish writers made more errors, making approximately twice as many errors as their US counterparts. Connor et al. observe that the 'US applicants were considerably better at word choice and word accuracy, whereas the Flemish participants made a lower percentage of syntactic errors' (469). In terms of clarity, as represented by the moves analysis, the Flemish writers wrote shorter moves in almost all the meaning categories (apart from I and IV), and they were more direct in applying for the position, and explicitly requesting an 'interview'. Move III in particular – where the applicant provides supporting arguments for the application – differed across the two cultures: 'The US letter included a lengthy discussion of the writer's qualifications, both personal and professional. In addition, it mentioned the benefit for the prospective employer as well as for the candidate. The Flemish letter, on the other hand, included a short and rather general statement of the qualifications and relied more heavily on this to convey information' (1995: 471).

Quote 3.9   The findings of the IBLC research project for application letters

This corpus shows that a typical US applicant writes more, but also that he or she produces fewer mistakes, predominantly at the levels of spelling and sentence grammar. By contrast, the Flemish job seeker tends to write a much shorter cover letter and is more likely to make a larger number of mistakes, especially in the areas of spelling and semantics.

These differences in error frequencies and error types do not point, however, in the direction of cultural differences between the US and Flemish applicants, but rather to native/non-native speaker contrast. Still, the fact that the typical US error is syntactic rather than semantic, ties in with our clarity findings: the US letters exhibit a larger degree of informativeness and functional transparency than the Flemish ones.

> Interestingly, differences found in the degree of clarity, i.e. content and length of information, that characterize both groups in this study correspond with findings from previous crosscultural research on business letters (Jenkins & Hinds, 1987). As in Jenkins and Hinds' study, the US letters are longer, are more individual in content, and pay attention to the welfare of the reader, i.e. the average US applicant directs his or her writing efforts towards the reader(s). For example, the US cover letters do not explicitly request an interview, but give information about how to get in touch. The Flemish cover letters, like the French business letters in Jenkins and Hinds' study, are rather brief and usually do not attempt to personalize. For example, they only rarely elaborate on the objective information contained in the résumé and they tend not to include closing expressions or pleasantries and/or appreciation.
>
> (Connor et al., 1995: 471–2, slightly adapted)

The 2001 follow up study by Upton and Connor shows how the research team used Wordsmith Tools to analyse how (student) applicants realized politeness strategies in the rhetorical moves found in an extended corpus of the IBLC application letters in English (for the 2001 study these included job application letters and curriculum vitae from business communication students in the US, Belgium, Finland, Germany and Thailand). The 2001 corpus consisted of 70 letters that had originated in Belgium, 26 in Finland and 57 in the US, making a total of 153, and the aims of the study were two-fold:

1. To demonstrate the efficacy of a multilevel analysis of a genre-specific learner corpus that included both a hand-tagged moves-analysis coupled with a computerized analysis of lexico-grammatical features of texts; and
2. To show how a pragmatic concept such as politeness can be operationalized to allow for computer generated counts of linguistic features related to that concept (Upton & Connor, 2001: 313).

Upton and Connor first manually tagged the moves that occurred in the corpus of letters and they then drew on the 1992 study by Maier of politeness strategies in native and non-native speaker business letters and looked for the linguistic realizations of the politeness strategies used in the IBLC application letters, analysing the texts using WordSmith Tools. Their multilayered study showed that 'none of the three groups used either positive or negative politeness strategies exclusively, or even more frequently than another group' (2001: 324). On the whole, the American writers 'tended to be much more patterned, even formulaic, in their politeness strategies' whereas the Belgians 'showed more individuality in their letters, incorporating a wider variety of sentence opening structures than the Americans, using more qualifying modals not tied to formulaic expressions, and much less frequently employed formulaic expressions and structures in general'. The Finnish learners combined characteristics of the other two groups, using 'the formula-oriented style of the American writers but also incorporating some of the more individualistic style of the Belgians' (2001: 325). Although exploratory in nature, as it was based on a relatively small number of texts, the study therefore generated a set of findings that could usefully be incorporated into teaching materials focusing on the application letter in general and politeness strategies in particular. In addition, Upton and Connor's concluding remarks (given in Quote 3.10) show how material like the IBLC can also be useful in increasing our understanding of the nature of (business) discourse (see also James et al., 1994, for an innovative investigation of the response of readers to crosscultural differences in application letters).

Quote 3.10   On the importance of specialized corpora

As illustrated by the corpus used in this study, we believe that specialized, genre-specific corpora will continue to grow in importance not only for instructional purposes in academic settings but also in professional and business contexts. That language use can dramatically differ from context to context or genre to genre has been clearly shown by Biber, Johansson, Leech, Conrad & Finegan (1999; *Longman grammar of spoken and written English*). Consequently, specialized corpora allow for a more thorough understanding of how language is used in particular contexts or in particular genres.

(Upton and Connor, 2001: 326, slightly adapted)

The CIBW teaching project

The CIBW Teaching Project (and its predecessor the AIP project) is discussed in detail in Connor, Davis, De Rycker, Philips and Verckens (1997) and in Verckens, De Rycker and Davis (1998). As Connor et al. (1997) describe, the CIBW project was a full semester course in international business writing, taught at all three of the participating institutions, with three course components;

1. instruction in international business writing;
2. a simulation, in which the students exchanged documents internationally; and
3. a case study of business people who communicate internationally in writing (Connor et al., 1997: 65).

Verckens et al. (1998), relate these three components to three underlying 'pillars'; a theoretical pillar, an experiential pillar and a practical field-research pillar. During the theoretical or instructional part of the course, the students became familiar with relevant background information by looking, for instance, at variations in national cultures in general (e.g. the work of Hofstede, 1991 and Trompenaars, 1993), together with crosscultural variations in business writing in particular (e.g. the work of Beamer and Varner (1995; 2004) as we will detail in Chapter 5, and the research findings of the IBLC project, as discussed above). After this, in the eight-week experiential part of the course, the students participated in a business game designed to give them 'authentic experience in initiating, and responding to, written communication with their counterparts in the other two countries' (Connor et al., 1997: 66). Verckens et al. (1998) describe how each of the institutions took on the role of a Publishing, Recruiting or Training company, and the students were then asked to complete a series of 'real' writing assignments, such as organizing and naming their own company, writing a request for a proposal from one of the other companies, and writing a proposal in response. The students produced the written documents, exchanged them (via fax!) with their counterparts elsewhere and then reacted to them, as if they were in a real business situation. Finally, in the case study or practical part of the CIBW course, the students were 'sent into the field to interview a business person who is faced with crosscultural communication as part of his or her everyday job. The questionnaire used in the field research deals with general and specific cultural issues. These issues could be the reason why, in actual (written) encounters, business persons write different messages than they would produce if the audience consisted of members of their cultural community' (Verckens et al., 1998: 253). The findings of the questionnaire were used to generate a case study report, which the students then circulated to their 'colleagues' at the other two participating institutions.

The added value in the CIBW project

Both Connor et al. (1997) and Verckens et al. (1998) provide information on the added value inherent in the CIBW project from two different perspectives (see also Quote 3.11). From a national crosscultural communication perspective, Verckens et al. (1998) show how the students' perception of the other two cultures changed to some extent as a result of participating in the course. Prior to the CIBW course, for instance, the Finns viewed:

1. US students as mixed (positive/negative characteristics) persons;
2. Belgians as (very) positive;
3. themselves as partly positive and partly negative (quiet, shy, lonely, insecure) (Verckens et al., 1998: 257);

whereas after the course, the Finns viewed:

1. US students as friendlier and more sociable than they expected, and less superficial, less patriotic, and less self-confident;

2. Belgians as (very) different from what they expected: only two characteristics were present both in the pre- and post CIBW evaluation: 'friendly' and 'well-educated'. Because of delays in sending documents, and because of letters looking 'too businesslike' the Finnish students drastically changed their opinion of the Belgian participants;

3. themselves as more positive than before the seminar: they were more polite, more 'well-educated', friendlier, but also less honest, and less shy. Moreover, the 'lonely' and 'insecure' characteristics were traded for 'reserved', 'stubborn', 'patriotic' and 'international' (Verckens et al., 1998: 258, slightly adapted).

Quote 3.11   The CIBW (a US–Belgian–Finnish) teaching project

Important assets of the CIBW include the opportunity to:

actually communicate in writing with people from different cultures;
actually compete in a crosscultural environment and thereby experience real anxiety and uncertainty; and

practise a foreign language in a normal-functional context that urges participants to do more than simply try to be correct or please the instructor.

(Verckens et al., 1998: 248, original emphasis)

Connor et al. (1997) comment on a second successful and unexpected outcome in the CIBW project, in that the students from all three national cultures wrote application letters that were similar in length, and which included similar arguments to provide support for their application. This was in direct contrast to the crosscultural variations found in the 1995 corpus-based project, as we have described above, when the US and Flemish writers differed in the length of their letters and the arguments they included. Two of the authors, Connor and Phillips, as instructors of the Finnish students 'speculate that the instruction about different cultural expectations offered as part of the [new] course caused students to adjust their writing towards the norms of the other countries' (Connor et al., 1997: 68).

The ILBC–CIBW project: research into practice

The complex ILBC–CIBW project is interesting for several reasons. First, in the ILBC project, it shows how electronic tools, such as a scanner and a concordancing programme, can be used to great effect in facilitating the analysis of a large set of data. Second, it builds on an extensive study of an important business genre, combining several methodological approaches to provide an account of the cross-cultural variations that exist between native English writers and (several varieties of) non-native writers. Third, it not only provides an example of a genre that is accessible and relevant to students across the globe, it also exemplifies how research may be used directly to inform teaching materials. In short, it is an excellent example of research-based practice. In the final box in this chapter, we will outline a more recent example of excellence in research-based business discourse teaching which also takes a multidisciplinary approach, combining insights from applied linguistics and insights from accountancy (e.g. Jones & Sin, 2004a; Jones & Sin, 2004b; Sin, Jones & Petocz, 2007; Sin, Reid & Jones, 2012).

Data 3.6   Teaching projects in BCQ and ESPj

Both the *Business Communication Quarterly* and the *English for Specific Purposes Journal* are useful sources of information on research-based teaching projects relevant for business communication. A few recent examples are:

Nickerson, Gerritsen & van Meurs (2005) provide an account of a large scale staff–student project focusing on the use of ESBP in print advertising within several of the EU member states. The collaborative research project between staff and students involved a survey of the use of English in print advertising in glossy magazines, aimed at young women in the Netherlands, Germany and Spain, together with an experimental investigation of the attitudes to and comprehension of English. The project was used to raise student awareness of the way in which English is present in the world around them, most especially in promotional genres.

  Gerritsen & Verckens (2006) report on a seven-week intercultural email project designed to raise Dutch and Belgian students' intercultural awareness. The purpose of the project was to allow the students to 'experience cultural differences, talk about cultural differences, and learn to cooperate with someone from a different culture' (2006: 50), using their shared language – Dutch – as a communication medium, together with email. Gerritsen and Verckens developed a questionnaire focusing on symbols, rituals and values, which the students completed individually, emailed to their project partner abroad, and then discussed via email and in a collaborative co-authored report.

  Connor, Rogers & Wong (2005) report on a series of collaborative research initiatives between Nanyang Business School in Singapore and the University of Michigan Business School in Ann Arbor, Michigan. They discuss how their coordinated efforts at the two institutions resulted in a change in teaching focus on both sides, such that at NBS the emphasis changed from (English) language proficiency to a focus on communicating effectively, and at UMBS there was an increased awareness of cultural and international issues resulting in the introduction of a new MBA course 'Communication for the

Global Manager'. The authors comment that as a result of the collaboration, 'NBS and UMBS faculty now have a keener sense of emerging global business communication imperatives' (2005: 443).

A research-based approach to teaching accountancy discourse

For the past decade, the applied linguist Alan Jones, at Macquarie University Sydney's Department of Linguistics, has been working together with an accounting colleague, Samantha Sin, from the Department of Accounting and Corporate Governance, on the teaching of accountancy discourse. Their approach integrates the set of generic skills that (Australian) accountants are required to obtain, such as analytical thinking skills and written communication skills, and places them within a linguistically scaffolded curriculum. Sin, Jones and Petocz (2007) provide the following details:

'The method used was to scaffold practice in analytical thinking skills through specially designed writing activities. Content-focused learning materials adapted from task-types currently used to teach language skills were used to facilitate the analysis and interrelation of accounting concepts, principles and problems in interpersonal communicative contexts typical of actual accounting practice. The materials, in three assignments, were designed to incorporate: (i) selected generic skills, taken from those listed by the professional accounting bodies; (ii) writing, both as communication and as an instrument for analytical thinking and learning; (iii) knowledge of accounting concepts and principles; and (iv) awareness of the interpersonal dimensions of professional communication' (2007: 143).

Sin et al. (2007) describe how they first identified a set of tasks designed to integrate the learning of accounting concepts with the development of the targeted generic skills, e.g. writing a letter to explain a breach of internal accounting control at the workplace and how a bank reconciliation statement is useful to safeguard cash (2007: 150). Each of these tasks was then preceded with a set of linguistically scaffolded exercises, designed 'to activate and structure key concepts through writing, raising awareness of co-occurring lexis and the syntactic patterns that accompany and constrain conceptual vocabulary' (2007: 250). Examples of these exercises include gap-fill exercises on key accounting concepts, short writing exercises involving a set of key words, and the classification of relevant information.

As Jones observes, the result is 'a content focused but language-enhanced curriculum' (personal communication, Alan Jones). And as Sin at al. (2007) report, this curriculum also resulted in a significant improvement in student performance, particularly for non-Australian students.

Further reading

Bhatia, V. K. & Bremner, S. (2012). English for business communication. *Language Teaching, 45*(4), 410–45. A state of the art review that suggests an integration of the frameworks used in English for Business Purposes and business communication in the design of English for Business Communication programmes.
Briguglio, C. (2005). Developing an understanding of English as a global language for a business setting. In F. Bargiela-Chiappini & M. Gotti (Eds.), *Asian business discourse* (pp. 313–44). Bern: Peter Lang. A discussion of the use of English as a *lingua franca* in multilingual companies in Hong Kong and Malaysia of relevance for teaching business discourse.
Connor, U., & Upton, T. (2004). *Discourse in the professions: Perspectives from corpus linguistics*. Amsterdam: John Benjamins. An edited collection on corpus linguistics with contributions of relevance for researching and teaching business discourse.
Nickerson, C. (2012b). Unity in diversity: The view from the (UAE) classroom. *Language Teaching,* DOI: http://dx.doi.org/10.1017/S0261444812000237. Gives an account of a research-based teaching program for senior business students in the Gulf Region, looking at various aspects of genre and discourse of relevance for the UAE economy.

Chapter 3 Tasks

1. Read Evans' (2012) account of the development of teaching materials to teach Business English email. Choose another common business genre, either spoken or written, and describe the research that you would do in order to design a set of appropriate teaching materials to teach that genre.

    Evans, S. (2012). Designing email tasks for the Business English classroom: Implications from a study of Hong Kong's key industries. *English for Specific Purposes, 31*(3), 202–12.
2. Refer to section 9.7 in Chapter 9 of this volume, which lists different corpora. Choose one of these, find out what its composition is, and decide how you would use it together with Wordsmith Tools to generate a set of teaching materials on one aspect of business discourse.
3. Refer to the final box in this chapter and read the account given by Sin, Jones and Petocz (2007) of their work in teaching accounting discourse. Choose another business discipline, e.g. marketing, strategy, human resource management, etc. and decide how you would integrate linguistic scaffolding with content presentation, in order to teach it.

    Sin, S., Jones, A., and Petocz, P. (2007). Evaluating a method of integrating generic skills with accounting content based on a functional theory of meaning. *Accounting and Finance, 47*, 143–63.

4
Research-based Consultancy Work

This chapter will:

- Profile five examples of *research-based consultancy work* involving business discourse from around the world;
- Discuss the *methodologies* used and the *implications* either for teaching or training, or the design of more effective documents;
- Show how each of the projects reflects the *developments* in business communication research now or in the future that we have discussed in Part 1.

This chapter will profile a number of examples of research-based consultancy work in business discourse from around the world, where the intention has been to provide research-based information to improve the effectiveness of the communication that takes place in a specific context. All the studies took place in real organizational settings and as in the previous chapter, they represent a variety of different methodologies and approaches, including survey and interviews, discourse analysis and conversational analysis and the use of experimental data in the design of more effective documentation.

4.1 The REFLECT project

The Review of Foreign Language and Cultural Training Needs project was a large scale needs analysis based consultancy project co-funded by the European Commission, designed to generate training information for European business to support European competitiveness. It took place over a two-year period, from December 2000 to December 2002, involved four research partners, and investigated language and cultural needs, competences and deficiencies in the UK, Ireland, Poland and Portugal. REFLECT was designed to promote and disseminate the importance of language skills in small to mid-sized companies by providing an email information service in English, Polish and Portuguese; and a reference guide in four languages (Gaelic, English, Polish and Portuguese). The objectives of the email service and guide were as follows:

- To promote the concept and use of the language audit (see Concept 4.1 on language audits);
- To promote the use of language skills for economic growth and mobility;
- To signpost companies to sources of language support and information;
- To publish the results and recommendations arising from the survey of language needs and strategies (see also http://salomao.info/wp/wp-content/uploads/2011/10/folheto.pdf).

The project was linked to similar previous studies in the European context (e.g. the REFLECT project in France, Germany, Spain and the UK) and it involved separate surveys for all four countries, a comparative survey of language use and cultural awareness across the four, and a series of case studies profiling the language and cultural strategies pursued within individual companies within the four participating countries. Data 4.1 presents the main comparative findings of the project as was the case at the end of 2002. As we will discuss below and elsewhere in the this volume, similar survey work on the use of different languages continues within the European context, for example in the work of researchers such as Eva Lavric (see Chapter 1) and Pamela Rogerson-Revell (see below).

Data 4.1   The findings of the Reflect Project

- European languages predominate in terms of use and barriers in all four samples. English is critical in Poland and Portugal, followed by German. French and German are the two critical languages in England and Ireland.
- The availability of language skills among the workforce is markedly greater in Poland and Portugal, 20 per cent higher than in England and 30 per cent higher than in Ireland. The two latter countries appear to be over-dependent on English.
- In each of the samples companies declare that they have encountered language barriers, cultural barriers and have lost business by lacking language ability.
- Cultural barriers occur mainly in dealings with Japan (England, Ireland and Portugal), Germany (Poland), the Middle East and China (England) or the UK (Portugal).
- England and Ireland do not show extensive use of language strategies. Polish and Portuguese companies appear to be taking languages much

> more seriously. Companies with English as their native language are less likely to establish language strategies.
>
> • 30 per cent–40 per cent of companies across the four samples expect to trade in new foreign-language markets in the near future. A similar proportion intend to carry out language training, significantly more, in each case, than in the past three years.
>
> • England and Ireland employ far more native speakers than either Poland or Portugal.
>
> (Source: www.reflectproject.com, retrieved in 2005)

Standardization versus adaptation?

European projects like the REFLECT project, its pre-cursors the ELUCIDATE project (1995–1997, England, Germany, France and Spain; Hagen, 1999) and the ELISE project (1999–2000, Denmark, Ireland, the Netherlands, Scotland and Sweden), as well as the more recent ELAN (2006) project that we discuss in Chapter 7 as an example of quantitative survey research, are concerned with whether or not companies 'standardize', i.e. the selection of a lingua franca such as English for all transactions, or 'adapt', i.e. conscious choice of using your business partner's language (Vandermeeren, 1999). In this respect, the PhD study by the Austrian economist Bernhard Bäck (Bäck, 2004) provides a comprehensive theoretical model which shows that language choice factors occur at three different levels: a macro-level (e.g. bilateral trade, language policies, degree of relationship between languages), a meso-level (e.g. degree of internationalization of a certain company, power balance between seller and buyer) and a micro-level, which distinguishes between 'dispositional factors' (e.g. knowledge of foreign languages of a certain employee), 'situational factors' (e.g. type of interaction, constellation of speakers) and 'motivational factors' (e.g. 'compliance' and 'natural choice'). Figure 4.1 shows the details of this model. Drawing on Vandermeeren's distinction between *adaptation* (using the customer's first language), *standardization* (using a 'lingua franca') and *non-adaptation* (using the exporter's own first language, i.e. German), Bäck's survey of Austrian companies communicating with their customers in French-, Spanish-, Portuguese- and Italian-speaking countries indicates that linguistic adaptation to customers in Romance countries is a particularly important strategy: the Austrian exporters use a standardization strategy, i.e. English, in Asia, a standardization i.e. English, or non-adaptation, i.e. German, strategy in Central Eastern Europe, but mainly an adaptation strategy in doing business with the Romance countries. This also belies the assumed dominance of English as a lingua franca in business communication and the corresponding attention that it has received in previous studies.

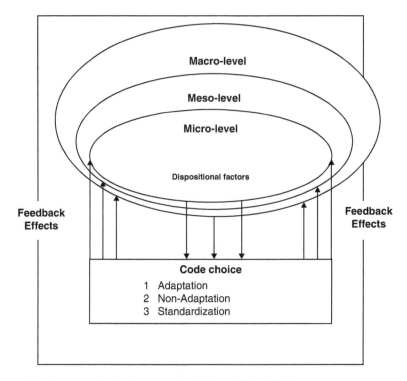

Figure 4.1 Language choice factors (adapted from Bäck, 2004)
Note: Reproduced with kind permission of Bernhard Bäck.

Quote 4.1 The importance of foreign language skills

Managers who dismiss the negative consequences of insufficient language skills as a marginal issue may not realize that a company's linguistic adaptation to its clients can make the difference between failure and success in establishing and maintaining a business relationship (Vandermeeren, 1999: 289).

Vandermeeren's work and Bäck's re-application of it, provide the theoretical underpinning for large scale needs analysis projects like those within the REFLECT, ELUCIDATE and ELAN projects. This is important, as it provides a way of avoiding the pitfalls of simply collecting large amounts of descriptive information in different unconnected contexts. In other words, it allows a series of case studies such as the use of languages in individual corporations to be viewed as contributing to a wider social phenomenon, i.e. the use of different languages in the business arena and the various factors affecting this use. This is supported by Cassell Johnson (2013) in his volume on language policy, when he observes that corporate language policies do not only affect the employees within a particular corporation, they may also then recursively impact language use within the host country, as has been the case, for instance, in countries such as Libya and Algeria where English is the *de facto* language of the oil and gas industry. The multilevel approach taken in Bäck's work provides a way of thinking about the various factors (like these) that contribute specifically to why an individual text or spoken event comes to exist in a particular language, e.g. German rather than English.

Pamela Rogerson-Revell: European Union projects

The British applied linguist, Pamela Rogerson-Revell, has been involved with a number of projects funded by the European Union to look at the use of English as an international working language in Europe. The most recent of these, for instance, is the COLA project (Construction-related language learning for low-skilled migrant workers) with partners based in Austria, France, Spain, Germany and the UK, which aims to improve language skills for migrant workers in the EU construction industry and therefore increase career opportunities, health and safety and social integration. The project is intended to develop language learning materials tailored to the specific needs of low-skilled migrant workers.

(http://construction-language-learning.eu/)

Much of Rogerson-Revell's published research reflects the European projects with which she has been associated, and as a result, it has generated a series of useful insights into the way in which English, in particular, is being used as an international language (EIL). Her work is an excellent example of the three way relationship that can exist between consultancy work, sound research, and teaching or training materials. Rogerson-Revell (2007), for instance, investigates the strategies used by the participants in business meetings in EIL at a European business organization, while Rogerson-Revell (2008) looks specifically at the difference between the strategies used by native speakers and non-native speakers of English in business meetings, and Rogerson-Revell (2010) at the accommodation strategies that occur in business meetings in EIL and how these can be incorporated into training materials (see also Chapter 7).

4.2 Horizontal corporate communication

The 2002 study by Mirjaliisa Charles and Rebecca Marschan-Piekkari is an extensive survey and interview investigation of middle-management at a major multinational designed to generate communication training. It provides an illuminating example of how it is possible to use survey data to reveal the interface between language policy on the one hand, and the communication practices within a business organization on the other. From the mid-1990s onwards, Marschan-Piekkari has explored the communication practices at Kone Elevators in Finland focusing on the impact of language on various aspects of organizational life including structure, power relations and the effectiveness of communication. In the 2002 study she and Mirjaliisa Charles analyse the horizontal communication within Kone Elevators, in order to make recommendations on the most appropriate content for language training at Kone Elevators specifically, and for corporate language training schemes in general.

Quote 4.2   Communication at Kone Elevators

The case study of Kone Elevators has exposed the power of language in the operations of this Finnish multinational. Although Kone has adopted English as its company language, this 'standardization' did not remove the barriers created by its crossborder activities. Instead, the data indicate that language acts as a barrier and a facilitator to inter-unit communication, and that those who possess relevant language competences may find themselves in more powerful positions than would normally be the case. Perhaps a more important finding from this case study is the existence of a shadow structure, based on language clusters and individuals who were language nodes and mediators. Because of the power of language they had the capacity to influence the formal communication lines and even threaten the intended functioning of the formal organizational structure.

(Marschan-Piekkari, Welch & Welch, 1999: 436–7)

Quote 4.3   A Finnish top manager interviewed at Kone Elevators

There is actually no other practical barrier than language when we have co-operation and meetings with each other. These Scandinavian units [in Sweden, Norway and Denmark] get along rather well, but for us [in Finland] it is a constant challenge to find staff who could participate because of language issues. The same persons tend to get overloaded by these duties.

(Charles & Marschan-Piekkari, 2002: 19)

Methodology and findings

One hundred and ten staff at Kone were interviewed, representing 25 corporate units in 10 different countries in Europe, Mexico and the Far East. The interviews were held in English, Finnish, Spanish and Swedish, and a further

six interviews were also held with key people within the organization for additional information on:

(a) the specific role that language is perceived to play in horizontal communication; and
(b) language training in Kone (2002: 14).

English had been adopted in the early 1970s as the official company language,
and the majority of the transactions that take place are between non-native
speakers of English. The interviews showed that communication problems were
caused either by the lack of a common language between interactants, or by the
insufficient language skills held by one or more of the interactants involved.
Somewhat alarmingly, the researchers report that 'A full 57 percent of those
interviewees who mentioned language viewed it as a barrier to communication
in their working context' (2002: 15). For written communication, problems with
translation were identified by the interviewees as being problematic, and for oral
communication, telephone conversations were viewed as difficult, together with
the fact that there were so many different kinds of English spoken within the
company. One of the most interesting findings in the study is the fact that the
non-native English speaking employees had less apparent difficulty understanding other non-native English speaking employees, than they did understanding
the native speakers such as the British. In the time since the study took place, the
fact that non-native speakers find other non-native speakers easier to understand
than native speakers, has now become well-established in research investigating
English lingua franca communication (see also Chapter 3 and Chapter 7, for
further discussion). A second finding is that employees with known language
proficiency, either in English or in other important languages within the organization, became focal points for communication, sometimes leading to an imbalance in the tasks required of them. Equally, employees who were not proficient
in the necessary language or languages felt marginalized or powerless, as they did
not have access to the information they needed. Other researchers have reported
that an imbalance in computer skills within an organization may lead to a corresponding change in the flows of communication through the organization
(e.g. Sproull & Kiesler, 1991), and it is easy to see parallels with the situation that
existed at the time in terms of language at Kone. Data 4.2 summarizes the main
communication problems that Charles and Marschan-Piekkari report.

Data 4.2   The communication problems at Kone Elevators

- The difficulty of finding a common language where none seemed to exist;
- Comprehension problems due to insufficient translation of documentation into subsidiary languages;

- Difficulty in understanding the various accents in which English was spoken internationally, particularly in the lower echelons of the corporate hierarchy;
- Centralization of power into the hands of those who were able to obtain and disseminate information through knowing the official corporate language or the parent company language;
- Feeling of isolation in those with lacking or inadequate skills in the corporate language, resulting in communication flows determined through language rather than job requirements.

(Charles & Marschan-Piekkari, 2002: 19)

Implications

The second part of the Charles and Marschan-Piekkari study consists of a discussion on the implications of the Kone research findings, not only for Kone Elevators in particular, but perhaps more importantly, for communication within multinational corporations in general. The authors outline the policies pursued by the majority of corporations, including recruiting new staff with existing language skills and providing language training, and they then go on to make five concrete suggestions as to how the horizontal communication within a multinational company could be made more effective (see Data 4.3). Marschan-Piekkari's work in general (e.g. Marschan, Welch, & Welch, 1996; 1997; Marschan-Piekkari, Welch & Welch, 1999; Piekkari, Vaara, Tienari & Säntti, 2005), and Charles & Marschan-Piekkari (2002) in particular, deserves a careful reading. Not only is it a useful research investigation that provides a great deal of information on the role played by language(s) in multinational communication, it is also an excellent example of how an empirical study can be used as the basis for a series of well-founded and innovative teaching suggestions.

Data 4.3   Recommendations for enhancing horizontal communication in multinationals

1. Conduct a linguistic audit to identify those specific situations where English (or another language) is needed,
2. Make specific comprehension proficiency a priority, such that comprehension could become a focus rather than production,
3. Encourage staff to understand and negotiate global Englishes to ensure that they are exposed to the communication strategies, expressions and accents they will be dealing with at their particular organization,

4. Include native English speakers in communication training to help them understand how to communicate effectively with non-native speakers, and
5. Make language and communication training a corporate level function, so that language training policy is implemented in the same way across the entire organization.

(Charles & Marschan-Piekkari, 2002: 23–6, slightly adapted)

Concept 4.1 A linguistic audit

Charles and Marschan-Piekkari recommend that corporations should carry out a linguistic audit in order to identify any problems in communication and language use. This means analysing the language communication needs of the corporation – both foreign language needs and local language needs – in a systematic way, including which languages are needed and in which situations and communicative genres, and what the existing language skills are and what still needs to be addressed. Identifying the gap between existing skills and required skills is an important part of conducting a linguistic audit, particularly in informal situations where there may not be a requirement to use an official company language (such as English). This information can then be used as the basis for language and communication training programmes. Charles and Marschan-Piekkari comment that an effective linguistic audit will reveal '(a) the situations in which staff engage (or would engage, if language skills existed) in [horizontal] communication, (b) the people between whom [horizontal] communication takes place (or would take place, if language skills existed), and (c) the language(s) currently used.'

(Charles & Marschan-Piekkari, 2002: 24)

English as a corporate language: strategy or hegemony?

The most important finding in the Charles and Marschan-Piekkari study is the disempowerment of some of the employees as a result of opting for English as the main corporate language. This is similar to findings by both Julio Gimenez (2002) and by Suan Kheng Chew (2005) for the Argentinean and Hong Kong contexts respectively (see Chapter 3 for a discussion of Chew's work in the Hong Kong banking sector), where there was also evidence of an imbalance in power. This is an area of business discourse that has received very little attention to date, since as we have observed in Chapter 1, business discourse researchers have tended to pursue a descriptive and largely neutral route in their analysis. Charles and Marschan-Piekkari's work challenges business discourse researchers to investigate further what the effect of using English rather than another language is in a given business context, starting with the systematic collection of a body of knowledge on the specific communicative situations in which English is used. It would be useful, for instance, to investigate the comprehensibility of different varieties of English in different business contexts, the attitudes towards English and the specific role(s) played by native speakers of English either in hindering or facilitating the effectiveness of the communication. Business discourse research could also consider further ways of counteracting the types of hegemonic situations that Charles and Marschan-Piekkari identify that are related to the use of English in international business, applying the findings of relevant research to the development of appropriate teaching or training materials.

Styling the worker: gender and the commodification of language in the globalized service economy

In 2000, the British sociolinguist Deborah Cameron published an account of the speech styles that were prescribed to telephone call centre operators at seven centres in the UK. Using a combination of observation, interviews and written materials such as employees' manuals, training packs and relevant memos, Cameron reveals that the speech styles recommended for use at the call centres were those most generally associated with what is known as 'women's language', such as showing rapport, asking questions, being expressive and being sincere. The study shows that 'the style is *gendered*, produced through a consistent and deliberate preference for ways of speaking that are symbolically coded as "feminine" (and that in some cases are also empirically associated with women speakers)' (2000: 333). The study is of particular interest, in that it is an example of the 'increasing tendency of employers to regulate even quite trivial details of workers' talk' which Cameron believes is a reflection both of increasing globalization and an increasing awareness of the role that language can play 'as a valuable commodity, potentially a source of "competitive advantage", which needs to be "managed" rather than simply left to take care of itself' (Cameron, 2000a; 324, drawing on Czarniawska–Joerges, 1998).

In the time since Cameron's study was published, the ITES industry, i.e. the Information Technology Enabled Services Industry, or BPO industry, i.e. Business Process Outsourcing industry, as exemplified by call centres in India and the Philippines, has attracted renewed attention from business discourse researchers. At the forefront of these developments is the applied linguist Jane Lockwood who has been involved with research, consultancy and textbook materials all related to the industry (http://www.futureperfect.com/home. html). Recent publications focusing on the call centre industry include Pal and Buzzanell (2008), who reveal the invocation of strategic identities in the Indian call centre context and discuss their hegemonic consequences, Forey and Lockwood (2007), who investigate the generic structure of call centre interactions, and Lockwood (2012), who argues for a research-based approach in the content and design of training materials. Lockwood and MacCarthy's (2010) textbook is included as a research-based, data-driven account in the next chapter.

Standardization and contextualization: the relationship between language and leadership

An alternative account of the relationship between language choice and leadership is provided by Zander, Mockaitis, Harzing et al. (2011) in their survey across 17 different countries (involving 24 different research collaborators). The respondents in the survey, who were all in senior positions, were presented with 15 different scenarios related to six common leadership tasks; Rewarding, Decision-making, Goal-setting, Face-saving, Conflict-resolving and Empathizing. Some respondents were presented with these tasks in English and others in their own language.

The abstract of the study reads as follows:

'With multinational corporations increasingly adopting English as a corporate language, the issue of language management and the pros and cons of language standardization have been widely debated in the literature. Our 17-country study considers whether the use of English as a common corporate language causes difficulties. We empirically examine whether managerial reactions to specific leadership scenario-based situations change as a consequence of the language they use. Our results show that the choice of language (native or English) does not matter much for the studied leadership scenarios. Instead, leadership decisions and reactions depend more on cultural and situational context.' (Zander et al., 2011: 296)

In Chapter 8 we will look in more detail at the study by de Groot (2012) who investigated the consequences of opting for a particular language at an international business organization with both Dutch and German employees.

(Zander, L., Mockaitis, A., Harzing, A. W. et al. (2011). Standardization and contextualization: A study of language and leadership across 17 countries, *Journal of World Business*, *46*, (3), 296–304)

4.3   The Language in the Workplace (LWP) Project

The Language in the Workplace Project (LWP) based at Victoria University Wellington, is a government-funded large scale study of communication in New Zealand workplaces. The project is particularly interesting because it uses real spoken data as the object of study, a type of data that is notoriously difficult for researchers to gain access to in business and organizational settings (see Poncini, 2004, for further comment on this). It has three main aims, which are to:

• Identify characteristics of effective communication between people;
• Diagnose possible causes of miscommunication;
• Explore possible applications of the findings for New Zealand workplaces.

The LWP started in 1996 with the collection or recordings at four government organizations, and it has since been extended in collaboration with UNITEC Institute of Technology and Eastern Institute of Technology (EIT) to include recordings in business organizations such as Telecom, Mobil Oil and Unilever Australia. In each organization spoken interaction such as everyday work-related meetings, telephone calls and social conversations were taped, and videotapes were made of a number of larger, more formal meetings. Approximately 2,000 interactions involving a total of 450 people in 20 different workplaces have been recorded so far (see Table 4.1 for details). The participants involved represent a diversity of backgrounds in terms of gender, ethnicity, age and first language spoken. The project team has eighteen permanent members representing three different institutions in New Zealand (Victoria, UNITEC and Waikato), with an additional team of four postgraduate students based at Victoria and four Research Associates based elsewhere in New Zealand and beyond. The project has resulted in a wealth of information on spoken interaction in workplace settings in New Zealand, much of which has been made available in the form of academic publications, general publications, information packs and brochures for employers, and a wide range of other resources for anyone interested in the area.

Table 4.1   The LWP Project: main datasets

	Government departments	Meetings dataset	Factory	Leadership sample	Skilled migrants
No. of interactions	352	156	837	184	294
No. of hours (approx)	30–40	100	30–40	90	100
No. of participants	251	151	31	99	93

(http://www.victoria.ac.nz/lals/lwp), data provided by the LWP Research Team, September 2012

Areas of interest

The LWP project website identifies fifteen areas of interest so far within the project. They are presented here in an abbreviated form with an example of each taken from the project website (http://www.vuw.ac.nz/lals/research/lwp/research/index.aspx):

Applied Linguistics, e.g. What are the practical implications of research on work-place language for speakers of English as a second language?

Cultural Identity, e.g. Do people from different cultural backgrounds have dif-ferent styles of interaction?

Directives, e.g. How do managers get their team members to do things in the workplace?

Email, e.g. How is the use of email changing workplace communication?

Gender, e.g. Is it true that men and women speak a different language at work?

Humour, e.g. What kind of humour occurs in different workplaces and why do people use it?

Management, e.g. What does the language of negotiation sound like?

Meetings, e.g. What discourse skills are involved in running an effective meeting?

Miscommunication, e.g. What causes miscommunication in the workplace?

Small Talk, e.g. Does small talk have any part to play in effective workplace communication?

Workplace Culture, e.g. Do all workers play an equal part in creating the com-munity of the workplace?

Investigating Māori Leadership, e.g. What is Māori leadership and what does it mean for a business?

Mentoring, e.g. How is the identity of mentor enacted in New Zealand work-place settings?

Nursing, e.g. How do the speech interactions between nurses and patients define the nature of their role as caregivers?

Skilled Migrants in the Workplace, e.g. How does working with socio-pragmatics aid skilled migrants in their ability to communicate effectively in New Zealand workplaces?

The project website provides further information on all these topics in the form of various publications, particularly in the series of LWP Occasional Papers which details the main aims and findings in the project so far, e.g. Holmes (2000a) provides an overview of the LWP project, Stubbe (2001) details the data collection methods used, Waldvogel (2001) looks specifically at the existing literature on the use of email in workplace communication (see also the discus-sion in Chapter 2 Part 1 of Stubbe et al.'s (2003) application of five different discourse analytic approaches to an extract from a business meeting). The most recent publications to come out of the project have included the edited collection by Angouri and Marra (2011) on how people construct identities at work, the volume by Holmes (2006) on how gender is constructed through talk, and the volume by Holmes, Marra and Vine (2012) on leadership, discourse and ethnicity. Quote 4.4 below shows information on small talk, as investigated in the project.

Quote 4.4   Small talk in the LWP project

The crucial role of small talk and social talk at work has become increasingly apparent with the growth of research in this area (e.g. Coupland, 2000). Small talk and social talk occurred in all the workplaces in which we recorded. People used small talk at the boundaries of interaction, at the beginning and end of the day, at the start and end of meetings, and sometimes at topic boundaries within meetings. Small talk in the workplace functions like knitting. It can be easily taken up and easily dropped. It is a useful, undemanding means of filling a gap between work activities, which also oils the social wheels. Our data illustrates how, at the beginning of an interaction, small talk assists the transition from interpersonal or social talk to work or task-oriented talk. Similarly, at the end of an interaction, small talk provides a means of finishing on a positive note, referring, however briefly, to the personal component of the relationship after a period when work roles and responsibilities have dominated the interaction. Small talk is flexible, adaptable, compressible and expandable. Interestingly, we found it can be as formulaic or as personal as people wish to make it. These characteristics make it eminently attractive as a discourse strategy in managing workplace relationships.

(Holmes, 2000b: 7, slightly adapted)

Data 4.4   An LWP project example

Brown and Lewis (2002) describe how they collected and analysed the conversations that took place in a pay clerk's office in New Zealand that they considered typical of the type of context that their target learners would enter on leaving the course. In the study, ten hours of conversation were collected and then analysed using the search facility in MS Word software. As a result, the researchers were able to identify six key work-related topics (money, job termination, accidents and illnesses, government departments, doctors, and form-filling) which were then used as the basis for the language classes that took place during an adult ESP pre-employment course. Brown and Lewis comment, 'Our work suggests that with minimal starting knowledge, teachers like ourselves who have no special expertise in computers can make productive use of a software program for analyzing authentic language.'

(Brown & Lewis, 2002: 96)

Project profile: the Talking it Through project

Ken Willing's 1992 report on the *Talking it Through* project at the National Centre for English Language Teaching and Research, Macquarie University, Sydney, Australia, on white collar immigrant interactions, is an early (and pioneering) example of a project based on real-life interactional data collected in the workplace. It was part of the CTPWP research project at Macquarie-NCELTR, which focused on Communication Tasks in the Professional Workplace. *Talking it Through* 'examines the interactive signalling used by people as they work together on problems and tasks'; it is 'a descriptive and analytical study of the means people use in order to stay reasonably clear about each other's meanings and intentions as they work towards solutions' (Willing, 1992: 1), and as such it provides an interesting contrast to corpus-based approaches, such as that taken by Mike Nelson that we profiled in Chapter 3.

Willing describes the data referred to in the study as 'a corpus of tape-recordings of task-oriented interactions (mainly two-person) between white-collar professionals collaborating in the course of their daily work. Most of these interactions involved at least one participant whose native language was not English (but whose -proficiency in English was of an intermediate to advanced level). Thus most of the communicative situations were potentially problematic to some degree, either linguistically or culturally' (1992: 1). He identifies four main functions that were associated with interactive signalling, or *interactivity*; *acknowledgement* ('*yeah*'), *guidance* ('*in a case like this*'), *clarification* ('*I mean*') and *repair* ('*I didn't mean that quite as badly as it sounded*'), and shows how it was through these functions, and the devices that realized them, that the interactants were able to define the problem inherent in the task they needed to complete, to explain and interpret it further and then create and select possible solutions. The study takes a multimethod approach and draws on insights from a number of different research traditions that were already established at that time, including schemata, speech act theory, conversational analysis and the pragmatics of crosscultural understanding. In this respect, it is a groundbreaking study that anticipates a number of the recent multimethod studies of spoken communication that we present elsewhere in this volume, e.g. Poncini (2004); Mullany (2003); Louhiala-Salminen et al. (2005). In 1995 Willa Hogarth and Linda Burnett produced a set of teaching materials based on the 1992 research study. We will discuss these in Chapter 5.

Business discourse research in authentic settings

The LWP has met a number of the challenges that have hallmarked business discourse research to date, as we have discussed in Chapter 1. First, it has gained access to and gathered information on a large body of real interactions in the workplace, no doubt as a result of the government funded status that the project enjoys (see also below for details on a similar project in the United Kingdom). Second, the researchers involved in the project have taken a data driven approach to the data available to them in order to say something useful about the interactions under analysis rather than relying on any one particular theory. And third, the project has generated a number of concrete suggestions for teaching and training in the workplace in the form of brochures on various aspects of workplace communication, and a handbook and video intended to improve the communication strategies used in effective multicultural workplace teams (Stubbe & Brown, 2002). Clearly not all business discourse researchers will have access either to the data or the resources available to the LWP team, but there is, however, much to be gained by considering several different approaches to the analysis of the same data set in order to understand it more fully, as well as in considering the practical applications of the findings of research and then translating them into teaching/training resources. As we discussed in the previous chapter, and in Chapter 1, there has been a curious disconnect between business discourse research and the language and communication training that many of those same researchers are involved with.

Leadership talk and gender in senior management business meetings in the UK

From January 2009 until May 2011 the British applied linguist Judith Baxter held a grant from the Economic and Social Research Council in the United Kingdom to investigate the speaking patterns of men and women leaders at a number of major companies. The project aimed to explore the role that discourse may play in impeding women's progress through to senior positions. Interviewed in *The Observer* in 2011, Baxter observed:

'I found very few differences between male and female leadership language, but there was this one key difference, which I call double-voiced discourse.* Women use this when they are facing criticism or when handling

conflict. While men tend to be direct and straight talking and if they are confrontational it is regarded as nothing personal, women avoid being directly confrontational and use a range of strategies to preserve a range of alliances, if not friendships, to achieve their agenda. I am not saying that women are more sharing and caring than men. I am not saying they are more altruistic. They are doing it to achieve their own agenda.'
(Source: http://www.guardian.co.uk)

Baxter's project has generated a series of recent publications looking at different aspects of men and women's discourse in the workplace, including the use of double-voiced discourse (e.g. Baxter, 2011), the construction of professional identities (e.g. Baxter & Wallace, 2009), and the language of female leadership (e.g. Baxter, 2010; 2012).

*Double-voiced discourse is a concept taken from Bakhtin, which refers to a speaker (or writer's) ability to carry more than one meaning at once, and in doing so to speak indirectly or to convey an underlying message while at the same time being direct. It has been referred to most frequently in literary studies and in critical feminist studies.

4.4   An ESP programme for management in the horse-racing business

The 2002 publication by Baxter, Boswood and Peirson-Smith is an account of an award winning collaborative ESP/management communication project designed and run by the Department of English at the City University of Hong Kong for the Training Department of the Hong Kong Jockey Club. It provides an example of a project where there is an obvious overlap between ESP on the one hand, and business discourse on the other. As we discussed in Chapter 1, there is a close relationship between ESP work and business discourse research, since many business discourse researchers – like Tim Boswood and Anne Peirson-Smith in this project – are involved in both.

The 'Jockey Club' project aimed specifically at 'developing the capacity of senior managers to write committee papers, the documents that drive top-level corporate decision making in the organization' (2002: 117). Baxter et al. describe the training programme that they produced as English for specific business purposes, characterized by such features as (1) a programme design based on an in-depth needs analysis involving corpus analysis, questionnaires and interviews (2), the generation of a set of training materials which reflected the specific activities of the participants and (3) the targeting of a highly specific genre which played a critical role within the organization. They also describe the project as characterized by a number of challenging additional features, as summarized in Data 4.5. '

Data 4.5   The challenges and opportunities in the Jockey Club project

- The participants were a demanding group of experienced and highly qualified senior managers from a wide variety of professional disciplines.
- Most of the participants were highly competent in the use of spoken and written English as their second language.
- The programme was an innovative, high-profile course for the corporation, involving a degree of risk, and demanding close collaboration and trust between client and consultants.
- A variety of delivery modes were employed, including seminars and individualized coaching to maximize the transfer of learning.
- A computer-based document template was developed, a printed style guide, and guidelines for managing collaborative writing processes.
- The contract was a collaborative one. The consultants designed programmes with the client and turned the course over to in-house trainers, who observed a sample of training sessions throughout the delivery period.

(Adapted from Baxter et al., 2002: 117–18)

The project originated in 1995 and involved 42 senior executives and 24 junior executives. As Baxter et al. describe, the club's communication culture depends on writing to a large extent, and within the writing that is carried out, committee papers are a crucial communicative genre through which a great deal of decision making process takes place. In order to develop appropriate training for the executives, an extensive needs analysis was first conducted consisting of (1) preliminary discussion with the directors of the Club, (2) a corpus analysis of 30 committee papers using a genre analysis approach at several stages in the drafting process, (3) a set of interviews with 20 Jockey Club executives (see Data 4.6 for a selection of the questions asked) and (4) a questionnaire survey of all the participants in the training course intended to find out more about issues such as the participants' perceived role in the writing process, their perceived writing ability and their attitude towards the task.

Data 4.6   A selection of the questions asked in the needs analysis interviews

What is your role in the Hong Kong Jockey Club?
What types of writing does your job require?
What is your role in the committee paper writing process?

How many people are involved in the process of writing committee papers?
How long does it take on average to write a committee paper?
How do you feel about writing committee papers?
What are the easiest aspects of writing a committee paper?
What are the hardest parts of writing a committee paper?
How could you improve on your committee paper writing skills/processes?

(Adapted from Baxter et al., 2002: 121)

Findings and implications

The needs analysis showed that not only did the executives need additional training on an individual basis, the process of writing the committee papers also needed to be developed. The team therefore focused on improving individual skills in developing an appropriate training course along with the development of 'streamlined systems for the collaborative writing of committee papers' (2002: 122). The needs analysis revealed difficulties in the structure and argumentation used in the committee papers and an over-long drafting process, rather than in problems with issues such as grammar and style, and further analysis showed that the drafting process was hampered by a lack of clarity in the audience requirement and in the correct format to be used, a lack of skills in writing strategically and in managing the collaborative writing process. The programme team therefore formulated the following three objectives to underpin the development of the training course:

1. educate executives about the particular features and functions of committee papers;
2. improve the strategic content and persuasive argument structure of the committee paper itself;
3. help executives manage the process of writing committee papers more efficiently in two respects:

- as paper writers, to think more strategically and systematically about the process of gathering information and drafting papers;
- as managers of other writers, to give guidance on the positioning and drafting of papers (2002: 123).

The training materials and training course that resulted from this included both a style guide and a training programme as a reflection of the need to improve the participants' own writing skills together with the writing process surrounding the creation of the genre of the committee paper. The training course itself consisted of a 2-day team-taught in-house seminar that included a range of different activities, such as case study scenarios presented through video, group case analysis, team presentations and extensive drafting of papers. The course participants worked with authentic committee papers and they were also presented with conceptual models for presenting the information most effectively, such as adaptations of Jordan's Situation-Problem-Solution-Evaluation structure (Jordan, 1984) and Blicq's Summary-Background-Facts-Outcome model (Blicq, 1993). The programme was evaluated both during and immediately after its completion, and the team also returned six months later to investigate the longer term impact on the organization. In this follow-up evaluation a process similar to the initial needs analysis was followed that included questionnaires sent to all the programme's participants, follow-up interviews with a sample of the participants and the director of the Club, and an analysis of committee papers produced after the programme compared to those produced beforehand. The evaluation showed that there had been considerable improvements in both the executives' understanding of the committee papers, and also in their presentation of strategic content and persuasive argument structure.

ESBP or business discourse?

In Chapter 1, we suggested that in comparison with ESP and LSP work, business discourse has generally been less motivated by pedagogical concerns and more with a concern with understanding how people communicate strategically in an organizational context. In the Jockey Club project, however, the authors look specifically at how the executives communicated (or failed to communicate) strategically through one very important corporate genre (the committee paper). To do so, they used a combination of survey, corpus and genre analysis and then used this to inform their training course. In addition, the team of researchers (and then trainers) combined their knowledge of the organization and their expertise as applied linguists and business discourse analysts, within what can certainly be viewed as a multidisciplinary project drawing on what we have referred to as 'partnership research' in Chapter 2, to great effect (from Bargiela-Chiappini & Nickerson, 2001). The Jockey Club project is therefore a rare example in which an extensive business discourse research project (combining many of the methodological approaches that we will discuss in detail in Part 3 of this book) is then 'translated' into research-based practice.

Research that sits between ESP/LSP and business discourse continues at the Department of English at City University in Hong Kong, as represented by the work of Bertha Du-Babcock and Jane Lockwood (discussed elsewhere in this volume). Similarly, the Research Centre for Professional Communication in English (RCPCE), at the Department of English at the Hong Kong Polytechnic University, aims to 'pursue applied research and consultancy so as to deepen our understanding of professional communication in English and better serve the communication needs of professional communities' (http://www.engl.polyu. edu.hk/rcpce). The Director of RCPCE, Winnie Cheng, is profiled in Chapter 1.

Corporate communication & corporate social responsibility

The past decade has seen an increase in research investigating the communication surrounding corporate social responsibility (CSR) as an important aspect of corporate communication. Since the beginning of 2010, for instance, the journal publication *Corporate Communications* has published 17 research papers involving various aspects of CSR, including Farache and Perks (2010) who look at how large corporations use CSR advertising to project an ethical image, Johansen and Nielsen (2011), who develop a framework for the initiation and maintenance of dialogue with stakeholders, and Schmeltz (2012) who investigates young people's opinions and attitudes to companies' CSR activities and communication.

Scholars interested in this type of research maintain close links with the organizations they study and it is likely that this will lead to an increasing number of business-discourse related consultancy projects in the future.

4.5 Forms as a source of communication problems

The final consultancy-based study we would like to profile in this chapter is the 1992 study by Carel Jansen and Michael Steehouder that investigates the problems encountered by people when filling in forms. Although it focuses on governmental forms, rather than on business texts, we include it here as a pioneering example of a relatively new area of interest in business discourse research, *document design*, which seeks to improve the effectiveness of certain types of documents using a combination of text analysis on authentic data, and the measurement of audience response to various manipulations in the document studied on an experimental basis. We will go on to describe more about the methodologies used in document design in Part 3.

Quote 4.5   The applications of document design

Our line of research can be considered an example of document design positioned between theoretical work and purely applied studies. We started with analysing the problems users have with certain types of documents; next we developed interventions (where possible on theoretical grounds) meant to help in reducing these problems, and, finally, we tested the effects of the measures taken. By applying this strategy to a number of documents and in a number of situations, we have tried to come up with heuristics for designers that would exceed individual cases.

(Jansen & Steehouder, 2001: 12, slightly adapted)

Methodology and findings

In the study, 98 people were first presented with one or two relevant forms, together with a written scenario describing 'their' current situation and they were asked to complete the forms while thinking aloud. Nine forms were used: three from the national Dutch tax authorities, five from the Dutch Ministry of Education and Science, and one municipal form from the Dutch city of Hengelo. After collecting information from the forms, the researchers' observations during the form completion task and the thinking aloud protocols, Jansen and Steehouder also carried out an interview with the respondents. Data 4.7 shows the problematic areas that could be identified in their order of importance (see also Jansen & Steehouder, 2001, for further discussion on form-completion problems).

Data 4.7   Problems encountered in completing forms

Ineffectiveness – the participant incorrectly omitted a step in the process of completing the form, or incorrectly performed a step;
Inefficiency – the participant took an unnecessary step;
Lack of understanding – the participant performed a particular step for the wrong reasons and/or did not really understand what he or she was doing;
Lack of autonomy – the participant requested the help of third parties when performing a particular step.

(Adapted from Jansen & Steehouder, 1992: 182, original emphasis)

Based on the respondent survey and observation, Jansen and Steehouder distinguish a series of tasks and sub-tasks that they identified as necessary in order to complete the forms. These existed at three levels, and consisted of (1) *functional tasks* that were directly connected with answering the questions on the form, such as generating information like a name or a date, (2) *interpretation tasks* which allowed the person to decide which functional tasks to perform, such as comprehending the text and correctly inferring its meaning, and (3) *monitoring tasks*, which involved decisions about whether or not to perform a particular sub-task, such as deciding which questions to complete. This series of sub-tasks allowed them to look systematically at what might be causing a problem in completing the forms, resulting in the following main problematic areas:

- Discrepancies between the assumptions made by the form compilers in terms of the attitudes, knowledge and skills of the respondents, and the real situation, e.g. the respondents did not read the information systematically, nor did they follow the instructions step by step;

- Lack of sufficient reading proficiency on the part of the respondents, in the formulation of the questions, in the structure of the explanatory notes and in the visual elements that were sometimes included;
- Too little background knowledge about the procedures necessary to complete the form successfully, including unfamiliarity with certain professional terms and a lack of understanding of the need for certain information (1992: 185)

Quote 4.6   Problems identified in completing forms

The analysis of the data showed that problems occurred in the case of each of the separate sub-tasks. For example, it was evidently very difficult for the respondents to obtain and keep an overview of the form, and of the activities that they were required to undertake in this connection. They also had little understanding of textual and graphic selection instructions, and found it difficult to understand terms and syntactic structures. The calculations were difficult, and many of the replies were given in the wrong format, particularly if unconventional coding systems were used in a form.

(Jansen & Steehouder, 1992: 185)

Implications

As a result of the underlying causes that Jansen and Steehouder identify, they suggest that the forms should be revised firstly, by presenting the information 'as much as possible in terms of specific situation, followed by instructions for the actions that have to be taken in each situation', secondly, by giving instructions that make clear to the reader exactly what is expected of them, including instructions for ignoring irrelevant questions and deciding which information should be generated, and thirdly, by providing the reader with 'adequate background knowledge' in the right place on the form, e.g. next to the relevant question, including a indication of the purpose of the form. What sets their study apart is the fact that they then went on not only to revise the forms in the way in which their research findings suggested, but also to re-evaluate the revised versions of the forms in an experimental setting (see also Jansen & Steehouder, 2001, for further discussion on the need for usability testing and revision in the improvement of forms).

Modifications were made in the forms in terms of the order in which the questions were presented, in grouping questions thematically, and in providing the reader with a route map which they should follow in order to complete the form in the most efficient way. In addition, the syntax of certain questions was changed, so that closed and positive questions were used (e.g. 'Have you worked continuously throughout this quarter?' rather than 'Was there any period in this quarter during which you had no work?') and the form was restructured using a three-column approach moving from left to right, in which the Explanatory notes were included in the first column, Questions in the second, and Answers in the third. A total of seven forms were revised and a further 86 respondents completed the same set of tasks that had been used with the original versions of the forms. Jansen and Steehouder report an increase in the correct completion of the forms from 12.3 per cent for the original versions, to 52.2 per cent for the revised versions. The research project therefore resulted in a demonstrable – and quantifiable – improvement in the usability of the forms.

The HACALARA project: An international document design project

The HACALARA project (2007–2010) investigated the use of spoken communication combined with printed visual and verbal information as a strategy to bring about effective comprehension and persuasion in the context of HIV/AIDS intervention programmes that are aimed at local and rural areas of the Limpopo Province in South Africa.

The project was carried out in cooperation between the University of Limpopo (South Africa), Radboud University Nijmegen (The Netherlands) and Tilburg University (The Netherlands) with financial support from SANPAD, the South Africa-Netherlands Research Programme on Alternatives in Development.

The project aimed to answer the following research question:

How can rhetorical devices be used in visual/verbal printed messages and in radio messages to create seminal conversations on health related behaviour, which in turn contribute to changes in relevant beliefs, attitudes and behavioural intentions?

Recent publications that discuss the findings of the project include Jansen and Janssen (2010), Lubinga and Jansen (2011), and Lubinga, Schulze, Jansen, and Maes (2010).

(*Source*: http://www.hacalara.org)

The HACALARA project, and the EPIDASA project which preceeded it from 2003 to 2006, resulted in a series of publications in South African and international journals, as well as a co-edited volume of papers (Swanepoel & Hoeken, 2008) and a PhD thesis (Saal, 2009). Conferences were also held within the context of the projects, which were attended both by academics and by representatives of the South African health promotion organizations.

One of the senior researchers associated with the project observes that although it is hard to know exactly how influential the findings of research projects such as HACALARA and EPIDASA have been, major changes have certainly taken place over the past decade in health communication in South Africa in general and in South African communication about HIV and AIDS in particular (personal communication, Carel Jansen).

A way forward for business discourse research

Projects like Jansen and Steehouder's study and revision of governmental forms, followed by an experimental re-evaluation of the revised form, have provided a promising area of enquiry for business discourse research. In the time since the study was published, researchers interested in document design have become increasingly concerned with all aspects of the design of an effective document, both textual and visual, providing ways of investigating the types of multimodal texts that have become endemic to communication within the business world. In Part 3 (Chapter 7) we will return to document design and discuss the main methodologies and approaches that have characterized the field.

Quote 4.7 The relationship between text evaluation and understanding

Redesigning documents is one thing, but the redesign is of little use if it does not improve understanding. Over the past decades, research on document quality has focused mainly on text evaluation. For example, readers might be asked to fill in seven-point scales or to be videoed thinking aloud while filling in a form. However, text evaluation is only one aspect. Research into real understanding seems more important: how many mistakes are made while filling in the old versus the new version of the form? A form with a photograph, for example, could be evaluated as more attractive than a form without pictures, but if the new version allows as many mistakes as the old version, how can the extra costs for the design of the renewed document be justified?

(Renkema, 2009: 174)

Quotation 4.7, taken from Renkema's discussion on improving two sets of governmental documentation in the Netherlands (Renkema, 2009), highlights both the power of document design as a research method and the need to implement (and then re-test) the findings of that research in order to justify the costs associated with redesign of a document. Research-based consultancy projects such as those discussed by Jansen and Steehouder (1992) and by Renkema (2009) are pertinent examples of collaborative research between academic scholars and the professional 'owners' of the documents, in this case the government officials responsible for improving the usability – and therefore efficiency – of a specific set of texts. Both studies also demonstrate how the research carried out led to an increase in the general public's understanding of the new version of the texts, and therefore to a reduction in the costs incurred if a person is unable to understand and use the document without outside help. Renkema concludes his discussion on a redesigned tax form and a redesigned letter referring to passport renewal, as follows: 'In both projects, it appears that the need for additional information diminished by about twenty percent. Financial experts in the municipality calculated the possible savings this represents. The average costs of a phone contact between a citizen and an employee (in Dutch society) is about €4.50. The passport letter in this municipality alone is sent yearly to about 100,000 citizens. If a new, reformulated version of the passport letter reduces the estimated chance of making a phone call by about twenty percent, then the savings could be as high as €90,000 annually' (Renkema, 2009: 190). In Part 3 of this volume, we will look at further document design research and the methodological approaches that document design researchers have followed in the course of the past decade.

Roe Delin: a language and information design consultancy

Roe Delin is a consultancy company set up in 2009 to improve communications for businesses through a process of redesign and simplification. It is a co-operative venture between Judy Delin, a linguist, and Iain Roe, a specialist in document design. Delin, in particular, maintains both commercial and academic contacts, and has published widely on a variety of subjects of relevance to the contemporary workplace, including multimodality (e.g. Delin & Batemen, 2002), branding (e.g. Delin, 2005), and trust in financial services (e.g. Delin, 2012/3).

(*Source*: http://delinroe.net/index.html)

Further reading

Holmes, J., Marra M., & Vine, B. (2012). *Leadership, discourse and ethnicity.* Oxford: Oxford University Press. A comprehensive account of the LWP project, together with the most recent findings on a range of different topics such as the construction of leadership through language, relational talk at work, and business meetings.

Lockwood, J., & Forey, G. (Eds.) (2012). *Globalization, communication and the workplace: Talking across the world.* London & New York: Continuum. A collection of papers looking at various aspects of the communication that takes place in the call centre industry around the world.

Paltridge, B., & Starfield, S. (Eds.) (2012). *The Handbook of English for Specific Purposes.* Oxford: Wiley-Blackwell. An extensive set of newly commissioned essays which surveys the most recent research findings in the field of ESP.

Schriver, K. (1997). *Dynamics in document design.* New York: John Wiley & Sons, Inc. A compendium on document design covering all aspects of the field, from the analysis of audience, through the impact of poor design, to the roles played by typography, space, words and pictures.

Chapter 4 Tasks

1. Read Delin (2005) on the relationship between branding and the use of a particular tone of voice. Explain how research like this can be applied in practice. Then think of your own project that could be used to improve the way in which a business organization communicates with its customers. (Delin, J. (2005). Brand tone of voice. *Applied Linguistics, 2*(1), 1–44.)

2. Read through section 4.2 in this chapter on horizontal corporate communication, in particular Concept 4.1 on linguistic audits. Decide on ten questions that you would ask either in an interview or a questionnaire survey, in order to conduct a linguistic audit within a major multinational corporation like Kone. Your audit will be used to make recommendations to the HR department on appropriate language training for staff.

3. Refer to the website for the European Commission's COLA Project on Construction-related language learning for low-skilled migrant workers (http://construction-language-learning.eu). Design a similar project focusing on language learning in a different industry or business sector. Explain which languages you will include, and why, and what the aims of your project will be.

5
Research-based Teaching Materials

This chapter will:

- Provide a brief *survey of published materials* for Language for Specific Business Purposes and Business Communication;
- Profile six sets of *research-based teaching materials*;
- Discuss the *approaches taken* in each case and show how these are related to business discourse research.

Introduction

This chapter will consider the relationship between published teaching materials and the findings of business discourse research. It will look at six sets of published teaching materials where research theory or the findings of empirical business discourse research have been used to underpin the information presented (see Data 5.1 for details). We will look at the theories and other research investigations underlying each book, the types of sources referred to and the approach taken in each case in communicating this information to students. As we will show in our brief survey of published materials in Language for Specific Business Purposes and Business Communication at the beginning of the chapter, research-based text-books like the ones we profile here are still few and far between in the vast array of teaching materials available to teachers and students of business communication, business language and business discourse. Three of the volumes are practice-driven accounts that focus on corporate and technical business communication in the US tradition (Argenti; Andrews; Beamer & Varner), one is theory-driven referring to one particular macro-theory in its presentation of the material (Tietze, Cohen & Musson) and two are data-driven and are grounded in the discipline of applied linguistics (Koester; Hogarth & Burnett). We will begin this chapter with a brief survey of current LSBP and business communication publications related to teaching and then continue by discussing each type of approach in turn.

Data 5.1   Teaching materials based on business discourse research

Paul Argenti (1998/2012) – *Corporate Communication* (McGraw-Hill/Irwin); a US textbook which shows how to apply macro-models of communication, making reference to various sources both academic and popular. It also includes use of the case-study method.

Deborah Andrews (1998/2001) – *Technical Communication in the Global Community* (Prentice Hall); a US textbook focusing (mostly) on written forms of communication (both verbal and visual), making reference to both academic and popular sources. It also includes reference to cultural differences in communicating effectively.

Linda Beamer & Iris Varner (1994/2005/2010) – *Intercultural Communication in the Global Workplace* (McGraw-Hill/Irwin); a US textbook on intercultural communication which shows the application of macro culture theory to real situations in business. Both authors are applied linguists and the volume includes specific reference to the role of language in intercultural business situations.

Susanne Tiezte, Laurie Cohen & Gill Musson (2003) – *Understanding Organizations through Language* (Sage); a UK-based publication which uses a discourse, i.e. social construction/semiology, approach to communication within (business) organizations. It also draws on academic and (some) popular sources.

Almut Koester (2004) – *The Language of Work* (Routledge); a UK-based publication written by an applied linguist (genre analyst) that provides a good example of European business discourse in an applied linguistics tradition. It includes numerous examples of the analysis of real text.

Willa Hogarth & Linda Burnett (1995) – *Talking it Through: Teacher's Guide & Classroom Materials* (NCELTR, Macquarie University); a pioneering Australian-based publication written by two TESOL/ESOL specialists, based on the research study with the same title by Ken Willing (1992). It includes numerous examples of discourse-based teaching activities that refer directly to the findings of Willing's study. Although this publication is now out of print, we include it in our discussion later in this chapter as an early example of how research may be used effectively to generate teaching materials.

5.1   A brief survey of published teaching materials

In this section, we will present a brief survey of ESBP, LSBP and business communication (BC) materials. We will discuss to what extent published materials have referred to empirical work in business discourse, business language or business communication through reference to the information available in August 2004 and June 2012 on the *Amazon* book ordering website, together with a survey of the book reviews that appeared in three relevant academic journals targeted at researchers and practitioners from 2002 to 2004, and from 2010 to 2012, i.e. the *English for Specific Purposes Journal*, the *Journal of Business Communication* and the *Business Communication Quarterly*.

Nickerson (2005) reports on the teaching materials available for the teaching of English for Specific Business Purposes (ESBP), first by comparing a previous survey by St John (St John, 1996) of ESBP textbooks available in 1996 to the situation in 2004, and then by using an advanced search of the *Amazon.co.uk* book site (Quote 5.1 contains a summary of her findings). She concludes that there was little reference to empirical research in the materials published up to 2004, despite the vast array of ESBP materials that were available. Two exceptions are the 2004 publication by Almut Koester, *The Language of Work* (and her two subsequent publications, *Investigating Workplace Discourse* (2007) and *Workplace Discourse* (2010; 2012)), and the 1995 publication by Hogarth and Burnett *Talking it Through* that we profile later in this chapter.

Outside of the ESBP world, we would suggest that there is a similar story for teaching materials designed for foreign languages other than English, since our survey of *Amazon.co.uk*, both in 2004 and 2012, using keywords such as *Language for Specific Business Purposes, French for Specific Purposes, Spanish for Specific Purposes, French for business, Spanish for business* etc. revealed that the majority of the volumes published since 1999 were either bilingual business dictionaries or textbooks in which there was little or no evidence of any reference to empirical research. And there was no apparent change in the eight year period between the two surveys. The volumes by Azuma and Sambongi (2001) on *Business Japanese* and the volume by Cui (2004) on *Business Chinese: An Advanced Reader* remained the only entries to show some evidence of reference to research, since Azuma and Sambongi state that 'this book focuses on the language used in real-life business situations', and Cui makes reference to authentic materials, including documents, forms and letters. The keywords *business communication* listed a total of 7404 volumes in 2004, and an astounding 49,421 entries in 2012 (87,773 on the main *Amazon.com* site), including both electronic and print sources. In 2004, out of 343 volumes then listed as published or due to be published from 2004 onwards, only the volume by Poncini (2004) on the discursive strategies used in multicultural business meetings that we have discussed elsewhere in this book, and the volume by Beamer and Varner (2005) on intercultural communication in the global workplace that we will discuss later in this chapter, showed evidence of drawing on existing research. In 2012, in the top 50 *Relevant* publications on *Amazon.co.uk* and *Amazon.com,* only three additional volumes show evidence of reference to research: the 2001 publication by Hartley and Bruckmann (Hartley & Bruckmann, 2001), which references work, for instance, by both Leena Louhiala-Salminen and Vijay Bhatia; the 2011 publication by Shwom and Gueldenzoph Snyder (Shwom & Gueldenzoph Snyder, 2011) which includes a set of both academic and business references for further reference; the 2011 Harvard Business Review collection on *Communicating Effectively* (Harvard Business Review, 2011) with contributions from academics such as Deborah Tannen, who references the work of Janet Holmes on women's leadership language. Two other recent textbooks, (Guffey & Loewy, 2010; Locker & Kaczmarek, 2010) are authored by prominent business communication scholars based in North America and make reference to some sources of business communication research alongside popular management writing (see Concept 5.1). Further searches using the keywords *business communication* prefaced with *French, Spanish, German, Italian, Japanese* and *Chinese*, also revealed very little change between 2004 and 2012; the ethnographic study of 550 workers in a Mexican industrial organization originally published in 2002 by Covarrubias (Covarrubias, 2002) has since been updated (Covarrubias & Hymes, 2005), the 1997 study of British and Italian business meetings by Bargiela-Chiappini and Harris (1997) that we discussed in Chapter 1 of this book, remains in print, as does Yamada's (2002) study of the difference between Japanese and US business culture and language. As we observed in the first edition of this volume, however, these are research investigations that are either most likely to be read by a specialized academic audience or to be used as supplementary materials for advanced research students. Of the research-based publications we found in 2004, for the keywords *business communication research, corporate communication research* and *corporate communication*, Hirsch (2003) on *Essential Communication Strategies* remains in print, as does Keyton (2004; 2005) on *Communication and Organizational Culture*, and the 2004 publication on *International Management* by Mead (Mead, 2004), has recently been updated as Mead and Andrews (2009). Other more recent volumes that refer to research in either business or corporate communication include Taylor and Van Every's text on the *Pragmatics of Communication* (Taylor & Van Every, 2010), Hirsch and Goodman's account of *Corporate Communication* (Hirsch & Goodman, 2010), Cornelissen's textbook which is also on *Corporate Communication* (Cornelissen, 2011) and Schnurr's 2012 publication on *Professional Communication* (Schnurr, 2012). We include further details on Cornelissen (2011) and Schnurr (2012) later in this chapter in sections 5.3 and 5.4 respectively. Finally, for the keywords *communication in organizations*, Argenti's *Corporate Communication* (1998/2003/2005/2008/2012) and Tiezte, Cohen and Musson's *Understanding Organizations through Language* (2003), both remain in print and are discussed in the next section as research based teaching materials.

Quote 5.1   Teaching materials for ESBP

A brief survey of twenty of the published materials that St John includes in her introduction to the 1996 Special Issue, reveals that seven are still available – all now between ten and twenty years old. Although, of course, these will certainly have remained in print due to popular demand, this must surely also be an indication that the market has remained somewhat static over the last two decades. In addition, although an advanced search of the *Amazon.co.uk* book site using the keywords, English for Specific Business Purposes, English for Specific Purposes, and English for Specific Purposes plus Business, results in 163, 611 and 143 publications respectively, the majority of the publications listed are either bilingual business dictionaries, are intended for learners at a low level of proficiency with a focus on business, or date from 1999 or before. The keywords ELT; English for Business, are more promising, yielding a total of 772 publications. Of the 31 listed that were published – or due to be published – in 2004, however, where content information was available, only two (Mascull, 2004; Collins Cobuild, 2004), specifically mention a link with (corpus-based) research as the rationale behind the volume, both of which are intended as advanced business vocabulary books. None of the books listed refer ostensibly to the findings of research in their descriptions, with the exception of the corpus-based accounts. This suggests that although we may certainly know more about the 'generic features . . . common features . . . and cultural influences' that St John (1996) identifies as areas that should be of interest in Business English, we do not draw any more on research in our development of teaching materials now, than we did a decade ago.

(Nickerson, 2005: 375–6, slightly adapted)

Outside of Amazon, when we surveyed all the reviews included in *ESPj* from 2002 to 2004, we found only four volumes related to researching and/or teaching in ESBP or LSBP. Of these four, the volume by Douglas (2000) on *Assessing Languages for Specific Purposes* (reviewed by Moore, 2002), and by Donna (2000), entitled *Teach Business English* (reviewed by Boswood, 2002), were intended as resource books for teachers rather than as teaching materials, and the remaining two were reviews of edited collections, i.e. the 1999 volume *Writing Business: Genres, Media and Discourses* (co-edited by Bargiela-Chiappini and Nickerson, reviewed by Lockwood, 2002) that we have discussed elsewhere in this volume, and the 1998 collection *The Cultural Context in Business Communication* (co-edited by Niemeier, Campbell & Dirven, reviewed by Du-Babcock, 2002) that contains the account of the research-based international business writing programme given by Verckens, De Rycker and Davis (1998) that we discussed in detail in the previous chapter. Similarly, in the period from 2010 to 2012, there were seven relevant reviews, three of which were edited collections (Bhatia & Gotti, 2006, reviewed by Dressen-Hammouda, 2010; Ruiz-Garrido, Palmer-Silveria & Fortanet-Gómez, 2010, reviewed by Cheng, 2011; Belcher, 2009, reviewed by Guthrie, 2011), three monographs (Handford, 2010, reviewed by Nickerson, 2011 and elsewhere in this volume; Gunnarson, 2009, reviewed by Valdez; Tardy, 2009, reviewed by Yigitoglu, 2011), and only one was a textbook (Basturkmen, 2005, reviewed by Vaughan & Voss, 2011). Basturkmen (2005) is a research-based textbook on the teaching of English for Specific Purposes which does include some reference to the teaching of English for Specific Business Purposes, as well as the relevant literature.

In a similar survey of the *Journal of Business Communication* from 2002 to 2004 we found only one review of relevance, the 2004 review by Tyler (Tyler, 2004) of Argenti and Forman's 2002 publication, *The Power of Corporate Communication* and in the *Business Communication Quarterly*, we found only three volumes that show a clear link to empirical findings: *Professional Communication in International Settings* (Pan, Wong Scollon & Scollon, 2002, reviewed by Gump, 2004), *When Teams Work Best* (LaFasto & Larson, 2001, reviewed by Melton, 2003) and *Technical Communication in the Global Community* (Andrews, 2002, reviewed by Blalock, 2002), although as Gump (2004) points out in his review, the Pan, Wong Scollon & Scollon (2002) volume is rather less of a convincing textbook, than it is a grounded research account. LaFasto and Larson (2001) is based on the empirical findings of a fifteen-year research initiative and is described as 'an ideal resource for teaching collaboration skills' (Melton, 2003: 133), and finally, Andrews (2002) is a research-based resource book intended for 'instructors of business and technical communication who understand the importance of focusing on the twenty-first century reality of crossborder research and who want to give students a resource that they'll find useful now and want to hold onto as a reference' (Blalock, 2002: 134–5), as we will discuss in the next section. In keeping with the journal's pedagogical orientation there were other reviews of textbooks in *BCQ*; these were books intended to provide useful information on how to improve specific skills, e.g. a *Guide to Meetings* (Munter & Netzley, 2002), rather than to make overt (or indeed any) reference to current research in the volume itself. For 2010 to 2012, the *Journal of Business Communication* carried only two reviews in total (perhaps as a reflection of a change in editorial policy), one a review of an edited collection (Garzone & Sarangi, 2007, reviewed by Clifton, 2010), and the other a review of Fairhurst's research-based textbook on leadership language and *The Power of Framing* (Fairhurst, 2010, reviewed by Aritz, 2012). The *Business Communication Quarterly* carried a total of 24 reviews in the same time period, although many of these were general business books rather than being textbooks, and almost all showed little evidence of reference to scholarly sources. Three that did, were Schein's volume on how to survive corporate culture (Schein, 2009, reviewed by Ford, 2010 and by Yugo, 2012), although this is not a textbook, and the textbooks by Zaremba (2010), which is a theory-based account of *Crisis Communication* (reviewed by Barclay, 2010), and the 5th edition of Chaney and Martin's textbook on *Intercultural Business Communication* (Chaney & Martin, 2010, reviewed by Ostendorf, 2012).

As we observed in 2007, when we looked for research-based text materials then, *Amazon* and the three journals we surveyed are not exhaustive, and there may certainly be other relevant publications in ESBP, LSBP, business discourse or business communication that *do* refer to empirical research that we have missed. They remain, however, four major sources of information available to practitioners around the world that have a vested interest in keeping their respective readerships up to date with the latest developments in the field. Blalock provides a telling comment on Andrews' volume when she writes, 'This book is a rare bird, indeed' (2002: 135), summarizing succinctly what we still believe to be the current state of affairs in research-based teaching materials for business discourse and business communication, at least in the sources we have reviewed here.

5.2   Practice-driven approaches

The three textbooks we profile in this section, Argenti (1998/2003/2005/2008), Andrews (1998/2002) and Beamer and Varner (1995/2001/2005/2010), are all examples of the (US) practice-driven approach, i.e. they are centred on a series of situations that commonly occur in business and technical organizations, such as *Intercultural Negotiation* (Chapter 9 in Beamer and Varner) and *Composing Visuals* (Chapter 8 in Andrews). In keeping with this brief, all three include either case studies or short cases to illustrate the material presented within each chapter. The latest editions of Beamer and Varner, and of Andrews, also include supplementary material for use with students either as a CD-ROM (Beamer and Varner) or in a (free) downloadable form from the publisher (Andrews) (see also Data 5.3 below).

As their titles suggest, Argenti, Andrews and Beamer and Varner provide research-based overviews of the fields of corporate communication, technical communication and intercultural communication respectively. All refer both to current theoretical frameworks and to relevant practical examples and all draw on various types of sources, such as published comments by captains of industry, business newspapers, e.g. the *Wall Street Journal*, academic business publications, e.g. the *Harvard Business Review*, academic business communication publications, e.g. the *Journal of Business Communication*, and academic theoretical accounts or macro-theories, e.g. *The Principles of Corporate Communication* (van Riel, 1995). In a chapter on Composing Text for instance, Andrews refers to Kaplan's macro-theory on cultural variations in structuring text (Kaplan, 1966), to a study by Joann Temple Dennett published in the *IEEE Transactions of Professional Communication* that builds on Kaplan's theory (Dennett, 1988) and also to university writing centres that may help students further in their writing, e.g. http://webster. commnet.edu/writing/writing.htm. Likewise, in a chapter focusing on Getting to Know Another Culture, Beamer and Varner refer to Hofstede's macro-theory on culture (Hofstede, 1984), to an article from the *Economist*, and to their own scholarly publications, e.g. Varner (2000) and Beamer (1994). In each case the authors use the different sources they include to provide supporting evidence for the information they present, and they illustrate this wherever appropriate with real examples or anecdotes taken from the business world. Although all four authors are active researchers within the community of business communication scholars, the intention in all three volumes is to present an overview of each (research) field and its practical applications rather than to showcase any one particular research approach or theory.

Concept 5.1   Popular management writing

Self-help books, e.g. *Getting to Yes* (Fisher & Ury, 1991)
Popular business magazine, e.g. *Fortune*
Multinational corporations writing, e.g. *Nike website*
Business newspapers, e.g. *Wall Street Journal*

Many best-selling management books rely on impression management and the packing of accessible ideas that are presented as relevant to the needs of the target readership of business managers and business people. Their widespread popularity and influence can create new fashions, models and ideas that are targeted at specific audiences but which in fact set trends that resonate beyond the business arena. Popular management writing has undergone critical scrutiny by management and organization scholars (e.g. May & Zorn, 2001; Greatbatch & Clark, 2005).

In Argenti and in Andrews in particular, each chapter concludes with a relevant Case Study. These provide an example or situation used to illustrate the particular aspect of corporate or technical communication in practice, together with a set of Case Questions (Argenti) or Exercises (Andrews). Quote 5.2 and Concept 5.2 provide further information on the use of case studies in the US tradition and their recent influence beyond US borders.

Quote 5.2   What are cases?

Cases are much like short stories in that they present a slice of life. Unlike their fictional counterpart, however, cases are usually about real people, organizations, and problems . . .

In cases, as in life, problems can be solved in a variety of ways. Sometimes one way seems better than others. Even if a perfect solution exists, however, the company may have difficulty implementing it. You may also find that you have a completely different solution to the problem than another student. Try to forget the notion of an 'answer' to the problem. The goal in using this method is not to develop a set of correct approaches or right answers, but rather to involve you in the active process of recognizing and tackling managerial problems . . . As a teaching device, the case method relies on participation rather than passive learning.

(Argenti, 1998: xiii–xiv)

Concept 5.2   Using case studies

The use of business situations for analytical and educational purposes started at Harvard University in the US in the 1920s (Argenti, 1998). It is now in widespread use, particularly in business education, and Harvard Business School still provide published case studies in their online business school cases (e.g., http://harvardbusinessonline.hbsp.harvard.edu). The effectiveness of using the case study method is discussed by Connor, Rogers & Wong (2005) in the groundbreaking collaborative project between the University of Michigan Business School and Nanyang Business School in Singapore (see Part 2, Chapter 3). The range of topics available and the variety of business problems discussed suggest that a case study approach could provide a useful resource for business language trainers looking for a convincing case to use as the basis for a business simulation in class or as a topic for (electronic) discussion. Almagro Esteban and Pérez Cañado (2004) explore this point in their interesting discussion of how the US case method can also be used in teaching ESBP. They comment, 'this demanding activity is a way of enhancing learning, together with the professional skills most business people possess . . . ' (2004: 158).

In Chapter 2 (Communicating Strategically) in Argenti, for instance, *Fletcher Electronics* is a fictional case drawn in part from real life cases, in which a newly appointed business executive Mr VanDyke, experiences problems as a result of the communication strategy he chooses to pursue with other employees. The case consists of background information on Fletcher Electronics, two examples of internal correspondence, and a set of four case questions. These questions ask students to identify any general or specific problems in the communication at Fletcher Electronics, and then to analyse the case making particular reference to the theoretical models of corporate communication that have been presented to them in the first stage of the chapter (see Data 5.2).

Data 5.2   Case questions: Fletcher Electronics

What problems does Fletcher Electronics have that will affect its communications?

What specific problems does Mr VanDyke have as a result of his communications to materials managers?

How would you analyse this case in terms of the Corporate Communication Strategy Model (Figure 2-3) and the Munter Communication Strategy Model (Figure 2-1)?

What advice would you give to Mr VanDyke to help solve his problem?

(Argenti, 1998: 46)

Similarly, Data 5.3 below provides details of how Andrews integrates the findings from current research into cultural differences, into the supplementary case study provided for the chapter in her volume that focuses on Letters.

Data 5.3   A supplementary case study

As the director of marketing for DJW, a software development company, you've received a letter from Lewis Tanaki, the marketing director for a client company, Kobi Concepts, based in Japan. Your company has contracts with Kobi, as well as other companies, to develop software for their business applications. Tanaki has written requesting you to provide him with a list of clients from your marketing database so that Kobi can solicit these clients, too.

This activity contains 1 question.

While Kobi is a client, DJW has a strong policy prohibiting access to client lists, which it considers proprietary information. Write a letter denying Tanaki's request, keeping in mind Kobi is a valued client and you want to keep their business. Also, consider cultural differences as you create your letter: what approach should you take when writing business letters to readers in Japan? Create your own addresses for both DJW and Kobi.

To research communication preferences in Japan, you may want to consult the Global Window Japan website from *UCLA's Anderson School of Management* (http://www.anderson.ucla.edu/research.xml).

(*Source*: http://wps.prenhall.com/andrews).

The volumes by Argenti, Andrews and Beamer and Varner are useful examples of the way in which information from macro-theories, empirical studies and popular sources may be combined with practical examples and case studies in the effective presentation of teaching materials. They make a small, but highly significant, contribution to the prescriptive possibilities afforded by research-based practice. In the next section we will consider a further textbook where one specific macro-theory plays a prominent role in the selection and presentation of the material.

Writing for different audiences

The 2002 volume co-authored by Paul Argenti and Janis Forman (Argenti & Forman, 2002), *The Power of Corporate Communication*, is a guide for managers which also focuses on corporate communication. It is also grounded in current theory although less obviously as a consequence of it target readership. In reviewing it for the *Journal of Business Communication*, Lisa Tyler writes; 'The authors draw on very current examples of communication successes and snafus, citing a range of popular and business periodicals and newspapers as their sources in their meticulously documented endnotes. The authors also draw on their own research and cite personal interviews among their sources . . . so as to produce a synthesis of the principles of corporate communication with varied examples to illustrate each' (Tyler, 2004: 100). *The Power of Corporate Communication* is worth looking at together with Argenti's *Corporate Communication*, as an example of the same authors presenting similar ideas in a different way for a different audience.

5.3   Theory-driven approaches

The 2003 volume by Tietze, Cohen and Musson – *Understanding Organizations through Language* – provides an interesting contrast to the three practice-driven volumes we discussed in the previous section. All three authors teach Organizational Behaviour at different UK business schools and the volume makes overt reference to the theories of semiology and social construction in its discussion of language as discourse in organizations. The volume therefore presents different facets of one meta-theory, by first introducing the principles of that theory, e.g. Chapter 2, 'A semiological approach to meaning making', and then exploring various themes within that theory, e.g. Chapter 3, 'Understanding organizations through metaphor', and Chapter 5, 'Understanding organizations through discourse'. As with the volumes we looked at in the previous section, Tietze, Cohen and Musson draw on both academic and popular sources, and they also provide numerous practical examples to illustrate their materials, but the emphasis on semiology and social construction clearly underpins the book throughout. To illustrate this point, Data 5.4 presents the objectives for Chapter 6, *Language, Culture, Meaning*, together with a theory driven discussion exercise taken from the same chapter. Finally, Quote 5.3 reproduces a paragraph from the first chapter in the volume, in which the authors discuss their intentions behind the volume.

Data 5.4   Chapter 6, *Language, Culture, Meaning*

Objectives

In this chapter we will:
define culture in semiological terms;
explore the relationship between language and culture;
discuss and assess the role and consequences of English as the main communicative tool in international encounters;
investigate the nature and role of non-verbal communication; and define and discuss ethnocentrism as the main barrier to effective communication.

A theory driven discussion exercise

Compare and contrast
'Management is getting things done through people.'
'Management is developing people through work.'

What are the implicit assumptions entailed in these two definitions?
Can you attribute them to different cultural frameworks?

(Tietze, Cohen & Musson, 2003: 91–3)

Quote 5.3   Understanding organizations through language

Our main concern is to enable readers to understand better the processes of construction of (their) organizational realities. It is possible that on the basis of better understanding, critical questions may be asked, taken-for-granteds may be queried, the normal may begin to appear strange or fabricated. These reflections may well be part of a process of individual or organizational change. However, we are wary about any exaggerated claims about the potential of this book to have an emancipatory effect. Rather, we hope to raise questions, offer illustrations and examples and put forward arguments to convince the readers that a working knowledge of semiology can be quite a useful thing!

(Tietze, Cohen & Musson, 2003: 13)

Corporate communication

Corporate communication: A guide to theory and practice (Cornelissen, 2011)

The 2011 textbook by Joep Cornelissen is a theory driven account of corporate communication, which combines both relevant theory and practical examples, including fifteen short case studies used to illustrate each important theoretical point. The volume looks at the historical development of the field, as well as the most important conceptual foundations that underpin this (e.g. Stakeholder management, Corporate identity, Corporate reputation, etc.), and the second part of the book then goes on to discuss how this theory can be applied in practice.

Corporate communication as a discipline is likely to be of increasing interest to business discourse scholars in the future. It includes genres such as advertising texts, annual general reports and corporate websites, alongside more general forms of communication such as marketing communication and the communication surrounding corporate social responsibility.

(Cornelissen, J. (2011). *Corporate communication: A guide to theory and practice*. London & New York: Sage)

5.4   Data-driven approaches

The 2004 publication *The Language of Work* by Almut Koester and the 1995 publication by Hogarth and Burnett based on Ken Willing's research project *Talking it Through* (see Chapter 4) provide two examples of data-driven ESBP/LSBP student books that are clearly based on research findings. In each case, they take a discourse approach to the analysis of business language, they illustrate each of the aspects of language they discuss with real data and they make specific reference to academic publications focusing on empirical data, mostly in the applied linguistics tradition. Koester's volume appears in a series of textbooks focusing on contemporary English Language Studies for UK students at the end of high school or at the beginning of tertiary education. The volume by Hogarth and Burnett is intended for NESB speakers (i.e. non-English speaking background students) at an advanced level or *'anyone whose work involves interactive problem solving'* (1995; v). In the remainder of this section we will illustrate how each volume refers to relevant empirical data in their presentation of the teaching materials.

Koester examines specifically how language is used in business and the workplace, referring to a variety of different situations and drawing on a diverse set of real life data. Meetings and negotiations are dealt with for spoken discourse, for instance, as are genres such as promotional letters and emails for written discourse, and the volume also deals expertly with the distinction between general language and business language. The extracts used to illustrate the volume are drawn from the empirical work of applied linguists such as Drew and Heritage (1992), Carter and McCarthy (1997) and Bhatia (1993), and Koester also suggests that students refer to the work of a number of others whose work we have discussed elsewhere in this volume, e.g. Cameron (2000b); Louhiala-Salminen (1999); Bargiela-Chiappini and Harris (1997). Data 5.5 shows an activity taken from Unit three, Written workplace genres, in which the students are presented with Bhatia's discussion of the move structure in sales promotion letters (not reproduced here) and are then asked to re-apply it to a new text (Bhatia, 1993), a UK printer's letter. Each activity is followed by a detailed commentary, e.g. in this case an analysis of the letter according to Bhatia (1993), and it often leads on to an additional activity, e.g. in this case an additional text to analyse, a US advertiser's letter, that forms an interesting cross-cultural contrast to the first text. Quote 5.4 shows part of the commentary that Koester provides in relation to this cross-cultural analysis. The activities and commentaries are clearly linked to the findings of research, and they are designed to introduce students to these findings and to encourage them to continue on to read them for themselves via the references and ideas for Further Reading.

Data 5.5   An example of a data-driven student activity

Activity

Read Text 9: Printer's Letter, which is a sales promotion letter from a British printer aimed at companies who might need their services for labels, stationery or other products.

Which of the above moves are used in the letter?

Where does each move begin and end? (Note that a move does not necessarily correspond to a paragraph.)

Based on your analysis of the letter, which moves would you say always occur in a sales promotion letter, i.e. are obligatory, and which are optional?

(Koester, 2004: 36)

Quote 5.4   Data-driven textbook commentary

All these features of the letter have the purpose of capturing the attention of the reader, and this is of course designed to serve the overall purpose of the genre – to persuade the reader to 'buy'. Does this mean that this letter is therefore a better sales promotion letter than the previous one? The answer is that it depends on the cultural context, as the differences we observe between these two letters may be due to national and/or business culture. Bhatia notes that Move 3, offering incentives, is particularly common in Singapore and other countries in the East. Neither of the letters we have looked at, both from western countries, have this move. But the features of the advertiser's letter identified above seem more typical of a North American than a British style of writing. In British culture, such a letter could be considered 'over the top', and might therefore not be successful. The differences may also have something to do with the type of business: advertising is typically associated with more 'hype', whereas this may not be considered appropriate in the printing industry. However, we would need more examples of sales promotion letters from each type of business to be sure.

(Koester, 2004: 42)

Investigating Workplace Discourse (2006), *Workplace Discourse* (2010/2012) & *the Business Advantage Series* (e.g. 2012)

In the past eight years, Almut Koester has gone on to publish two further volumes on workplace discourse, which take a data-driven approach to research. She has also collaborated on the *Business Advantage* series of textbooks, designed to teach international business English. In *Investigating Workplace Discourse* (2006), for instance, she outlines the different analytical approaches that can be taken in the investigation of both written and spoken forms of (business) discourse, and in *Workplace Discourse* (2010/2012) she continues this account, looking not only at specific aspects of how people communicate in the workplace including the use of humour, and the impact of English as an international language, but also at how to teach workplace discourse. And in the *Business Advantage* series, Koester and her co-authors show how research like this may then be applied in the generation of appropriate teaching materials through reference to established corpora like the CANBEC corpus that we have discussed elsewhere in this volume.

Koester's work provides an excellent introduction to the research and pedagogy that underpins the European approach to understanding more about how people get their work done in business organizations.

Koester, A. (2012). *Workplace discourse*. London: Continuum.
Koester, A. (2006). *Investigating workplace discourse*. London: Routledge.
Koester, A., Pitt, A., Handford, M., & Lisboa, M. (2012). *Business Advantage: Theory, Practice, Skills* (intermediate level). Cambridge: Cambridge University Press.

Hogarth and Burnett's teaching materials are also clearly linked to empirical research findings, in general to the work of applied linguists such as Kaplan (i.e. Kaplan, 1966), Thomas (i.e. Thomas, 1983) and Williams (i.e. Williams, 1988), and specifically to the study of interactive strategies by Willing (i.e. Willing,

1992). Although they were produced almost twenty years ago, they remain a pertinent (and singular) example of how research may be used directly to generate a set of teaching materials. The materials centre on the four main functions that Willing associated with interactive signalling, i.e. *acknowledgement ('yeah'), guidance ('in a case like this'), clarification ('I mean')* and *repair ('I didn't mean that quite as badly as it sounded')*, and they present learners with a series of activities designed to focus on and practise the discourse markers that realize each one, in the process of interactive problem solving. In Part 1, for instance, which aims 'To increase students' awareness of how discourse can be structured in English to increase clarity when presenting information or discussing problems during work consultations' (Hogarth & Burnett, 1995: 1) the students are first asked to listen to an interaction between an Australian-English speaker and an NESB speaker and to answer a series of questions designed to raise their awareness of the differences between the speakers. They are then asked to listen to a second transcript of the same Australian-English speaker summarizing the same problem, followed by a similar series of awareness raising questions (see Data 5.6). The section continues with a worksheet focusing on Kaplan's concept of different cultural thought patterns (Kaplan, 1966) in which students are asked to consider their own thought patterns compared to Anglo-Saxon thought patterns, e.g. a circular or indirect way of organizing information compared to a linear way of organizing information, and it concludes with a series of further transcripts and related activities, all designed to present and practise the discourse markers identified in Willing's study. Data 5.7 reproduces one of the Worksheets taken from the section.

Data 5.6   An example of a data-driven student activity

Section 1, Unit 1 – Presenting Information
Transcript 2 (Improvised)

1. Students listen to *Transcript 2* and discuss the following questions:
   a) Do you feel the facts of the problem are presented clearly? Why?
   b) What differences do you notice between Lai Xen and Anna in how they present their information?
   c) Have you had any difficulties either understanding information being presented by Australians or presenting information or a report yourself? What do you feel were the causes of the difficulties in either case?
   d) What difficulties do you think you might have when presenting information to a colleague in the Australian workplace?

(Hogarth & Burnett 1995: 4)

Data 5.7 An example of a data-driven worksheet

Match the discourse markers with the different ways they can be expressed:

A) The main problem is	1) asking for information
B) What you have to do is	2) giving an opinion
C) Just let me explain	3) clarifying what you have said
D) The point is	4) emphasizing the next point/ statement
E) What I think is	5) indicating the main point/problem
F) Something I'd like to ask you	6) indicating you want to explain something
G) What we need to do is	7) giving an example
H) What I meant was	8) interrupting
I) Could I just come in there?	9) giving instructions
J) One example is	10) indicating what needs to be done

Read the following conversation and fill each space with one of the discourse markers below.

Discourse markers: *the most important thing, I'll tell you why, what we've got to do, the other thing was, the trouble is, the problem was.*

A: Listen how did you go yesterday?

B: Oh it was a bit of a disaster actually

A: Yeah? What happened?

B: Well _____ I didn't have all the info really, didn't have time and I was as sick as a dog, couldn't think straight

A: You should have put it off.

B: No couldn't

A: Listen _____ today sometime let's get together and go through that proposal.

B: Yeah look, I'm just really flat out. How about tomorrow?

A: Ah well umm I'd like to get into it pretty quickly actually _____ we're supposed to have the whole proposal done by the 20th, doesn't give us much time.

B: Look _____ for me at the moment is to finish what I'm on. Can we just leave it for a couple of days and . . .

A: Yeah Alright I guess we can wait till then.

(Hogarth & Burnett, 1995: 11, slightly adapted)

Two recent data driven textbooks

The 2012 publication by Stephanie Schnurr on *Exploring Professional Communication* is a data-driven textbook for advanced students of applied linguistics and communication with an interest in looking at what plays a role in the communication that takes place in the contemporary workplace. Schnurr looks in turn at a number of important aspects of professional communication, including gender, leadership, culture and identity, using authentic data first in order to then lead 'back to front' to the relevant theory.

Likewise, the 2010 publication by Jane Lockwood and Heather McCarthy also begins each chapter with a piece of authentic data, but this time for a very different audience: the growing population around the world who aspire to work in the call centre industry. Each chapter of *Contact US* begins with the text of an authentic call which students are encouraged to discuss, and the volume also grounds itself in the general principles of sociolinguistics, including discussing the relationship between language and culture, as well as in the specific work by Earley and Ang (2003) on how to approach intercultural training.

Schnurr, S. (2012). *Exploring professional communication: Language in action.* London & New York: Routledge.
Lockwood, J., & McCarthy, H. (2010). *Contact US.* Cambridge: Cambridge University Press.

These are clearly very different textbooks designed for a very different audience. What they share, however, is a reliance on authentic data in the presentation of examples, together with the disciplinary knowledge of the authors concerned as a result of their own research work in the same area.

5.5   Commentary

The approach taken in the six sets of published materials that we have reviewed in this chapter also reflects some of the hallmarks of and developments in business discourse research that we discussed in Part 1. In Chapter 1, for instance, we discussed the fact that many business discourse researchers have chosen a neutral stance in their analytical approach and in the presentation of their findings. The practice-driven US-based materials reviewed in the first part of this chapter also reflect this largely neutral, i.e. non-critical, approach. In contrast, in both Chapters 1 and 2 in Part 1, we have identified a relatively recent tendency for business discourse researchers to turn to qualitative methods of analysis, together with a critical, and often purposely emancipatory, approach.

The theory-driven materials in the second part of this chapter also reflect this tendency from within the context of the UK-Business School environment. Finally, in Chapter 1 in Part 1, we observed that many business discourse researchers, particularly those concerned with the analysis of language, have chosen to work exclusively with authentic data. The two final sets of materials discussed in this chapter are clearly a reflection of this data-driven approach, with their reliance on empirical studies of what people actually say and write in different business organizations.

Further reading

Bremner, S. (2010). Collaborative writing: Bridging the gap between the textbook and the workplace. *English for Specific Purposes, 29*, 121–32. A discussion on how textbooks may help students make the transition from the classroom to the workplace.

Brett, P. (2000). Integrating multimedia into the Business English curriculum: a case study. *English for Specific Purposes, 19*, 269–90. An author's account of a research-based evaluation of his own published teaching materials.

Clampitt, P. (2000). *Communicating for managerial effectiveness* (2nd edn.). Beverly Hills: Sage. A classic practice-based textbook in the US tradition.

Jones, A., & Sin, S. (2004b). *Generic skills in accounting: Competencies for students and graduates.* Sydney: Prentice Hall/Pearson Education. A research-based textbook for accountants in the LSP tradition that focuses on how communicative skills contribute to professional expertise.

Lucas, U., & Tan, P. (2011). Developing a capacity to engage in critical reflection: students' 'ways of knowing' within an undergraduate business and accounting programme, *Studies in Higher Education, 38*(1), 1–20, DOI:10.1080/03075079.2011.569706. A study of what business and accountancy students consider to be knowledge at a business school in the United Kingdom.

Chapter 5 Tasks

1. Look at the series of publications that Almut Koester has been involved with over the past decade (e.g. Koester, 2004; Koester, 2006; Koester, 2012; Koester, Pitt, Handford & Lisboa, 2012) and decide how her research-based work is related to her authored and co-authored teaching materials. Choose a specific example related to written business discourse to support your discussion.
2. Read pages 250 to 260 in Handford (2010a), *The language of business meetings*. Explain how you would use a corpus of spoken business discourse to generate a set to teaching materials. Illustrate your discussion with examples.

Part III
Researching Business Discourse

6
Themes and Research Strategies

This chapter will explore the link between business discourse research and the real world. It will:

- profile selected studies to illustrate a number of central themes and research strategies (survey studies, corpus research, ethnographic studies and experiments) in practice-based research on business discourse;
- consider what practice-based research has revealed about business discourse, business communication practices and the nature of the business environment;
- provide suggestions for further reading by referencing similar and relevant practice-based research throughout.

Introduction

Practice-based business discourse research is aimed at describing organizational communication *in situ* and gaining an understanding of the factors that shape it. Practice-based studies have been inspired by the need to characterize business discourse and business communication practices in an ever-changing business environment, impacted by advances in communication technology and increased globalization. Another aim of practice-based research has been to inform business language teaching and corporate training by determining what core communication skills business practitioners require to be successful, with particular emphasis on international business. This focus on contextualizing communication practices has been a hallmark of business discourse research since the mid-1990s. Among other things, practice-based studies have investigated practices in a variety of discourse communities and corporate communication contexts, the nature of business discourse in different genres, and how various new media and technologies have affected interpersonal organizational communication and the business message.

This chapter will consider central themes in practice-based business discourse research, by showcasing example studies that have contributed to our knowledge of business communication practices and of business discourse across genres. In doing so, the chapter will illustrate the research strategies such studies have employed – often in combination – to gain access to authentic data and insights from members of relevant business discourse communities. These include (needs analysis) surveys, text-based corpus studies, ethnographic (case) studies and, more rarely, experimental studies. In addition to reflecting a high degree of multimethodology, approaches to the study of business communication practices have tended to be multidisciplinary as well. In Chapter 7, we will therefore go on to consider in some detail methodologies and analytical frameworks from a variety of disciplines that have been used in business discourse research, including practice-based research. We will also provide suggestions for individual, collaborative or group research projects.

6.1   Corporate communicative practices in Brazil (Barbara, Celani, Collins & Scott, 1996)

An important focus of practice-based research has been to describe business discourse practices and skills needs in relevant business communities, and to identify and describe salient patterns of communication in or across different corporate contexts. The study of communication patterns and skills needs in Brazilian firms by Leila Barbara and colleagues (1996) identified users of business English and Portuguese in different types of business organizations and determined the communication types (written and oral) most widely used for national and international business dealings. The investigation was part of a larger international project (DIRECT: the Development of International Research in English for Commerce and Technology) concerned with describing and analysing business discourse in relevant contexts in order to provide a research base to support training programmes in the specific skills identified, as well as the development of teaching materials.

This investigation is an example of a survey-based study (see also Chapter 4) that not only provides an extensive overview of the written and oral communication tasks undertaken by Portuguese-speaking business practitioners in a specific region in Brazil, but also promotes our understanding of the influence aspects of the wider corporate context can have on communicative practices in organizations which operate internationally.

Concept 6.1   Survey research and needs analysis

Conducting a survey is a strategy for systematically gathering information from a potentially large group of informants relatively quickly, especially when human behaviour, opinions and attitudes are under study. A written survey can generate both *quantitative* and *qualitative* data that are collected from relevant informant groups through self-completion questionnaires. Questionnaires are quicker to administer than interviews, and the data are generally easier to process in terms of quantification and analysis. Because the information is controlled by the questions, questionnaire data allow for a high degree of clarity and precision. However, questionnaires need to be carefully constructed and must always be piloted to test their reliability, avoid ambiguity, and to ensure a balance between generating sufficient data and not overtaxing informants. In business discourse research, surveys are commonly used to determine members of a corporate community's attitudes, preferences and judgments regarding aspects of business discourse and, in particular, to study communication practices and needs in different types of organizations (see e.g. Deneire, 2008; Erling & Walton, 2007; Randall & Samimi, 2010).

Methodology

Barbara and colleagues surveyed 214 organizations located in and around São Paulo, a large industrial city in Brazil. The survey was based on a written questionnaire designed to collect information about the communication tasks undertaken by the organizations, the purposes of – and media employed – within those tasks, and the language(s) used in national/international business settings. Another aim was to obtain information about the organizations themselves (see Data 6.1 for an overview of variables). The researchers chose the questionnaire format in favour of interviews as their study involved a large number of respondents, and written questionnaires generally allow for easier and quicker data collection than interviews, without the researcher having to be present. Of the 1347 questionnaires that were mailed initially to organizations in the greater São Paulo area, 222 questionnaires were returned (16.5 per cent). A number of these were found to be incomplete and subsequently excluded from the study. As a result, the final sample consisted of 214 questionnaires.

Data 6.1   The variables studied in Barbara et al. (1996)

- Organizational profile (that is, number of employees, type, location);
- Type of documents – written and oral (that is, report, memo, meeting, presentation, and so on);
- Purpose of documents (that is, promotion, information, negotiation, decision, analysis, and so on);
- Target group of documents (that is, shareholders, clients, factory, and so on);

- Medium of delivery (that is, fax, email, telephone, and so on);
- Frequency of use of documents (that is, frequent or infrequent);
- Language of documents/oral communication (that is, Portuguese, English or other);
- Number of documents produced in different languages.

Main findings

The data revealed a number of communication patterns in the business community under study. Of the seven (written and spoken) document types distinguished, reports, memos and meetings were the most frequently used types in the 214 organizations surveyed. Overall, over 90 per cent of document types were produced in Portuguese, although for the same document types, foreign languages (and English most often) were used as well. In short, although the Brazilian organizations in the survey obviously used native Portuguese most often in their business dealings, the large majority used English too, not only for conducting business externally, but also internally. Other foreign languages were used in international contacts, but to a much lesser extent.

The survey results also suggested differences in corporate and communication activity between companies with different profiles. Size and type of organization (that is, industrial versus non-industrial) determined the use of English: the larger, industrial organizations in the region used English more than the smaller non-industrial corporations. Companies in these categories also reported using the widest range of document types.

Implications and relationship with similar studies

This survey-based investigation, as well as providing an extensive overview of communication patterns in Brazilian organizations in and around São Paulo, promotes our understanding of the influence that aspects of the business environment (that is, business sector, size) can have on communicative practices in organizations which operate internationally (see also the discussion of Nickerson, 1998, and Vandermeeren, 1999, below). Also, the findings confirm the status of English as a widely used lingua franca in international business. In the organizations surveyed, it was reported to be the most commonly used language (other than Portuguese) in both written and spoken contexts, and in external and internal communication. The widespread use of English as a lingua franca in business has also been observed in practice-based studies by, for example, Nickerson (1999), Louhiala-Salminen (2002), Louhiala-Salminen, Charles and Kankaanranta (2005), Evans (2010), and Kankaanranta and Planken (2010).

Quote 6.1

> [I]f the discourse community is central to the notion of genre (Swales, 1990b) and the discourse community itself uses a variety of terms with no straightforward one-to-one relationship between term and function, this raises questions about the potential fuzziness (fuzzy edges or fuzzy membership) of the discourse community itself. (Barbara et al., 1996: 69)

From a methodological perspective, Barbara et al.'s (1996) study throws light on some of the difficulties involved in research involving data collected from informants using indirect methods, such as the written survey (interviews or telephone surveys would be regarded as direct methods of data collection). For example, the researchers report noting a mismatch between what they meant by the labels used for different document types in the written questionnaire and the respondents' perception of the meanings of these labels. This disagreement in terminology existed not only between the researchers and informants, but also between practitioners in different organizations and effectively raises an interesting theoretical point. If it is assumed that the discourse community (in this case, the business community of São Paulo) is central to the notion of genre (that is, document type) as it is defined by Swales (1990b), and the discourse community is found to be using different labels to refer to one and the same document, with no clear or consistent relationship between label and purpose, this raises a question about the robustness of the concept of discourse community itself, and more specifically, of its boundaries and its role in defining genres within organizational genre systems. We will further discuss the concepts of genre and discourse community in Chapter 7, and consider genre theory in more detail as an analytical framework in Chapter 8.

Further examples of studies that have used (needs analysis) surveys to investigate business discourse practices in international or multinational contexts include Deneire's (2008) investigation of managers' and employees' English language proficiency needs in French companies in which English is the corporate language, Erling and Walton's (2007) study of (foreign) language use and needs in multinational companies based in Germany, Randall and Samimi (2010) who trace the transition from Arabic to English as a lingua franca by investigating the languages needed by the Dubai Police Force, Chew's (2005) analysis of language needs in banks in Hong Kong and the interplay between English and Cantonese in daily communicative tasks, and Jackson's (2004) study investigating the language and communication skills needs of pre-experience business practitioners (students at the bilingual Hong Kong university). Chew's and Jackson's studies were in fact part of a larger project (reported in Bhatia & Candlin, 2001, see Chapter 3 for a detailed discussion), whose main impetus was to gain an understanding of the learning situation and skills needs of business practitioners of the future in bilingual Hong Kong, in order to subsequently develop relevant course content – with a specific emphasis on English for Specific Business Purposes – for tertiary level programmes. Other examples of needs-focused studies whose complementary aim was to inform curriculum development are Cowling's (2007) investigation of workplace language and communication needs to develop English language intensive courses for a large Japanese industrial firm and Kaewpet's (2009) investigation of Thai civil engineering students' (English) communication needs (for course development in tertiary education). Finally, Evans (2010), in a study of the role of written and spoken English in relation to local languages (written Chinese, Cantonese and Putonghua) in four different service industries in Hong Kong, pinpointed learner needs that might be addressed in teaching English to future employees in this specific sector.

Early examples of studies, like Barbara et al.'s (1996), that investigated business discourse practices specifically in light of corporate characteristics include the investigations by Sonja Vandermeeren (1999) and Catherine Nickerson (1998) at the end of the nineties. Vandermeeren (see also Chapter 1) determined the use of foreign languages in written communication between companies in a number of German, French and Dutch companies, and considered the relationship between aspects of the corporate profile and the language used with foreign trading partners. Her findings illustrate clear differences in language use between companies in the three countries, and unexpectedly perhaps, that English was not the dominant lingua franca in correspondence. In Dutch–German contacts, German as a business language clearly dominated, while French and German companies seemed to alternate between two competing strategies, either using English as a lingua franca, or choosing to 'adapt' and communicate in the first language of the business partner. Nickerson conducted a survey-based study to investigate how corporate culture (defined as the relationship between a corporation's head office and its subsidiaries) impacted on non-native corporate writers of English working in a multinational context. She examined whether characteristics of this relationship, such as the degree of operational autonomy allowed to subsidiaries, influenced business discourse practices within subsidiaries. The study provides evidence that written communicative practices within British-owned Dutch subsidiaries are, at least in part, a product of the larger corporation's culture. Corporate culture determined whether head office insisted on receiving corporate documents in English, even when these were relevant only to Dutch employees. Also, Dutch subsidiaries were required to report back in English to head office regularly, even when they enjoyed a high degree of operational autonomy. Finally, in subsidiaries where head office had placed a British employee in a senior position, many of the documents originating within that subsidiary were in English to allow the British senior manager access, despite the fact that he or she may have been the only non-Dutch speaking employee.

The investigations in this section are all examples of practice-based business discourse research whose primary aim was to characterize communication practices in multilingual corporate contexts and to identify factors that influence those practices. In doing so, they have also provided potentially relevant input for business discourse teaching in tertiary education and corporate training settings.

6.2   Email and English in an Anglo-Dutch multinational (Nickerson, 1999)

As evidenced by a number of the studies referenced under 6.1, an important point of interest in studies of business discourse in international contexts has been the use of English as a lingua franca in, mostly written, text types. Nickerson's (1999) study provides an insight into the use of English in one division of a large Dutch multinational corporation, and combines a case study approach with a text-based corpus investigation (see Concept 6.2) featuring what was a relatively new computer-mediated business discourse at the time, namely business email (but see also e.g., Collot & Belmore, 1996; Gains, 1999; Mulholland, 1999; Gimenez, 2000, 2002, 2006; Louhiala-Salminen, 2002; Kankaanranta, 2006). Nickerson's study provides many illustrative examples of how Dutch and English interplay in email communication in the Dutch multinational context, and pinpoints why and when English is selected as the appropriate code in favour of the local language.

Methodology

The emails for the corpus were supplied by a Dutch-speaking manager working in a large Dutch-owned multinational. Initially, they were collected during a period of two months, from six managers in the technological department of the Dutch division of the multinational.

Concept 6.2   Corpus-based approaches

Collecting a *corpus of discourse* is a useful research strategy in situations where the researcher wants to engage in an in-depth linguistic analysis of a specific genre of business discourse or a particular text type, or where the researcher wants to test assumptions or hypotheses about language use on an empirical (quantitative) basis. By studying a corpus (or corpora), the researcher aims to make generalizations about aspects of discourse (or language). A corpus is a body or *collection* of (written or spoken) texts. There is no fixed size for a corpus, or a specific description of what it should contain. Depending on the focus of the study, for instance, a corpus could contain the annual reports for 2004 of the top 50 companies in the Fortune 500, transcriptions of a series of board meetings at a Swedish bank, the emails sent and received in a given month by a customer service employee, or the corporate blogs published in a given financial quarter by every fifth company on the Corporate Social Responsibility Index. In practice-based business discourse research, studies investigating specific types of business discourse and how they evolve commonly incorporate corpus-based analysis as a methodology, where the corpus is ideally a collection of *authentic* examples, that is, examples of the discourse type produced by members of a business discourse community, in a business context, or as part of a business activity. More recently, corpus-based analysis has increasingly been used in combination with other quantitative and/or qualitative methodologies to study not only how business discourse is instantiated and used, but also how it is shaped and received (see Chapter 8 for examples of multimethod studies that incorporate corpus analysis, amongst other methods).

Common approaches: (manual or computerized) text analysis (language and/or content), moves analysis (structure), contextual analysis to determine the situational factors that play a role in text construction (on the basis of desk research on related corporate documents, observation of collaborative corporate writing processes, interviews with writers and readers, and so on), contrastive analysis (e.g., of two text types), cross-cultural analysis (e.g., of the same business discourse in two or more countries, or two or more corporate contexts).

- Hyland, Huat and Handford (2012) provide many examples of applied corpus analysis, while Baker discusses approaches to discourse analysis (Baker, 2006) and to sociolinguistic research (Baker, 2010), using techniques from corpus linguistics;
- Flowerdew's (2012) volume illustrates the interdisciplinary nature of corpus linguistics, as well as best practices and central themes in this field, by highlighting the role of corpora as a data source in a variety of disciplines;
- For an overview of a large number of studies that have used Wordsmith Tools to investigate a variety of discourses, see Mike Scott's online resource: www.lexically.net/wordsmith/corpus_linguistics_links/articles_using_wordsmith.htm

Two of the managers were native speakers of Dutch and four of English, although all spoke and wrote both languages at a level of proficiency that allowed them to participate in departmental meetings in either language. From the initial corpus, the incoming and outgoing messages from one of the

Dutch-speaking managers were selected for further investigation, since he had provided a large number of messages from which a random sample of 100 emails could easily be drawn. These messages (the corpus) were analysed with respect to the situations in which English was required, the communicative purpose of the messages in English, the use of English in the structure (that is, in the layout) of the emails, and one discourse feature, the use of corporate-bound lexis, that is vocabulary that refers to the way business processes and activities are organized.

Main findings

Nearly a quarter of the messages in Nickerson's corpus contained English. Of the three message types (incoming, outgoing and forwarded) the majority that used English were addressed to multiple recipients (between two and fifty), while additional groups of employees were copied in to more than half. According to Nickerson, the fact that a proportion of English messages in the corpus were addressed to more than 200 recipients in total, and the fact that all department managers and senior managers in a given division were copied in as part of the circulation list, suggests that email was not only used as a source of information exchange, but that a considerable amount of information, at all levels of the organization, was circulated in English, regardless of whether recipients were English-speaking or not. Taken together, the findings provide clear evidence that the use of email in general, and the use of English email in particular, were already clearly embedded in the organizational practices of this Dutch multinational at the time, where the large majority of management executives and employees were (and are) Dutch-speaking.

Data 6.2   Aspects of English use studied in Nickerson (1999)

- Code (that is, Dutch, English or another language) used per message type (that is, incoming, outgoing or forwarded messages);
- Situations in which English was required (that is, the corporate unit or department involved in the communication);
- Communicative purpose of messages sent and received in English;
- Use of English in the structure of the emails in the corpus (that is, in their layout);
- Use of corporate-bound lexis (that is, the use of lexis or vocabulary that refers to corporate procedures, units and designations).

Nickerson's study also throws light on the interaction between the local language, Dutch, and the lingua franca, English. Within forwarded chains of email transmissions in the corpus, considerable reference was made – as part of the organizing process – to written (electronic) internal sources of information.

In the specific department under investigation, those electronic reference sources were both in English and in Dutch. With respect to corporate writers' reasons for using English in favour of the local language, Nickerson's analysis suggests that this decision was minimally determined by two situational factors. First, Dutch employees tended to communicate in Dutch within their division, unless a non-Dutch speaking employee also required access to the information, in which case they used English. Second, and in accordance with corporate policy, any corporate electronic communication to external parties (outside the division, but not necessarily outside the organization) was always in English, regardless of the originator or the recipient. Finally, the selection of English versus Dutch seemed to relate to the communicative purpose of a given transmission: if the purpose was to report officially on the organizational process, the message tended to be in English, even if all those involved in the communication were Dutch-speaking.

Quote 6.2

> One practical outcome of future research is expected to be insights on the nature of the writing tasks which many non-native corporate users of English are required to complete in order to be effective members of the growing multinational and multilingual business community.
>
> (Nickerson, 1999: 53)

Implications and relationship with similar studies

Although the business discourse practices Nickerson describes and motivates are based on the findings of a single case study, and pertinent only to a specific division in a Dutch multinational, they provide useful information on several aspects of corporate e-communication, the use of English in a largely non-native corporate environment, and the role of (computer-)mediated discourse and English in managing divisions of corporations. The case study illustrates that email, still a relatively new genre at the time, was already a major source of information exchange within (multinational) corporations, forming a 'fluid database of corporate knowledge' that was frequently referred to in the management process. In this way, the findings provide a strong indication that, within this particular multinational at least, the structuring of the organization itself is achieved in part through the production and distribution of information by email, and in particular by email in English.

Nickerson's findings regarding the use of English by non-native corporate writers have clear implications for corporate training policy in multinationals. They serve to highlight the fact that employees in multinationals need to be able to communicate effectively – in this particular instance by email – about a variety of different tasks, to achieve a variety of different communicative purposes, with people from at least one other culture than their own, and in at least two languages, one of which is a foreign language (i.e. English). Not surprisingly, Nickerson found that the non-native writers in her study felt the need for skills training (particularly in the foreign language) and would have welcomed corporate training in these areas had it been made available to them. This indicates that organizations that choose to introduce a corporate language other than the native language(s) of their employees would do well to put in place a corporate policy that affords 'non-native' employees the opportunity to train for the required skills. Other studies since Nickerson (1999) that have underlined the communication skills needs of employees in organizations that operate internationally, and have subsequently made recommendations regarding corporate training policy, include Louhiala-Salminen, Charles and Kankaanranta's study of the communication (and English) skills required by employees in two large Scandinavian corporations (2005, see Chapter 8 for a detailed discussion), Chew's needs analysis of the English language skills required by new graduate employees in four Hong Kong banks (2005), and Cowling's (2007) study of communication needs in a Japanese company. More recently still, Kaewpet (2009) investigated Thai engineering students' (English) communication needs and Evans (2010) examined the interface between English and 'local' languages in the Hong Kong service industry. It would seem, therefore, that needs analysis continues to be a fruitful approach to investigate different corporate communities of practice in various business sectors and across cultural and language situations, in business discourse research aimed specifically at yielding insights that can form the basis for directly relevant (in-company) training recommendations.

6.3   Between text and context: the mission statement (Swales & Rogers, 1995)

Practice-based studies of business discourse aimed at investigating the nature of specific business discourse types have not only considered textual aspects, but also how a text type is socially constructed by members of the corporate discourse community in which it occurs. Such investigations necessarily involve a consideration of how the wider corporate context plays a role in the development of the discourse type; they aim to explain discourse from a socio-cultural and institutional perspective, and often combine linguistic or textual analysis with ethnographic methods to determine why corporate discourse community members write and use certain text types in the ways that they do. Another objective of these investigations, particularly of newer business discourses (such as email, corporate blogs, online consumer reviews, webpages), has been to determine whether such text types can be regarded as 'genres', or systemically distinct discourses (see Chapter 7 for a discussion of genre analysis and the emergence of new genres). John Swales and Priscilla Rogers' study of the genesis and construction of the mission statement as an organizational text type is a classic example of a genre-based investigation that combines corpus analysis, case study research and ethnographic methods (desk research and interviews). Its primary aims were to characterize the mission statement and to determine whether it constitutes a genre, and to trace the creation and development of a specific set of mission statements within their wider corporate context.

Methodology

The study employed a multimethod approach that combined a text-based analysis of a corpus of 100 mission statements with a detailed contextual analysis of the organizational 'framing' of three such texts. The contextual analysis considered the history, authorship and institutional function of the texts within the corporation in which they originated. Employees involved in creating the mission statements were interviewed, in order to establish the reasons for writing such documents, and to determine what role they played in organizations. Corporate policy documents were studied to gain insight into the corporations' histories and corporate processes and philosophies. The study thus incorporates many methods that could be considered ethnographic in their approach (see Concept 6.3).

The initial corpus of mission statements was collected from 100 large US organizations associated with the University of Michigan School of Business Administration (the researchers' employer at the time of the study). The corpus texts were used to arrive at an initial characterization of the text type. The texts appeared under a variety of different headings, such as 'Our Mission', 'Our Commitment', 'A View to the Future', and most often 'Mission Statement'. In terms of message content, they were geared less towards structuring or prescribing everyday corporate procedures and activities (that is, placing an order, handling a complaint, negotiating a contract, and so on) but rather towards carrying and projecting a corporation's culture and ideology. Although the terminology and style of the texts did not appear to be fully stabilized, the researchers regarded them sufficiently similar to consider them as a single genre, distinct from other text types.

Concept 6.3   Ethnographic research and case study research

Ethnographic research is *collaborative* and *contextual*. It is collaborative because it involves various participants, including the researcher and relevant (groups of) informants, and it is contextual because it is carried out in the environment in which the informants work, or in which the phenomenon under investigation manifests itself. In business discourse research, for example, ethnographic researchers locate their investigations within (departments in) organizations and gauge the perspectives and opinions of informants who work in business, and of the counterparts, customers and clients they communicate with. A much-used method in ethnographic research is the *case study*: a means to characterize a particular situation or process by describing in detail the reality of participants' experiences, attitudes and thoughts in the situation, or while conducting the process. In business discourse research, *cases* may include companies, departments, or business people. Ethnographic approaches to data can be characterized as *interpretive* and *organic*. It is the researcher who interprets the data, and hypotheses and generalizations emerge during the phases of data collection and analysis, rather than being predetermined. Throughout the ethnographic, iterative research cycle, it is important that the role of the researcher remains as *unobtrusive* as possible; she can observe and participate in the activities being investigated, but should do so without intruding on the informants or manipulating the phenomena under study.

Commonly used data collection methods, often employed in combination (see also Concept 7.3), include: observation, interview, fieldwork, informants' self-report (that is, diary or logbook), questionnaire, think-aloud protocol, desk research (e.g., of related documentation or relevant corporate information).

More information on linguistic ethnography, ethnographic research and training can be found on the Linguistic Ethnography Forum's online resource: http://www.ling-ethnog.org.uk

From the corpus, a sample of 30 representative texts was analysed further with regard to content and textual features (see Quote 6.3). In general, the mission statements seemed to be extensions of the goals, values and purposes of the corporations that published them, and originated at the level of the CEO and senior management. All the mission statements shared the aim of encouraging and fostering identification with the corporation, serving as a management tool for promoting corporate culture and values, and for encouraging employees to 'buy into' that culture and values.

Quote 6.3   General characteristics of mission statements

The Mission Statements in the sample are pithy and up-beat . . . , somewhat like inspirational speeches. . . . There is an almost total absence of . . . 'support' (that is, examples, comparisons, quotations, statistics, visuals and the like). [T]he content of these texts largely consists of general statements, claims and conclusions. It is not surprising then that the verb forms are predominantly the present, the imperative ('Return to underwriting profit – Chubb & Son) and the purpose infinitive ('To provide a caring environment for staff' – Bank of Ireland; 'To be the safest carrier' – Conrail). If modals occur they are typically of the un-hedged variety such as Kodak's 'We *will* be a globally competitive high growth company . . . ' or EID-Perry Farm Products' 'All the business activities *must* maximize satisfaction to customers . . . '. Frequently used nouns are goals, principles and values, and the texts draw their colour mostly from a variety of adjectives that are used to characterize activities in a positive light, such as *competent, creative, enthusiastic, leading* and *profitable.*

(Swales & Rogers, 1995: 226–7)

The final stage of the study centred on the case histories of three mission statements from two large US corporations. Interviews with relevant informants within the corporations (e.g., policy committee members and senior management) were held to determine the motives and strategic corporate goals underlying the statements and to gain an overview of the development of, and textual changes in, the text over time in relation to the corporations' histories and performance. To gain insight into the framing of these mission statements within the corporate environment, the researchers consulted a large number of other corporate policy documents.

Main findings and relationship with similar studies

The main picture that emerged was that mission statements are indeed a genre that is clearly distinct from other corporate text types in a number of ways (see Quote 6.3). They have the strategic objective to inspire commitment and involvement in a workforce that may number thousands of employees, potentially distributed around the globe.

In terms of its methodology, Swales and Rogers' study remains an excellent early example of how a detailed corpus-based content and text analysis, in combination with an in-depth consideration of the corporate and wider historical context in which a text type is situated, can provide a comprehensive insight into the genesis, creation and impact of a specific genre as a situated response to an emerging rhetorical need. In the case of the mission statement, this is the need to 'creat[e] allegiance and inspir[e] commitment within and to a constructed discourse community' (Swales & Rogers, 1995: 237).

Other examples of corpus-based business discourse research include an investigation of Chinese sales genres by Zhu (2000) and Flowerdew and Wan's (2006) genre-based study of tax computation letters, which were both conducted in the tradition of Swales (1990a) and Bhatia (1993). Using a corpus of authentic sales letters, requests raised by subordinates and official approvals, Zhu's study provides a discussion of the development of these specific sales genres in relation to the changing social and economic context in China. By considering the genres in the periods before and after the reform and economic opening-up in 1978, she illustrates how their use over time reflects China's gradual move towards a market economy and how sales letters in particular emerged to meet the communicative needs of the Chinese business community in the period following economic policy change. Zhu also uses an analysis of authentic examples of the three sales genres in terms of communicative purpose and moves structure to show that their use has been largely determined by the changing nature of reader–writer relationships in the two economic climates (before and after 1978). For an extensive methodological description of Zhu's cross-cultural genre research into rhetorical patterns in Chinese versus English sales genres, see Zhu (2005). In Flowerdew and Wan's (2006) study, a corpus of authentic computation letters was analysed in terms of the letters' structure (i.e. moves), the communicative purposes of different categories of moves, and the lexico-grammatical realizations of moves. Here too, genre was approached from a contextualized, ethnographic perspective, by considering the behaviour and writing practices of tax accountants in situ, by studying how they prepared information to be included in the letters as well as the way in which they structured and wrote the letters (through observations of writing practices in the workplace and interviews with tax accountants). Like Swales and Rogers' study of mission statements, Flowerdew and Wan's multimethod and multiperspective investigation of computation letters offers a comprehensive view of how this particular genre comes about and is manifested within and by the specific accounting discourse community under study, as well as providing a detailed, genre-based description of the moves, communicative purposes and lexico-grammatical realizations (of moves) that constitute and characterize the genre.

Implications of Swales and Rogers' study

Swales and Rogers' (1995) study concludes that mission statements can be regarded as a generic discourse type that is clearly distinct from other texts that project corporate philosophy, such as ethical codes or standard practice guides. Thus, their investigation constitutes an early demonstration of the usefulness of genre theory (see Concept 7.7) as a descriptive framework that allows for a specific text type to be identified as an appropriate response to a recurring communicative situation by the community that uses it, that is, an email communication will be considered as an appropriate way of disseminating information of a certain type in one corporation (or culture), but not necessarily in another (see also Markus, 1994, for a discussion on this). Above all, the study is an excellent illustration of the added value of a contextualized approach that considers (a) text (type) not only on the basis of linguistic or content analysis, but incorporates an investigation of the context in which a document is produced, in order to gain insight into its creation, the rationale behind it, and its purpose and role in the organization it originates in (see Quote 6.4).

Rogers continues to investigate the relationship between the organizational context and the discourse of the mission statement, and has most recently revisited the changes made in the Dana Corporation's mission statement over a twenty-one year period from 1990 (Rogers & Swales, 1990) to 2011 (Rogers, Gunesekera & Yang, 2011). Rogers et al. (2011) compared Dana's Philosophy and Policy Documents from 1987 and 2004 in order to analyse, on the basis of upper management's revisions and substitutions in the two documents, the language components managers opt for when faced with reformulating the mission statement in such a way as to reflect shifts over time in corporate strategy. In doing so, the researchers identify and suggest the language options (e.g. verbs, thematic devices, modifiers, sentence subjects) that managers can, and should, employ when formulating corporate messages about strategic change. As a follow-up to their study, Rogers et al. suggest an audience-based, experimental study, in which the communicative impact of management's manipulation of language strategies and rhetorical devices such as identified in their study could be tested on relevant target audiences (see section 6.4 and Case Study 8.7 for examples of reader-based experimental research that uses the findings of corpus-based analysis as input).

Quote 6.4   The added value of a 'contextualized' analysis of text types or genres

Although there may be a value in purely textual studies for crosscultural or stylistic purposes, we . . . argu[e] that a useful understanding of the role of genres in institutional and community affairs requires more sociocognitive input than the texts themselves provide. Certainly, the rationales for the three Mission Statements did not leap off their pages, but were enmeshed within the context of corporate history, culture and legend.

Beyond . . . differences in purpose, theme and self-definition, the contextual aspect of the study also reveals that the first two mission statements operate to prevent change, while the third, viewed as both product and process, is designed to encourage it.

(Swales & Rogers, 1995: 236–37)

6.4   English in Dutch job ads: evaluation and comprehension (Van Meurs, Korzilius & Hermans, 2004)

The use of English as an international language is steadily increasing in various communication domains in non-English speaking countries around the world. In Germany, Luxemburg and the Netherlands, for example, English is not 'just' a lingua franca, but also consistently serves functions 'in various social, cultural, commercial and educational' domains (Kachru, 1995: 8–9). An emerging trend in business discourse research on English as a lingua franca has been to consider the effects of using English in business messages aimed at non-English speaking target groups. Here we profile such a study, whose main aim was to determine whether using English in recruitment advertisements aimed at Dutch-speaking applicants affected Dutch readers' comprehension of the text, and their attitudes towards the quality of the text, the job advertised and the company that placed the ad.

Some of the reasons suggested in the literature for the use of English in advertising for non-English speaking target groups is that the language has prestige value, bolsters the image of the company and the product advertised, may affect applicants' motivation to apply, and makes jobs sound more appealing and exciting (van Meurs et al., 2004). The study we profile here set out to empirically test these assumptions and followed previous investigations in the same vein that considered non-native readers' comprehension and appreciation of English in product advertisements in magazines, newspapers and television commercials, and English in job ads in newspapers. These studies are all examples of investigations that used either a corpus analysis, survey or an experimental approach to conduct practice-based research (that is, research involving actual relevant target groups and investigating aspects of business discourse 'in use') with the aim of evaluating business messages and offering practical advice as to how to maximize their effectiveness.

Examples of corpus studies on the use of English in business discourse in non-English speaking countries

- Larson (1990): a corpus study showing that English is frequently used in Swedish job ads, especially in job titles and descriptions of work areas;
- Korzilius, van Meurs & Hermans (2007): a corpus study showing that 39 per cent of job ads in a Dutch national newspaper contained one or more English words, and that 2.4 per cent of job ads were completely in English;
- van Meurs, Korzilius, & den Hollander (2007): a corpus study showing that 88.5 per cent of job ads on the Netherlands Monsterboard.nl recruitment site included one or more English words, while 4 per cent of ads were completely in English;
- Gerritsen, Nickerson, van Hooft, et al. (2007): a comparative (cross-country) corpus study showing that 65 per cent of product advertisements in the glossy magazine *Elle* (published in the local languages) in Belgium, France, Germany, the Netherlands and Spain contained one or more English words.

Methodology

Design and respondents

The study used an experimental design (see Concept 6.4) in which three different manipulated versions of the same job ad were presented to three groups of potential applicants (30 respondents per group). One version of the ad was completely in English, the second version contained 11 English words (the rest of the text was in Dutch), and the third version was completely in Dutch. In terms of content, layout and structure, the three versions were exactly the same. The 90 respondents for the study were students in their final year at the faculties of Arts or Social Sciences at two Dutch universities, or students who had recently graduated from these institutions, as it was thought that these respondents would be about to – or involved in – applying for a job and would therefore be interested in job ads. All respondents were native Dutch-speaking and all had had seven to eight years of formal training in English.

Concept 6.4   Experimental studies

An experiment is essentially a 'test' under defined and controlled conditions to determine an unknown effect, to illustrate or verify a known law or theoretical premise, or to test a hypothesis.

Usually, experiments involve carefully changing one variable and observing the effect on another variable (e.g., altering the order of information elements in a text, and asking members of a relevant target group which version of the text – changed versus original order – they perceive as clearer, more appealing, more user-friendly, and so on).

Key characteristics:

The researcher *manipulates* an independent variable (that is, a text or stylistic feature) in order to establish the effect of that variable on one or more dependent variables (that is, text comprehension, text clarity, and so on). Where possible within the experiment, other variables – besides the dependent and independent variable(s) – are kept *constant*. This is to control potential effects from these variables, which might cause 'white noise' in the experiment. The researcher then *observes* (or measures) the effect of the manipulation of the independent variable on the dependent variable(s).

Experimental studies have been rare in business discourse research, but more recent studies aimed at testing the effectiveness of specific business text types (with respect to aspects of design, content and style) have started using experimental approaches involving evaluation of the text under study by relevant target groups, that is, product advertisements, information leaflets, tax forms, manuals, patient information, and so on (see also case study 8.7). For much of their methodology, these studies rely on the discipline of Document Design.

Materials

The job advertised in the three versions of the ad (English, partly English or Dutch) was that of a management trainee of a fictitious bank, which the researchers assumed to be suitable and appealing to university graduates. The English used in the partly English ad (the second version of the ad) was based on a corpus analysis of 119 ads from a major Dutch national newspaper. Seven of the 11 words used in the partly English ad were among the most frequently occurring words in the corpus and included assessment, business, team player and professional. The remaining four words were less frequent in the corpus. The completely English version of the ad was a direct transla-tion of the partly English and the Dutch versions of the ad and included the 11 English words from the partly English version. As the researchers were all native Dutch speakers, the idiomaticity and naturalness of language in the (partly) English texts in the experiment was checked by two native speak-ers of English. The English text was also back-translated (see Concept 6.5) to ensure that the three versions of the ad were as equivalent as possible. Finally, the three texts were pre-tested, with respect to authenticity and clarity, on personnel officers and human resource managers at a number of Dutch companies.

Concept 6.5   The back translation technique

Back translation is a commonly used technique in cross-cultural research, and involves looking for equivalents in languages through the translation of stimuli, survey items, interview data, central research concepts, and so on. For example, in experiments involving cross-cultural comparisons (e.g., testing the effectiveness of certain language strategies in two target cultures) back translation can help improve the validity and reliability of experimental stimuli in the different languages involved. It requires that the quality of translated stimulus material is verified by an independent translator translating back into the original (source) language. The original and back translated texts are then compared to determine how equivalent the different versions are, and to clarify or remove ambiguities. The higher the equivalence achieved between the two versions of the experimental stimulus, the more valid and reliable the stimulus is considered to be. Back translation is also used in business to develop equivalent advertising texts across cultures, and to minimize language problems and cross-cultural gaffes commonly associated with international marketing campaigns (see e.g. Brislin, 1980).

To collect information on potential applicants' perception of the ads, the respondents were asked to fill in a written questionnaire after they had been presented with the ad (either version 1, 2 or 3). The questionnaire contained seven-point semantic-differential scales to test the effect of English or Dutch in the ad on text evaluation (the intelligibility, attractiveness, and naturalness of the ad), attitudes towards the organization and the job (the organization's image, respondents' attitudes towards working for the organization and the job being offered), and their estimated comprehension of the Dutch or English items in the ad. Respondents were also asked to paraphrase these items, so that their actual comprehension of these items could be determined.

Data 6.3   Part of the English version of the ad used in the experiment

> Van Breederode isn't a bank like other banks. We believe that banking isn't only about finance, but also about style and personal contact. Van Breederode is a trusted name and has an excellent reputation when it comes to client-oriented banking. Offering high-quality service focusing on advice and personal attention is our core business. In order to guarantee this high level of quality, we pay particular attention to the wishes of our customers. Our Communication department has a special role in this. For this department we are seeking a *Management trainee with an eye for service*.
>
> (van Meurs et al., 2004)

Main findings and relationship with similar studies

A statistical analysis (One-way Analysis of Variance: ANOVA) was used to test whether the three versions of the job add differed with respect to the three dependent variables (text evaluation; attitudes towards the ad, company and job; and text comprehension). With regard to text evaluation, no statistically significant differences emerged between the scores on the three versions with respect to attractiveness and intelligibility. However, the naturalness of the three versions of the ad was assessed differently by the three groups of respondents. Overall, the completely English version of the ad (see Data 6.3) was regarded to be more natural than the other two versions.

No statistically significant differences were found between the three versions with respect to the potential applicants' attitudes towards the company or the job offered. For comprehension, it was found that respondents' comprehension of English words in the partly English version of the ad was worse than their comprehension of their Dutch equivalents both in terms of their own estimation as to how well they understood the item and in terms of their success at paraphrasing correctly the meaning of those items. These findings are similar to the results of Renkema et al. (2001) who found that the use of English versus Dutch terms in partly English and completely Dutch job ads had no statistically significant effect on the perception of the ad, the organization's image and the appeal of the job offered, and are in line with Gerritsen et al. (2000), who found that only a minority of respondents could paraphrase correctly the meaning of English words and phrases in Dutch TV commercials.

A number of more recent experimental studies of target groups in Western European countries (e.g. Gerritsen, Nickerson, van den Brandt, et al., 2007, Nickerson, Gerritsen & van Meurs, 2005, for product ads; Smakman, Korzilius, van Meurs & van Neerven, 2011, for radio commercials) seem to confirm that the use of English instead of the local language, on the whole, does not result in differences in attitudes towards the product advertised or towards the advertisement. In addition, with respect to comprehension, these studies found that respondents had relatively little trouble paraphrasing the English used.

Quote 6.5   Limitations and suggestions for further research

One [limitation] relates to the way we tested actual comprehension . . . . The question is whether a paraphrase task is a very precise way of testing whether respondents have understood a particular word or phrase. It may well be that they know what it means, but cannot put it into different words. . . . In our case, the difficulty of the task may have been compounded by the fact that some items did not consist of one word, but of combinations of words. In future research, additional methods may be used to measure comprehension, such as Cloze tests and recording reading time . . . . Another limitation . . . is that . . . we only tested the effects of the use of English in versions of one advertisement. In this one advertisement, the attitudes of the respondents towards the position offered and the organization may have outweighed the effects of the use of English instead of Dutch. Further research should test the effect of the use of English in job ads aimed at potential applicants belonging to various age groups and with different educational backgrounds, with more than one job ad per target group. It would also be interesting to test the effects of the use of English on potential applicants from other countries where English is not spoken as a first language. . . . Cross-cultural research of the kind proposed here has obvious relevance for the decisions of organizations in different non-English-speaking countries regarding their use of English when trying to recruit new personnel.

(van Meurs et al., 2004: 104–05)

Further experimental (perception) studies on the effect of using English in business discourse in non-English speaking countries

- Hornikx, van Meurs, & de Boer (2010): a study of Dutch readers' appreciation of easy and difficult English slogans in product ads, showing that degree of difficulty of English slogans affected readers' preference for English (English slogans were preferred to their Dutch equivalents when they were easy to understand; English slogans, when difficult to understand, were appreciated as much as their Dutch equivalents);
- van Meurs, Korzilius, Planken & Fairley (2007): a study of the effect of English (vs. Dutch) job titles in recruitment ads, showing that Dutch potential applicants assessed jobs more positively, associated them with a higher salary, and regarded them as more international when they were presented with job titles in English (vs. in Dutch);
- Planken, van Meurs, & Radlinska (2010): a study showing that Polish readers presented with product ads in English did not evaluate the product/brand image or the ad differently than readers who were presented with the equivalent ads in Polish, their native language. The use of English (vs. Polish) also did not affect product-buying intention, and led to only few statistically significant differences in comprehension;
- Smakman, Korzilius, van Meurs, & van Neerven (2009): an experiment showing that the use of English in Dutch radio commercials (vs. the use of Dutch only) did not significantly affect target group's attitudes to the company, the product advertised or the commercial, nor their estimated understanding of the commercial.

Studying the use and effects of foreign languages other than English in advertising discourse

Although English seems to be the most frequently used foreign language in multinational advertising across the globe (Bhatia, 1992; Piller, 2003), multilingual advertising involving other foreign languages has also become commonplace. Kelly-Holmes (2005) argues that the use of a foreign language in multinational advertising has a symbolic function, in that it can evoke specific associations, emotions or connotations among receivers of the message (i.e. consumers). She hypothesizes that receivers will associate the foreign language with a particular country (where the language is spoken), and that this will trigger associations with particular qualities or competences that country is (stereotypically) taken to possess, which are then transferred to the product being advertised. Kelly-Holmes (2005) calls this the 'country-of-origin effect', and examples include Germany/German as a trigger for e.g. reliability and engineering competence, French/France as a trigger for e.g. elegance and haute cuisine, and Swedish/

Sweden as a trigger for e.g. minimalism and quality furniture design. According to Kelly-Holmes (2005), the use of a foreign language in advertising is evident particularly in cases where the product 'fits' the country in which the language is spoken (for example, cars and German/Germany, wine and French/France, beds and Swedish/Sweden). Its use is therefore not arbitrary but strategic; foreign languages are used in advertising because marketeers assume that positive language or country-related connotations will boost the product's image, distinguish it from others and persuade consumers to purchase it.

While we have seen in this chapter and elsewhere in this book that a number of studies have empirically investigated the occurrence of English as a foreign language in corpora of persuasive discourse (e.g. product and recruitment advertising), and that a number of experiments have investigated the effects of English used in persuasive discourse on non-native English receivers' attitudes and intentions, relatively few studies on the use and effects of foreign languages in persuasive discourse have involved foreign languages other than English. Rare exceptions include the corpus studies by Haarmann (1989) and Piller (2000), who investigated the use of European languages in Japanese advertising and German TV commercials respectively. A rare example of a study that investigates the effects on readers of using a foreign language other than English in advertising, is an experiment by Hornikx and Starren (2006), who examined the effects of French in Dutch advertising discourse, and more specifically, the relationship between the appreciation and comprehension of easy versus difficult French (and equivalent Dutch) slogans. When participants found French slogans difficult to understand, they preferred the Dutch equivalent slogans. However, when participants could understand the French slogans, they marginally preferred them over the Dutch equivalents. The researchers tentatively conclude from their findings that French does seem to carry a symbolic (as well as a literal) meaning.

How the process of symbolic meaning association actually works in advertising or other persuasive contexts remains an open question. Very few studies to date have systematically investigated whether and what types of association people (e.g. consumers) have with regard to different foreign languages in general, and with respect to foreign languages in persuasive discourse in particular. One exception is the experimental study by Hornikx, van Meurs and Starren (2007), which showed that different languages (German, Spanish and French) can indeed trigger different associations. Dutch consumers in their study associated German, for example, with adjectives such as 'businesslike', 'reliable' and 'boring', French with e.g. 'beautiful', 'businesslike' and 'elegant', and Spanish with e.g. 'modern', 'elegant' and 'boring' (Hornikx, van Meurs, & Starren, 2007). Furthermore, the study found that the associations consumers had with the three foreign languages were mostly positive, and that they preferred the language (out of the three) with which they had the most positive and least negative associations (Hornikx, van Meurs, & Starren, 2007). However, the study did not go on to test empirically whether and how these symbolic associations affected perceptions and attitudes when the foreign languages were used in persuasive discourse.

In sum, studies of the use, and particularly of the effects, of foreign languages other than English in multinational advertising (and other persuasive business discourses) remain relatively sparse, and we suggest that these topics could become a fruitful line of investigation for business discourse researchers in the future.

In conclusion

In this chapter we have profiled and cited a selected number of practice-based studies that illustrate some of the central themes in business discourse research as well as the main strategies (needs analysis survey, corpus analysis, ethnographic study, and experiment) used in this field. An important incentive for practice-based research is an awareness on the part of researchers, business practitioners and teachers alike that advances in communication technology and increased internationalization have brought about developments in organizational communication that need to be described and understood if (international) organizations are to continue to operate successfully, and students are to be adequately prepared for the business arena. Because it is essential that such research involves business discourse in use in relevant discourse communities, business discourse researchers have increasingly opted to choose the professional workplace as the site of their investigations in order to gain access to authentic business discourse data and first-hand information about business practices.

In the next chapter, we will consider in some detail various methods and analytical frameworks that have been used in business discourse research, and provide suggestions for further research in individual, collaborative or group projects.

Further reading

Black, T. (1999). *Doing quantitative research in the social sciences: An integrated approach to research design, measurement and statistics.* Thousand Oaks, CA: Sage Publications. A 'how-to' book for students and researchers that focuses on designing and conducting quantitative research: it deals with aspects of the research cycle such as planning, sampling, designing data collection instruments, choosing statistical tests, and interpreting results.

Field, A. (2009). *Discovering Statistics Using SPSS (Introducing Statistical Methods series).* Thousand Oaks, CA: Sage Publications. A comprehensive text that takes students through a varied collection of statistical methods, tests and procedures for conducting research in the social sciences, using vivid examples of research problems and data

sets, as well as self-assessment tests to reinforce methodological and statistical knowledge throughout. The book deals with concepts from introductory to advanced level,
illustrating the use of SPSS Statistics in such a way as to accommodate a readership
ranging from relatively novice to more experienced in research design and inferential
statistics.

Oppenheim, A. N. (2000). *Questionnaire design, interviewing and attitude measurement.*
Amsterdam: Continuum International Publishing Group – Academi. A practical text
that deals in detail (and on the basis of examples) with the construction of a variety
of data collection instruments (questionnaires, interviews, and so on) for use in both
qualitative and quantitative research.

Silverman, D. (2001). *Interpreting qualitative data: Methods for analyzing talk, text and
interaction.* Thousand Oaks, CA: Sage Publications. A text that presents recent developments, methodologies, and interpretative strategies used in qualitative research aimed
at investigating spoken and written discourse in various contexts.

Chapter 6 Tasks

1. Refer to Concept Box 6.3 on Ethnographic research and case study research. Explain
   how you could combine several different methods in a study of how a particular type
   of discourse is *used* within a business organization. What data could each method
   provide? And how would the methods you select complement one another?
2. Do an on-line study of corporate mission statements using a corpus-based approach.
   Refer to the studies by Rogers and her colleagues that we have discussed in this
   chapter and describe the genre of the mission statement.
3. Collect a corpus of advertising texts (e.g. magazine or online ads) that contain one or
   more languages. Use it as a basis to design a study that could investigate the *effects* of
   using foreign languages in advertising. Formulate a research question (or hypotheses),
   determine the main variables you would research, and create a set of experimental
   materials and a questionnaire.

7
Research Methodologies, Frameworks and Project Ideas

This chapter will:

- Profile and cite replicable studies from a number of key research areas: contextualized business discourse research, research on business writing and business talk, and studies of business document design;
- Present some of the theoretical frameworks and methodologies business discourse researchers have used;
- Provide examples of project ideas that could form the basis for individual, collaborative or group research.

7.1   Investigating the business environment: studies of business discourse in context

In business, communication is not an end in itself; there is always an underlying business purpose or objective to be achieved as a result of the communication. To study and understand organizational communication researchers need to take into account the specifics of the context, including business strategy, the business environment and professional practices, and how that context influences communication practices in a given discourse community (e.g. Varner, 2000; Bhatia, 2004). Business discourse researchers that have investigated the link between business discourse practices and the business context have taken different approaches, depending on the aims of their research, and have used various methodologies to collect and analyse their data. Using a selection of representative studies in the field, we will outline and discuss some important approaches and methods in business discourse research, and present some of the theoretical frameworks that researchers have used as the starting point for their enquiries or as a basis for analysing their data.

Business discourse practices and communication needs in organizations: quantitative approaches

Elsewhere in this book, we discuss examples of large-scale quantitative studies of business practitioners' communication skills and language needs that have investigated the interface between language use and business discourse practices, and the organizational context in which they occur (see Part 2). We note, for instance, that quantitative surveys conducted in Europe since the 1990s have indicated a clear relationship between the geographical scope of exporting companies' corporate activities and foreign language use and skills needs in these firms (e.g. van Hest & Oud-de Glas, 1991; Hagen, 1993; 1999; Christie et al., 2001; ELAN, 2006). The ELAN (2006) surveys, for instance, commissioned by the European Union at the turn of the millennium to investigate the relationship between language needs, corporate language strategy and economic performance in internationally operating companies across 29 European countries, showed that English is the most widely required and used lingua franca for international business in over 20 markets, in Europe and beyond. It is used relatively more extensively by larger European companies than SMEs, a reflection of the wider scope of these companies' business dealings, and partly the result of their frequently adopting a single corporate language, which has led to English being the official corporate language in many post-merger and multinational companies in Europe over the past decades (cf. Fredriksson, Barner-Rasmussen & Piekkari, 2006). At the same time, however, a number of studies have shown that French, German, Spanish and Russian also continue to be used relatively frequently for international business dealings, despite the advent of English as the international language of business (e.g. ELAN, 2006; Kankaanranta & Planken, 2010; cf. Vandermeeren, 1999).

What large-scale quantitative studies such as ELAN and its pre-cursors (ELUCIDATE, 1999; ELISE, 2001; REFLECT, 2002) clearly show is that the language factor, and in the European context, multilingualism, is essential not only in achieving international success and a competitive edge at the level of individual companies, but also in economic development and increased affluence in the region more generally (see also Hagen, n.d.; Dhir & Savage, 2002). A significant proportion of European companies lose or fail to land contracts and underperform internationally due to a lack of foreign language expertise (see also Christie et al., 2001). Over half the companies surveyed for ELAN (2006), i.e. in 13 of the 29 countries, and even higher percentages of companies in the new(er) member states such as Bulgaria, Romania and Hungary, expected to see the demand for foreign language skills grow in the near future as globalization continues to increase. Also, the effects of globalization have not been restricted to the larger, Europe-based multinational companies, but have impacted smaller to medium-sized enterprises located throughout the region.

Furthermore, as the international business European companies are involved in extends around the world, this means that European business professionals must regularly engage with business partners whose cultural, corporate and linguistic backgrounds are likely to be very diverse.

Concept 7.1   Quantitative research

Quantitative research aims at systematically and cumulatively collecting large amounts of quantifiable (that is, countable) data from a sample of the population (e.g., a subset of the business community under study, a subset of the business text type under study, and so on) that can be used to explain or even predict characteristics, outcomes and effects in the wider population (e.g., the wider business community, the text type in general, and so on).

Important characteristics:

Quantitative research aims to answer predetermined research questions (and the hypotheses derived from them) and uses precise definitions and replicable methods for collecting and analysing data.

In business discourse research, quantitative research is often conducted via a survey of a sample, and more rarely in experiments. The sample for surveys and in experiments should be representative so that the results can be extrapolated to the wider population.

As quantitative researchers know what they are looking for, the study (e.g., research question and hypotheses, research design and methods) is carefully designed before data is collected.

Quantitative researchers should be objective observers who do not participate in or influence what is being studied.

Ideally, quantitative methods should be designed to be detached from, and independent of, a specific situation under study in a particular organization, department, or institution in order to ensure objectivity and promote generalizability of the results. This poses a problem for business discourse researchers, whose investigation site is often a single organization, department, or business unit.

Applicability:

Quantitative methods are appropriate where measures of variables are quantifiable, hypotheses can be formulated, and inferences can be drawn from samples to wider populations. Quantitative analysis can determine which phenomena are a reflection of communicative behaviour in a specific business community, and which phenomena occur by chance.

Proviso:

Quantitative data are generally collected on the basis of a question-and-answer procedure between the researcher and a sample of participants (e.g. in the context of surveys and experiments). According to some researchers, they therefore lack (ecological) validity because they may not take sufficiently into account the context in which a phenomenon is manifested, or the discourse community's or subject's daily encounters with and social knowledge about the phenomenon. In other words, the questions being formulated and asked by the researcher may be too abstract, narrow or limited in scope to be able to generate data that fully and reliably reflect the subject's privileged perspective on, or situated knowledge of and experience with the phenomenon being studied (cf. Cicourel, 2007; see also Quote 7.1 and Concept 7.3).

Survey-based investigations that have focused on individual corporations, business units or discrete corporate communities (e.g., in a given business sector or geographical region) have considered business discourse types in relation to foreign language use, aspects of corporate activity, and corporate profile. In earlier chapters we have noted that such studies have found evidence of a relationship between company size and sector, and the use of written text types and foreign languages (e.g., Barbara et al. 1996, see Chapter 6) or between corporations' use of foreign languages and export sales performance on the one hand, and the volume of documentation and company size and sector on the other (e.g., Vandermeeren 1999, Chapter 1). Overall, large-scale quantitative research into business discourse (see Concept 7.1) has provided convincing evidence of the interaction between contextual factors and practices, and how such factors impact on practitioners, for example on language and medium choice, in internationally oriented organizations in particular.

As we pointed out in the previous chapter, studies of business discourse like those discussed above have largely aimed at descriptions of discourse (practices) *in situ*; in other words, they have been practice-based. As a result, they have been pragmatic and data-driven rather than theory-driven in their approach and methodology, drawing on authentic examples of business discourse produced in relevant business settings, and on the opinions and perspectives of informants from the business communities under study. Perhaps because business discourse is still a relatively new and hybrid research field, there has been surprisingly little effort – or perhaps need – to come up with an overreaching theoretical framework that accommodates determinant factors in the wider business context and their relationship with, and impact on, business discourse and business discourse practices (for an extensive discussion of the field, its origins, and where it stands today, see *The Handbook of Business Discourse*, edited by Bargiela-Chiappini, 2009, see also Chapter 1). The working model presented by Bäck (2004) which locates the situational factors that can play a role in determining language choice in business discourse by organizations in international business, remains a promising exception (see Chapter 4 for a detailed discussion). As Bäck's model is derived primarily from the findings of his survey study on code choice in communication between Austrian exporting companies and their partners, it would be interesting to test its applicability in characterizing and contextualizing code choice in other (international) business settings, for example involving companies from other countries, or different business sectors.

Concept 7.2　Qualitative research

Like any and all human behaviour, communicative behaviour is influenced by the setting in which it occurs. In business settings, aspects of the immediate physical and wider corporate setting form contextual variables that can shape business discourse. Therefore, business discourse should ideally be studied *in context*, and research should be located in settings (organizations, departments, and so on) where contextual variables are operating.

Important characteristics:

The researcher is the primary instrument for data collection and analysis.

Qualitative research involves *fieldwork*. The researcher goes to the business practitioners, communicative setting, or organization personally, to observe or record behaviour in its natural environment.

Qualitative research is *descriptive*: the researcher gains insights into process (communicative behaviour and actions, and so on) and meaning (practitioners' perspectives, motives, and so on) on the basis of words (e.g., through interviews) and texts (e.g., through desk research), and tries to identify patterns of communicative behaviour.

The qualitative research process is *inductive*: abstractions, concepts, hypotheses and theories follow from the researcher's interpretations of the data.

Applicability:

Qualitative methods are appropriate when the phenomenon under study is complex, social in nature, and does not lend itself easily to quantification. For example, they can be useful when studying business discourse *processes*, for instance, the process of collaboratively writing an annual report.

Qualitative research is suitable where meaning is central, that is, in studies that aim to gain insight into business practitioners' perspectives on, and

> motives for, communicative tasks and actions, their experiences, and the
> social and corporate networks within which they operate (e.g., their profes-
> sional field, the corporate culture, and so on).
>
> Qualitative approaches are recommended for earlier, exploratory phases
> of research, when the researcher may have only a rough idea of what she
> is looking for.

Business discourse practices and business discourse in context: qualitative approaches

A number of researchers have employed qualitative approaches to investigate
the interface between aspects of the business environment and the use of specific business text types. These studies have gleaned their methodology and
analytical approach more obviously from other research disciplines, including
ethnography (of language), sociolinguistics and applied linguistics (see also
Chapter 2). A concern with how the organizational, i.e. sociocultural, context
shapes the discourse used in business, seems to have been evident especially
in European business discourse research, which is traditionally grounded in
the ESP and LSP fields, and in ESP genre analysis in particular. Therefore, it is
European researchers working in the discipline that have relatively frequently
studied the interplay between contextual variables, such as the economic
conditions or corporate language policy, and how these factors influence code
choice, that is, which language is selected for a specific genre or task, and discourse characteristics, for example, which genre, medium or linguistic realization or communication strategy is selected (Nickerson & Planken, 2009).

The studies by Leena Louhiala-Salminen (2002) and Didar Akar (2002),
which we profile briefly below, are typical examples of European researchers'
efforts in this area and illustrate how a contextualized interpretative approach
not only provides a comprehensive characterization of aspects of business
discourse phenomena but also serves as a potential starting point for broader
generalizations on business discourse practices. In her case study, Louhiala-
Salminen combined qualitative fieldwork methods such as observation and
interviews (see Concept 7.2) to explore the potential relationship between the
corporate environment and the communicative tasks undertaken by a manager
(that is, the case) working in a Finnish computer company. In interpreting the
motives for the manager's communicative tasks on the basis of observation in
the workplace and interviews with the manager and his co-workers, Louhiala-
Salminen demonstrates how the discourse activities undertaken by her informants are embedded in the social context formed by the organization on the
one hand, and the department in which they take place on the other. She also
shows that these activities can be seen to contribute to the restructuring and
reinforcing of corporate – social and communicative – networks and as such,

to the structuring and running of the organization itself. She suggests that aspects of the corporate context partly determine communicative practices; within the Finnish company, for instance, corporate culture and corporate language policy determine English use, as well as the types of activity undertaken. Taken together, these interpretative analyses provide confirmation that the relationship between the social corporate context and the discourse activities undertaken within is indeed a reciprocal one (see also Boden, 1994, discussed in Chapter 1).

Quote 7.1   Qualitative research and 'the analyst's interpretive burden'

An example of a challenge facing applied researchers positioned as outsiders to the professional practice and knowledge under study is the need to remain au courant with the discoursal shifts within a given workplace context . . . . However, recognizing and describing such shifts in discourse is not just a matter of making a link to shifting workplace practices, but, more fundamentally and problematically, that of the non-transparence of the significance of these shifts to the outside researcher to whom such professional practices based on tacit knowledge will always remain inaccessible unless collaborative interpretation is taken seriously. . . . It is also what Sarangi (2002) refers to as 'the analysts' paradox', where analysts need access to participants' insights in order to be able to understand the participants' practices and tacit knowledge structures but at the same time they have to report on them explicitly in the language of research (see e.g. Becker, 1993; for illustrative confessional accounts). Most basic to collaborative interpretation is the alignment of the participants' and analysts' stances, i.e. the fusion of emic and etic perspectives (Sarangi & Candlin, 2001).

Taken from: Sarangi & Candlin (2003: 274: slightly adapted)

In Didar Akar's study, different qualitative research methods were used to provide insights into the socio-historical context of written business discourse in Turkey (Akar, 2002). By combining an interpretative textual analysis of the content of memos and faxes from Turkish companies with interviews with business text writers from those companies (some of whom wrote the texts in the corpus), Akar shows how the political history and the economic business context of the country are reflected in the business discourse. More specifically, she demonstrates that bureaucratic traditions and professional attitudes dating back to the time of the Turkish state not only influenced all aspects of the discourse in the corpus, including the genres opted for; it also determined stylistic aspects of the texts, such as formality level and degree of directness, which varied depending on the management style (authoritarian versus open) used in the department in which messages originated. Like Louhiala-Salminen's study, Akar's investigation is an example of what can be revealed by a 'thick' multi-layered, ethnographic analysis of text in context (see Concept 7.3).

Concept 7.3   Multimethod and multiperspective approaches: using multilayered analysis to contextualize business discourse

To understand business discourse phenomena and the factors that shape them, researchers can use multilayered analyses to frame their findings. Framing – or contextualization – takes into account the *social embeddedness* of practitioners and communicative activities not only within the dynamics and norms of personal relationships, but also within broader networks of social and corporate systems that include discourse community member-ship, corporate policy and philosophy, corporate profile, and so on. For a comprehensive understanding of a phenomenon, and to promote the effec-tiveness of practical advice regarding it, a researcher needs to understand the phenomenon in context, by observing closely the real world in which it is situated. According to Geertz (1973), observation of the real world implies doing 'thick descriptions', or detailed, small-scale, analytically informed characterizations of social life through observational fieldwork. Such micro-level descriptions can subsequently lead to broader generalizations about the phenomenon being studied. Fairclough's (1993; 2003) framework goes a step further, by combining macro- and micro-phenomena in discourse analysis to examine the impact of ideology and hegemony.

In business discourse research, contextualization has meant locating research in the business practitioners' everyday world, highlighting con-texts of communicative practices and tapping into participants' viewpoints on those practices. Quantitative surveys or content analyses of business documentation, and case studies that use participatory, qualitative research techniques (observation, narratives or accounts, interviews, logbooks, and so on) form important methods of data collection, and are often used in combination within a single study.

Multimethod (or multilevel) approaches (see e.g. Cicourel, 1992; Wodak & Krzyznowski, 2008): supplementing observations from in-depth case stud-ies (for instance, a company, department, practices of a key informant, and so on) with qualitative data (from for instance, interviews, logbooks, focus groups, and so on) or quantitative data (from surveys, corpus analyses, and so on).

Contextualizing quantitative data (for instance, survey findings) on the basis of qualitative data (e.g., findings from key informant interviews, real participant observation, or desk research on documents reflecting corporate strategy, history, policy, and so on);

Multiperspective approaches (see e.g. Fairclough, 1993; Candlin & Crichton, 2012; Crichton, 2010): collecting (and analysing) data on a particular phenomenon from multiple subjectivities (or points of view), including the discourse community's view of generalized behaviours relating to the phenomenon, the participant's individual experience with the phenomenon, the researcher's (objective) observation of the phenomenon in practice, and a collaborative perspective involving comparisons of the researcher's and individual's points of view. Multiperspected approaches are *integrative* in the sense that they combine analytical perspectives and research traditions relevant to the study of 'language, interaction, the perceptions of participants and analysts' and the factors that shape the wider context (Crichton, 2010: 20). They are *reflexive* in that the researcher should strive throughout the research cycle to create alignment between his own perspective and that of the participants, while establishing how this 'new' collaborative viewpoint, in turn, relates to practices, in an effort to generate relevant, practical insights into the phenomenon under study (see also Quote 7.1). The latter echoes Sarangi and Roberts (1991) who posit that the researcher is at all times *situated* within the wider social context and is therefore obliged to conduct research that is at once aimed at 'theory-building', while also meeting participants' local needs.

Investigating context: the impact of ICT and new media on corporate practices

Due to the rapid advances in ICT over the past two decades, organizations have at their disposal a wide and ever-expanding range of new, electronically mediated communication tools to manage business processes and to reach audiences. As developments in ICT are fast, still ongoing and relatively recent, little is known about the impact of such technologies and of new communication, and particularly 'social' media, on corporate communicative practices in general, on the quality of communicative practices, and on interpersonal business discourse in particular.

Studies of computer-mediated communication tools and their impact on (business discourse) practices

Arnfalk and Kogg (2003) explored the contextual factors that influence the use of, and communication and meeting behaviour in, virtual audio and video meetings in Swedish telecommunications companies;

Wong and Aiken (2003) investigated the effectiveness of automated facilitation modes versus human (expert and novice) facilitators in electronic business meetings;

Van den Hooff (2004) considered the use and effects of electronic calendaring on organizational connectivity (an increased ability to reach other members of the organization) and communality (more information on location and activities of co-workers);

Turner, Qvarfordt, Biehl, Golovinchky and Back (2010) used surveys and in-depth interviews to study media usage trends in a small US-based organization, investigating what mix of communication tools employees use (e.g. IM, Twitter, Wiki, Blog) to communicate on the workfloor, and how employees perceive these tools, i.e. in terms of strengths and weaknesses.

The study we profile here investigated the impact of introducing what was a relatively new – and up and coming – communication medium at the time of the study, namely Instant Messaging (or IM) in the workplace (Cameron & Webster, 2005). IM is a facility, much like online chat, that can be used to send and receive instantaneous messages over the Internet, and although similar to the idea of a telephone conversation, it involves text instead of speech. Geographically dispersed corporations first began installing IM when it came to be recognized by managers as a tool that could facilitate long-distance teamwork (e.g., Nardi, Whitaker & Bradner, 2000; Pauleen & Yoong, 2001). The study by Cameron and Webster is a good example of a multimethod approach that combines various quantitative and qualitative methods to investigate the use and impact of a new technological medium in four large US organizations (or cases). In all four companies, IM systems were officially sanctioned by management and available to all employees.

By interviewing and observing employees and management at work, the researchers collected both quantitative and qualitative data about general patterns and frequency of IM use, experiences regarding IM, and perceptions about the impact of IM on the corporate environment. These data were interpreted in the light of insights from theories – including critical mass theory and media richness theory – that can be used to explain the acceptance and use of (new) communication media in organizations (see Concept 7.4).

The findings of the study suggest that critical mass (that is a sufficient number of participants) is an important factor for IM success (i.e. use), that the medium symbolizes informality, and that it is perceived to be much less 'rich' than face-to-face communication. Employees had not only begun to use the facility instead of existing media (suggesting an impact on medium choice) but were also using it as an additional method to reach colleagues, as IM allowed employees to 'multitask' different communication activities, and to 'jump the communication queue' (Cameron & Webster, 2005: 14).

With regard to the impact of new technologies, such as IM, on the workplace, the data suggest further-reaching implications of introducing a quick and easy communication medium. While IM-type technologies have the potential to increase connectivity and facilitate teamwork, they also appear to encourage increased interruptions to the work of others, with the potential for decreased performance. Also, there is a risk that employees will begin to use informal media like IM, and more recently social media like Twitter, and social networking platforms like Facebook, etc., for formal (workplace-related) communication as well (see also Guan & Alkinkemer, 2002). Furthermore, as few IM-type systems automatically save messages, it seems wise for organizations that make such media available to train their employees to use more traceable (and firewalled) formats (email or other online electronic databases) for storing sensitive information. Finally, employees who use social media and online networks (for/at work) should be made aware of the ins and outs of social media privacy law and legal liabilities. Cox, Martinez and Quinlan (2008), for example, use brief case studies as examples to discuss the potential advantages as well as the risks of corporate blogging for companies, and recommend a number of guidelines for creating corporate blog policy. They warn that personal views aired in uncontrolled corporate blogging by employees can pose a risk to the company's reputation. The suggestion of companies monitoring and 'controlling' corporate blogging, however, also raises an ethical issue in itself. The whole idea of the Internet is that users can share content and freely express their opinions and thoughts online. The question as to whether and to what extent organizations can – and are entitled to – control their employees' blogging content is therefore a sensitive one (see also discussions on this topic in e.g. Cox et al., 2008 and Lee et al., 2006).

With the increased use of new technological tools and media, multi-communication has become an increasingly prevalent behaviour, particularly in organizations. Multi-communicators perform a number of communication tasks with a number of people simultaneously. In practice, this requires the use of a combination of technological 'tools', such as Smartphone apps, social networking platforms (like LinkedIn or Yammer), chat programmes, email, and more recently tablet computers. Studies of multi-communication have been rare to date but there has been some exploratory research which has investigated the impact of multitasking on communicative practices (in business and academia). For example, Turner and Reinsch's (2010) study used an analysis of critical incidents to explore which media individuals (in this case MBA students) combine when multi-communicating, and to establish what factors determine successful and unsuccessful incidents of multi-communicating. They found that multi-communicators most frequently paired the telephone with electronic text. Furthermore, multi-communicators provided a number of different reasons for categorizing a particular multi-communication episode as 'unsuccessful'. A particularly salient reason was when the multi-communicator or a communicating partner had exceeded their ability to maintain different conversations while multi-communicating, as manifested in communication errors, i.e. a decrease in communication quality. In an earlier study, Turner and Reinsch (2007) used qualitative and quantitative data to explore factors that influence multi-communicating behaviour itself, using concepts of media richness (see Concept 7.4) and social presence. They describe how contemporary workers try at all times to efficiently assign their personal presence across the various interrelated interactions that multi-communicating involves and identify message equivocality and interlocutor status as two factors that would seem to encourage (or discourage) individuals to multi-communicate.

Although most users would seem to multitask and multi-communicate because they see such behaviours as efficient (and necessary) in today's working environment, some studies show that multitasking behaviours do not necessarily improve 'task' performance. Kraushaar and Novak (2010), for example, found that students multitasked extensively (using laptops) during lectures (often to engage in behaviours, i.e. reading personal email and chatting online, that were not class-related). They were found to be distracted more and to perform less successfully academically, in terms of e.g. an in-class quiz, a project exam and final grade scores, than classmates who multi-communicated less during lectures. Conceivably then, multi-communication may affect, that is, constrain or impede, communication performance of tasks in workplace contexts too.

To date, systematic studies on the impact of CMC tools on communication practices, the quality of business discourse and communication effectiveness, as well as investigations of the ethical implications of allowing the use of new (social) media at or for work, have been relatively rare. By the same token, the phenomenon of multi-communication and its impact on personal efficacy and effectiveness in the workplace has rarely been researched. It is likely, therefore, that investigations of the impact of ICT tools in the workplace, on discourse practices, on individuals and their communication effectiveness, will be a fruitful avenue of research into business discourse (practices) in the near future.

Concept 7.4   Media Richness Theory

The core idea of Media Richness Theory is that different communication media have varying capacities for resolving (message) ambiguity and facilitating understanding in organizations. The main assumptions are that people want to promote transparency and overcome uncertainty in organizations, and that the various media they can use are better suited to certain (communicative) tasks than to others. Using four criteria, Daft and Lengel (1984) presented a so-called 'media richness hierarchy', arranged from high to low degrees of richness, to illustrate the capacity of media types to process ambiguous communication: availability of instantaneous feedback, capacity of the medium to transmit multiple cues (such as body language, pitch and voice tone), use of natural language, and focus of the medium. The hierarchy regards face-to-face communication as the richest medium, and fliers and bulletins as least 'rich'.

Media richness theory posits that the more ambiguous a message is to a receiver, the richer the medium needed to communicate it. Different media have varying benefits and drawbacks; some communicate non-vocal cues more accurately than others, for example (i.e. a Skype video call versus a 'regular' telephone call). In general, media richness is used to select the 'most effective' medium for an individual or an organization to communicate a message. With the increasingly virtual nature of organizational communications, and the expansion of media and channels, media richness theory is again gaining relevance. As the media landscape becomes ever richer, both organizations and the people they target (consumers, employees, clients, etc.) become spoilt for choice, making strategic communication (i.e. choosing the 'right' medium and channel to reach a particular target group) increasingly complex.

Investigating the connection between context and business discourse: example projects

Individual: An analysis of English language use in one business genre (e.g. email or meetings) at one division or department of a multinational corporation or exporting company (cf. Nickerson, 1999; Barbara et al., 1996);

An investigation of register and/or style in email (genres) as a manifestation of the discursive reality and of power relations in an organization (cf. Kankaanranta, 2006; Gimenez, 2001, 2002).

Collaborative: An investigation of one genre as it is used in two different national or professional contexts, for instance, business letters of request in two different countries (cf. Jenkins & Hinds, 1987), or a sales genre across two cultures or languages (cf. Zhu, 2005), or email in business versus academia (cf. Gains, 1999).

Group: An analysis of foreign language use in different divisions or units located in different countries, of one multinational corporation (cf. Hagen, 1999; the REFLECT project; the ELUCIDATE project; the ELAN project);

An exploratory investigation of a group of employees' multi-communication practices and the factors that govern successful/unsuccessful multi-communication practices (i.e. through observation, critical incident analysis, or interviews);

An experiment with two conditions (one condition with multiple e-tools, one without) to investigate the impact of multi-communication on a particular task (e.g. solving a puzzle, making a decision), by measuring task outcomes (e.g. time on task; number of errors made, etc.).

7.2 Researching written business communication

Since the early 1980s, a growing body of research on business discourse has considered the nature and construction of written communication in organizational or institutional contexts (e.g., the collections by Odell & Goswami, 1985; Spilka 1993; Bargiela-Chiappini & Nickerson, 1999). Methodological approaches have included surveys on the use of business writing in organizations, contextualized text-based studies of specific written text types, ethnographic case study accounts of writing activities undertaken within the context of specific organizations or specific corporate activities, and linguistic investigations of written business discourse, often involving specific text types and contrastive analyses on a crosscultural or intercultural basis.

Survey-based research into business writing: quantitative approaches

Surveys of business writing (practices) include Cassady and Wasson (1994) and Gallion and Kavan (1994), both on the use of written documents in US corporations, Barbara et al. (1996) on written documents and (foreign) language use in the Brazilian business context, Louhiala-Salminen (1999) on texts used in a Finnish business community, Vandermeeren (1999) on the use of written documentation and (foreign) language use in German, French and Dutch companies, and Nickerson (2000) on the use of English by non-native writers in British multinationals in the Netherlands. Studies such as these have provided useful information about the specific text types used in organizational settings, the way in which specific business texts contribute to the construction of social and communication structures within organizations, and the use of foreign languages – especially English as a lingua franca – in written business discourse in multinational and intercultural contexts. In Part 2 we talked about studies like these as an important source of information for teaching and training purposes.

Interpretative approaches to business writing: How like you our Fish? (Connor, 1999)

Like studies that have investigated the relationship between communicative practices and the business environment, researchers of business writing have also used interpretative methods to contextualize organizational writing processes and to determine how writing tasks are accomplished. Ulla Connor's case study (1999) on the role of English in written business discourse in an international fish brokerage company in Finland demonstrates how interpretative text analysis can be used to describe not only the occurrence of a particular phenomenon (that is, the use of English in the firm's written communication), but also to determine a business practitioner's underlying motives for communicative choices such as the selection of languages, media and text types. The data were supplied by the company's owner and consisted of the firm's written correspondence, generated in two non-consecutive weeks, one week in the most intensive business period of the year, the second in the slower selling season. Connor's starting point was to explore the communicative needs of a non-native English-speaking business person (the owner) in selling and buying products around the world. To do so, she analysed the corpus of writing to identify the media, genres and languages used in international communication, and more specifically, to determine the types of English used by the owner, depending on his role in sales transactions (buyer or seller).

Connor shows that most of the written communication generated by the company was in English with non-native speakers of English (but also in Finnish, Swedish, Estonian and Norwegian) and that communication was exclusively conducted by fax. Furthermore, Connor's qualitative consideration of these faxes suggests a complex interaction between the owner's choice of linguistic and rhetorical styles and a number of contextual factors. Specifically, the faxes showed evidence that the owner accommodated his fax communication to the expectations of the receiving party, depending on the task, his own role in a transaction, the cultural background of the receiving party, and personal relationship characteristics.

Examples of qualitative, text-based studies of business writing

Catherine Nickerson (1999) and Joan Mulholland (1999) used case studies to investigate the relationship between aspects of email use and the institutional environment, conducted in a multinational corporate context and a university respectively. Both used text-based qualitative analysis of emails to show that workplace procedures and conventions, in combination with corporate or institutional culture respectively, affect and influence not only the distribution processes and languages used (native or foreign), but have caused email to become deeply embedded in the managerial process and the communicative practices of corporate and educational institutions.

Louhiala-Salminen (1997) used an exploratory analysis of business faxes from a Finnish export company to distinguish five distinct types of fax that differ in their textual realizations and communicative purpose. She also shows that the professional role of the writer and the relationship between sender and receiver influences the textual realizations of rhetorical moves used in faxes.

Gimenez (2002) used a case study approach to investigate the role of email and fax in communication between a multinational and its Argentinean subsidiary. The study combines an interpretative corpus analysis with interview data from employees involved in producing such texts to illustrate how communication conflicts as a result of globally-adopted and locally-constructed identities are reflected in the communication practices and conventions used between head office and the subsidiary.

Jensen (2009) used a case study-based, contextualized (qualitative and quantitative) approach to identify the discourse strategies used in email negotiations between a Danish company and its Taiwanese clients over a three-month period. The analyses show how rapport between participants develops through the use of specific discourse strategies in e-mail communication over time, and as the relationship advances from first contact to doing business. Drawing on Hyland's (2005) concept of metadiscourse (see also Concept 8.2) and Charles' (1996) categories of 'old and new relationship negotiations', the study provides insights into naturally occurring language in intercultural professional e-mail communication. During the period observed, the frequency of occurrence in the use of interpersonal strategies converges, as the relationship moves towards a more contextually stable and personal level of communication as trust increases and participants' power relations are 'co-defined' within the legal framework of the contract.

Connor's findings point to a number of trends in international business in general. Firstly, they confirm the increasing importance of technology (e-tools) in doing business around the world. Secondly, they point to the emergence of an international English for business, the features of which deviate from standard Englishes, such as British English or General American English (see also Crystal, 1997). According to Connor, this highly flexible variety of English appears to be characterized by accommodation and convergence between speakers and is geared above all to optimizing intelligibility (see also Concept 7.5).

Concept 7.5 The notion of BELF – Business English as a Lingua Franca

BELF refers to English used as a 'neutral' and shared communication code. BELF is neutral in the sense that none of the speakers can claim it as his/ her mother tongue; it is shared in the sense that it is used for conducting business within the global discourse community, whose members are BELF users and communicators in their own right – not 'non-native speakers' or 'learners'.

(Louhiala-Salminen et al., 2005: 403–4)

Louhiala-Salminen et al. (2005) found that the strategy of introducing BELF as the corporate language (in favour of a local language) in a recently merged Swedish–Finnish company alleviated at least some of the professional and linguistic problems that employees typically face following a cross-border merger. Making one of the merged corporations' first languages (and most commonly the first language of management) the new corporate language can create asymmetry among employees; the 'native' speakers have the advantage over the non-native speakers, and non-native speakers often feel – and are – excluded from decision-making, and so on as a result of their relative lack of communicative competence. However, with the introduction of a 'neutral' language (like BELF), the idea is that all employees, regardless of their language background or hierarchical position, start off on a similar footing in 'the post-merger communicative challenge' (Louhiala-Salminen et al., 2005: 417: slightly adapted).

In order to determine the characteristics of BELF, Kankaanranta and Planken (2010) investigated how internationally operating business professionals perceive using BELF and how they think it contributes (or not) to success at work, based on data from an online survey and in-depth interviews conducted in Europe-based multinational companies in Finland and the Netherlands. Their findings indicate that BELF can be characterized as a 'simplified, hybridized, and highly dynamic communication code'. Also, competence in BELF 'calls for clarity and accuracy of content rather than linguistic correctness, and knowledge of business-specific vocabulary and genre conventions rather than only "general" English' (Kankaanranta & Planken, 2010: 380). Because BELF encounters can involve non-native speakers from a variety of cultures, the relational orientation (communicating appropriately and 'socially', making small talk, etc.) is perceived by BELF users as an integral aspect of their BELF competence. Finally, the findings show that BELF competence is seen by users as an essential component of the business knowledge required in today's global business environment.

The studies cited in this section have all explored business discourse from a socio-semiotic perspective, that is, they have considered the writing process and product in context (see Concept 7.6). Each study, in its own way, shows us that business writing is a dynamic process in which the situational context and the elements that make up that context (the medium, the power and role of sender and receiver or target group, the corporate environment, the cultural background against which writing activities take place, and so on) define communicative practices and norms. They also demonstrate that the relationship between the social context and the product of organizational writing is reciprocal and mutually constructive. Furthermore, they have collectively provided evidence that business writing facilitates a corporate discourse community's common goal of doing business, and helps define such communities by forming part of the set of practices that the community recognizes and uses, and through which it is 'managed and constituted' (Giddens, 1987; Orlikowski & Yates, 1994).

Concept 7.6 Social semiotics

Social semiotics is the study of human meaning-making practices (see also Chapter 2). The premise is that meanings are socially constructed, and the task of social semiotics is to develop analytical constructs and a theoretical framework to show how this occurs. Meanings are taken to be jointly constructed by participants (for instance, a group of marketing executives), for a relevant 'social' activity (e.g., meeting about a product launch), within a relevant 'social' network or structure (for instance, a marketing department). In social semiotics, the fundamental concept is that of contextualization. No semiotic form, event, text, or action has meaning in and of itself. The meanings these have are made in and through the social meaning-making practices which construct semiotic relations among forms, material processes and entities, and social actions. A given (business or professional) community or sub-community has regular and repeatable patterns of meaning-making and interactional (discursive) strategies to achieve 'tasks'. These patterns and strategies are typical of the community, help to define and constitute the community, and distinguish it from other communities. Another notion which is central to semiotics – and highly relevant to contextualized investigations of business discourse – is that of *intertextuality*. This notion implies that texts (and relationships between them) can be located on two axes of connection: a horizontal axis between the author and reader(s) of the text, and a vertical axis connecting the text to other texts.

For detailed treatments of social semiotics and its applications, see Jewitt (2009), Kress and van Leeuwen (2001), Kress and van Leeuwen (2013), and van Leeuwen (2005).

Identifying text typology: genre-based studies of writing (Van Nus, 1999; Sless, 1999)

A sizeable number of studies of business writing have been geared to investigating (new) written business text types, in relation to aspects of the corporate context in which they are produced. These studies have explored the interface between text construction, the people who write the texts, and aspects of the wider business environment. Two examples are provided by Miriam van Nus (1999) who uses a genre-based approach (see Concept 7.7) and David Sless (1999) working in the multidisciplinary tradition of document design. Van Nus (1999) explored the relationship between discourse practices in direct sales letters and the corporate context in which they are produced. Following a survey of 600 Dutch organizations to establish what factors in the corporate context determine a company's media selection in general and direct mail selection in particular, she uses a moves analysis (e.g., Bhatia, 1993; Swales 1990a) to investigate a corpus of direct mail letters (sales offers) sent out by the Dutch subsidiary of an international ship broker's firm. She characterizes the genre by considering the texts' structural elements and their functional components (that is, acts and moves).

Her findings confirm earlier results regarding a similar genre, but used in another language and against a different cultural background (see Bhatia, 1993, on Singaporean companies' and western multinationals' sales promotion letters), suggesting that there are similarities in the way direct mail letters achieve their communicative purposes across countries. Using examples from the corpus, van Nus also demonstrates the methodological relevance for genre research of a model of corporate context that considers different situational levels (business community, organization and campaign) in the analysis of business documents.

Concept 7.7   Genre analysis

Genre analysis aims to situate texts within their textual, corporate, cultural or historic contexts, so as to describe the social nature of the production and reading of text. The term *genre* is widely used in rhetoric, literary theory, media theory, and more recently linguistics, to refer to a distinctive *type* of text. Genre analysis is principally geared to *categorizing* systems of texts into types, and to *naming* those types. Within the field of business discourse, researchers have used genre analysis to identify and meaningfully classify systems of *recurrent practices* as they are manifested in texts between and within companies, and to characterize and describe potentially new genres, such as fax and email. Genre studies in business discourse research have tended to use two approaches: they have centred on the development of a single text in context, or have investigated the characteristics of a specific text type on the basis of a *corpus* (a collection of authentic texts, seen as representative for the type being investigated and used for linguistic analysis).

Analytical approaches: moves analysis (structure), text analysis (language and/or content), contextual analysis (desk research, observation, interviews with writers and readers), contrastive analysis (for instance, of two genres), cross-cultural analysis (e.g., of the same genre in two countries or two corporate contexts).

David Sless' investigation centres on a potentially new genre of business text, the mass-produced commercial letter (Sless, 1999). Mass produced letters are an interesting text type because they are not actually 'written'. Instead, the information elements in mass-produced letters are assembled from a database according to a set of algorithms. Furthermore, before such letters are sent off to customers, they are pre-tested, adapted and refined to ensure their comprehensibility and acceptability in tone to a company's customers. Based on a text-based analysis of the structure, content and sequencing of information elements in an authentic example of a mass-produced letter, Sless shows that such letters are dissimilar to traditional business letters in terms of their overall structure, layout and temporal sequencing of information, and with respect to the use of certain visual cues. For example, mass-produced letters clearly distinguish, typographically and by using different locations on a page, between the different types of information readers need in order to carry out various tasks (for instance, read information, fill out a payment slip, and so on). Because different types of information in mass-produced letters are presented as distinct, readers can easily select the information that is relevant to them. From the point of view of document design, consistently applying such visual cues helps readers use these documents appropriately.

The applicability of genre theory to emerging genres

Business practitioners have been seen to creatively combine discourses into hybrid texts that cut across conventional genre boundaries, often mixing spoken and written discourse in the process, for example, in fax and email (Akar & Louhiala-Salminen, 1999). It is likely that such trends will make the identification of distinct genres in business discourse increasingly complex. A further complicating factor is that communicative practices associated with new media, such as weblogs, have not been documented as extensively, and are as yet more flexible and less conventionalized than practices associated with more traditional media such as business letters, and so on (see also the edited collections by Gotti & Gillaerts, 2005, and Garzone, Poncini & Cattenacio, 2007, for series of papers taking a genre approach that are centred on this theme). Furthermore, web-based genres in particular are inherently *multi-modal*, combining different semiotic resources to communicate a single 'event'. According to Garzone (2007), as communicative events are increasingly being transferred to a computer-mediated environment (i.e. online), and as the 'semiotic coordinates' of such events are undergoing profound changes as a result, this will give rise to 'new – or modified – genres, whose genetic identity needs to be defined and classified' (p. 8). In Garzone's view, genre theory itself will need to undergo a multi-modal turn, in which researchers adopt an analytical approach that requires them to apply a wider focus accounting not only for the language in use in business contexts, but also for the non-verbal, visual and sound components of the interaction. In a multimodal perspective, notions such as organization and organizing, textuality and intertextuality, or context and contextualization acquire new meanings and significance. As a result, genre theory will continue to be on the move for a while yet (cf. Planken, 2012).

Perhaps the most significant challenge for researchers will lie in finding ways to accommodate the changes that new media and communication technologies continue to have on business communicative practices, without sacrificing the genre model's explanatory force as an analytical tool that is 'discriminating enough to highlight variation rather than uniformity in functional language use' (Bhatia, 1993: 11).

Sless' analysis identifies another way in which mass-produced letters differ from traditional business letters. They do not include the opening salutations (e.g., 'Dear Sir') and the closing salutations (for instance, 'Yours faithfully') that traditional letters use, because they are directed at a mass audience rather than an individual customer, and the person 'signing' the letter is not necessarily the same as the employee who will deal with the customer if they contact the organization. Thus it would seem that, for practical reasons, the mass-produced letter differs from traditional business letter genres; it does not reflect the relationship between sender and receiver.

Quote 7.2   Social media: new genres, new research opportunities

The emergence of social media, and social network sites in particular, has provided researchers interested in discourse, language, genre, rhetoric, interpersonal and cross-group interaction, etc. with a rich source of interactional data (Beer 2008), readily available online, produced by a potentially vast population, from various communities of practice and backgrounds, organizational, cultural or otherwise. Social media and networking sites provide an excellent data resource for discourse and conversation analysts (socio-) linguists, and critical discourse analysts to investigate how people discursively co-construct individual – and organizational – identities, and build (or mediate) relationships and create interpersonal and intercommunity rapport. And emergent media such as social media are always of interest to genre analysts, who are challenged to identify new genres, and define their characteristics (Planken, 2012: 34, slightly adapted).

Investigating written business discourse (genres): example projects

Individual: An investigation of the structure and (multimodal) content of locally produced direct mail letters (e.g., sales promotion or fund-raising letters) (cf. van Nus, 1999), online corporate press releases (cf. Catenaccio, 2007), corporate weblogs (cf. Herring, 2004; Poncini, 2007), webpages (cf. Askehave & Nielsen, 2005; Bargiela-Chiappini, 2005b), or annual reports (cf. de Groot et al., 2006).

Collaborative: A genre analysis of a written business text type as it is used in two different national contexts, for instance, application letters (cf. Connor et al., 1997).

Group: An analysis of the use of English in print advertisements in glossy magazines in non-English speaking countries (cf. Nickerson, Gerritsen, & van Meurs, 2005).

7.3   Researching spoken business discourse

Talk is central to doing business and business conversations play an important role in both the performance and the coordination of corporate activities. They can be conceived as a type of discourse, because the coherence and order in such conversations are not found at the level of linguistic expressions, but at the level of the interactional moves or speech acts that speakers make by uttering those expressions. The field of business discourse distinguishes a number of generic spoken discourse types that have been investigated from different perspectives using various approaches (see Chapter 1). Some discourse types have been studied more than others, while research methods have been inspired by a broad range of disciplines and theoretical constructs, including Conversation Analysis (CA), discourse studies, pragmatics and speech act theory, negotiation studies and applied linguistics. As has been the case for research into written business discourse, investigations of spoken business discourse have increasingly incorporated international or intercultural business talk, as well as business interactions in which English is used as a lingua franca, in order to determine the effects on business communication of globalization at economic, political and corporate levels.

Studying business talk: approaches inspired by CA (Conversation Analysis)

CA has provided a methodological starting point for many studies of spoken business discourse. The aim of CA is to see how people, through talk, carry out their daily routine, whether casual or institutional. Inspired by ethnomethodology (Garfinkel, 1967), CA was developed principally by the sociologist Harvey Sacks (Sacks, 1963). The idea behind it is that conversations are orderly and structured, not only for observers, but first and foremost for participants (e.g., Schegloff & Sacks, 1973). This orderliness is seen as the product of the systematic use of identifiable interactional devices, such as turn-taking, adjacency pairing of conversational turns (e.g., question–answer), and temporal and spatial sequencing that participants in interactions use as solutions to discourse organizational problems. Although these devices are quite general, they also allow for adaptation to local circumstances. As a result, they can be considered to be both 'context-free' and 'context-sensitive' (Schlegoff & Sacks, 1973). The basic reasoning in CA is that methodological approaches should be appropriate for dealing with the interaction data at hand and for the problems the individual researcher is dealing with at that time, rather than being pre-specified. As such, CA is a specific analytical route that may be followed to gain a systematic insight into the ways in which everyday business is conducted 'at the level of talk', as well as into the interactional and organizational business that is accomplished through that talk (Boden, 1994: 15).

Concept 7.8   Discourse analysis

Discourse analysis focuses on a description of the organization of language in terms of linguistic units larger than the sentence or clause, such as conversational exchanges or texts. Within business discourse research it has been used to establish what patterns exist between longer sections of business talk or text in terms of, for example, typical patterns of initiation or response, what constraints there may be on conversational exchanges, and how business talk is organized more generally (that is, in speaker turns, content episodes, and so on). It follows that discourse analysis is therefore concerned with language use in its social context, and in particular with interaction between speakers. Conversation analysis shares many features with discourse analysis; both investigate structures beyond the sentence and the way stretches of talk cohere and relate to each other. However, whereas conversation analysis tends to be purely descriptive in nature, discourse analysis tends to also be concerned with discovering constraints on conversation patterns. A methodological approach related to both CA and DA is Critical Discourse Analysis. CDA is an approach that assumes a critical point of view in the study of 'politicized' language use in natural speech situations of social relevance (Wodak & Meyer, 2001). By systematically exploring the underlying relationships between discursive practices, texts, and events and wider social and cultural networks and processes, the critical discourse analyst examines issues of social relevance in order to try to draw attention to power imbalance, social inequality, non-democratic practices and other injustices (Fairclough, 1993). In terms of method, CDA can be considered to be supra-linguistic, in that it takes into account the broader discourse context or the meaning beyond the grammatical structure. This includes a consideration of the political, the historic and even the economic, context of language usage and production. CDA has been applied to examine ideologies, power relations and political policy as these are reflected in the media (for instance, by looking at how minority groups are portrayed in newspaper discourse) and in certain types of institutional discourses (usually in [local] governmental institutions, and more rarely in business contexts). In Chapter 1 we discussed Sharon Livesey's work on corporate discourse using a combination of CDA and DA.

A seminal study of spoken discourse in work settings that uses insights from ethnomethodology and CA is provided by Deirdre Boden (1994). We briefly mentioned her landmark work in the introductory chapter of this book. The business talk that formed the data for Boden's investigation originated in a variety of service-industry organizations, including a travel agency, an investment bank, a radio station and a hospital. Based on detailed and rich analyses of structural characteristics (e.g., moves in openings and closings of conversations) and conversational procedures (e.g., adjacency organization and turn-taking) in a variety of business interaction types, Boden illustrates how organizations are effectively 'run' by talk, in that who talks to whom, when, how and why determines how the organization works on a day-to-day basis and how it develops over time. Her work thus substantiates the notion that the relationship between business talk and the organizations in which it occurs is reflexive and reciprocal. Also, her analyses demonstrate that business talk is 'an autonomous domain of action that . . . unfolds independently', but also that talk instantiates and 'creatively extend[s] the organization in which it occurs or about which it deals' (Boden, 1994: 215). What Boden's work demonstrates above all in linking business interaction with large-scale properties of the organizational context is how methodologies generated by CA can be an effective means of studying organizational settings from the perspective of the spoken communication that occurs in them. As we pointed out in Chapter 1, her work is an accessible and readable account of use to anyone interested in how people communicate within organizations.

Using CA to investigate structure in business talk (Halmari, 1993; Marriot, 1995)

Helen Halmari (1993) used CA to identify intercultural differences in the organization of discourse in speech in naturally occurring business conversations over the phone conducted by Finnish and Anglo-American business people. She recorded a corpus of twelve phone conversations, conducted by one and the same Finnish businessman. Five conversations were conducted in Finnish with Finnish business partners, and seven in English with counterparts from the US. Using the model of speech event negotiation developed by Neu (1985) Halmari first analysed the episodic structure of each of the negotiations. She found that there was a clearly identifiable episodic pattern for all of the negotiations, regardless of the cultural backgrounds of the speakers involved. Per episode, Halmari then identified differences in discourse organization between the Finnish–Finnish and Finnish–US data, in terms of openings and side sequences (Jefferson, 1972). Halmari found differences between the two groups of calls in the way opening sequences were structured, and in the importance Finnish and English speakers attach to the transactional episode. Whereas English speakers emphasize the business episode, Finns want to embed business dealings in a positive atmosphere, and therefore attach greater importance to non-topical episodes. According to Halmari, this latter motivation is also the reason why humour was found to be a much-used filler in the Finnish negotiations. Halmari further identified differences in interruption behaviour; for example, the native speakers of English initiated overlaps more than three times as often as native speakers of Finnish, and whereas Finns tended to initiate overlaps close to the end of utterances, the native English speakers tended to initiate overlaps in the middle of utterances or turns. Although such differences may seem insignificant, Halmari suggests that their cumulative effects could have significant outcomes on intercultural encounters, and especially in business-related talk, where mutual understanding and acceptance are prerequisites for doing business successfully.

In another example of a CA-inspired investigation, Helen Marriott (1995) examined the management of discourse in naturally occurring business negotiations between an Australian seller and a Japanese buyer. She used the notions of structural element and discourse topic as the central analytical units, where topic described the speech function performed by linguistic expressions in an interaction. In this way, her methodology clearly draws on CA work in topic organization and development (Atkinson & Heritage, 1984) and topic maintenance and change (e.g., Gardner, 1987). Marriott identified the main structural elements (that is, greeting, introduction, seek information, agreement, and so on) in the case study negotiation, and made a sequential overview of their relative occurrence in the interaction as a whole. In addition, she used information from interviews with the two participants immediately after the negotiation, to identify communicative features that had not been recoverable from surface speech or by observing negotiators' conduct. Marriott's analysis provides a detailed description of the characteristics of negotiation discourse in terms of its recurring structural elements. In addition, the interview data enabled Marriott to determine the underlying reasons for differences between the negotiators' discourse with respect to the sequencing and frequency of structural elements, and topic management. These latter insights in particular provide support for the idea that a multimethod approach is recommended in the study of naturally occurring talk, as it can lead to a better understanding of the communication process, some of which is not observable at surface level.

Further examples of CA approaches to studying the sequential and collaborative construction of meaning in work-based talk (negotiations and meetings)

Björge's (2010) study of verbal and non-verbal backchannelling (i.e. active listening, manifested as 'uhuh', for example) in conflictive or cooperative negotiations in which English was used as a lingua franca (51 participants, 16 nationalities). The study showed that non-verbal backchannelling in the form of head nods was most frequently used, while verbal backchannelling was mainly restricted to 'yes/yeah' and to items not exclusive to English, such as 'mhm' and 'okay'. Backchannelling behaviour also varied depending on conflict level, and giving or withholding support seemed to be used as a negotiation strategy.

Rogerson-Revell's (2008) investigation of the interactive characteristics (with respect to e.g. topic and turn management, turn length and participation levels) of users of English as a lingua franca in international, multi-party meetings. Rogerson-Revell uses a combination of quantitative and qualitative data, and discourse analytical and CA tools, to illustrate how participants in such meetings employ 'a variety of interactive resources and strategies to achieve substantive goals and to establish a sense of normality in situ despite generic and linguistic constraints' (p. 338). Her analyses show that, in terms of procedures and language, both native and non-native speakers engage in 'interactive accommodation', which 'indicat[es] an underlying awareness of some of the issues involved in . . . lingua franca communication' (p. 357).

For an illustrative overview of recent developments in CA as it is applied to intervention programs in medical communication, speech therapy, mediation, welfare interviewing, telephone helplines, and a number of other institutional encounters, see Antaki (2011).

Multimethod approaches to business talk (Charles, 1995; Neu & Graham, 1995)

There are several further pertinent examples of studies of spoken business discourse that have used CA, at least as a methodological starting point, in combination with insights from other disciplines. Charles (1995), for instance, used CA to investigate manifestations of organizational power in authentic business negotiations between native speakers of English. Based on an analysis of discourse topic development as an indicator of power shift in the negotiations, she demonstrates the power differential that characterizes the positions held by buyers and sellers. Furthermore, she demonstrates that negotiations are subject to constant change, both in terms of the power balance between participants at various stages, and the business relationship between organizations over the long term. She makes a convincing case for the need to develop a methodological framework that can accommodate the dynamics of negotiations, and that acknowledges them, not as one-off events, but as steps in a sequence of events that make up the business relationship.

Concept 7.9   Content analysis

Content analysis is a systematic, replicable technique for compressing many words of text into fewer categories of content based on explicit, predetermined coding rules. Researchers use it to make inferences by objectively and systematically identifying specific characteristics of a message. Content analysis is useful for examining trends and patterns in documents. It is not restricted to the domain of text, however, and can be applied to nonverbal communication, including photographs and drawings (for instance, in annual reports or product advertisements), or actions observed in (videotaped) case studies (e.g., negotiations or meetings). Content analysis enables researchers to systematically sift through large volumes of data with relative ease. It is useful for determining and describing the focus of individual, group, or institutional communication events and allows inferences to be made which can then be corroborated using other methods of data collection (triangulation). Krippendorff (1980) notes that content analysis is mostly 'motivated by the search for techniques to infer from symbolic data what would be either too costly, no longer possible, or too obtrusive by the use of other techniques' (1980: 51).

Joyce Neu and John Graham (1995) investigated the verbal behaviour of sellers in sales negotiations to determine whether there is a relationship between language use in negotiations and the tangible outcomes of such encounters. Their study, though informed by CA for the selection of its conversational variables, also involved quantitative statistical procedures to examine the strength and significance of the relationship between language use and negotiation outcomes. Neu and Graham used a content analysis scheme (see Concept 7.9) developed specifically to categorize language strategies in bargaining encounters (Angelmar & Stern, 1978) in order to analyse 24 simulated negotiations. Descriptions of verbal negotiating activities, for example bargaining strategies, were regarded as process measures that functioned as indicators of the efficiency of the negotiation. Additional process measures that were analysed included features of the conversational structure of the negotiations, such as repairs, pauses, pitch changes, laughter and side sequences. The outcome variables the researchers considered were the sellers' profit levels (the direct results of the agreement reached in the simulated negotiations) and the buyers' expressed level of satisfaction (measured post-negotiation in a brief questionnaire). Neu and Graham's results provide evidence of a strong relationship between seller's verbal behaviours and negotiation outcomes. The more the sellers in their study said, the less were their economic rewards and the buyers' satisfaction level at the end of the negotiation. In addition, Neu and Graham found that the conversation structure variables they analysed were more important to the negotiation outcomes than the content variables, suggesting that *how* sellers said things was more important than *what* they said.

Studying business talk: approaches inspired by pragmatics and speech act theory

A number of studies have looked at spoken business talk from the perspective of pragmatics, and more specifically, speech act theory (see Concept 7.10). Broadly speaking, speech act theory considers what people *mean* when they use language. In other words, the focus is on what people do with language rather than on what they say. Speech act theory is partly taxonomic and partly explanatory. It aims to systematically classify types of speech acts, or acts of communication, and the ways in which they can succeed or fail. In doing so, it must take into account the fact that the relationship between the words a speaker uses and the meaning of a particular utterance is often oblique. For instance, a speaker may formulate an utterance literally (directly), for example, 'Open the door', or non-literally (indirectly), for instance, 'It's warm in here'. Essentially, the theory of speech acts tries to account for the fact that speakers succeed in what they do despite the various ways in which linguistic meaning underdetermines use.

Concept 7.10 Pragmatics and speech act theory

At the heart of pragmatics lies the study of meaning. Closely related to semantics (the study of word and sentence meaning), pragmatics concerns itself with the meaning of utterances (that is, spoken language) in the specific context in which they are used. Three levels of meaning can be distinguished:

Abstract meaning (the meaning of words and sentences in isolation, e.g., the various meanings of the word 'bank');

Contextual or utterance meaning (for instance, when a mother says to her small child 'You're a little angel', the utterance 'really' means 'You're a sweet child'); and

> *Utterance 'force'* or how a speaker intends an utterance to be understood (for instance, when X says to Y 'It's raining quite hard now', X may intend the statement as a request to borrow Y's umbrella).
>
> Pragmatics concerns itself primarily with utterance meaning and force, and in doing so, takes into account the interrelationship between speaker and hearer, utterance and context. The notion of force comes from Austin's work (1975) on speech act theory and his distinction into the locution of a speech act (the actual words used in an utterance), its illocution (the force of the intention of the speaker behind the utterance), and its perlocution (the effect of the utterance on the hearer). Speech act theory sees language as action, the basic idea being that when we say something we are simultaneously doing something. It aims to explain the effects of a speaker's utterances on the listener. Speech acts are the 'units' of talk that constitute the action inherent in language (that is, greeting, questioning, joking, [dis]agreeing, apologizing, complimenting, and so on). A speech act may involve more than one move from only one person. For example, 'taking leave' usually involves a sequence of two 'moves' on the part of speaker and hearer (X: 'Well, goodbye then'; Y: 'Bye bye.').
>
> Archer, Aijman and Wichmann's (2012) advanced resource book on pragmatics offers a recent and broad overview of the field of pragmatics, considered from a range of perspectives. It is illustrated with various examples and tasks.

Native and non-native realizations of speech acts (Stalpers, 1995; Neumann, 1997)

An example of a study of spoken business discourse that uses speech act theory as a methodological starting point is Judith Stalpers' comparison of the speech act of disagreement in corpora of native negotiation data (same-culture French and Dutch negotiations), and non-native negotiation data (from mixed, Dutch–French negotiations) (Stalpers, 1995). Stalpers investigated how these potentially 'face-threatening acts' (Brown & Levinson, 1987) are realized linguistically and how disagreements were mitigated, that is, whether and how they were formulated politely, and whether there were differences in the way the non-native and native speakers in her study used mitigation. For her analysis, she used the list of characteristics associated with so-called 'dispreferred acts' (Levinson, 1983) such as disagreements, adapting it to include ten features that can reduce the unwelcome effects that a dispreferred act may have on the hearer. Her analysis showed that disagreements in negotiations are usually mitigated, although not to such a great extent as they are in everyday conversations. This leads her to suggest that business negotiations may exhibit certain features that distinguish them from other types of interaction, and that the relatively low degree of mitigation found in business talk indicates that politeness requirements are more relaxed in negotiation settings than in casual conversation. In other words, business people may prioritize conversational clarity over politeness considerations.

In an analysis of requests in German and Norwegian managers' business talk, Ingrid Neumann considered the speech act of request (Neumann, 1997). Using a corpus of audio-taped authentic business talk (face-to-face negotiations and business calls) between Norwegian and German buyers and sellers nego-tiating in German, Neumann analysed both qualitatively and quantitatively the distribution of, and differences in, request forms selected by the native and non-native speakers. Then, using the directness scale for the speech act of request that was developed as part of the linguistic Cross Cultural Speech Act Realization Project (Blum-Kulka, House & Kasper, 1989), she ranked the request forms she identified in the corpus on a continuum involving directness and indirectness. Neumann's analyses clearly show that in business contexts, with German as the language of communication, Norwegian speakers choose more indirect linguistic strategies than native speakers of German to realize the speech act of request. Furthermore, the Germans in the study were found to have used twice as many requests as the Norwegians. Overall, Neumann found that there was high density of direct request strategies in this business corpus compared with the corpora of everyday language that were investigated by Blum-Kulka, House and Kasper (1989). This latter finding may be a further indication that business people are indeed inclined to override politeness con-siderations for the sake of conversational clarity.

A crosscultural perspective on speech acts in intercultural meetings (Bilbow, 2002)

A final example of a study of spoken business discourse that uses the speech act as a central unit of analysis is Grahame Bilbow's crosscultural investigation of commissive speech acts in intercultural business meetings (Bilbow, 2002). Bilbow's corpus-based study focused on the use, and lexico-grammatical form, of promises and statements of commitment (that is, commissive speech acts) in a series of meetings recorded in a large multinational airline company in Hong Kong. The participants in the meetings belonged to various cultural groups (English-speaking westerners and Cantonese-speaking Chinese). With respect to the overall use and distribution of commissive speech acts in his corpus, Bilbow found that both Chinese and western participants used these types of acts frequently, and to a similar degree. However, there were a number of crosscultural differences between the two groups in terms of the circumstances under which these speech acts were uttered, and how they were realized lexico-grammatically. Interestingly, Bilbow noted that meeting-type may also play a part in determining how, and how often, commissive speech acts are used in business meetings. Within the corpus, crossdepartmental cooperation meetings were found to contain the highest number of commissives, involving the greatest range of linguistic realization strategies. In contrast, weekly departmental meetings and brainstorming sessions contained fewer commissive acts, and a more restricted set of lexico-grammatical realizations for them.

Studying business talk: impression management and socialization in interviews

Jonathan Clifton (2012) conducted a thick, CA-based analysis of the face-work strategies employed by participants in a performance appraisal interview to deal with the inherently face-threatening nature of such encounters. With his consideration of talk-in-interaction, Clifton aims to demonstrate how the analysis of practices in situ (i.e. first order descriptions of discursive practice) can complement and 'enter into dialogue with' the theoretical, static knowledge that resides in the community's 'black box', its Stocks of Interactional Knowledge, or SIKs, which Clifton regards as constituting second order descriptions of practice. Peräkylä and Vehviläinen (2003) defined SIKs as 'normative models and theories or quasi-theories about interaction as part of the knowledge base of many professions [that . . .] can be found in professional texts, in training manuals and in written and spoken instructions in the context of professional training or supervision' (729–30). Although SIKs comprise valuable information on professional practice in a particular community, Clifton argues that only detailed analyses of actual discursive practice (like the appraisal interview) in a particular community can help clarify the apparent gap (or mismatch) between actual practice and practitioners' theory, and by extension, 'disprove or confirm assumptions inherent in existing SIKs, provide more detailed descriptions of SIKs-in-action, and add . . . unexplored dimensions to SIKs' (2012: 303).

Caroline Lipovsky's (2006) study of intercultural (French–English) job interviews shows how candidates negotiate their expertise to make a good impression on their interviewers. The investigation establishes a methodologically useful link between lexico-grammatical analysis and impression management theory. Lipovsky bases her analyses on discourse generated in five role-played interviews in French and four authentic interviews in either French or French and English, focusing on the candidates' comments on the impression they tried to convey and the interviewers' comments on the impression they had of the candidates. Using a systemic functional approach and the theory of politeness, she highlights how candidates' lexico-grammatical choices in particular play a role in their interviewers' impressions of them. Her analysis also shows that the candidates' discourse and therefore the impression they make is linked to their ongoing interaction with the interviewers.

Jan Scheuer (2001) looks at authentic Danish job interviews to explore the relationship between success (or failure) of applicants in relation to communicative style. Drawing on critical discourse analysis and sociolinguistics, and through qualitative and quantitative analyses of spoken language, he demonstrates that certain communicative styles and recontextualizations formed by a combination of lifeworld and job-related perspectives would seem to lead to (greater) success in job interviews. Interviewers are shown to be sensitive to the applicant's communicative style and distinguish between applicants on the basis of particular attributes of social identity, that is attributes that are a consequence of their social background. Universal attributes, acquired by people regardless of their social background, such as education level, are consequently placed in the background. Thus, the interviewers do not distinguish between individuals, but rather between types of communicative socialization.

Studies of business negotiation

Compared to other types of business talk, negotiation has been – relatively speaking – a much-researched genre. For decades, interest in the analysis of business negotiations has been evident in various disciplines, including behavioural decision theory, economics, political science, communications, and anthropology. The primary motivation has usually been purely practical, and this has resulted in a sizable body of research-based, prescriptively-oriented literature that covers training in negotiation skills, including crosscultural negotiation training, and that offers tactical advice for business practitioners on how to maximize negotiation outcomes and individual negotiator effectiveness (e.g., Raiffa, 1985; Fisher & Ury, 1991; Bazerman, Lewicki & Sheppard, 1991; Bazerman & Neale, 1992; Ury, 1993). Other dimensions of interest in business negotiations have been ethnographic, ethnological and social-psychological. Here, research into business negotiation has offered crosscultural comparative analyses of the role of negotiation in various cultural contexts, focusing for the most part on negotiation types that differ from western negotiation culture, and analyses of the role of individual participants in the negotiation activity, seen from the perspective of negotiators, and within the socio-psychological context in which they operate (see Rubin & Brown, 1975; Putnam & Roloff, 1992, for overviews of negotiation literature in these areas). Overall however, these areas of negotiation research, in focusing mainly on negotiating effectiveness and end results, have offered only limited insight so far into the structural or discoursal elements of business negotiations.

Discourse-based studies of negotiation as communication

In comparison to the wealth of negotiation studies generated in other disciplines, there are relatively few studies that have considered negotiation at the level of language or discourse, as a type of spoken business discourse. However, since the 1990s, there has been a steady increase in language-based studies of business negotiation, such as those profiled in the collections edited by Ehlich and Wagner (1995), Firth (1995), and Bargiela-Chiappini and Harris (1997a). Other notable examples of discourse-based negotiation studies include:

Pedro Garcez (1993): a crosscultural investigation of differences in point-making styles between US and Brazilian business negotiators;

Mirjaliisa Charles (1996): a study of discourse organization and rhetorical strategies in new relationship versus old relationship negotiations involving English native speakers;

Julio Gimenez (2001): a crosscultural exploration of emerging discourse patterns in negotiation interactions involving non-native speakers of English.

Face concerns in business negotiations: language-based studies of negotiation discourse

A small, but very useful, group of language-based studies of business negotiation has specifically considered face-related issues in negotiation and how such concerns manifest themselves in negotiation discourse. Face, the speaker's need to be respected and liked, and the social recognition of the listener's positive self-image, are salient in any type of communication, but particularly so in settings where participants may encounter potential conflict. Business negotiations constitute such a setting, as they are associated with both cooperation and (potential) conflict. In such situations, negotiators have to risk threatening each other's face while simultaneously maintaining a good business relationship with the other party at the same time. As a result, negotiators will need to engage in a considerable amount of linguistic 'diplomacy', or facework. Facework is defined as 'the actions undertaken by a person to make whatever he or she is doing consistent with face' (Goffman, 1967). Face can be created and given by the communicative moves, or the linguistic facework, interactants undertake. Facework can be engaged in to maintain or enhance face, or to repair face loss. Concern about face has been found to be an important determinant of negotiation behaviour. Various social psychological studies have shown a relationship between face concerns and negotiation strategies (e.g., Brown, 1977; Folger & Poole, 1984). In general, the greater the concern for face loss, the more defensive the tactics a negotiator will employ.

Many of the language-oriented studies of face-motivated behaviour in business negotiation have used insights from Brown and Levinson's politeness theory

(Brown & Levinson, 1987). Using a cross-cultural analysis of how face-threatening speech acts are realized linguistically in three different languages, Brown and Levinson posited a universal theory of politeness, and presented a universal taxonomy of linguistic output strategies that constitutes a speaker's politeness – or facework – repertoire. Discourse-based studies of negotiation that have used an approach based on Brown and Levinson's theory include van der Wijst (1996) who explored the relationship between linguistic facework and negotiator relationship factors (e.g., power difference and social distance) in Dutch business negotiations to test the predictions of politeness theory, and Charles (1996) who analysed, among other things, face-saving hedging devices in authentic English business negotiations to arrive at an explanation for certain role-bound buyer and seller behaviours. Grindsted (1995) focused on the use of joking as a strategy for creating rapport and affiliation in Spanish and Danish naturally occurring negotiations, while Planken (2002) used Brown and Levinson's taxonomy of politeness strategies to investigate aspects of rapport management in simulated intercultural business negotiations involving English as a lingua franca. Finally, van der Wijst and Ulijn (1995) analysed polite linguistic behaviour in the different stages of simulated negotiations in French (between Dutch and French negotiators), Villemoes (1995) compared facework in naturally-occurring Spanish and Danish negotiation data, and Stalpers (1995) considered differences in the mitigation strategies used in disagreements in native (Dutch and French) and non-native (Dutch–French) negotiation encounters. All these studies show the wealth of important information that can be gleaned by considering not only the language choices that speakers make in negotiation situations, but also their underlying intentions in doing so (see also the Language in the Workplace project that we profiled in Chapter 4; for an overview of studies of face, and what constitutes face in interaction, see also Bargiela-Chiappini & Haugh, 2010).

Investigating spoken business discourse: example projects

Individual: An investigation of the differences between buyers' and sellers' verbal behaviour in sales negotiations (cf. Charles, 1996; Vuorela, 2005); an investigation of politeness in face-threatening speech acts (e.g. refusal, criticism, directive) in authentic workplace communication (cf. Planken, 2005; Vine, 2009).

Collaborative: A cross-cultural investigation of aspects of meetings (that is, structure, language, and so on) in different national contexts (cf. Yamada, 2002; Bilbow, 2002).

Group: A contrastive analysis of business telephone calls (structure and language) in different national contexts (cf. Halmari, 1993; Sifianou, 1989; Planken, 2005).

7.4　Investigating text quality and text production: studies in (business) document design

An emerging body of research that incorporates studies of business discourse is that of document design. This discipline combines insights and methodologies from language and communication studies and is aimed at 'creating comprehensible, persuasive and usable functional documents' (Jansen & Maes, 1999: 2). Broadly speaking, document design studies aim to test the communicative quality of functional texts in order to improve them. Unlike most of the research approaches we have looked at so far in this volume, it is therefore prescriptive rather than descriptive in its rationale. The document types that form the focus of research can generally be distinguished on the basis of their purpose: they are informative (aimed at presenting information), instructional (aimed at guiding behaviour) or persuasive (aimed at eliciting behaviour). Methods that are used to determine text quality can be categorized as either text-focused or reader-focused (see Schriver, 1989, for an extensive overview of text evaluation methodologies). Within a business and institutional (government) context, such texts tend to be aimed at external target groups (shareholders, customers, citizens, recruitees, consumers, and so on). A growing number of document design studies aimed at testing variables determining the documents' effectiveness have involved business and institutional discourse, including annual reports (e.g., Courtis & Hassan, 2002; de Groot, Korzilius, Gerritsen & Nickerson, 2011), business proposals (for instance, Lagerwerf & Bossers, 2002), product advertisements (e.g., Hoeken, van de Brandt, Crijns, Dominguez, Hendriks, Planken & Starren, 2003; Hornikx, van Meurs, & de Boer, 2010), tv and radio commercials (for instance, Gerritsen, Korzilius, van Meurs & Gijsbers, 2000; Smakman, Korzilius, van Meurs, & van Neerven, 2009), job advertisements (e.g., Yüce & Highhouse, 1998; van Meurs, Korzilius & Hermans, 2004; van Meurs, Korzilius, Planken & Fairley, 2007), public documents (for instance, Steehouder & Jansen 1992, on forms), product manuals (e.g., Jansen & Balijon, 2002 on patterns of use of instruction guides), and patient package inserts (Gerritsen, Nederstigt & Orlandini, 2006).

Examples of contextualized studies of document design

Document design research also investigates the *process* of text production, and particularly how complex functional texts come into being through collaborative writing, in both institutional and corporate settings. Such studies have promoted our understanding of:

- how and in what context writing takes place in various stages of the writing process (e.g., Bock, 1994; Swales & Rogers, 1995; Janssen & van der Mast, 2001; van der Mast & Janssen, 2001);

- what strategies writers employ to bring about consensus in the collaborative writing process (e.g., Janssen, 1991);
- how policy writers collaboratively revise and edit documents (e.g., van der Mast & Janssen, 2001; Flowerdew & Wan, 2006).

In the remainder of this section we will profile two studies from the field of document design in some detail. The first investigation uses a multimethod approach to test the functional and textual quality of a multilingual public information brochure about motor vehicle tax, published by the Dutch Ministry of Finance (Hulst & Lentz, 2001). The second study adopts a longitudinal, ethnographic approach to investigate the collaborative construction of a management report in a Municipal community of practice in the US (Wegner, 2004).

Text evaluation: testing a public document in a multilingual context (Hulst & Lentz, 2001)

Jacqueline Hulst and Leo Lentz report on a research project carried out for the Dutch Ministry of Finance. Although the Dutch government communicates with residents of the Netherlands in Dutch, it also translates around six per cent of information in brochures and leaflets into other languages, to facilitate communication with the growing segment of the population whose native language is not Dutch. For document designers working in such a multilingual context it is relevant to determine which criteria apply in the decision to translate government information or not, to decide which languages information should be translated into, and how the quality of such translations can be assessed. Following on from these practical questions, and particularly the third question, Hulst and Lentz's methodological aim for this project was to integrate knowledge from the field of document design with approaches from translation studies, in order to widen the scope of quality control of public documents, which are generally tested and improved a number of times before final publication, from *monolingual* to *multilingual* communication.

Concept 7.11   Text analysis

Text analysis methodology includes a broad variety of approaches to researching text, including stylistics, rhetorical moves analysis and corpus analysis. Although the main focus is on the systematic analysis of naturally occurring, that is authentic (usually written) data, text analysts also take into account the social nature of text. Essentially, they investigate how speakers and writers employ language and linguistic strategies to achieve particular communication purposes, and what this tells us about given communication contexts or the relationships between participants. In business discourse research, text analysis has helped us to characterize and better understand communication in various business-related contexts, involving a broad range of genres and media, and has allowed us to observe and describe corporate discourse communities, including their practices, philosophies, ideologies, intentions and internal relationships.

We focus here on the part of the project in which the researchers evaluated the quality of one specific document that is published by the Ministry in five languages besides Dutch (French, English, Spanish, Turkish and Arabic). The information in the document is about motor vehicle tax and is published in a single multilingual brochure entitled 'Your car and Dutch motor vehicle tax'. With regard to the choice of other languages besides Dutch, the researchers note that the decision to translate the brochure into these five languages had been taken ad hoc. As there was no multilingual policy in place, at least not while the study was conducted, the person responsible for communicating tax information to the general public simply made the decision to translate the document into these five languages. The only plausible reason given was that the document had been presented in this way for years, suggesting that tradition, rather than any clearly defined criteria, seemed to legitimize the choice of languages, for this particular brochure at least. With respect to translation policy too, none of the Ministry officials responsible for publishing the documents could clarify who had translated the Dutch text, or how, and whether any pilot-tests had taken place. Furthermore, there was no explanation for the fact that German, a much-used foreign language in the Netherlands and within the European Union, had not been considered for inclusion in the brochure.

Concept 7.12   Document design

Simply put, Document Design as a field of research can be explained as the study of what makes a document work, whether it is a brochure circulated by the local council, an online complaints form, an instructional manual or a mission statement. Document Design studies the instruments and tools that can be used to convey the correct and appropriate message to the readers the message is aimed at, using potential readers as 'informants' in the cyclical design process. It entails 'paper' communication but also communication via other media, including electronic media (for computer-based learning, e-marketing, online help, and so on), video, signage, hypertext and multimedia.

   Patricia Wright's research is a good example of recent developments in document design, in that it has examined the effectiveness of linguistic as well as visual design cues in aiding users of online information to carry out certain ' tasks' (e.g. find information, make decisions or follow instructions). For example, together with her colleagues, she has investigated the trade-off between using multimodal design features and the cognitive demands their use puts on readers working with (online) information to achieve task goals. Her research centres on documents aimed at various types of users, including the elderly, audiences whose first language is not English and adults with low literacy rates (e.g. Wright, 2012; Wright, 2011; Wright et al., 2010; Wright et al., 2008).

To evaluate the actual translations in the brochure, Hulst and Lentz combined two methods, a text-focused evaluation aimed at determining the functional quality of the document (that is, to assess whether the information in the document helps achieve the communicative goals formulated for the document by the Ministry), and a reader-focused evaluation to test the quality of the document from the target groups' perspective, consisting of a combination of open interviews and a performance test. For the text-focused evaluation, Hulst and Lentz used a team of excellent students of translation studies at Utrecht University, the Netherlands, who were also native speakers of the five target languages. Although these students could be regarded as translation experts, they had not been trained specifically in document design. Therefore, to prepare them for the text-based evaluation, they started the project with a training session aimed at familiarizing them with common methods of text evaluation and principles of effective document design. For the reader-focused evaluation, Hulst and Lentz used an instrument that combined an open individual interview with a structured questionnaire on text comprehension. In the open interview, relevant readers (that is, members of the intended target groups of the document) were asked to read the text and to mark passages that evoked positive or negative feelings with a plus or a minus sign respectively (for details on the so-called 'plus-minus' method, see for example, de Jong & Schellens, 1997). They were then asked to explain their motives for assigning positive or negative marks in the text. Finally, the readers were asked a number of comprehension check questions, to ascertain that they had understood the text, and to determine which information from the brochure they used for their answers.

Hulst and Lentz's findings clearly show that both the functional and the textual quality of the translated documents left something to be desired. For example, several bilingual Turkish readers involved in the reader-focused evaluation were forced to turn to the original Dutch text in an attempt to understand the Turkish translation. The Arabic expert evaluators qualified the Arabic text as very bad on all aspects of text quality. The quality of the Spanish text was judged to be well below the level of an average student of Spanish in the Netherlands. The English and French texts were found to be less problematic, but even here, the text quality was deemed to be below standard.

Hulst and Lentz's observations regarding the lack of translation and multilingual policy, together with the findings of the evaluation of the brochure texts by experts and readers, strongly suggest that there is an urgent need in government institutions to manage the quality of the process of multilingual communication systematically and responsibly. It seems plausible that the findings from this study of multilingual government communication would be similar in corporate contexts in which multilingual translations (of instruction leaflets, product advertisements, and so on) are the order of the day. Therefore, companies that employ multilingual written communication (both external and internal) could do worse than to take heed of the methodological recommendations made on the basis of studies such as these, regarding translation procedures, criteria for language choice, and the evaluation of the functional quality of information texts. There is also clearly scope for further research of a similar type but in different contexts in the future.

Quote 7.3 Ethnomethodology as an approach to workplace studies

Known primarily as the author of a *method* for studying work, Harold Garfinkel – and ethnomethodological studies of work, or workplace studies – also offer an important alternative *theory* of work. First articulated in the late 1940s and early 1950s as a theory of communication, organization and information, it has been Garfinkel's proposal that mutual understanding . . . requires constant mutual orientation by participants in the discourse community to situated constitutive expectations – *taken-for-granted methods of producing order that constitutes sense* – accompanied by displays of attention, accounts, competence and trust. Based on this premise, researchers need to enter worksites to learn the order (i.e. structured and structuring) properties of work (actions). Conventional theories tend to treat social orders (including work) as resulting from individual interests, external constraint, and/or some conjunction between the two. For Garfinkel, however, individual motivation, power, and constraint must be managed by workers in and through the details of work. He insists that the need for participants to mutually produce order on each next occasion adequately explains the details of orders and sense-making. Thus, any worksite exhibits details required to produce, manage and understand local orders of work, including power and constraint – details that are local matters, lost to general formulation, required on a research approach focused on the order properties of those details.

Garfinkel maintains that each action in the workplace must exhibit an order that is recognizable to other members of the same situation in order to be meaningful. It is the achievement and display of such recognizable orders that allows for mutual understanding – sense-making – and coordinated action. The argument that meaning requires order, and the empirical investigation of how the construction and recognition of activities (i.e. situated practice) is achieved by discourse community members through sequential devices and reflexive attention, are Garfinkel's unique contribution to social action theory.

(Taken from Warfield Rawls, 2008: 701, 703, slightly adapted)

Text production: the collaborative construction of a new text form (Wegner, 2004)

In the final study we discuss in this chapter, Diane Wegner provides a fascinating ethnographic account tracing the genesis and development over time of a collaboratively constructed policy text to examine how managers in the Parks Division of a growing US municipality tackle the writing of a new type of management report, for which no textual model is available. The management report in question is described by Wegner (2004) as 'a municipal plan for managing natural areas' and has a broad scope, encompassing – for the first time – the municipality's policy regarding the management of all the natural areas and parks they administer. As a result of the extensive brief of the management plan, its different components (17 in all) were assigned to (groups of) different members of staff, departments and environmental interest groups, both inside and outside the Parks Division. It was therefore truly a collaborative – and indeed complex – undertaking.

Wegner's multifaceted and detailed analysis essentially centres on two key features of the situation: the role of the participants in the project, and the role of audiences whom the participants see as resistant to the plan. To determine how the writing process developed over time and how the document itself took shape through various cycles of production and revision, Wegner employed ethnographic methods, involving, among other things, a detailed study of related internal documentation (minutes of meetings, memos, guidelines, interim reports, and so on) and observations of and interviews with participants, to collect their comments regarding the text in production, and to track how they negotiated the development and transformation of draft versions in project meetings and written revisions. The study involved 17 of the participants involved in writing the plan, which was produced over the period 2000–2001.

Examples of studies of collaborative writing in workplace settings

Sandra Gollin (1999) investigated the interactive cycles involved in the collaborative writing of a number of documents (that is, information paper,
questionnaire, progress update, final report) in an Australian consultancy
firm specializing in projects with an environmental focus. Over the course
of three months, she used a largely ethnographic approach (case study;
interviews; observation; text analysis) to study how the participation of different types of contributor to the writing process (that is, designated writers,
stakeholders, steering committee, client) affected and shaped the development of the texts under study. By modelling the writing process (in terms
of 'circles of collaboration', 'planes of negotiation', and power relations
between contributors), Gollin formulates a number of recommendations for
the teaching of writing in professional contexts, which she regards a necessity in a business world that is becoming increasingly reliant on networking
and (virtual) teamwork 'online'.

Geoffrey Cross (2001) reports in detail on an ethnographic study of collaboration in a large financial conglomerate based in the US. Cross's research
centred around three months of fulltime observation in the corporation,
during which he collected 1,500 pages of transcribed data, and 500 pages of
field notes and documents to analyse the collaborative writing (involving
20 business units) of a Service Level Agreement (SLA) for the Technological
Services unit. The SLA was to detail services, provide quality control and
define the relevance of Technological Services to the corporation's future.
Cross's study is a model of ethnographic research, and can be considered
to be one of a kind, as this type of large-scale collaboration has not been
studied before in such detail. The work also provides an example of a contextualized approach to researching business communication: by tracing
the creation of the SLA document within the context of the corporation's
history, corporate strategy, corporate culture and the main players and units
involved in the collaborative effort, Cross models the cycles of collaborative effort (and their obstacles and catalysts) at various levels, and circles, in
the corporation. His analyses offer insights into many collaborative writing
activities, such as meetings, drafting and using feedback.

Based on her analyses, Wegner broadly offers insight into two cycles of activity,
one historical, the other immediate. Firstly, she demonstrates how a description
of the cycles – or drafts – of the management plan show how successive groups
of participants, with overlapping membership, collaborate in successive 'zones of
development'. As they complete each cycle of activity, they transform the text
and achieve another step toward the development of the final version. Secondly,
through small-scale analyses of concrete and immediate problem-solving episodes

between the participants in project meetings, Wegner shows how text production involves the use of the text as a mediational tool. From their different perspectives, participants respond to the text, which functions in turn as a tool for problem solving and for achieving the document's functional and rhetorical goals. According to Wegner, what unifies these processes of construction is the concept of genre, in both its textual and contextual dimensions. In collaborative deliberations and learning, genre involves the text both as the product the participants create and as a mediational tool. As a process, genre advances the writing process through successive stages of the text's development.

Quote 7.4   On the cyclical nature of collaborative problem solving

[I]n expansions of work cycles, team members solved problems using familiar tools and concepts. [. . . A]s participants responded to the draft, which functioned as a mediational means, they solved problems to achieve the goal of audience acceptance. In other words, they used the need to produce text to learn textual and situational dimensions of the genre, producing a textual revision that was a partial and preliminary strategy. At the same time, participants were also renegotiating the problem of audience reception to recontextualize the problem as an issue to be addressed in the next cycle of problem solving.

(Wegner 2004: 444)

What makes Wegner's study particularly interesting is that it contributes to our understanding of the interface between text and context, and to our understanding of recent conceptualizations of genre as an activity system that can help provide greater insights into the inherently complex relationship between genre and learning.

Investigating text quality and text production: example projects

Individual: An investigation of the production of one corporate document (e.g., mission statement, annual report, and so on), including the collaborative writing process it involves (cf. Gollin, 1999; Pogner, 1999; Wegner, 2004).

Collaborative: An investigation of reader response to the use of English in local job advertisements, in which researchers representing different fields collaborate to combine multidisciplinary research methodologies, such as linguistic discourse analysis and different experimental approaches (cf. van

Meurs, Korzilius & Hermans, 2004; van Meurs, Korzilius, Planken & Fairley, 2007).

Group: An analysis of reader response (that is, with respect to clarity, comprehensibility, etc.) to user manuals translated for different national audiences (cf. Hulst & Lentz, 2001; Jansen & Balijon, 2002; Gerritsen, Nederstigt & Orlandini, 2006).

In this chapter we have looked at four main areas of interest that can be identified in business discourse research, particularly where language and communication are viewed as 'socially constructed' discourse. We have highlighted some of the methodologies and analytical approaches researchers have used, and discussed some of the theoretical frameworks that have formed the starting point for their enquiries. For each area of research, we have also suggested projects in the same vein that could be undertaken individually, on a collaborative basis or in a group.

In Chapter 8, we will look in detail at ten key research studies, or research initiatives, that showcase the work of a number of researchers of business discourse from around the world, as well as a wide range of recent business discourse research topics. Within this volume, these studies serve as illustrative examples of how the various theories and methodologies that we have highlighted throughout may be applied (and combined) in a specific research project. The ten investigations can thus be used by students, researchers and educators alike as a basis for replication studies, or as inspiration for further investigation in current and emerging areas of interest in the field of business discourse.

Further reading

Cameron, D. (2001). *Working with spoken discourse*. London: Sage Publications. This critical text discusses current approaches, concepts and debates in the field of spoken discourse, providing a grounding in the practical techniques of discourse analysis and how these can be applied to analysing real data in a variety of social contexts.

Fairclough, N. (2003). *Analyzing discourse: Textual analysis for social research*. London & New York: Routledge. An introduction to text and discourse analysis, providing a step-by-step guide to investigating authentic language data that allows students and researchers to get the most out of their data.

Gee, P. (2005). *Introduction to discourse analysis*. London: Routledge. This volume considers how language (spoken and written) embodies social and cultural perspectives and identities. It incorporates perspectives from a variety of disciplines, including applied linguistics, education, psychology, anthropology and communication to help students formulate their own views on discourse and to conduct their own discourse analysis.

Have, P., ten (2007). *Doing Conversation Analysis (Second edition)*. London: Sage Publications. This textbook has been substantially revised to bring it up-to-date with the many changes that have occurred in Conversation Analysis over recent years. The book has a twofold purpose: to introduce readers to Conversation Analysis (CA) as a research approach in the human (social) sciences, and to provide students and novice researchers with methodological and practical suggestions for doing their own CA-based research.

Richards, K. (2009). *Language and Professional Identity: Aspects of Collaborative Interaction.* Basingstoke: Palgrave Macmillan. This volume draws on recordings and interviews to reveal how professional groups communicate to construct and reinforce shared identity and professional dividends in subtle and surprising ways. The chapters deal with various aspects of professional talk, such as humour, argument and storytelling, and show how these are used as resources to create and promote collaborative communication in professional groups working in academia.

Wooffitt, R. (2005). *Conversation analysis and discourse analysis: A comparative and critical introduction.* Thousand Oaks: Sage Publications. This book provides a critical and comparative overview of the fields of conversation analysis, discourse analysis, critical discourse analysis and discursive psychology. It illustrates the various methodological approaches through detailed analyses of data.

8
Research Cases

This chapter will present ten research studies that showcase the work of business discourse researchers from around the world. The studies reflect many of the themes, research sites and approaches discussed in the rest of this volume, and illustrate the different facets of business discourse research today. For each study, details will be given of the business genre or genres under investigation, the research methodology(ies) used and the theories and paradigms referred to in the approach to analysis. Each study will be presented using the structure of a research article:

- Summary;
- Introduction and aims;
- Method;
- Findings;
- Commentary (Discussion & suggestions for future research).

The studies can be used by students, researchers and educators alike as a basis for replication studies or as inspiration for further investigation into current and emerging topics of interest in the field.

8.1 Customer-friendly e-service? How Dutch and American companies deal with customers' email inquiries

Summary 8.1

Van Mulken, M., & van der Meer, W. (2005). Are you being served? A genre analysis of American and Dutch company replies to customer enquiries. *English for Specific Purposes*, 24, 93–109.

The authors use inductive genre analysis to determine whether customer service email is a distinct genre (in terms of moves structure), and to establish whether there exist differences in the way Dutch and American companies (Old and Newly established) deal with email enquiries relating to customer service. They conclude that email customer service replies are not distinct from their paper-based counterparts, and that there appear to be only few differences between Dutch and American companies' e-replies overall, with respect to preferences for certain moves. The study also investigates the use of rhetorical interpersonal strategies to build rapport in e-replies, and of indicators of customer-friendly behaviour (response time, response quality, and so on).

Introduction and aims

Customer service plays an important role in quality management. It can contribute to establishing a relationship between customers and the organization, and can help build trust and customer loyalty. This corpus-based investigation focuses on an important domain of customer service that involves electronic discourse, namely Internet-based, one-to-one written contact between (potential) customers and companies. By means of what the authors term 'an inductive sample analysis', this genre analytical study aimed to determine the proto-typicality and structure of the 'e-service reply' as a potentially distinct genre. More specifically, it aimed to determine whether the e-service reply is a potential subgenre of the pre-genre of business email in general (see e.g. Louhiala-Salminen, 1997), and whether it is distinct from its paper-based counterparts. In addition, the study considered the overall customer-friendliness of the companies who sent the e-service replies that formed the corpus. Finally, it investigated whether there are differences in the way Dutch and American companies, and established and relatively new companies, deal with e-inquiries, in order to gain insight into whether cultural preferences (at the level of both national and corporate culture) play a role in shaping the structural moves and rhetorical strategies used in e-service replies.

On the one hand, the literature on cultural differences and contrastive findings from studies of Dutch versus American business letters led the researchers to expect differences between the American and Dutch companies in the way they react to customer inquiries via email. On the other hand, as marketing theories around the world would now seem to have employed a largely Anglo-American perspective, the researchers also kept in mind the possibility that this universal approach to marketing would have erased regional differences between Dutch and American customer e-service.

Quote 8.1   The importance of customer e-service

In the era where 'competition is just a click away', customer e-service has become an important issue in marketing policies. Many customers that buy on-line goods, base their opinions of the company on the way their inquiries are responded to. . . . Internet-based contact between (potential) customer and company can be a very cost-effective means of getting to know the individual customer's wishes, and at the same time informing them of a company's latest developments (Hanson, 1999). . . . Garbarino and Johnson (1999) have shown that for customers, trust and commitment are of the utmost importance for future contact and future intentions. . . . One way to improve the relationship between customer and Web-based company is through one-on-one communication via e-mail. (Van Mulken & van der Meer, 2005: 95)

Method

To establish whether e-replies to customer inquiries constitute a distinct genre, the researchers first located the company reply within the promotional discourse framework. They regard the customer inquiry as part of a genre of promotional discourse, an element that occurs in a sequence of interrelated communicative actions (that is, customer inquiry–company reply–[customer reaction]). The customer e-inquiry and the company e-reply are phases in the so-called pre-order sequence, which forms part of the commercial transaction genre system (Yates & Orlikowski, 2002). The communicative purposes that motivate such email exchanges are the customer's need for information and the company's interest in engaging with a potential customer. The company reply can therefore be characterized as mostly informational and to some extent promotional. According to the researchers, the communicative form of the initial action is crucial, as subsequent actions in the sequence are unlikely to change in terms of channel choice, formality level and address form.

Data

To elicit authentic company e-replies, the researchers constructed a 'typical rhetorical situation' that Dutch and American companies were likely to react to using a 'typified response' (Yates & Orlikowski, 2002). They created a standardized email inquiry, supposedly from a potential international customer (Dutch or American), implying interest in a particular product, and asking for specific information (the distributor's address, the cost of shipping, and conditions of guarantee). The inquiry was kept simple and straightforward, in order to make it as easy as possible to reply quickly and without much effort on the part of a company's customer service personnel. As the level of formality used by the customer in the email inquiry could potentially have been an important determinant of the company's reply, the researchers aimed to formulate the inquiry using neutral language. To this end, they ran a pre-test, in which they asked three independent judges to choose the most neutral message out of three versions containing the same requests for information. The judges unanimously picked one version, which was used as the stimulus inquiry in the data collection phase of the study (see Data 8.1). The e-inquiry was sent to 20 Dutch and 20 American companies. All were manufacturers of personal computers and peripheral equipment (speaker sets, wireless keyboards, and so on). Given their product field, they were all expected to be familiar with email communication. Within each group of 20, ten companies were Old and ten were Newly established. The determinant for classifying a company as Old or New was the year it was founded (before or after 1990). Both types of companies were included in the study for the following reason. If e-replies to customer service inquiries were indeed a newly emerging genre, then it was thought that older companies, with a well-established customer service policy in place, would be likely to 'borrow' elements of established genres (e.g., customer service letters) in their e-replies. In contrast, newer companies, unhampered by established communication patterns and traditions, would be expected to create a more prototypical e-reply.

The participating companies were deliberately not told beforehand of the survey, so that any company e-replies to the standardized e-inquiry could be regarded as an authentic sample text. The Dutch computer companies received the e-inquiry from a potential American customer, while the American computer companies received the inquiry from a potential customer from the Netherlands. The communication sequences between the potential customer and the computer companies could thus be regarded as examples of intercultural business discourse.

Data 8.1   Standardized e-inquiry used to elicit e-replies from Dutch and US IT companies

Hello

I visited your website and am curious if you have a distributor in my country (the Netherlands). If so, could you direct me to his address, or provide any other contact information? I also wonder if you can indicate the average cost of shipping from the US to the Netherlands, if I choose to order over the Internet? Furthermore, what guarantee do you offer on your products for a potential international customer like myself?

Thank you,
John Petersen
The Netherlands

(Van Mulken & van der Meer, 2005: 100)

In answer to the 40 inquiries sent out, 24 replies were received. Six Dutch New, seven Dutch Old, seven American New, and three American Old companies replied; all but one (who posted their reply on an Internet webpage) replied via email sent to the address of the customer. Some of the replies were automated responses; all 24 emails were included in the subsequent analysis.

Analysis

The corpus of e-replies was analysed in terms of the moves that occurred in each text. In this way, the researchers investigated the proto-typicality of the structure of the set of e-replies. As a rule, a move was included in the move structure when it occurred in 75 per cent or more of the e-replies, and when it seemed characteristic of the communicative action in question. Moves that seemed typical but occurred in less than 75 per cent of responses were typified within the structure as subsidiary moves. Any additional moves were considered to be idiosyncratic, and as such were assigned to the class of 'unexpected moves'.

Quote 8.2

> We opted for an essentially inductive way of determining genre: we let the data – a sample of responses, written by members of one discourse community that share 'structure, style, content and intended audience' and that share text characteristics decide on their generic properties. In this essentially iterative process, we defined the most common denominator for company replies via email, that is, we looked for 'family resemblances'. . . . This is the process that Paltridge (1995: 404) has called 'genre assignment, [which] happens on the basis of both pragmatic and conceptual conditions of "sufficient similarity"'.
>
> (Van Mulken & van der Meer, 2005: 100)

Main findings

The overall structure to emerge from the analysis of the corpus identified four typified moves that were seen to combine to serve the overall communicative purpose of the genre, that is, to establish a customer friendly contact. According to the researchers, the moves can be viewed as discriminative for the genre, as they are non-optional elements that characterize the e-reply's rhetorical structure; the four moves were each found in 75 per cent or more of the sample texts.

The cross-company type analysis showed that only one of the ten Old companies in the sample used the Presentation of Self move, as opposed to four of the 14 New companies. Three of these New companies were Dutch. The researchers suggest that the New companies were also fairly small and might therefore feel a greater need to develop a close relationship with potential customers. Only two of the 13 Dutch companies (both Old) thanked the customer, whereas nearly all the American companies that replied expressed their gratitude to the customer (eight out of ten replies). This leads the researchers to suggest that Expressing Thanks seems to be a typically American move. Overall, New companies were more keen to invite Further Contact (seven out of 14) than Old companies (two out of ten) and there were no differences between Old and New, and American and Dutch companies' replies with respect to including the Justification move. In sum, there were no intrinsic differences between Old and New and American and Dutch companies with regard to move structure, that is, the occurrence of a particular move was not restricted to one or more of the subsets of e-replies (from Old versus New companies, or American versus Dutch companies).

In an effort to determine companies' overall customer-friendliness, the researchers took a number of indicators of customer-orientedness and responsiveness into account. First, they looked at the response rate of the 40 companies contacted initially; a total of 24 (60 per cent) replied, leading the researchers to conclude that the 16 companies who neglected to reply failed to meet the basic requirement for customer friendliness, by essentially ignoring a potential customer. Second, the researchers looked at e-response time; it took US companies an average of 0.9 days, and Dutch companies an average of 1.3 days to respond to the e-inquiry. This would seem to be fairly slow, as the response time for business emails averages as little as 1–2 hours (e.g., Zemke & Connellan, 2001). Further indicators of customer friendliness that were taken into account were whether companies sent an automated acknowledgement that they had received an inquiry (most of the companies did) and how 'complete' and 'concrete' the 24 e-replies were. With respect to the latter, four companies who replied did not in fact answer the customer's questions at all (instead providing promotional information and a hyperlink to the products page of their website). On the whole, Old companies and New companies (both Dutch and US) put in similar efforts in terms of the number of questions dealt with in their e-replies (answering an average of 1.5 of the 3 questions posed in the standardized e-inquiry).

Data 8.2   Example of a company reply

[John]_Salutation
[Thank you for contacting Company-Name Customer Service] _Thanks
[Unfortunately, we are not set up to ship to Europe from here.]_ Apologize
[We don't have a branch in Europe for these sales. I would go to: http://webpage and see if they can help you.] _ Answer

[If you have any further questions, don't hesitate to ask.]_ Further contact
[Thank you!
Charley]_ Close
Customer Service

(Van Mulken & van der Meer, 2005: 100)

The researchers also determined the degree of customer friendliness expressed in the e-replies at the rhetorical level. To this end, they analysed the corpus with respect to a number of interpersonal rhetorical strategies that writers can use to establish a personalized relationship between them and the reader/customer. For example, the researchers looked at the use of 'hedges', a rhetorical means of 'softening' or minimizing face threat and damage to personal credibility that simultaneously contributes to an atmosphere of professional openness (Hyland, 1998). In the e-replies, such hedges were used mostly in suggestions (e.g., 'You *may* wish to try www.companyname.com' or 'I *would* go to Company X's website'). Other textualizations that were regarded as indicators of a personalized approach in the e-replies included the use of politeness markers (e.g., '*Please* let me know if I can be of further assistance '), the use of active versus passive constructions (passives are often used as a 'distancing' device between writer and reader, to impersonalize messages), and the use of so-called 'attitude markers' including attitude verbs (that is *to hope, to be sorry*, and so on) and attitude adverbs (e.g., *unfortunately, thankfully*, and so on) that writers use to signal their attitude to the content of a message (e.g., '*Unfortunately*, we don't sell products in the US'). Although the researchers found evidence of the use of 'customer-friendly' rhetorical strategies in the e-replies in the corpus (for an example, see Data 8.2), there appeared to be no striking differences in the use of individual or sets of rhetorical strategies between the e-replies of the different companies (Old/ New; US/Dutch).

Quote 8.3   Electronic format as a discourse medium: implications for the categorization of genre

Since the move structure [of e-replies] does not differ intrinsically between the two groups [of companies], and since variation in customer friendly behaviour and rhetorical interpersonal strategies concern only minor differences, we conclude that there is no necessity to distinguish the electronic company replies from their paper-based counterparts. The electronic format is . . . a channel choice, a medium of discourse, and this format entails register consequences: the style is informal, salutations and closings are often omitted, and form of address is direct and straightforward, as is characteristic for electronic communication in general . . . . We also suggest, on the basis of these findings, that in order to assign genre, one has to abstract from register, i.e., medium characteristics imposed by the channel choice. It is conceivable that medium characteristics have implications for the move structure, in the sense that moves are omitted (such as openings and closings in e-communication) or added (such as literal citations in e-mail, often preceded by _>_). These channel variations allow the move structure of the overarching genre to become more flexible and more dynamic.

(Van Mulken & van der Meer, 2005: 106)

Commentary

This study shows how a multifaceted, multimethod approach to genre (part experiment, part inductive corpus analysis) can help to throw light on how text-external factors, as well as text-internal features, contribute to the achievement of a text type's communicative purpose(s). In the case of the e-replies in this study, the researchers provide convincing evidence to suggest that, within the text, providing concrete and relevant information to answer the customer's question(s) can contribute to the communicative purpose of establishing a promising contact with a potential customer, as can the use of rhetorical strategies that express a personalized and customer-friendly approach by the company behind the message. Factors external to the actual message, however, such as a company's response rate and response time are likely to determine, at least to some extent, how potential customers view that company in terms of customer-orientedness and reliability. Thus, text-external factors are likely to interact with text-internal features in that both can contribute to achieving the text's communicative purpose – to a greater or lesser extent.

Quote 8.4   Suggestions for further research

[W]e investigated whether American and Dutch companies differ in their reply to customer inquiries via electronic mail. We have seen that there are some culturally different preferences, but these concern proportional differences: some moves are more favored than others. We found no idiosyncratic moves. We therefore have reasons to believe that De Mooij (2004) is right in suggesting that globalization, at least in the Anglo-Saxon world, allows genres to cross borders. . . . Whether this also holds true for other cultures, such as Mediterranean countries or African or Asiatic cultures certainly deserves to be investigated. . . . In future research, it would also be interesting to set up an experiment to investigate how Dutch and American customers appreciate this type of customer service. Do Dutch customers expect another type of customer policy than American customers? How do Dutch customers respond to a prototypical American customer service reply and vice versa? On the basis of this study, we may conclude that, in an era where '(international) competition is just a click away', a detailed analysis of customer service policy is worthwhile in the battle for customer retention.

(Van Mulken & van der Meer 2005: 107)

8.2   Standardize or adapt? Audience reaction to localized product advertisements

Summary 8.2

Hoeken, H., van den Brandt, C., Crijns, R., Dominguez, N., Hendriks, B., Planken, B., & Starren, M. (2003). International advertising in Western Europe: Should differences in uncertainty avoidance be considered when advertising in Belgium, France, the Netherlands and Spain? *Journal of Business Communication, 40(3)*, 195–218.

This study surveyed potential target (consumer) groups of different nationalities to test experimentally whether international advertising texts that use appeals to values regarded as important in a given target group's national culture are more persuasive than advertising texts that appeal to values considered as less important in a target group's national culture. The study aimed to provide insight into the ongoing debate among scholars of intercultural business discourse, and international advertising in particular, as to whether cultural differences between target audiences necessitate adaptation of advertising to local circumstances.

Introduction and aims

Cultures differ with respect to which values (or 'life rules') are considered important (e.g., Hofstede, 2001). Such variation in assigning importance to values lies at the core of cultural differences. With respect to international advertising, a number of authors have suggested that adapting advertising texts to cultural differences and local circumstances may make such texts more successful (for instance, de Mooij, 1998). For example, if an advertising text appeals to values that a given target group regards as important in their culture, it is likely that it will be perceived more favourably by that target group than if such an advertisement appeals to cultural values that the target group regards as less important. Using a reader-focused, experimental design, Hoeken et al.

tested that assumption. Reader-focused research, which surveys an intended audience's reactions to elements of a given document or text, is a much-used method in document design research to determine aspects of text functionality (see Chapter 7).

The central aim of the study was to investigate whether product advertisements that appeal to a value regarded as important in a given target culture are more persuasive than advertisements that appeal to values that are less important in that culture. The study involved a survey of target groups from Spain, Belgium, France and the Netherlands, in which the researchers gauged respondents' reactions to a product advertisement for a watch. According to Hofstede (2001), the four countries under study differ with respect to the cultural dimension 'uncertainty avoidance', which is defined as 'the extent to which members of a culture feel threatened by uncertain or unknown situations' (161). Spain, Belgium and France can be regarded as high uncertainty avoidance cultures (where people feel uncomfortable about unexpected situations), while the Netherlands, in contrast, is a relatively low uncertainty avoidance culture.

In Hoeken et al.'s investigation, an experiment was set up to test specifically whether appealing to 'security' (a value regarded as important in high uncertainty avoidance cultures) indeed made the advertisement for the watch more persuasive in the high uncertainty avoidance cultures involved in their study (that is, France, Belgium and Spain) than in the low uncertainty avoidance culture (that is, the Netherlands). By the same token, they tested whether the same advertisement with an appeal to 'adventure' (a value regarded as important in low uncertainty avoidance cultures) made the text more persuasive in the low uncertainty avoidance culture in the study (that is, the Netherlands) than in the high uncertainty avoidance cultures (that is, France, Belgium and Spain).

Concept 8.1   Geert Hofstede's dimensions of culture

The lack of a universally applicable framework for classifying cultural patterns has been pointed out by a number of researchers. The most often cited work in this area is the research by the organizational anthropologist Hofstede who derived five dimensions of culture from a large-scale survey of work-related values among IBM employees from countries around the world. In his original study (conducted in the 1970s) he conceptualized cultural differences in terms of four dimensions: power distance, individualism/ collectivism, masculinity/femininity and uncertainty avoidance (Hofstede, 1984). Based on follow-up research, he conceptualized a fifth dimension, long-term orientation (Hofstede, 2001; for information on the results of Hofstede's surveys and an overview of individual country scores, see also: http://geert-hofstede.com).

Method

Materials

For the experiment, two versions (in Dutch) were constructed of an advertisement for a watch. A fictitious brand name (Tempus) was used in the ad to avoid evoking established attitudes towards existing watch brands. Hoeken et al. opted to use an advertisement for this specific product because research shows that cultural values are especially influential in the consumer's evaluation of products that are 'socially visible', that is, products that consumers can be seen to wear or to use by peer group members whose opinions they value (Zhang & Gelb, 1996). In the advertisement, consisting of a short text superimposed on a photograph of someone entering a restaurant, a person (supposedly the person in the photograph) describes his or her favourite night out. The two versions of the text that were constructed for the experiment only differed with respect to which aspects of an evening out were described. In one version, the evening was described as uneventful, without any surprises (*we went to our favourite restaurant and to a classical concert that received positive reviews only*). This version appealed to 'security' values, which members of high uncertainty avoidance cultures, such as Spain, Belgium and France have been found to regard as important (Schwartz, 1992). The second version of the advertisement described the evening out as unpredictable and full of surprises *(a new restaurant we've never tried before; an experimental music concert)*. This text appealed to a sense of 'adventure', a value regarded as important by members of low uncertainty avoidance cultures, such as the Netherlands. The pair of advertisements was pre-tested by (Dutch) representatives of the intended target group, who offered further suggestions about the choice of photograph, the wording of the text, and the appeal to the different values. This process eventually resulted in two versions of the watch advertisement that were the same with respect to the visual elements, the overall layout and the number of sentences, and differed only with respect to the values appealed to (see Data 8.3 for an English translation of the two versions of the text).

Data 8.3   The text of the two different ad versions (Hoeken et al. 2003: 205)

Appealing to high uncertainty values (or 'security')	Appealing to low uncertainty values (or 'adventure')
Tonight?	Tonight?
First: dining out. In our favourite restaurant. We've gone there for years. It is a place we definitely like. Then on to the theatre. A classical composition. It got rave reviews.	First: dining out in that new restaurant. Never been there before. Are not sure we will like it. Then on to the theatre. An experimental composition. The reviews were mixed.

| For us, an evening out is an evening in familiar surroundings – where we don't have to keep track of the time. My Tempus does that. | For us, an evening out is an evening full of new experiences – where we don't have to keep track of the time. My Tempus does that. |

Next, using the translation-back-translation method, equivalent translations in Spanish and French were made: one translator translated the Dutch version into French or Spanish and another translator then translated the French or Spanish versions back into Dutch. The original Dutch text and the translations into Dutch were compared; the versions were very similar, suggesting that the French and Spanish translations were sufficiently equivalent to the original Dutch version of the advertisement to be used in the experiment. Finally, the French and Spanish versions were presented to native speakers of those languages who checked the naturalness and idiomaticity of the texts, as well as the extent to which a text appealed to the intended values.

Respondents and procedure

A between-subjects design was used for the experiment. That is, participants read only one version of the advertisement, in the language that was relevant to them. The different versions of the advertisement were distributed randomly across the respondent groups in the four countries. A total of 476 volunteer respondents took part (142 from Belgium, 125 from France, 108 from Spain, and 101 from the Netherlands). All participants were students in humanities departments at various universities in the four countries (mean age: 21). The researchers chose a homogeneous pool of respondents (students) across the four countries (similar in terms of age, background, and potentially, interests) to limit the risk of potential variation as a result of independent background variables as much as possible (e.g., vastly different age groups in the sample might have regarded different sets of values within their 'cultural value set' as important, relative to each other, or might have responded differently to the leisure events described in the ads, and so on). This is, of course, common practice in experimental research. However, it is also true that students are a much-used source of respondents in research, as they tend to be accessible, particularly to researchers based in universities who work within the academic, rather than the practice-based, tradition.

  The dependent variables associated with the research questions were measured through items in a written questionnaire. The translation-back-translation method was used to create equivalent questionnaires in Dutch, French and Spanish. To assess the persuasiveness of the advertisement, respondents' attitudes towards the advertisement and towards the product were measured using seven-point semantic differentials and seven-point Likert scales (see Data 8.4; and Concept 3.1).

Data 8.4 Examples of items used by Hoeken et al. (2003)

Examples of *semantic differentials* (scales with adjectival opposites at either end):
I think this watch looks . . .
Very attractive 0 0 0 0 0 0 0 Very unattractive
Very modern 0 0 0 0 0 0 0 Extremely old-fashioned

Examples of *Likert scales* (scales that allow respondents to indicate [dis]agreement with statements):
I would consider buying this watch.
Completely agree 0 0 0 0 0 0 0 Completely disagree
If I needed a watch, I would definitely buy this watch.
Completely agree 0 0 0 0 0 0 0 Completely disagree

A number of control questions were also included in the questionnaire. These aimed to determine the external validity of the experimental materials, that is, whether respondents regarded the advertisement as typical for a watch advertisement and typical for a product advertisement in a given country. Finally, the questionnaire included a shortened version of Schwartz's (1992) value list to determine individual respondents' value hierarchies. In this way, the researchers could determine whether the relative importance of different cultural values (relating to high or low uncertainty avoidance) assumed in the literature for the countries under study could be confirmed with respect to individual respondents in the four groups that represented the countries in the investigation. Thus, this list of items served as a 'check' to see whether the supposed cultural differences also applied to the respondents in the study at an individual level (that is, to determine cultural versus personal preference).

The experiment was conducted over a number of weeks at various universities in the four countries in the study, and always during class seminars on a topic that was not relevant to the investigation (for instance, linguistics or communication skills training). The researchers introduced the experiment as a survey that was being carried out to determine consumers' opinions about a new watch brand to be introduced on the European market.

Main findings

The main research aim was to determine whether appealing to a high uncertainty avoidance value (security) would result in a more persuasive watch advertisement for the Belgian, French, and Spanish respondents and, conversely, whether appealing to a low uncertainty avoidance value (stimulation) would make that same watch advertisement more appealing to the Dutch participants. The prediction that a security appeal would yield a more persuasive advertisement in a high uncertainty avoidance culture whereas a stimulation appeal would yield a more persuasive advertisement in a low uncertainty avoidance culture was based on two assumptions. The first was that appealing to a value higher in the individual's value hierarchy would yield a more persuasive advertisement. The results showed that this assumption appeared to have been well-founded: when the data were analysed using differences in *individual* hierarchy (based on the Schwartz's list) instead of *nationality* as a factor, the interaction between advertising appeal and value hierarchy became significant. That is, an appeal to security proved to be more persuasive for people who valued security more than stimulation, whereas it was far less persuasive for people who valued stimulation more than security. For the security appeal then, the findings confirmed the expected relationship between an individual's value hierarchy and advertising appeal.

The second assumption was that respondents from countries that Hofstede (1984; 2001) regards as different with respect to uncertainty avoidance would hold different value hierarchies, specifically with respect to the value categories security and stimulation. This assumption proved to be unfounded. The number of respondents from the three high uncertainty avoidance cultures that preferred security values was exactly the same as the number of participants that preferred stimulation values. For the respondents from the low uncertainty avoidance culture, the preference ran counter to the researcher's prediction: the number of respondents that preferred security to stimulation exceeded the number of participants that showed a reversed preference. These results seem to support the observation made by a number of researchers recently that western European cultures are becoming more homogeneous.

Commentary

Research on cultural differences in relation to the persuasiveness of value appeals has tended to focus on only one cultural dimension (individualism–collectivism) and on only one set of countries (the US versus Asian countries). The findings from these studies have indeed indicated that there are cultural differences in persuasiveness (e.g., Zhang & Gelb, 1996; Aaker, 2000). However, Hoeken et al.'s findings seem to suggest that the results of such studies may be restricted to appeals relating to the dimension individualism–collectivism only, and to cross-cultural comparisons of Asian countries versus the US. Also, their results suggest that using appeals associated with one of the other cultural dimensions (in this case uncertainty avoidance) in countries that are much more alike in terms of culture than the US–East-Asian countries does not bring about country by advertising appeal interactions. Clearly, studies like this have great relevance for the international business community in general and for international marketing in particular. However, for business professionals who are not directly involved in international marketing communication, the results may be of relevance too. Business people frequently have to communicate with counterparts from other countries, about whom they often know little more than what their nationality is. Hoeken et al.'s results show that Shelby (1998) provides good advice when she suggests that a persuasive document should be adapted to suit the audience's preferences: in Hoeken et al.'s study, appealing to security did indeed yield a more persuasive advertisement for those valuing security more than stimulation. However, Hoeken et al. also point out that caution should be exercised with regard to business communication practices in the western European context, in that it would be risky (and perhaps simplistic) to take Hofstede's cultural dimensions as a point of departure for adapting external business messages to different cultural target groups within this region. In other words, a relative 'micro study' such as this can be useful in building a case for or against overarching claims and generalizations made on the basis of large-scale macro studies such as Hofstede's (Hofstede, 1984; 2001).

8.3 Tailor-made teaching: the English workplace needs of textile merchandisers in Hong Kong

Summary 8.3

Li So-mui, F., & Mead, K. (2000). An analysis of English in the workplace: the communication needs of textile and clothing merchandisers. *English for Specific Purposes 19*, 351–68.

This survey-based study combines various methodologies to investigate the workplace English needs of textile and clothing merchandisers in Hong Kong who communicate in an international marketplace. By combining different methodologies and data sources, the researchers gained a detailed understanding of the communication demands on merchandisers and used that knowledge to develop learning and teaching materials (for courses in English for specific business purposes) to suit the specific workplace needs of Hong Kong clothing merchandisers.

Introduction and aims

The authors of this needs analysis study are both business discourse researchers who also teach English for specific business purposes to students taking textile and clothing related courses at two Hong Kong institutions. Their investigation is a typical example of practice-based research arising from a pedagogical need to obtain a detailed understanding of the business discourse and workplace

English needs of a specific industry target group, with the aim of developing up to date, relevant, needs-based teaching materials for that group. The investigation incorporated two independent but complementary multiperspective needs analyses, focusing on the communication required by graduates working as merchandisers in the textile and clothing industry, who had studied at the two institutions at which the authors were teaching at the time.

Quote 8.5   A characterization of merchandisers

A merchandiser requires considerable business communication skills in addition to specialist technical knowledge and his/her role is defined by Hay (1976: 7) as 'a junior or middle manager whose responsibility is mainly the marketing and financial side of the buying/selection operation, quantities, size breakdown, distribution, contracts, etc.' The position of merchandiser normally involves communication with several customers and may include:

- the buyer who places the order for the consignment of garments;
- the supplier of fabric, yarn and accessories;
- the manufacturer/factory involved in producing the garments.

Since the buyers and, suppliers and manufacturers are normally based in different countries, it is frequently necessary for the merchandiser to communicate with the different parties in the international language of business, English.

(Li So-mui & Mead, 2000: 353)

Method

The respondents in this study were 360 graduate students from two institutions: The Hong Kong Polytechnic University (PolyU) and the Kwun Tong Technical Institute (KTTI). All the graduates had been working as merchandisers for at least one year and had taken English and Communication units as part of their degree courses. The design of the investigation followed the methodological approach proposed for communication needs analysis by Hutchinson and Waters (1987), who distinguish target needs (or what a learner needs to be able to do in the target communication situation), and learning needs. As learning needs were being addressed separately in simultaneous investigations within the larger project, Li So-mui and Mead focused only on target needs, further operationalized as necessities, wants and lacks (cf. Allwright & Allwright, 1977, and their so-called 'deficiency analysis'). The design further involved a broad range of ethnographic methodologies and data from multiple sources: information was collected through questionnaires and follow-up telephone interviews, by analysing authentic workplace texts, and by visiting and observing respondents at work.

The researchers essentially conducted two written surveys, each aimed at graduates from one of the two educational institutions. Although the time period in which the two surveys were administered differed (1995 and 1996), and the questionnaires used in the two surveys varied in terms of length and question 'depth', both questionnaires were similar to the extent that they contained questions relating to the six main topic areas relevant to this study: the extent of English usage at work, the countries with which business was conducted, the most common communication channel(s), the preferred communication channel(s); the main purpose(s) of written communication, and the use of abbreviations in written messages. This last topic was included as recent graduates had indicated that the use of abbreviations in written communication in the workplace was widespread, and that they had found this aspect of writing style particularly difficult to understand and to use themselves.

The overall response rates for the written survey were 43 per cent (that is, 130 questionnaires) for graduates from PolyU and 33 per cent (that is, 20 questionnaires) for graduates from KTTI. The researchers then used telephone interviews to follow up on the questionnaire responses of a subset of 18 respondents from both institutions. In addition, they conducted 15 telephone interviews with the workplace supervisors of these respondents in order to collect information regarding company communication profiles, and to establish the supervisors' views about the graduates' specific communication needs. The interviews with the respondents and supervisors were used both to supplement the questionnaire data and to achieve greater validity and reliability overall.

Throughout the investigation, the respondents provided authentic samples of correspondence (their own as well as texts received) which were analysed in terms of writing style (including the use of abbreviations). In addition, the researchers made a number of workplace visits to gather macro-contextual data: to a Hong Kong-based buying office to observe merchandisers at work and to gain an understanding of this type of company, and to a local textile factory in order to observe how garments are produced and what communication is required in the process.

Main findings

The results from the written surveys showed that English was used extensively at work, but far more in written than in spoken contexts. Still, evidence of the use of at least some spoken English was found for over 50 per cent of respondents. With respect to the countries with which graduates commonly conducted business (and communicated) it was found that China was most frequently mentioned (mentioned by approximately 60 per cent in both surveys), followed by the USA (mentioned by approximately 40 per cent in both surveys). Other countries with which graduates conducted trade included Japan, Macau, Taiwan, Korea, Canada, Italy and the United Kingdom. English was used by the merchandizers in communication with most of these countries. Chinese was used extensively in contacts with China, Macau and Taiwan.

Fax was rated as the most frequently used channel of communication in both surveys (mentioned by 59 per cent of graduates from PolyU and 50 per cent from TTTI), followed by the telephone (23 per cent and 35 per cent) and email (15 per cent and 5 per cent). The results further showed that fax was also the most preferred communication channel (by approximately 50 per cent of respondents in both surveys). There were some differences between the two groups of graduates surveyed in terms of preferences for email, telephone and face-to-face communication but almost no (differences in) preferences with respect to letters, telex and forms.

Quote 8.6

E-mail was not very widely used at the time these surveys were conducted . . . ; however, it is becoming an increasingly popular channel and further investigations are being carried out to determine current usage. This is in line with Hutchinson and Waters' advice (1987, p. 59) that needs analysis 'should be a continuing process, in which the conclusions drawn are constantly checked and re-assessed.'

(Li So-mui & Mead, 2000: 357)

With respect to the main purposes of written communication, the surveys showed that the written activity ranked as highest (that is, most frequently used) was 'describing products'. Three further activities that were ranked highly were 'following up and order', 'advising updated order status' and 'clarifying order queries'. Activities that were reported in both surveys as occurring less frequently included 'negotiating for better order terms', 'negotiating or settling a claim' and 'making a claim'. With respect to the final topic of investigation, the use of abbreviations in written communication, respondents reported using abbreviations themselves (88 per cent of PolyU respondents versus 85 per cent of TTTI respondents), and provided examples of the abbreviations used (e.g., 'pls' for 'please'; 'cfm' for 'confirm'; 'adv' for 'advice'; 'gmt' for 'garment'; 'px' for 'price'; 'b/4' for 'before'). An analysis of authentic workplace texts supplied by the respondents corroborated the findings from the surveys with respect to the frequent use of abbreviations in writing. From the follow-up telephone interviews with workplace supervisors it emerged that they were satisfied on the whole with graduates' language and communication skills, but that they felt that graduates were equipped inadequately to deal with more demanding communicative tasks in English, such as negotiating

and making claims. This impression was confirmed by the data from the follow-up interviews with graduates, where interviewees expressed the need for a
better command of English in complex communicative activities, as coping well
in such contexts was seen as a prerequisite for advancement in the organization.
The interviews also pointed out differences in opinion between graduates and
their supervisors. Whereas the graduates mainly expressed concern about the
need for grammatical accuracy in their writing, the supervisors regarded correctness of content and appropriateness of tone as more important needs. In
their comments relating to these two aspects, they expressed concern about
the legal implications that could result from miscommunication at the level
of content, and the fact that the use of an unfriendly or unsympathetic tone
could spoil the business relationship. Grammatical errors were of no concern
to the supervisors as long as they did not interfere with the reader's comprehension.

Data 8.5   Example of an authentic text

NOW RE-SEND THIS MSG TO U. PLS CFM RECEIPT BY RTN.

1. U/STAND WE R TO FLW THE WASHG STANDARD OF JOF SMPLS TO PROCEED W/BULK
   WSHG.
2. EST WHOLE ORD CAN COMPLETE WASHG NXT WK-END 8/29/30. AFTER WASH GMTS W/B
   TRIMMED N CHECKED B4 SENDG TO PRESSG DEPT.
3. OUR PRESSING DEPT W/B PRETTY BUSY 1ST WK IN SEPT RUSHG OUT THE JOP CORDUROY
   ORD. B'COS OF THE DELAY OF THIS LL BEAN ORD. ALL GMTS WL NOW B IN THE PRESSG
   DEPT AT THE SAME TIME. BELIEVE WE CANNOT COMPLETE BOTH JOP N LL BEAN IN
   1 SHOT.
4. AS THIS IS OUR FIRST CORDUROY ORD FOR LL BEAN WE WANT GMTS TO B INSPECTED IN EOT
   B4 SHPG. WE T/F RQST THAT VAL VISIT EOT ON/ABT 9/10 FOR BULK SHPT ON 9/12 VSSL.
5. FYI WE CAN PROPOSE SPLIT SHPT FOR 9/9 + 9/12\SSL (1/2 QTY EA). HWR NOT SURE IF
   BYR WL ACPT. IF ACPTABLE, THEN WE WUD WANT 9/6 AUDIT FOR 9/9 PORTION N 9/10
   AUDIT FOR 9/12 PORTION.

TKS N RGDS.

(Li So-Mui & Mead, 2000: 365)

The researchers' analysis of 100 authentic texts, mostly faxes, showed that the
type of written communication required in the textile industry is unlike the
'standard' exemplified and taught on the basis of textbooks. The sample texts,
on the whole, were hard to read because they were printed entirely in upper-
case letters, were often not divided into paragraphs (but presented as one solid
block of text), used few or no (sub)headings, and contained many abbreviations.

With respect to tone, there were numerous examples in the texts where writers had failed to adopt a positive, cooperative tone, using instead an accusative tone that could endanger the relationship with the reader/ customer.

Finally, the company visits conducted by the researchers confirmed many of the observations made by respondents in the interviews and impressions gleaned from the surveys. In addition, as these visits gave the researchers a fuller understanding of the complexities of communication in the workplace, they could introduce language learning activities to their courses which reflect more accurately the communication tasks required of future graduates in this particular industry.

Quote 8.7

These [workplace] visits have enriched our understanding of the complex work involved in the production and merchandising of garments and have enabled us to introduce language learning activities which more closely match the working environment our students will enter.

(Li So-Mui & Mead, 2000: 363)

Commentary

This study is an example of a multifaceted analysis of graduate communication needs in a specific industry, combining perception data (from surveys), analyses of authentic communication, and workplace data (through observation and interviews). It shows convincingly how such an approach can be used to provide directly relevant and up-to-date input regarding language and communication skills needs in relevant international environments for developers of teaching materials who want to provide more specifically focused business English courses for their students.

Needs-based studies of organizational discourse practices

A number of studies that have used needs analysis (surveys) like Li So-Mui and Mead to investigate business discourse practices in (international and multinational) organizational contexts were already discussed in Chapters 3 and 6 (e.g. Jackson, 2005; Chew, 2005; Cowling, 2007; Erling & Walton, 2007; Deneire, 2008; Kaewpet, 2009; Evans, 2010; Randall & Samimi, 2010).

A further example is a recent study by de Groot (2012), which examines the implications of a corporate language strategy on communication efficiency in a Dutch international company, by using a cross-national survey of (foreign) language use and language needs of around 800 Dutch-based and German-based employees in the organization's international business units. One of the things the study demonstrates is that although English is used most frequently (and successfully) with international colleagues for internal communication it is not perceived as equally effective in external communication contexts across national borders. The overall findings of the study indicate that employees' individual language background affects their language skills (both active and passive), which in turn suggests that introducing English as the corporate language is feasible, as long as provisions are made at the same time to promote and facilitate language use for specific language groups within the organization. What this investigation demonstrates perhaps above all is what the value of quantitative research (in this case, a cross-national employee survey) can be as a starting point for formulating a relevant corporate language policy that contributes to achieving an organization's strategic communication goals on the one hand, while responding to employees' communication needs on the other.

8.4   English as a lingua franca in corporate mergers

Summary 8.4

Louhiala-Salminen, L., Charles, M., & Kankaanranta, A. (2005). English as a lingua franca in Nordic corporate mergers: Two case companies, *English for Specific Purposes, 24*, 401–21.

This multimethod study investigates the use of English as a lingua franca in two Swedish–Finnish corporate mergers. It combines a questionnaire survey, interviews and the analysis of both spoken and written forms of communication used within the corporations, to identify the similarities and differences between the Swedish and Finnish employees, and it discusses the cultural and communicative challenges that those employees were faced with in order to get their work done.

Introduction and aims

Leena Louhiala-Salminen and her colleagues begin their article by underlining the recent increase in the number of crossborder mergers and acquisitions between corporations, most especially within the Nordic countries (Denmark, Finland, Iceland, Norway and Sweden). Within these countries in particular, this has caused a number of corporations to opt for English as their official corporate language, rather than what has been the traditional lingua franca within the region, that is, a variant of Swedish referred to as 'Scandinavian' (*skandinaviska*), which is a combination of the closely related languages of Swedish, Norwegian, Danish and Icelandic (see Quote 8.8 for further details).

This study looks at the consequences of opting for English for the employees working within two crossborder mergers between Swedish and Finnish companies, focusing in particular on the perceptions that the two different cultures hold of each other and the spoken and written discourse they produced within the corporation.

The study focuses on two crossborder mergers dating from the late 1990s, involving Finnish and Swedish partners and their corporate language policies. The first company was a paper manufacturer, Paper Giant, which had been formed in 1998 from the Finnish company 'Paper' and the Swedish company 'Giant', and the second was a banking group, 'PankkiBanken', formed in 1997, from the Finnish 'Pankki' and the Swedish 'Banken'. Paper Giant opted for English as their corporate language from the beginning, whereas PankkiBanken originally opted for Swedish, as this was seen as a first language for the Swedish employees and an official second language for the Finnish speaking staff, and since much company documentation was already in Swedish, it was felt that it would save both time and money to use it. As Louhiala-Salminen et al., point out, however, despite the fact that Swedish is an official second language in Finland, 'many Finnish people's ability to speak Swedish is not at a standard which allows even general communication to take place easily, let alone professional communication' (2005: 403), and indeed the PankkiBanken decision to use Swedish as an official reporting and management language, caused a number of problems for the Finnish speaking staff. In 2000, when the group expanded to Denmark and Norway, to become Scandi Bank, the language policy issue was re-evaluated and the decision was made to adopt English as the official corporate language.

The central aim of the study was to identify the 'cultural and linguistic challenges' that were faced by Finnish and Swedish speaking employees at Paper Giant and PankkiBanken/Scandi Bank as a result of the decision to use Business English Lingua Franca (BELF) (2005: 403). In order to investigate this, Louhiala-Salminen et al. identified three key areas of interest:

1. the communicative practices at Paper Giant and PankkiBanken/Scandi Bank;
2. the perceptions that Finnish and Swedish employees had of each other's communication cultures and communicative practices;
3. the discourse produced in spoken and written crosscultural interactions in BELF within the corporations, for example, in meetings and in email (2005: 403).

These three aspects of the communication at Paper Giant and PankkiBanken/ Scandi Bank were investigated using several different sets of data and different methods of collection and analysis, as we will detail below.

Quote 8.8   The shift from 'Scandinavian' to English as a business lingua franca

The switch from 'Scandinavian' to English as the regional lingua franca is reflected in the fact that today, pan-Nordic corporations increasingly choose English as their corporate language. [T]his language choice means that corporate level documentation and all reporting is done in English, and communication between different units is also mostly in English. Though standards of English are generally high in Scandinavia . . . the use of English – a foreign language in all Scandinavian countries – to this extent and in these kinds of demanding professional activities nevertheless puts great pressure on staff, particularly in competitive international business, where the requirements and stakes are high. These pressures become particularly acute in merger situations.

(Louhiala-Salminen et al., 2005: 402)

Method

In the first part of the project, in order to investigate the communicative practices at Paper Giant and PankkiBanken/Scandi Bank and the perceptions that Finnish and Swedish employees had of each other's communication cultures and communicative practices, the researchers used a questionnaire survey, together with a set of interviews. The questionnaire was circulated to 520 Paper Giant employees (260 in Sweden and 260 in Finland) and 400 Finnish (200) and Swedish (200) Scandi Bank employees, in the first half of 2001. These were selected at random from the complete corporate population in each case, to provide a representative sample of different positions and corporate units. The questionnaire consisted of 30 questions, covering issues such as the daily routines of communication, language choice in specific situations, and the characteristics of what the respondents considered to be 'typically Swedish' and 'typically Finnish' communication (see Louhiala-Salminen, 2002, for further details). Fifty-five per cent of the Scandi Bank sample responded, as did 33 per cent of the Paper Giant sample. Louhiala-Salminen at al. comment that 'Although the Paper Giant response rate of 33 per cent cannot be regarded as fully satisfactory, the rates were, however, considered acceptable for the purposes of this study, since the aim was to look for general trends among the views of the employees, not for exact information on the distribution of the population's views' (2005: 405). The research team then followed up the questionnaire with 31 interviews at the two companies to clarify the information that they had received from the wider populations.

In the second part of the project, the research team investigated whether the characteristics that the respondents had identified as being 'typically Swedish' and 'typically Finnish' were reflected in the discourse associated with each national culture. In order to do this, they analysed the discourse characteristics of four videoed meetings (around nine hours of talk) with a total of 16 Finnish and 15 Swedish participants at both corporations, as well as the discourse characteristics of 114 English messages written by 27 Finnish and 23 Swedish Paper Giant employees. The meetings were analysed using an ethnomethodological or Conversational Analysis (CA) approach, and the email messages were analysed using a genre approach (see Table 8.1 for an overview of the methods used by Louhiala-Salminen et al.).

Main findings

The questionnaires and interviews

In the questionnaires and interviews, the respondents reported that 'the daily routines of communication and the use of languages in both companies, and in both countries, were largely similar' (2005: 406). For example, both nationalities and both corporations reported that around 80 per cent of their time was spent in internal communication, and more than half of the respondents across the board reported that they were involved in crossborder communication on a weekly, or even, daily basis. In addition, the use of English had increased in both countries and both companies from the pre-merger situation to the present (2001), and accounted for around 20 per cent of all communication in all four contexts, and in both companies, the Finns spent more time on email whereas the Swedes attended more meetings. The choice of language depended

Table 8.1 Overview of methods used by Louhiala-Salminen et al. (2005)

Data	Method of analysis	Aim
920 questionnaires 31 interviews	Open & Closed questions Statistical analysis (percentage distributions, mean values, cross-tabulations)	Identification of communicative practices and perception of own and other's culture
4 (BELF) meetings (video)	CA	Identification of discourse realizations reflecting the national cultural characteristics identified in the questionnaires/interviews
114 (BELF) emails	Genre Analysis	Identification of discourse realizations reflecting national cultural characteristics identified in the questionnaires/interviews

on a variety of factors, including the target group and the group members' language skills, the status of English as the corporate language, and the medium of communication (see also the discussion of Bäck's work on code choice in Chapter 4). The respondents reported difficulties related to the use of foreign languages in situations such as using the telephone, in detecting nuances, and in giving an opinion suddenly (and effectively) in meetings (see also the discussion of Charles and Marschan-Piekkari (2002) in Chapter 4 for more details on the communication difficulties encountered in horizontal communication in multinational corporations).

Quote 8.9 The use of BELF in multinational organizations

Contrary to expectations . . . the proportion of English used did not correspond directly to the respondents hierarchical position in the organization; at all levels there were individuals who reported that practically all their company-internal communication (all written material, the majority of meetings and telephone calls) was in English, and there were those who almost entirely used their mother tongue. Although this survey did not give us data to examine what kind of tasks in the organization require more proficiency in English than others, it was possible to see that in these multinational organizations, such positions exist at all organizational levels and in all business units.

(Louhiala-Salminen et al., 2005: 406, slightly adapted)

The questionnaire and interviews revealed descriptions of what was 'typically Swedish' and 'typically Finnish' communication: 'Swedes were seen to be "discussive" and "wordy", Finns "direct" and "economical with words" ' (2005: 408). Louhiala-Salminen et al. report that the respondents' answers were consistent in reporting on Swedish 'discussion' and Finnish 'directness'. Data 8.6 shows some of the perceptions of Swedish and Finnish communication by each group in turn (translated into English from the original Finnish and Swedish replies). As Louhiala-Salminen et al. comment, 'the views of Finns and Swedes of their own and each other's communication often seem to refer to the same characteristic feature, but they used very different evaluative language to describe it. For example, Finns considered themselves as "factual" and "direct" communicators, implying that they are effective, while Swedes referred to essentially the same characteristics as "blunt", "pushy" and "few-worded". Swedes, again, described themselves as "discussive" and "democratic", implying that they are effective, while Finns thought they were "wordy" and "talked endlessly" ' (2005: 409).

Data 8.6   The perceptions of Swedish and Finnish communication

---

Finnish communication by *Finnish respondents*

- Directness and factuality, no small talk, equality
- Effectiveness, efficiency
- To the point, no unnecessary chatting

Finnish communication by *Swedish respondents*

- Quick, sometimes too quick decisions that may be later changed, the boss is the boss
- 'Few-worded', economical with words; reserved
- Communication is direct, sounds harsher than is intended

Swedish communication by *Swedish respondents*

- Dialogue
- Consensus, everybody participates, a lot of discussion, everybody talks
- Discussion so that everyone is happy

Swedish *communication by* Finnish respondents:

- Endless discussion
- Polite talk without practical measures, avoiding conflict
- A lot of extra talk before getting down to business.

(Louhiala-Salminen et al., 2005: 408, slightly adapted)

The meeting analysis

The findings of the analysis of the four video-taped meetings would seem to suggest that 'culture bound discoursal features can be identified and would seem to be transferred into a BELF situation' (2005: 413). The Swedish speakers in the corpus exhibited an interpersonal orientation, characterized by the use of queries, questions, hedging and other forms of metadiscourse intended to orient the hearer to the discourse, whereas the Finnish speakers tended towards issue orientation, and a relatively low level of interpersonal orientation. Furthermore, the Swedish speakers relied much less than their Finnish counterparts on shared context or shared values, such that they used 'more explicit rhetoric and conversational gambits than do Finnish speakers' (2005: 413). The example in Data 8.7 shows the difference between the 'discussive' Swedish style of communication, as opposed to the 'direct' Finnish style. Louhiala-Salminen et al. describe this encounter as follows:

> In Example 1, the key idea is the name of an important person – Pelle Svensson. Using a question to address his interactants, the Swedish speaker (S) offers to write it down (lines 1–2), obviously to assure himself that the Finns will get the name right. The offer – made in question form – introduces a dialogic element into the conversation. This dialogue, however, is rejected by the Finns, with their monosyllabic 'No´ (lines 3–4). To the Finns, the 'no' obviously signifies that writing the name is unnecessary as they already know it. S, however, continues in a discursive manner, explaining why the name is important (lines 5 & 7), repeating the name (line 7) – to make sure the Finns remember it – and is then joined by the Chair (also a Swede, incidentally) who mentions the name for the third time in a very short period (line 10). Throughout, the Finns backchannel (lines 6, 8, 9) – thus, in effect, avoiding dialogue, and not confirming that they know and remember the name. . . . we see the Finnish speakers being economical with words and issue oriented, relying on shared information (i.e. the Swedes finally knowing or realizing that the Finns know the name as they do not want it repeated), and the Swedish speakers being 'wordy', taking their interactants into account, and being less reliant on what is taken to be shared assumptions. Examples of this type abound in our data. (2005: 412–13, slightly adapted)

Data 8.7 Swedish and Finnish BELF interaction in meetings

Example 1		
1	S:	And my contact person in Stockholm. His name is Pelle Svensson.
2		**Should I write it down?**
3	F1:	No.
4	**F2:**	**No**
5	S:	If if Mats Mats wants to know *who
6	**F2:**	***ya-ah**
7	S:	who are you talking to (*pause*) **Pelle *Svensson**
8	**F2:**	***ya-ah.**
9	**F1**	***ya-ah**
10	C:	You can't talk to so many others and **Pelle Svensson** I suppose it is (.) project
11	S:	He is Mister Project
12	C:	Yes. He is . . .

C = Chair, F = Finnish speaker, S = Swedish speaker, * = overlapping speech, (.) = short pause.

(Louhiala-Salminen et al., 2005: 412)

The email analysis

The analysis of 114 Finnish and Swedish BELF messages from Paper Giant revealed both similarities and differences between the two different cultures. For example, all included a Salutation, (almost) all a complimentary close, and the messages were characterized by similar content, by the frequent use of first names, and by the use of the Swedish *Hej* (*Hello*) and *Med vänlig hälsning* (*With kind regards*), by both Finnish and Swedish writers. When the research team looked at the way in which requests were formulated, however, they found that the Finnish writers tended to make direct requests, whereas the Swedish writers preferred indirect requests. For example, almost 50 per cent of all the requests made by the Finnish writers used an imperative form (Please comment on this), as opposed to only 20 per cent of the requests made by Swedish writers. The Swedish writers, in contrast, used indirect requests, such as 'Could you please comment on this?; that is, they used a strategy that is *not* consistent with the minimalist politeness forms that other researchers have found to be characteristic of email discourse (e.g., Mulholland, 1999; Nickerson, 2000). Louhiala-Salminen et al.'s findings of the analysis of the email messages in relation to the rest of the study can be summarized as follows:

> the generic similarity of the BELF email messages examined supports our survey findings on the similarity of communicative practices in general between the Finns and the Swedes, i.e. the email messages share a number of features related to their form and content, and in the way in which the three [email] genres were used. In addition, no differences were found in the use of names in salutations, such that both writer groups were equally interpersonal. (Louhiala-Salminen et al., 2005: 417, slightly adapted)

Commentary

The study by Louhiala-Salminen et al. is a useful example for a number of reasons. Firstly, it shows how a number of different methods and different types of data can be combined to great effect to build up a multilayered picture of the communication that takes place within a given social context. The combination of survey data and the analysis of different types of discourse all contribute to a richer understanding of the challenges posed by opting for BELF as the official corporate language at Paper Giant and Scandi Bank, than would otherwise be possible in a more narrowly focused study. Other business discourse researchers have combined different methods, or have looked at different genres carried by similar media, such as fax and email, but few have combined the analysis of both written and spoken media in this way, together with information on the wider social and individual corporate context. Secondly, the study pinpoints at least one important difference between the Finnish (direct) and Swedish (discursive) employees at the two corporations, causing the research team to observe that BELF cannot 'be taken to be "neutral" or "cultureless". Rather, it can be seen to be a conduit of its speaker's communication culture' (2005: 417). In this respect, it points the way forward to a fruitful line of enquiry within the many other corporations around the world where BELF is used between speakers that represent different national cultures. Finally, as well as this difference, the study also highlights the many similarities between the two national cultures and the two corporations under investigation, both in their daily routines of communication and in their use of languages, suggesting that it may be possible to identify a number of the features that characterize international business discourse, regardless of where (or in what language) that discourse takes place.

8.5   The use of metadiscourse in the CEO's letter

Summary 8.5

Hyland, K. (1998). Exploring corporate rhetoric: Metadiscourse in the CEO's letter. *Journal of Business Communication, 35*(2), 224–45.

This study looks at how CEOs try to build a relationship with the readers of an annual general report, as well as projecting a positive image of their corporation.
It looks specifically at the role of metadiscourse, that is the textual and interpersonal aspects of the text, in 137 CEO's letters to shareholders at the beginning of the annual report, using a close text corpus analysis facilitated by Microconcord. Hyland maps the various metadiscourse devices he identifies to the realization of three aspects of classical rhetoric: rational appeals, credibility appeals and affective appeals, and in doing so he shows how this non-propositional information in the texts is a fundamental way in which CEO's seek to persuade their readers.

Introduction and aims

Ken Hyland begins his study of CEO's letters by selectively reviewing the existing literature at the time of publication, from the late 1980s and early 1990s. In doing so, he points out two important reasons as to why his study is important, i) the CEO's letter is widely referred to and is used to 'construct and convey a corporate image' (1998: 224), ii) very little research had been done to investigate the rhetoric used in CEO's letters to project a positive corporate image, concentrating instead on issues such as readability, gender representation and content related to performance. These two factors provide both a societal motivation (the texts are important and widely read), and a research motivation (as little or no work has been done to date), for the study which looks at 'critical features of text-level rhetoric to determine how writers project themselves into their texts in order to present an effective corporate picture' (1998: 225).

The specific aim of the study is to examine the role of metadiscourse in 137 CEO's letters originating between 1992 and 1994 in international and Hong Kong-based companies registered with the three most important Chambers of Commerce in Hong Kong. As Hyland observes, metadiscourse is an important aspect of how persuasive a text is, as it signals a writer's attitude to the propositional content of the text, as well as contributing to building a relationship with the readers of the text (see Concept 8.2 for further details). The study goes beyond simply describing the metadiscourse devices used however, in that Hyland builds on his analysis to show how these devices contribute to three aspects of classical rhetoric, 1) rational appeals to signal meaning relations, 2) credibility appeals, to create an ethos, and 3) affective appeals that relate to the reader. The study therefore combines a quantitative analysis (using Microconcord) to identify the frequency of occurrence of the various metadiscourse devices, and a qualitative analysis looking at the contribution made by each device within the context of the text.

Concept 8.2   Metadiscourse according to Ken Hyland

Metadiscourse is a term from discourse analysis which is generally seen to refer to aspects of a text that explicitly relate to the organization of the discourse or to the writer's stance towards either its content or the reader. It is the author's manifestation in a text to 'bracket the discourse organization and the expressive implications of what is being said' (Schiffrin, 1980: 321). It consists of features which are largely independent of propositional content, but which reveal the writer's conception of audience and the types of appeal that he or she considers most persuasive for that audience. Metadiscourse thus comprises a range of linguistic devices to convey a writer's personality, credibility, reader sensitivity and evaluation of propositional matter (Crismore, 1989; Van de Koppel, 1985).

Metadiscourse involves linguistic elements that help realize the rational, credible, and affective appeals that contribute to the persuasiveness of a text. It is an important means of supporting the writer's position and building writer–audience relationships. In its role in the CEO's letter, it is also rhetorical, galvanizing support by building credibility, resolving uncertainty, and avoiding disputes.

(Hyland, 1998: 225–6, slightly adapted)

Although the notion of metadiscourse has enjoyed considerable popularity among applied linguists and teachers alike, Hyland and Tse acknowledged

as early as 2004 that it had failed to some extent to 'achieve its explanatory potential due to a lack of theoretical rigour and empirical confusion'
(Hyland & Tse, 2004: 156). In the same 2004 article, and based on an analysis of 240 L2 postgraduate dissertations (a corpus of four million words),
they therefore reassess the notion of metadiscourse and discuss some of its
limitations. They subsequently present an adapted model of metadiscourse,
and show on the basis of their analyses how insight into metadiscourse can
help us understand 'the interpersonal resources' student writers employ in
their work, and how such insight provides a way to investigate 'the rhetorical and social distinctiveness of disciplinary communities' (Hyland & Tse,
204: 156).

Method

The corpus used in the study was a random selection of the annual reports
published in Hong Kong between 1992 and 1994, and consisted of 137 CEO's
letters. These ranged in length from 16 to 116 pages. The annual reports as
a whole were scanned electronically to produce a corpus of just over half a
million words, and it was then divided into three sections:

1. CEO's letters;
2. directors' reports;
3. other disclosures.

The CEO's letters comprised 175,152 words, and these were compared within
the analysis with 110 randomly selected Directors' reports from the same corpus, consisting of 122,511 words. Hyland comments on the difference between
these two types of texts and the usefulness of their inclusion within the analysis as follows: 'It [the directors' report] reviews the year and describes important
events affecting the company, changes in fixed assets, details of directors, and
so on. Such an objective digest of statutory information provides a useful contrast to the CEO's letter, which is voluntary and not subject to official audit. So
while the quality of information provided in the letters may very enormously,
the CEO's letter is likely to play a more rhetorical role in company communication' (1998: 227).

Before the data was analysed, an inventory of 250 metadiscourse items was
compiled, first by two experienced applied linguists referring to reference
grammars and the existing research literature on metadiscourse (e.g., Holmes,
1988; Hyland, 1996; Kjellmer, 1994), and then by supplementing this list with
additional suggestions made by Hyland's colleagues within the Business Studies
and English department at City University in Hong Kong. The CEO's letters
and Directors' reports were then analysed using Microconcord to identify the

frequency and range of the 250 items listed in the inventory. Hyland completed the analysis by working with two other colleagues – all three working independently – to code the items using the classification of functions of metadiscourse adapted from Crismore et al. (1993) specifically for the CEO data. Once this quantitative coding had been completed, Hyland then looked at the various metadiscourse devices in the context of the CEO's letters to identify how these contributed to the rational, credible and affective appeals made by the writers.

Main findings

The quantitative comparative analysis of the CEO's letters and Directors' reports

Hyland's analysis revealed a number of key differences in use of metadiscourse between the CEO's letters and the Director's reports. Although metadiscourse occurred in both, and there were also more textual devices than interpersonal devices in both, the CEO's letters contained 'about two and a half times more metadiscourse per 100 words' than the Directors' reports, and they also included 'six times more interpersonal metadiscourse' (1998: 231). Hyland summarizes the findings of this part of the study as follows:

> The CEO's letters contain about one metadiscourse device every 50 words. These are typically connectives or hedges (comprising 66 per cent of all items) with little endophoric or attributional signalling. The directors' reports show a similar overall percentage of connectors and hedges, although with fewer than half the occurrences per 100 words. The strikingly different frequencies demonstrate the distinct nature of the two documents, with the directors perceiving less need to exercise control over the discourse by marking the organization of their prose or its affective implications. The CEO's, on the other hand, clearly see a need to intervene by displaying an alignment to their readers and informing them of their intentions, meanings, and attitudes. (Hyland, 1998: 231)

He goes on to say that although devices such as the logical connectives *and*, *also*, and *but*, and the hedge *would*, were the most frequently occurring devices in both corpora, the ten most frequently occurring items accounted for 81 per cent of all devices in the Directors' reports as opposed to only 51 per cent in the CEO's letters. The reports are therefore much more formulaic than the letters. In addition, whereas 85.5 per cent of the metadiscourse devices in the Directors' reports belonged in the textual categories, with 14.5 per cent in interpersonal categories, only 62.3 per cent of metadiscourse devices were textual in the CEO's letters, and 37.7 per cent were interpersonal. Relatively speaking as well as being less formulaic, the CEO's letters are also more interpersonal than the Director's reports. Hyland summarizes the reasons for this by saying, 'While directors' reports are often a simple record of company particulars, the CEO's letter represents corporate communication decisions which involve attempts to influence the audience' (1998: 232).

The qualitative analysis of the CEO's letters

In the qualitative analysis, Hyland looks at the rhetorical effects of the different metadiscourse devices in the CEO's letters, in particular how these contribute to the realization of rational appeals, credibility appeals and affective appeals. Rational appeals in the text are about 'how writers choose to define problems, support claims, validate promises, state conclusions, and so on', and their persuasive force is dependent to a large extent on 'the logic connecting these elements' (1998: 233). Textual metadiscourse elements, such as logical connectives and frame markers, play a fundamental role in this process, since 'textual metadiscourse helps readers understand how the text is organized by explaining, orienting them to, and guiding them through the information. It functions rhetorically to point readers in the direction of the argument intended by the writer' (1998: 233).

In his discussion of metadiscourse and credibility appeals, Hyland looks at how metadiscourse is used to realize a writer's ethos, that is, the projection of 'the writer into the document to present a competent, trustworthy, authoritative, and honest *persona*' (1998: 235). Not surprisingly, credibility appeals are enhanced in the CEO's letters through interpersonal devices, such as hedges, emphatics, relational markers and attributors, 'all of which help to indicate writers' assessments of truth and their convictions in their views' (1998: 235). And likewise in affective appeals, where the persuasiveness of the text is achieved if the writer effectively relates to the reader, interpersonal devices, such as 'attitude markers, and hedges, together with the manipulation of pronoun reference' are again shown to make an important contribution to the effectiveness of the text, this time in 'the development of a relationship with the reader' (1998: 238).

Hyland's analysis of the role played by metadiscourse in the different appeals in the CEO's letters allows him to conclude that 'metadiscourse is a ubiquitous feature of the way CEO's portray their awareness of how best to represent themselves and their companies' (1998: 241). He goes on to call for further investigation of metadiscourse in other business genres including variations between different genres, for instance reports versus letters, and variations within the same genre in different circumstances, for example CEO's letters in high versus low performance companies, in more profitable versus less profitable years for the same company, and in companies working in different sectors. And in his concluding remarks, he makes a connection with the teaching of business discourse and underlines the importance of raising student awareness of the type of strategic rhetoric that metadiscourse facilitates in corporate writing in addition to a careful selection of appropriate propositional information:

> Finally, the analysis may help students of business communication under-stand and gain control of metadiscourse in their own reading and writing of business genres. Such studies can help learners gain a better understanding of the strategies used in corporate messages and develop a more effective rhetorical and verbal repertoire to use in the professional domains in which they will find themselves. CEO's letters are among the most widely read and easily accessible documents companies produce. Often readily encountered by shop-floor employees and small investors, annual reports are now distrib-uted internationally. They thus represent part of the growing hegemony of English and the increasingly insistent undercurrent of a promotional culture in informative discourse. Analyses such as the one presented here can there-fore help consumers of these documents develop a rhetorical awareness of written managerial persuasion. (Hyland, 1998: 241–2)

Commentary

Hyland's study, which can now be considered as an early example of busi-ness discourse analysis, is still worth looking at in detail for two important reasons, one methodological, the other epistemological. Firstly, the project is expertly put together, combining existing theory, i.e. the classification systems for metadiscourse, applying this in a new context, i.e. business discourse as opposed to academic discourse where most work on metadiscourse had been done up until 1998, and drawing on both quantitative and qualitative method-ologies in the process. The texts under analysis are shown to be relevant both from a societal perspective and a research perspective, such that the findings contribute to our existing knowledge about CEO's letters; as well as making a ground-breaking contribution to the literature on business discourse, the research carried out is both valid and reliable, incorporating important meth-odological decisions such as random sampling, the adaptation of an existing classification system and the co-operation of several coders in the analysis, and the research is shown to have useful and far reaching research and pedagogi-cal implications. Secondly, as we have detailed above, Hyland's investigation of textual and interpersonal metadiscourse and their contribution to a series of different appeals to the reader, uncovers the crucial role played by rhetori-cal strategies in the construction of (persuasive) corporate messages. Since the study was published, many business discourse researchers have turned their attention to communication strategies in both written and spoken genres (e.g., Nickerson, 2000; Poncini, 2004; Vuorela, 2005), and for financial report-ing in particular, the influence of the study is clear on the growing interest in the rhetorical strategies used by the writers of annual reports to communicate effectively with their stakeholders (for instance, Garzone, 2004; Garzone, 2005; Nickerson & de Groot, 2005; de Groot, Korzilius, Nickerson & Gerritsen, 2006, case study 8.6 below; de Groot, Korzilius, Gerritsen & Nickerson, 2011, case study 8.7 below).

8.6 A multimodal analysis of text and photographic themes in annual general reports

Summary 8.6

De Groot, E., Korzilius, H., Nickerson, C., & Gerritsen, M. (2006). A corpus analysis of text themes and photographic themes in managerial forewords of Dutch-English and British annual general reports. *IEEE Transactions on Professional Communication, 49*(3), 217–35.

This study uses genre theory and semiotics as the basis for a comparative analysis of textual and pictorial content in a corpus of Dutch-English and British managerial forewords (in annual general reports). The multimodal analyses indicate that Dutch-English CEO statements differ significantly from British CEO's statements and British Chairman's statements in terms of their thematic content. The researchers suggest that these differences may be attributable to contextual variables that play a role in this specific community of practice, such as historical and communicative conventions, as well as current affairs. They conclude that the managerial forewords examined comparatively cannot be seen as similar, even though they are part of the same comprehensive, multimodal text (i.e. the annual report). The study indicates that practitioners and instructors in international communication should be aware of both the textual and contextual dimensions of the professional genres employed strategically in intercultural discourse settings.

Introduction and aims

De Groot et al. set the scene by introducing the annual general report as an instantiation of a genre of organizational communication that comprises textual elements about non-financial business aspects such as 'the organization's mission, its objectives, its policy, its relations with the surrounding world, and the management review of the past year', which are used to explain and support financial information, as well as 'to establish a positive corporate image' (218). The researchers explain that the annual report is clearly a multimodal genre, in that rhetorical action is established through a combination of 'textual and (photo)graphic or visual modes' (218). They go on to argue that, as companies' financial statements have become more and more standardized over the years, the non-financial (English) content of annual reports will be used increasingly as an informational (and promotional) resource through which organizations can distinguish themselves from their international competitors. They note that the annual report is thus becoming a 'crucial, internationally oriented corporate communication instrument' (217), as a result of, amongst other factors, stricter European disclosure requirements, globalized operations and the need to compete internationally.

With these developments, the researchers argue that it has also become increasingly important to study the differences and similarities between corporations in different countries and their 'international (i.e. English) presentation of information in the annual report' (217), because although the annual report may be aimed at a similar audience internationally, different cultures may still use different discourse strategies to communicate with this audience. Furthermore, the authors note that the distinction between genres across cultures in terms of a substantive (i.e. content) perspective has received scant attention by genre researchers, even though it is substance which gives meaning to a genre and, in doing so, is crucial to the realization of a genre (see also Concept 8.3).

Basing themselves on the premise that different social communities (whether national or professional) may opt to employ and emphasize different 'aspects of their experience in the same situations involving the same participants in order to achieve the same social action' (221), the researchers hypothesize that it is therefore plausible to assume that an analysis of textual and photographic themes in non-financial information in annual reports in two distinct national and business cultures (i.e. Dutch vs. British) may manifest variations in the prominent substantive or content features used in the same document/genre across cultures. In line with this reasoning, the specific aims of the study were: 1) to describe the typified substantive characteristics (realized as themes in texts and photographs) in the English managerial forewords in annual reports originating in Dutch and British corporations, and 2) to determine to what extent the substantive characteristics used in Dutch-English annual reports differ from the substantive characteristics in British-English annual reports.

Method

The corpus for this study was collected using a combination of purposive and cluster sampling techniques. It consisted of 44 English annual reports (from 22 Dutch companies in 15 different industries and 22 British equivalents). The selection criteria included company size, English language policy and merger history. All CEO's and Chairman's statements were then selected from the corpus, yielding 20 CEO's statements from the Dutch corporations' reports, and 16 Chairman's statements and 18 CEO's statements from the British annual reports. Thus, a total sample of 54 statement/texts was selected for the analysis of textual and visual themes.

Text themes in the management statements were defined as clusters of keywords/key phrases with coherent meanings (see Concept 8.3). They were identified and categorized 'when the meaning of several words or word strings could be grouped together to establish a higher order thematic concept' (de Groot et al., 2006: 223). Visual themes were analysed only for the documentary photographs in the management statements. Following Kress and van Leeuwen (2001), photographic themes were identified by associating objects that were displayed in the pictures, and, 'if necessary, relating them to complementary descriptive texts, by using objects-as-mode (and possibly the written language-as-mode) to acquire a set of thematically related signs' (de Groot et al., 2006: 223).

Data 8.8   Examples of text themes and photographic themes

De Groot et al. distinguished four text themes on the basis of their corpus analysis: 'Shareholder Confidence', ' Marketing', 'General Financial Results' and 'HRM/People'. Constitutive elements, or keywords/phrases, that were labelled 'Shareholder Confidence' include, for example, 'the plan to recovery', 'mindful of our responsibilities', 'progress', and 'potential'. Keywords/phrases reflecting the theme 'HRM/people' include 'motivating', 'we have asked our people to dig deep', 'they have delivered', and 'employees'.

Examples of photographic themes identified by de Groot et al. include: 'Work area', 'CEO' and ' Male Employee'. Constitutive elements, or signs-as-objects, labeled 'CEO' are, for example, 'desk + paperwork + electronic planner', 'adult male', and 'suit + neat shirt + tie'. Examples of constitutive elements reflecting the photographic theme 'Work Area' include 'steel construction for building', 'yellow work coat', and 'helmet'.

(De Groot et al., 2006: 223)

An inter-rater reliability analysis was conducted to determine the quality of the thematic coding. This analysis determines the degree to which two or more coders agree (independently) on the implementation of a particular coding or rating system. Two raters analysed 10 per cent of the corpus independently from each other (amounting to 21 pages of management statements each). Cohen's Kappa was used to measure the degree of inter-rater agreement per theme type. Kappas were found to be substantial, and the mean agreement percentage between coders of both text and photographic themes was found to be above 96. Therefore, it could be concluded that the coding system used in the study was sufficiently reliable.

Main findings

Text themes

A total of 97 different text themes were identified in the Dutch and British CEO's statements and the British Chairman's statements, covering a diversity of topics such as Marketing, HRM, Finance, Operations, Corporate Strategy, CSR, Share Management (see Data 8.8 for selected examples). The large number of themes categorized seems to indicate that these statements are highly complex documents covering varied substance/content and fulfilling various rhetorical functions, for a variety of participants. Fifteen themes appeared most prominently across the three statement types (i.e. they occurred in more than 50 per cent of one, two or three types). These included the HRM/People, General Operational Results, Future, Corporate Strategy and Shareholder Confidence themes for the Dutch CEO's statements, and the Corporate Strategy, Future, General Operational Results and Shareholder Confidence themes for the British CEO's statements.

Furthermore, significant differences were found across statement types for four of the top score themes and two other main text themes. Cross-culturally, for example, it was found that the Dutch CEO's statements revealed significantly higher frequencies for both the HRM/People theme and the Corporate Governance theme than the British CEO's statements. The British CEO's statements, on the other hand, were found to significantly more often disclose information on the CSR theme than the Dutch CEO's statements. Also, the British Chairman's statements included significantly more details on the Dividend theme than either the Dutch or the British CEO's statements.

Photographic themes

A total of 23 photographic themes could be identified in the Dutch and British CEO's statements and the British Chairman's statements (45 documents included documentary photographs that could be analysed). The content of the documentary photographs centred around three company-related items: Management members, Workplace and Employees (see Data 8.8 for selected examples). A limited number of pictures with main themes were used in the three types of statements, including the CEO and All Executive Board Directors themes for the Dutch CEO's statements and the Male employee and Female Employee themes for the British CEO's statements. The Chairman theme was identified in all (i.e. 100 per cent) of the British Chairman's statements.

With respect to cross-cultural differences, the Dutch CEO's statements were found to be characterized primarily by clustered photographic themes referring to Members of the Management, while the British CEO's statements mainly reflected clustered themes centering on Members of the Board. Furthermore, significant differences were found in that the Dutch CEO's statements contained a high number of photographs displaying all executive directors in the company, while in the British CEO's statements, female employees were depicted significantly more frequently than in the other two statement types. Finally, a significantly larger number of British CEO's statements were found to include pictures portraying company employees as well as a significantly higher frequency of photographic themes referring to the workplace.

De Groot et al.'s study of the substantive or content characteristics of managerial statements in Dutch-English and British annual reports, in terms of textual and photographic themes, yields several insightful findings from both a cross-cultural and cross-textual perspective. De Groot et al. contextualize these results as follows:

> The general implication that can be drawn from [this study] is that the Dutch-English and British-English management statements are not generically identical in so far as substance is concerned. In spite of some overlap in textual and photographic content, the many subtle significant variations in both text and photographic themes suggest that 1) the British CEO's statements and the British Chairman's statements are not generic equivalents and that 2) the Dutch-English and the British managerial forewords also differ generically. With regard to distinctions in textual substance, much of the diversity observed seems to stem from the fact that the supposed writers of the text, the CEO's and chairmen, fulfill distinct functions within Dutch and British organizations. As for the distinctions in photographic substance, it seems as if British CEO statements in particular tend to focus on visual representations of the company's profile and its performance. [. . . T]he results of this corpus analysis are congruent with the basic genre assumption that the thematic, structural, and lexico-grammatical nature of texts strongly depends on the communicative purposes, the participants, and discourse communities that use them. (de Groot et al., 2006: 231)

Furthermore, according to the researchers:

> [. . . T]he present investigation has important implications for educators, researchers and practitioners teaching or engaging in intercultural communication. It suggests that texts originating in a particular discourse situation do not exist in isolation; on the contrary, they emerge on the basis of continuous interaction with the social community in which they are realized.

Commentary

De Groot et al.'s study is worthwhile for a number of reasons. The project combines the classification systems for analysing genre and for establishing multimodal meaning-making (semiotics), while also extending them to analyse a new semiotic resource, i.e. visual substance (or visual genre content). The analyses are shown to be relevant both from an organizational perspective and a research perspective, and the findings they yield contribute to our existing knowledge about promotional corporate communication; as well as making contributions to genre methodology (extending it to encompass multimodal analysis) and to the literature on business discourse (specifically in annual reports; see also 8.5 above). Furthermore, the research is both rigorous and reliable, incorporating careful sampling techniques, the adaptation of an existing classification system as well as the cooperation of multiple coders.

The research also has usable research and pedagogical implications. As we have detailed above, De Groot et al.'s investigation shows how rhetorical strategies in the construction of (persuasive) corporate messages can be seen to differ not only across text types, but also across (business) cultures. In doing so, the study makes a clear contribution to earlier work on identifying rhetorical strategies in corporate (promotional) 'texts'. As we have seen, financial reporting in particular has enjoyed growing interest from business discourse researchers intent on establishing how the writers of annual reports can communicate effectively with their stakeholders (see also, for example, Garzone, 2004; Garzone, 2005; Nickerson & de Groot, 2005; de Groot, Korzilius, Gerritsen, & Nickerson, 2011, see case study 8.7 below). Finally, de Groot et al.'s concern with analysing multimodality to characterize genres, particularly in light of the high degree of multimodality evidenced in emerging (online) genres (see Chapter 7) is both useful and timely. Studies such as this make an important contribution to advancing genre research beyond 'text', to examine how genre substance and discourse strategy are instantiated using multiple semiotic resources (for another example of a visual analysis applied in financial reporting, see Ditlevsen, 2012).

8.7   Investigating international audience reaction to the annual report in English: UK-based financial analysts' response to Dutch-English and British letters to stakeholders

Summary 8.7

De Groot, E., Korzilius, H., Gerritsen, M., & Nickerson, C. (2011). There's no place like home: UK-Based financial analysts' response to Dutch-English and British-English annual report texts. *IEEE Transactions on Professional Communication, 54*(1), 1–17.

This study uses the findings from an earlier comparative analysis of textual and pictorial content in Dutch-English and British managerial forewords in annual general reports (De Groot, 2008 and De Groot et al. 2006, discussed above as case study 8.6) as input for an experiment in which the effectiveness of texts and photos in Dutch-English and British-English management statements is tested with a relevant audience for annual reports, namely financial analysts in the UK. The potential target was surveyed to test experimentally whether management statements that use nationality-appropriate texts and photos in management statements (i.e. multimodal substance that the 2006 corpus study had shown to be either typically Dutch or typically British) are more persuasive than management statements that do not use nationality-appropriate multimodal content. The experiment showed that the UK-based financial analysts in the study, on the whole, indeed responded more positively to typically British communication features in management statements than to features typical of Dutch-based management statements.

Introduction and aims

The authors begin by noting that Investor Relations (IR) communications are no longer solely about supplying financial information to potential investors, but also about managing relationships with a variety of different stakeholders and maintaining corporate reputation within the broader financial community. A case in point is the annual financial report, which was originally created as a 'financial fact sheet' for national audiences. It has since evolved into a report that today's multinationals spend large sums of money on in order to make it 'verbally and visually appealing to a variety of international stakeholder groups' (de Groot et al., 2011: 1). Annual reports nowadays include multimodal elements, such as texts, graphics and images that 'frame' the financial content and contribute to the relational function of the report.

Most multinationals tend to publish an international annual report that is largely standardized in content, that is, largely similar to the annual report published in the corporation's home country, in terms of textual as well as visual features. Often, the only local adaptation that takes place in the international report is that the textual information is presented in a different (local) language, but more often than not, English as an international language is used for international audiences across borders. The use of English in the annual report is believed to facilitate external investment because it enables the company to directly address investors from various cultural (and language) backgrounds. English is also perceived as a means to increase an organization's international prestige, and as essential in gaining approval for annual reports in corporations managed by international boards.

Earlier studies have indicated that companies from different national business cultures would seem to apply culture-specific conventions in the textual and visual design of their international annual reports. Such 'culturally typical' conventions would seem to be followed despite the use of English as an international language in those reports, which suggests that corporations from native and non-native English business cultures draw on the sociocultural norms they associate with their own first language (de Groot et al., 2011: 2). According to the researchers, members of a given culture can generally be assumed to have specific notions about what communicative behaviour they expect in specific interactional contexts, and by extension it can be hypothesized that cross-cultural variation in the textual and visual features of English annual reports (see e.g. de Groot et al., 2006) may evoke different responses in audiences from different national business cultures. So far, however, not much is known about the communicative effectiveness of culture-specific disclosures in international annual reports. The researchers posit that research on this topic is needed, particularly in the European context, as European-based annual reports tend to be used as an IR tool with companies and stakeholders from a variety of cultural backgrounds.

The researchers conclude on the basis of their literature review that it is as yet unclear whether standardized verbal and visual elements in an annual report actually bring about desired responses among international audiences. In the same way, it has not been determined whether adapting annual report content (at textual and visual levels) to the information needs and expectations of local audiences yields better (i.e. more positive) outcomes than standardized reporting. To gain insight into such questions, de Groot et al.'s 2011 study focused on the effectiveness of multimodal texts in English annual reports originating in two Western European countries: the UK and the Netherlands. The study investigated UK-based analysts' evaluations of nonfinancial texts (i.e. management statements) containing multimodal features that are typical of English annual reports produced in either the Netherlands or the UK. De Groot et al.'s earlier study (2006, see also de Groot, 2008) had shown that there are cross-cultural differences in themes, structure, and lexico-grammar between Dutch-English and British-English multimodal annual reports (see case study 8.6 above).

In line with the similarity-attraction paradigm (Byrne, 1971; see also e.g. Lee & Gudykunst, 2001) which posits that individuals assess the attractiveness of a perceived phenomenon on the basis of whether or not they are able to recognize it, De Groot et al. expected that British-based texts and photos would be more effective than Dutch-based texts and photos among British analysts. In other words, it was hypothesized that financial analysts in the UK would rate annual report sections designed in accordance with British-English communication conventions more positively than annual report sections that follow Dutch-English conventions. The following variables were investigated:

- perceived corporate reputation;
- willingness to invest;

- attitude towards the text;
- perceived credibility of the text;
- perceived comprehensibility of the text;
- overall text preference;
- preference for individual textual and visual features.

Method

Respondents

Thirty-five financial analysts, who worked in investment companies in the financial centres of London (the City and Canary Wharf), took part in the experiment (convenience sample). The majority worked as analysts or advisors (85.7 per cent), the remainder as brokers or traders (14.3 per cent).

Materials/stimuli

The independent variables included in the research materials for the experiment (Dutch-English and British-English communication strategies) were manipulated on the basis of findings from de Groot (2008), who found cross-cultural differences in textual and visual features between Dutch-English and British-English management statements. Culture-specific textual and visual features were integrated into the experimental materials in four forms: '(1) as part of the text of full management statements, (2) as part of propositions about the text of management statements, (3) as part of text fragments in management statements, and (4) as part of photographs representing the visual design of management statements' (de Groot et al., 2011: 7). The design of the materials was based on authentic English management statements taken from 2003 annual reports (Dutch and British firms in the financial services industry). They featured generic, non-identifiable business names (i.e., CorpA, CompanyX) to diminish the possible impact of the participants' existing views on real companies.

Two full management statements were created containing either typically Dutch-English or British-English features. Both texts were entitled 'Letters to the Shareholder.' Apart from the cross-cultural differences that were manipulated in the text versions, all other aspects were exactly the same in both texts. Thus, they contained the same 'corporate story', with respect to profit summary, operational review, economic situation and markets. The materials prepared for the experiment also included text *fragments* that were used to present participants with individual features typical for either the Dutch-English or British management statement. Participants were confronted with pairs of such fragments, each one including a Dutch-based or British-based feature and each one excluding a Dutch-based or British-based feature.

Finally, the research materials included photographs representing the visuals typically found in either Dutch-based or UK-based management statements.

The photographs replicated images used in real management statements of Dutch or British companies, with respect to elements such as gender, posture, clothing, number of subjects or props, etc. (see e.g. de Groot, 2008, for examples). In the experiment, photos were also presented to the respondents in contrastive pairs.

Data collection: the questionnaire

The UK-based analysts' responses to the culture-specific communication strategies in the full texts and fragments were measured in terms of corporate image, text persuasiveness and preference (see above). Measures for these dependent variables were mostly based on scales used in earlier research. All items consisted of statements accompanied by 5-point Likert scales.

Corporate image was assessed with regard to the full English letters to the shareholders (Dutch-English and British-English), using two instruments. First, the Fortune corporate reputation scale (Fombrun & Shanley, 1990) was used to gauge participants' opinions about the company, based on corporate attributes reflected in the full text. Respondents were asked to indicate how they would rate the company on the following aspects: (1) quality of management; (2) quality of products / services; (3) long-term investment value; (4) innovativeness; (5) financial soundness; (6) ability to attract, develop, and keep talented people; (7) community and environmental responsibility; and (8) use of corporate assets (de Groot et al., 2011: 9). The 5-point scales accompanying each aspect ranged from 1 (poor) to 5 (excellent). Second, Smith's purchase intention scale (Smith, 1993) was used to measure willingness to invest after reading a letter to the shareholders. Based on the full text of a letter, analysts were asked (1) how likely it would be that they would invest money in the company and (2) how likely it would be that they would recommend the company to a professional colleague. The degree of likelihood was indicated on a 5-point scale ranging from 1 (zero likelihood) to 5 (certain).

To test the persuasiveness of the full Dutch-English and British letters to the shareholders, attitude towards the text, credibility of the text, and text comprehensibility were measured. Attitude towards the text and perceived text credibility were measured on the basis of MacKenzie and Lutz (1989), with the items (1) good/bad, (2) pleasant/unpleasant, and (3) favourable/unfavourable for attitude to text, and the items (1) convincing/unconvincing, (2) believable/unbelievable, and (3) unbiased/biased for text credibility. The scale used to measure text comprehensibility was based on van Meurs, Korzilius, and Hermans (2004), and featured the items: (1) difficult/easy, (2) simple/complex, (3) unclear/clear, (4) poorly organized/well organized, (5) logical/illogical, and (6) concise/lengthy.

Participants were also asked to indicate to what degree (on a five-point scale) they had an overall preference for the full letter to the shareholders of either

CorpA or CorpB, where the cultural origins of the letters and the companies– that is, Dutch or British, varied. They then indicated their preference for individual culture-specific features on the basis of five text-related propositions prompted by: 'The Letter to the Shareholders should include details about . . . ' and ending with the following text features: board details, corporate social responsibility, dividend, corporate strategy and future aims. Answers were indicated on a 5-point scale (1 (absolutely agree) to 5 (absolutely disagree). Their preference for culture-specific text features was tested (again, using a five-point scale) by means of three pairs of text fragments, each featuring one excerpt with, and one excerpt without, a typically Dutch-English or British feature. A similar measurement was applied to three pairs of management photographs, typical of either the Dutch-English or the British management statements.

The authenticity of the (manipulated) culture-specific research materials was checked in a pretest by four experts in finance or business communication (full versions and text fragments). They also evaluated the authenticity of the management portraits and the comprehensibility of the questionnaire. The pretest results led to only minor changes to the questionnaire and materials.

Design and procedure

The experiment used a within-subjects design. This means that each of the 35 participants evaluated the Dutch-English as well as the British version of the letter to the shareholders. They were not given information about the cultural origins of the two texts they evaluated. This allowed for a research setting that was ecologically valid, in that financial analysts commonly compare corporate information sources. In the questionnaire, the order in which the materials (full letters and paired text fragments) were presented was reversed, in order to counterbalance potential sequence effects. This resulted in four questionnaire versions. Participants filled in the questionnaire individually, during work breaks, taking about 15–20 minutes on average.

Main findings

Paired samples t-tests were used to analyse the experimental data. First, it was determined to what extent the two different versions of the letter to the shareholders (British-English versus Dutch-English) influenced perceptions of corporate image and persuasiveness. With respect to corporate image, it was found that the two letters affected the analysts' perceptions of corporate attributes differently, in that the corporate reputation reflected in the British-English letter was rated significantly more positively than that represented in the Dutch-English letter. Intention to invest, the second measurement of corporate image, was not affected by the letter version. With regard to the perceived persuasiveness of the text, it was found that the analysts' found the British-English letter to be significantly more comprehensible than its Dutch-English counterpart. Effects of version on the other measurements of persuasiveness (attitude towards the text and text credibility) were not found.

Second, paired samples t-tests were used to analyse differences in reported preference with regard to the text overall, and with regard to textual and visual fragments, presented to participants in pairs (a British-English and Dutch-English version).

With respect to overall text preference, it was found that the financial analysts had a significantly higher preference for the British-English version of the full letter than for the Dutch-English version. Furthermore, for individual fragments too (both textual and visual), a substantial number of significant differences were found with regard to these UK-based analysts' preference across versions. In relation to textual content features, for example, they significantly preferred letter fragments following typically British themes. This was the case for board details, CSR and dividend. As far as structure was concerned, participants significantly preferred British-English style fragments (i.e., with headings) to Dutch style fragments (i.e., without headings). Finally, with respect to the three visual features investigated, the financial analysts were found to significantly prefer British style pictures of managers (i.e., looking away from the camera) to Dutch style photos of managers (i.e., looking straight at the camera). No other significant differences were found.

Commentary

De Groot et al.'s study is a very good example of a carefully conducted experiment that is based on an extensive corpus analysis of cross-cultural, multimodal reporting practices. The study provides consistent and compelling evidence that cultural adaptation beyond using a lingua franca (English) is worthwhile in intercultural stakeholder communications, to evoke desired (i.e. positive) responses in audiences. The UK-based analysts in the study evaluated the British-English letter to the shareholders (reflecting their own cultural conventions) more positively than its Dutch-English counterpart, at the level of full text, as well as on a substantial number of the textual and visual fragments. Typically British-English features had a stronger positive effect on UK analysts' perceptions than typically Dutch-English features. In other words, culture-specific multimodal features in text can influence readers' appreciation of the text. Also, the findings indicate that text appreciation is related to perceived corporate image, as the British text version led to significantly higher ratings on this variable than its Dutch-English counterpart, although it did not affect investment intention (the second measurement of perceived corporate image).

This investigation is naturally limited to giving insight into a UK-based target group's response to Dutch-based companies' reporting in English. Other corpus-based studies (similar to this case study) could answer the question as to what textual and visual features are conventional in Dutch-based annual reports in other cultures (than the British). Further reader-based studies (like the current case study) could then use the corpus-based findings as a basis for systematically investigating the persuasive effects on readers from these other cultures of culturally adapting multimodal texts to match their cultural expectations. See Quote 8.10 for further suggestions by the researchers themselves.

Quote 8.10   Suggestions for further research

According to de Groot et al., the findings from their experiment suggest many ways of extending research on the reception and assessment of international annual reports among relevant target groups (de Groot et al. 2011: 14). For example, follow-up studies could assess the effect of textual and visual features in Dutch-English annual reports on readers' perceptions in additional international markets that are important to the Dutch business community, for example other European markets (France or Germany) or even markets beyond Europe (e.g., the US or China). Additional studies might also investigate the response of different target groups of the English annual report than the UK-based financial analysts featured in de Groot et al.'s (2011) study.

Investigations might also focus on a more finely segmented selection of financial analysts (e.g. sell-side and buy-side analysts), or on another relevant audience, such as private investors or financial journalists. Finally, the authors note that their investigation could prompt further reception-oriented, experiment-based research into the effect of international annual reports published in other business cultures. A number of cross-cultural text analyses of English annual reports have uncovered reporting practices typical in other nations (e.g. Hooghiemstra, 2008 for textual attributions in Japanese versus US reports; Beattie and Jones, 2001, for graphics in annual reports across six countries, including France and Australia). However, the authors note that the readership and intercultural reception of such reports has not been investigated experimentally yet.

(de Groot et al., 2011: 14, slightly adapted)

8.8   Social media in corporate communications: an analysis of the corporate blog as a relationship-building tool

Summary 8.8

Cho, S., & Huh, J. (2010). Content analysis of corporate blogs as a relationship management tool. *Corporate Communications: An International Journal*, *15*(1), 30–48.

This study explored the evolution of the corporate blog, a relatively new corporate communications tool, by analysing the adoption trend of corporate blogs by large US corporations in the *Fortune 500* or *Interbrand Top 100* over time, establishing the key characteristics of such blogs and changes over time, and examining the extent to which corporate blogs feature relationship maintenance strategies. The approach taken was a longitudinal, comparative content analysis, which focused primarily on the interactive features and functionalities (i.e. modalities other than text) afforded by this specific social media tool. Analyses were conducted on a sample of corporate blogs originating in 2006 and 2008 respectively. The study is one of the first attempts to examine the development of corporate blogs, and one of only few studies to date that has considered how and to what extent corporations use blogs to maintain corporate-stakeholder relationships.

Introduction and aims

Blogs are essentially diaries on the internet that contain an author's personal reflections on a potentially wide range of themes and topics. Blogging can help authors to create a virtual community, or allow them to ventilate a viewpoint, interact with other bloggers or simply circulate information. The personal diary is still the most common type of blog, which means that blogs, on the whole, can be characterized as 'an individualistic and intimate form of self-expression' (31). However, as blogging has become more popular, different types of blogs have emerged, one of which is the corporate blog. More and more organizations have begun to experiment with blogs, because they see blogging as a potentially effective relationship-building tool (e.g. Kelleher & Miller, 2006; Smudde, 2005). For the time being, however, research on corporate blogs, and the discourse of corporate blogs in particular, remains relatively sparse (but see Chapter 7, where we referenced some examples, including this study).

While corporate blogging seems to be on the increase, Cho and Huh note that, at the same time, corporate blogs are still regarded somewhat cautiously by many organizations. The issues associated with social media as corporate communications tools were briefly discussed in Chapter 7. Blogs, like social platforms such as Twitter, YouTube and Facebook, blur the boundaries between private and corporate voice, and in doing so carry with them certain inherent dangers, for example, when potentially sensitive corporate information, or personal disclosures, comments or opinions that reflect negatively on the company end up in the public domain. Given the unrestricted, open and interconnected nature of the internet, and of the blogosphere in particular, organizations are very aware that they can never fully control the content posted on organizational blogs (i.e. in newsletter blogs, employee blogs, etc.). They are also acutely aware that they should not be seen to control such content, as this would be regarded as going against the fundamental – democratic – principles of the internet, as well as most organizations' own commitment to open and two-way communication with stakeholders. In other words, company blogs inherently pose a risk to organizational reputation and credibility, and efforts by a company to anticipate or counter such risk (by e.g. developing blogging policy) are likely to be met with scepticism.

Because few studies had previously examined corporate blogs systematically, Cho and Huh's 2010 exploratory investigation aimed to investigate the current state of corporate blogging by large US corporations (at the time of writing), by examining corporate blogs within the context of relationship management. To gain insight into the potential usefulness of corporate blogs as a relationship maintenance tool, the researchers set out to identify features of corporate blogs that reflect established relationship management strategies and to analyse whether and how such features (or modalities) are used (Cho & Huh, 2010: 33). They formulated three research questions:

1. How many major US corporations use a corporate blog and what are the key features of such blogs?
2. To what extent do corporate blogs employ relationship maintenance strategies and what specific strategies are most frequently used?
3. Does the use of these strategies differ across industry types?

Concept 8.3 Characteristics of the corporate blog

Blogs (including corporate blogs) have unique characteristics that distinguish them from other forms of computer-mediated communication. Amongst other features, they have an easy-to-use content management system, use archive-oriented structure and latest-information-first order, include links to other blogs, and offer ease of response to previous blog postings (e.g. Herring et al., 2004; Huffaker & Calvert, 2005), Smudde (2005: 35) described the corporate blog as 'a hybrid of the personal blog' presenting 'the insights, assessments, commentary, and other discourse devoted to a single company'. Corporate bloggers, the authors behind corporate blogs, are defined by Sifry (2004) as 'people who blog in an official or semi-official capacity at a company, or are so affiliated with the company where they work that even though they are not officially spokespeople for the company, they are clearly affiliated'.

Based on these descriptions, Cho and Huh, in their study, define the corporate blog as a blog that is 'endorsed explicitly or implicitly by the company' and 'posted by a person (or group of people) affiliated with the company'.

(Cho & Huh, 2010: 31–2)

Method

Corpus and analysis

The researchers conducted a broad search of the blogosphere to determine which companies listed on the *Fortune 500* or *Interbrand 100* maintained a corporate blog. Non-English blogs were excluded from the analysis. Two corpora were collected: 31 blogs published in 2006 and 59 in 2008.

Next, the researchers developed a coding scheme based on relationship management strategies distinguished in the literature on interpersonal relationships (e.g. Stafford & Canary, 1991). Four strategies were selected for this study (positivity, openness, social networking, and sharing tasks), which were operationalized further so they could be applied within a blogging context, using Ki and Hon's coding scheme for analysing user-friendliness and usability on corporate websites (Ki & Hon, 2006). Positivity, for example, was defined as 'any attempt to enable ease of use' and measured by the presence of various interactive features (e.g. podcast, video, animation, audio, etc.) and user-friendly navigation tools (e.g. search, archive, tags, and calendar, etc.). Openness referred to features that 'encourage and facilitate two-way communication between bloggers and visitors' and was measured by the presence of e.g. trackback and comment functions. Social networking was defined as 'networking with common friends and affiliations' and measured by the presence of the blogroll feature and the blogs and websites in the blogroll list. Bloggers use the blogroll to expand their social network, by linking their blog to other blogs and websites, and listing their favourites and mentioning blogs and websites they frequently visit. Finally, sharing tasks was measured by the frequency with which blogs were updated and new postings were uploaded. The rate at which a blogger is active on his or her blog will affect the reader's perception of how well that blogger is doing the tasks expected. In other words, it indicates whether and to what extent the blogger is prepared to invest time in maintaining a relationship with visitors.

For each blog, two independent coders analysed the content of the first blog page. They then assigned overall scores for each of the four relationship management strategies, indicating to what extent a particular strategy had been implemented in the blog (see Data 8.9). In addition, type of blog (multivocal, univocal), blog topics (industry/company, brand/product, personal/public/other issues) and designation and affiliations of the blogger (in the company) were identified. The researchers discussed the coding scheme and operationalizations of the variables with the independent coders prior to the analysis, and the coders were given an initial training. Intercoder reliability (tested using Holsti's formula) was found to be acceptable for both corpora (2006 and 2008).

Data 8.9　Operationalization of relationship strategy implementation

For each of the four relationship strategies Cho and Huh distinguished in their study, they analysed to what extent the strategies had been implemented in the corporate blogs under study. To do so, the researchers operationalized three levels of implementation, with '3' indicating a relatively high level, '2' a relatively medium level, and '1' a relatively low level. For example, with respect to the relationship strategy 'Openness', a '3' (high level of implementation) was assigned when a corporate blog offered 'both trackback and comment functions', a '2' (medium level of implementation) when a blog featured 'only the comment function', and a '1' (low level of implementation) when a blog offered neither of these functions.

(Cho & Huh, 2010: 37)

Main findings

Key characteristics of corporate blogs (industry types, blogger characteristics, topics)

A comparison of blogs between 2006 and 2008 showed a number of differences (only a few of which were statistically significant). For example, in terms of industry types, the analysis showed that the types of company adopting blogs appeared to be diversifying over time. While the majority (ca. 70 per cent) of corporate blogs in 2006 were found in the electronics, computer or communications industries, only 42 per cent of blogs in 2008 were in these same industries, suggesting a shift over time to a situation in 2008 where blogs were found in a more diverse set of industries. The topic-oriented blog was the most popular type (in both 2006 and 2008), followed by community blogs and personal journals, with the latter clearly in the minority in both years. With respect to blogger characteristics, it was found that the percentage of blogs maintained by multiple authors (multivocal) showed a substantial (and statistically significant) increase over time, from 42 per cent in 2006 to 78 per cent in 2008. This, according to the authors, suggests a shift from personal journals to a group-maintained form of online publication. Finally, with respect to the affiliations and positions held by the bloggers, it was found that in both years, staff-level employees were the most common bloggers (around half in both years), followed by managers and executive officers. The bloggers most commonly worked for the development department (both years), although the number of bloggers working in communications or PR slightly increased from 2006 to 2008.

Relationship management strategies in corporate blogs (positivity, openness, networking and sharing tasks)

Most corporate blogs (in both years) provided a large variety of navigational features, an indicator of the positivity strategy, with multimedia features (e.g. podcasts, video links, video clips, animation) becoming more popular in 2008 than in 2006. At the same time, the use of a number of positivity indicators declined slightly over time (e.g. the calendar feature). With regard to openness, it was found that while openness strategy indicators were evident in most blogs, there was in reality little opportunity for two-way communication (in both years). For example, a majority of blogs did not provide the author's contact details and leaving comments was the only way for visitors to share opinions with the blogger. Furthermore, comments seemed to be monitored in most cases and around 50 per cent of blogs (both years) provided an explicit policy statement stating that the corporation reserved the right to monitor and erase reader comments. Between 2006 and 2008, there was a slight decrease in the percentage of blogs that used blogrolling, an indicator of the social networking strategy (77 per cent in 2006 to 63 per cent in 2008). Upon closer inspection their use as a networking tool was relatively limited, however, as the links featured in the blogroll tended to refer to internal, company locations rather than to external locations, communities or websites, etc. With respect to the last relationship strategy, sharing tasks, it was found that the blogs in 2008 seemed to be updated relatively more frequently than the blogs in 2006.

When the potential differences in the use of relationship strategies between industry types (manufacturers versus services/retailers) were investigated, few statistically significant results were found. Only the sharing tasks strategy was found to have been employed differently, and then only in 2006, with service/retailers using it in their blogs significantly more than manufacturers. The use of the other three strategies did not differ significantly, across industry types or across years.

Commentary

The analysis of corporate blogs over time (2006 versus 2008) indicates that a growing number of major US corporations seem to be adopting blogs as a communications tool, although the proportion of companies that maintain corporate blogs overall is still relatively small. Furthermore, the practice of blogging seems to have diversified to other industry types besides the computer and technology industry between 2006 and 2008. Topic-oriented blogs would seem to be preferred over community or personal diary blog types (see Lee et al., 2006, for a taxonomy of blogs), which, the researchers suggest, may indicate that corporations prefer to maintain a blog type that allows them a maximum degree of corporate control over content and communication with their publics. While two-way communication (comment) features seemed to be widely used in the corporate blogs in this study (an indicator of the openness strategy), the researchers note in their conclusion that using this functionality on its own does 'not facilitate true two-way communication' (43).

With respect to the four relationship management strategies overall, they conclude that while all four featured in a proportion of the corporate blogs studied, and in some cases, increasingly did so over time, their use tended to be concentrated on a specific strategy (e.g. positivity). Some of the other strategies were used relatively scarcely, or were not used to their full potential (e.g. the blogroll functionality for social networking). In sum, the use of relationship management strategies in corporate blogs remains limited. Furthermore, despite the increase in corporate blogging from 2006 to 2008, many corporations still do not seem to be making optimal use of the potential advantages of corporate blogging suggested in the management literature, namely as a dialoguing tool that could be used to maintain and enhance relationships with a corporation's external publics.

As we already suggested in Chapter 7, we expect that new (social) media, such as the corporate blog or Twitter, etc., are increasingly likely to become the object of study for business discourse researchers in the near future (see also Quote 8.11), particularly because corpus data are now readily available online. In this respect, we suggest that such media can be studied in a number of ways. For example, new (social) media can be examined in terms of their genre characteristics, in terms of how they are incorporated into corporate communications practices (or individuals' multi-communication practices), with respect to the (discourse) strategies used in them, and in terms of what effect such strategies have on relevant stakeholder groups.

Quote 8.11   Limitations and suggestions for follow-up research

In terms of key measures, because this study is the first attempt to apply the relationship maintenance strategy framework to the blog context, the operationalization of the relationship maintenance dimensions is exploratory and the measurement validity needs to be further tested. Another measurement-related limitation is that because our content analysis focused on analysing blog features found on the front page, some of the relationship maintenance strategy dimensions could not be properly measured . . . . To further examine relationship maintenance strategies used in corporate blogs, we encourage future researchers to use different research methods such as content analysis of blog postings, qualitative analysis of blog content, a survey or in-depth interviews with corporate bloggers.

Lastly, because of the mostly descriptive nature of this study and the limitations of the content analysis method, this study cannot offer empirically tested strategic recommendations for better corporate blogging. Another important question that cannot be addressed by this study is the link between relationship management strategies used in corporate blogs and relational outcome . . . . These questions call for an experimental study.

(Cho & Huh, 2010; 44, slightly adapted)

8.9   The storytelling organization: a narrative analysis of change accounts

Summary 8.9

Löwstedt, M., & Räisänen, C. (2012). 'Playing back-spin balls': Narrating organizational change in construction. *Construction Management and Economics 30*, 795–806.

This article reports on a longitudinal, interpretative case study of organizational change in a Swedish construction company over two decades. The study aimed to investigate how organizational members experience and 'live' change. The researchers used a discursive approach, and more specifically narrative interviews, to elicit managers' stories of change episodes. They then compared these stories with corporate narratives about the same episodes in corporate documents (e.g. business plans, corporate pamphlets, CEO statements). This multi-perspective, qualitative approach allowed the researchers to gain a greater understanding of the way in which a '20-year change trajectory' (796) was understood, experienced and represented at two levels of the company. In doing so, the study demonstrates the usefulness of narratives (or storytelling) as a methodological means to connect macro-level and micro-level phenomena. It also shows how a discourse-analytical approach can contribute to a fuller understanding of change as a socially constructed sense-making process that is inherent to what has been termed 'organizational becoming' (Tsoukas & Chia, 2002).

Introduction and aims

Organizational change is now all-pervasive and regarded as essential to an organization's survival. It is a complex process that has been studied extensively in management and organizational studies. An established method to study how change practices are understood and constructed at the micro-level is to analyse the organizational discourse(s). The idea is that to gain a fuller understanding of how change happens and is experienced by practitioners, researchers must view change as a process that is constructed discursively, on the basis of multimodal (textual) representations. In this view, change is a 'socially constructed reality' and an 'intertextual phenomenon' (796). The purpose of this study was to use narrative analysis to study representations of change and organizational members' 'sense-making' of change at two levels, and from two perspectives, in a large, Swedish construction company. The following research questions were formulated:

1. How has change been represented in the organization's official documents over a twenty-year period (1990–2011)?

298 Business Discourse

2. How do organizational actors (middle managers) interpret and enact the change trajectory?
3. How can a comparison of formal and experienced versions of change (see questions 1 and 2) inform theories of change?

A secondary objective of the study was to gain insight into the difficulties involved in creating strategic coherence throughout the organization.

Method

The case study centred on strategizing and organizational change in a construction company over a twenty-year period (1991–2010), by combining retrospective and real-time accounts. The researchers chose to focus on change in the two decades prior to the study because these constituted one of the 'most turbulent periods so far in [the company's] 100-year history' (797), punctuated by reorganization, strategic redirection and expansion, to promote growth and increase efficiency. The data on which the narrative analysis were applied consisted of retrospective accounts of change, elicited in in-depth, open-ended narrative interviews with 27 upper-middle level managers conducted over a two-year period. The researchers opted to collect accounts from managers at the intermediate level because they were regarded as having 'interpretative priority' in comparison with other employees; as a result, they were also seen as more directly relevant for a researcher investigating how 'collective meaning in an organization' is framed (798). In short, managers were seen as 'interpreters' of events within the organization. To ensure that the sample of managers reflected as diverse a population as possible, the participants were invited randomly (through snowballing), came from various geographical units, and reflected the line organization, as well as central and product functions.

The approach taken in the interviews was 'free storytelling', which means that there were no predetermined categories or a theoretical framework to guide the interviewers and the data collection. Instead, perspectives were expected to emerge spontaneously through the accounts of change given by the managers in the interviews. The idea behind such an approach is that the personal stories that evolve in this way constitute a more genuine, that is reliable, reflection of the underlying beliefs and assumptions that guide certain actions or influence certain perceptions, because interviewees are not being prompted by pre-formulated questions about constructs identified (and defined) by the researcher beforehand, but are given free rein to describe experiences, attitudes and viewpoints in their 'own discourse' and from their own perspective (see also Chapter 7 for a discussion of the advantages of such an approach over quantitative methods).

All the interviews were audio-recorded and transcribed. Two researchers independently applied a narrative analysis by coding fragments of change accounts and creating plots that identified the sequence of events described in the managers' stories. The analysis was done in three steps. First, accounts were ordered chronologically to obtain an overview of time perspective. It was found that the accounts did not orient so much to years and events as to persons (i.e. 'I remembered that this took place when Z had just become CEO'). Second, a close reading of the storytelling transcripts was conducted to gain an understanding of the managers' perceptions of the changes described. From these readings, a clear pattern emerged on the basis of seven discrete organizational change episodes that featured consistently in all (27) interviews. According to the researchers, the consistency found in the interviews with regard to these seven episodes suggests the managers were drawing from a 'common organizational memory' (798). Third, corporate narratives on the seven change episodes were identified in official corporate discourses (i.e. in the business plans, corporate pamphlets, annual reports, and CEO statements covering the 20 years under study). Next, the lived narratives (from managers) and the narratives from official documents were aggregated into one archetypical change narrative for each perspective (manager and corporate: per change episode). The lived versus official versions were subsequently compared per episode and overall, as an indication of how the change trajectory over 20 years was experienced at the micro and macro levels (see also Data 8.10). In cases where the two researchers' analyses were found to deviate from one another, differences were resolved through discussion between the coders and a careful reconsideration of the data.

Concept 8.4   Methodological approach: narrative accounts

One of the ways learning in organizations is achieved is through narrative exchanges between employees, that is, through storytelling which allows them to make sense of their situation and of the organization (Weick, 1996). It is through such stories or accounts that employees share their experiences and insights, which they subsequently use as reference points and frames to interpret similar situations that occur in the future (Räisänen & Gunnarson, 2007). For the researcher, stories, narratives or accounts are a potentially powerful means to uncover experiences 'lived' by employees, to investigate how they position themselves and to study how they accommodate their identities to the different situations they encounter, from their own perspective and 'in their own words', rather than through the researcher's interpretative lens (see also Chapter 7). From an epistemological perspective, narratives are constitutive of organizations and organizing; they shape the events they describe, often in a circular and fragmented manner and from perspectives distributed in time and space. The narrative interview is a particularly useful methodology for studying organizational processes and practices in general, and change in particular, because change is regarded as socially situated, as a 'multi-authored' reality that is constructed on the basis of often competing, interrelated accounts (Buchanan & Dawson, 2007).

(From Löwstedt & Räisänen, 2012: 796, slightly adapted)

Main findings

The interpretative analysis of the managers' accounts revealed that all 27 of them consistently described the occurrence of the same seven change episodes in the two decades under study. We cannot report in full here what the results of the narrative analysis were, but Löwstedt and Räisänen, in their results section, show how the seven episodes 'unfolded' in the different data sources as two 'representative narratives of change', one reflecting an amalgamation of the lived accounts (told by managers) of the change episodes, the other reflecting corporate accounts of these same change episodes, as expressed in official documentation. See Data 8.10. for summaries of data for two of the seven change episodes.

Data 8.10   Overall summary of differences between narratives (lived versus official), and for two of the seven changes studied

According to Löwsted and Räisänen, the episodes they identified represent seven distinct and different changes, while their aggregation represents an overall change over time. Furthermore, when the researchers compared the *rationales behind these changes* in the two versions of events (the lived versus the official narrative), they noted a clear difference in the overall mode and characterizations of organizational change over time.

For example, for one of the seven change episodes (labeled 'Safety', and dating from 2003), the researchers found that the rationale for the change offered in the formal narrative was 'to achieve the goal of zero accidental events'. However, the lived narrative was found to reflect a different rationale, namely that the change 'related to the CEO that introduced it'. For another of the seven change episodes (labeled 4XX, and dating from 1991), the rationale in the formal narrative was 'to increase operational efficiency', while in the lived rationale it was seen as a 'reaction to global economic crisis'.

(Löwsted & Räisänen, 2012: 801–2)

Commentary

This study shows how there are indeed clear discrepancies between the reality depicted in formal, corporate discourses (reflected in official documentation on change) and the reality experienced by managers, as reflected in their personal accounts. While the formal narrative can be said to reflect a 'symbolic' representation of corporate strategizing, the lived version reflects a more reactive, 'emergent' representation of how change is experienced. The study thus shows how using a narrative lens to examine organizations and organizing (in this case with respect to strategizing and change) can provide multi-perspective insights into the socio-cultural system that constitutes the organization, and into how the potential tensions within that system affect organizational members differently, to evoke different experiences and perceptions over time. It also demonstrates that a narrative approach can provide insight into how the macro and micro (i.e. employees' and corporate experience and views) are linked, and how the topics of narratives are situated in, and bear testimony to, the wider contextual space in which organizational members operate. In this way, storytelling in combination with narrative analysis provides contextualized, 'situated' insights that more rigid, quantitative approaches cannot. The researchers themselves note that a discursive approach to the organization essentially acknowledges that 'objectivity or "truth" is impossible to achieve' (see also Chapter 7) and that there are instead 'multiple truths, i.e. narratives, competing for articulation and legitimacy (e.g. Buchanan & Dawson, 2007)' that need to be taken into account by the researcher (Löwstedt & Räisänen, 2012: 802).

In recent years, there has been increasing evidence of researchers (particularly in business and management studies) using narratives and storytelling as a complementary approach to investigating how organizational actors 'make sense' of and experience organizational events in general, and change in particular. Because narrative analysis acknowledges the situated, social and 'discursive' reality organizational actors find themselves in, such an approach can be a potentially suitable (complementary) method in studies of business discourse practices too, as we have already seen with respect to the contextualized, multi-perspective and 'thick' analyses referenced in earlier chapters. A recent study by Oliveira, Vilhena and Vilhena Novaes (2012) for example, draws on a Garfinkelian analysis of narrative accounts collected in a Brazilian company, to show how the quality of internal communication contributes to employees' (lack of) trust. The analysis demonstrates that self-confidence is grounded in communicative practices that reinforce the feeling that the employee is recognized and understood. Without this feeling of self-confidence, trust – and with that teamwork within the organization – is likely to be seriously compromised.

Another example of a study like Löwstedt and Räisänen's, in that it also employs and demonstrates the potential usefulness of organizational storytelling and narrative analysis, is Cardel Gertsen and Søderberg's (2010) investigation of expatriates' accounts of cultural business encounters. Their analysis not only provides greater insight into the way expatriation is actually experienced and constructed (i.e. made sense of) by expatriates, but also suggests pedagogical applications for narratives. Based on their analysis of critical incidents in particular, the researchers suggest that narration could stimulate cultural learning by challenging the storyteller's established views on 'culture', and making them reflect on cultural encounters in new ways. This, in turn, might help expatriates to cope better with such encounters in the future (see also Cardel Gertsen & Søderberg, 2011).

8.10   What's your style? Does adapting communication style to local audiences make business newsletters more effective?

Summary 8.10

Hendriks, B., van Meurs, F., Korzilius, H., Le Pair, R., & Le Blanc-Damen, S. (2012). Style congruency and persuasion: A cross-cultural study into the influence of differences in style dimensions on the persuasiveness of business newsletters in Great Britain and the Netherlands. *IEEE in Transactions on Professional Communication 55*(2), 122–41.

This cross-cultural study explored the effect of writing style congruency (succinct-elaborate style and instrumental-affective style) on the persuasiveness of business newsletters in two European countries. The question was whether a writing style in a country with cultural values that are congruent with this writing style is more persuasive than a writing style which is not. Two experiments were conducted among the business-to-business clients of a company in the Netherlands and the United Kingdom. Participants were presented with different versions of a business newsletter and were asked to evaluate each of the versions with respect to text comprehensibility, text attractiveness and intention to purchase goods from the company.

Introduction and aims

Due to increased internationalization, most organizations now need to consider how to create effective corporate communications that address and reach different international audiences (see also Case study 8.2 on international advertising and Case study 8.7 on international investor relations). The challenge these organizations face is whether to standardize their communications or to localize (i.e. adapt communications to local audiences). Hendriks et al. note that scholars in favour of localization have suggested that increased globalization will encourage cultures to reestablish their local identity and emphasize their uniqueness in the face of a converging world market, and that companies should therefore adapt their advertising to local values if they wish it to be effective. Researchers that have empirically investigated the merits of localization versus standardization, on the other hand, have called for a situational approach in which companies decide on the basis of contextual factors to what extent (marketing) communication needs to be adapted to the intended target group.

Previous research reviewed by Hendriks et al. in their introduction shows that content, structure and style features can all affect the persuasiveness of communication. A number of such studies have investigated differences in direct versus indirect style, and for cultures that vary widely (i.e. Asian versus US cultures) differences on Hofstede's individualism–collectivism dimension. However, Hendriks et al. note that few studies to date have investigated other style dimensions (than direct vs. indirect), or cultures that differ on dimensions other than individualism–collectivism (for example western European cultures). In addition, very few studies have explored whether style congruency in writing (i.e. adapting writing style to the style referred in a particular culture) leads to positive outcomes in intended audiences. Therefore, Hendriks et al.'s investigation focused on two rarely investigated style dimensions (the instrumental-affective and succinct-elaborate dimension). Based on the fact that the Netherlands and the United Kingdom differ with respect to Hofstede's dimensions of femininity-masculinity (The United Kingdom is relatively more masculine than the Netherlands) and high-low uncertainty avoidance (with the Netherlands higher in uncertainty avoidance than the United Kingdom), Hendriks et al. argue that the instrumental-affective style dimension can be linked to the femininity-masculinity cultural dimension (in that affective style has been associated with relatively more feminine cultures, and instrumental style with relatively more masculine countries). In addition, the succinct-elaborate style dimension can be linked to high-low uncertainty avoidance (in that succinct style can be associated with relatively high uncertainty avoidance cultures and elaborate style with relatively low uncertainty avoidance countries). Based on these assumptions, a number of hypotheses were formulated for the study, of which only the main hypotheses will be discussed here:

H1:   In the UK, a business newsletter with an instrumental style will be more persuasive than in the Netherlands;

H2:   In the Netherlands, a business newsletter with an affective style will be more persuasive than in the UK;

H3:   In the Netherlands, a business newsletter with a succinct style will be more persuasive than in the UK;

H4:   In the UK, a business newsletter with an elaborate style will be more persuasive than in the Netherlands.

Concept 8.5 Style dimensions (Gudykunst & Ting-Toomey, 1988) whose relative persuasive effects were studied by Hendriks et al.

Cultural differences in value orientation are reflected in how members of a culture communicate, and, by extension, in different preferences for communication styles across cultures. Gudykunst and Ting-Toomey (1988) distinguished four communication style dimensions on the basis of Hofstede's cultural dimensions (2001; see also Case study 8.2), two of which were featured in this study. The first style dimension, instrumental versus affective communication, can be linked to Hofstede's masculinity-femininity dimension and differs with respect to whether a message is goal-oriented and sender-oriented (instrumental style, associated with a masculine culture) or process-oriented and relationship-oriented (affective style, associated with a feminine culture). The second style dimension, elaborate versus succinct communication, can be linked to Hofstede's uncertainty avoidance dimension, and is reflected in the extent to which different cultures value information quantity. Cultures with moderate to low uncertainty avoidance have been found to prefer a relatively more elaborate communication style than cultures with high uncertainty avoidance, which prefer a more succinct (i.e. brief and to the point) communication style.

(Hendriks et al., 2012: 124,126, adapted)

Method

Two experiments were conducted; one to test the persuasive effect of instrumental versus affective style in a business newsletter in the Netherlands versus the UK (experiment 1) and one to test the persuasive effect of the succinct versus elaborate style in a business newsletter in the two countries (experiment 2). See Concept 8.5 for further explanation of the style dimensions studied, and why. In both studies, participants were asked to react to different versions of the same newsletter (in their own language), in which the style features were manipulated as the independent variables. Participants' reactions to the newsletters were measured using a written questionnaire.

For both experiments, participants were the actual business-to-business customers of a company based in the Netherlands and the UK. The participants were recruited randomly for the experiments on the basis of the company's mailing list. Experiment 1 was conducted online; ca. 7000 Dutch and ca. 8000 UK participants were sent a link to the questionnaire and asked to click on the link if they wished to participate (in total, 142 Dutch and 100 British participants responded to the request to take part). For experiment 2, paper questionnaires were presented randomly to 135 Dutch and 135 British customers (not the same customers as in experiment 1).

To determine whether the Dutch and British participants actually differed as assumed with respect to masculinity-femininity orientation in experiment 1, their value orientation on this dimension was measured as part of the experiment. Paired samples t-tests showed that Dutch and British participants differed significantly from each other, and that the Dutch were indeed oriented significantly more to feminine values than the British. Similarly, for experiment 2, measurements were included to determine whether the Dutch and British differed with respect to uncertainty avoidance. As assumed, the British were found to attach significantly more importance to values that could be associated with low uncertainty (stimulation) than with high uncertainty (security). However, the Dutch were found not to differ significantly in the importance they attached to these values, meaning they were neither high nor low on uncertainty avoidance (but still different from the British participants).

Materials

The texts that served as the basis for the newsletters that formed the materials in both experiments was taken from English websites of companies in the same sector of industry as the company (a manufacturer of diaries and time-management devices) whose customers took part in the investigation. The texts were manipulated to include style features that reflected instrumental or affective style (experiment 1) and succinct or elaborate style (experiment 2). In experiment 1, for example, the instrumental text version included references to "achievements, successes, and quantities, locatives and first person pronouns", while the affective style version included relatively "fewer references to achievements, successes, . . . quantities, and locatives" as well as "second person pronouns" (Hendriks et al., 2012: 129). For each of the two experiments, the manipulated sets of texts were created in both Dutch and English.

Questionnaire (dependent variables)

For both experiments, written questionnaires were created with seven-point scales to measure the persuasiveness of the letter, measured as intention to purchase goods (i.e. "After reading this newsletter I would consider purchasing products from the company": totally agree – totally disagree). To measure attitude to the newsletter, participants were presented with a statement: "I think the text is . . . ", followed by eight seven-point semantic differentials (e.g. engaging-boring; monotonous-lively; not enjoyable-enjoyable, etc.). To measure comprehensibility of the newsletter, participants were presented with the statement "I think the text is", followed by a set of four, seven-point semantic differentials (e.g. clear-unclear; incoherent-coherent, etc.). In each experiment, the questionnaire also included questions to check whether the manipulations of style had been successful. It was determined on the basis of statistical testing that the differences in communication style were perceived as such by the Dutch and

British participants in both experiments, and that the manipulation of the two style dimensions instrumental-affective (experiment 1) and succinct-elaborate (experiment 2) had thus been successful.

Main findings

The results showed that the instrumental version of the newsletter was more persuasive in the UK than in the Netherlands, at least where the dependent variable intention to order goods was concerned, as expected (H1). However, with respect to the other two dependent variables, attitude to the text and comprehensibility of the text, the instrumental version was not found to be more persuasive in the UK than in the Netherlands. For the affective version of the newsletter, the analyses revealed no differences on any of the three dependent variables (H2). In sum, although the manipulated style differences (instrumental versus affective) were recognized by the participants in experiment 1, style had only limited effect on the persuasiveness of a business newsletter.

In experiment 2, in which the effect of a succinct versus elaborate style on the persuasiveness of a business newsletter was investigated across the two cultures, it was found that the succinct newsletter was indeed evaluated as more attractive in the Netherlands than in the UK, as expected (H3). Other significant effects across cultures of succinct style were not found, however (i.e. with regard to intention to purchase goods and text comprehensibility). With regard to the effects of elaborate style across nationalities, no effects on any of the dependent variables were found (H4). Similar to what was found for experiment 1, although the different styles (succinct versus elaborate) were recognized by the Dutch and British participants in experiment 2, style had only a limited effect on the persuasiveness of a business newsletter.

Commentary

For both experimental studies, it was hypothesized on the basis of an extensive literature review, that a culture-congruent communication style in business newsletters would be more persuasive than a culture-incongruent communication style. Only partial support was found for the hypotheses (H1–H4) that were formulated. Overall, the style differences investigated were found to have had only very limited effect on the persuasiveness of the business newsletters. From a practical perspective, this study indicates that in some respects at least, audience reactions to differently styles messages vary across cultures. This might suggest, according to the authors, that organizations should localize the style of their messages to 'match' international audiences' expectations (see also Case study 8.7). The results of the study are, however, necessarily limited to this particular genre (business newsletters), to two communication styles (succinct-elaborate and instrumental-affective) and to the two countries investigated (the Netherlands and the UK). The researchers suggest that future studies might therefore investigate style preferences (and their effects) in other genres (than the business newsletter). As the authors point out, this would provide insights into the 'interplay between genre-specific style conventions and cultural and individual preferences for communication styles' (138). Follow-up studies might also incorporate complementary qualitative methods to establish what readers note and pay attention to when reading corporate messages (for example, a business newsletter or annual report).

Part IV
Resources

9
A Guide to Resources for Business Discourse Research

9.1 Books, edited collections and special issues

A number of important references have been added at the end of each of the previous chapters, together with a brief description of each one. The following are additional book-length studies, edited collections and recent journal Special Issues that are also worth consulting. The publications listed in this section have been instrumental in shaping the field of business discourse. Many of them also present empirical research that has helped to build up our current body of knowledge on how people in business organizations use language in order to get their work done.

Book-length studies

Bargiela-Chiappini, F., & Harris, S. (1997). *Managing language: The discourse of corporate meetings.* Amsterdam and Philadelphia: John Benjamins Publishing Company.

Basturkmen, H. (2005). *Ideas and options in English for specific purposes.* Hillsdale, NJ: Lawrence Erlbaum Associates.

Baxter, J. (2010). *The language of female leadership.* Basingstoke: Palgrave Macmillan,

Bhatia, V. K. (1993). *Analysing genre: Language use in professional settings.* London: Longman.

Bhatia, V. K. (2004). *Worlds of written discourse: A genre based view.* London: Continuum Publishers.

Boden, D. (1994). *The business of talk: Organizations in action.* London: Polity Press.

Clyne, M. (1994). *Inter-cultural communication at work: Cultural values in discourse.* Cambridge: Cambridge University Press.

Cornelissen, J. (2011). *Corporate communication: A guide to theory and practice.* London & New York: Sage.

Covarrubias, P., & Hymes, D. (2005). *Culture, communication and cooperation: Interpersonal relations and pronominal address in a Mexican organization.* Lanham, MD: Rowman & Littlefield Publishers.

Fairhurst, G. (2010). *The power of framing: Creating the language of leadership.* San Francisco, CA: Jossey-Bass.

Goodman, M. B., & Hirsch, P. B. (2010). *Corporate communication.* Bern: Peter Lang.

Graddol, D. (2006). *English next.* London: British Council.

Guirdham, M. (2005). *Communicating across cultures at work.* Basingstoke: Palgrave Macmillan (2nd edn).

Gunnarsson, B. L. (2009). *Professional discourse.* London & New York: Continuum.

Handford, M. (2010).*The language of business meetings.* Cambridge: Cambridge University Press.

Holmes, J. (2006). *Gendered talk at work: Constructing gender identity through workplace discourse.* Malden, MA: Blackwell Publishing.

Kameda, N. (2005) *Managing global business communication.* Tokyo: Maruzen Co., Ltd.

Kelly-Holmes, H. (2005). *Advertising as multilingual communication.* Basingstoke: Palgrave MacMillan.

Koester, A. (2006). *Investigating workplace discourse.* London: Routledge.

Koester, A. (2010). *Workplace discourse.* London: Continuum.

Lampi, M. (1986). *Linguistic components of strategy in business negotiations.* Helsinki, Finland: Helsinki School of Economics, Studies B-85.

Nair-Venugopal, S. (2000). *Language choice and communication in Malaysian business.* Bangi: Penerbit Universiti Kebangsaan Malaysia.

Nickerson, C. (2000). *Playing the corporate language game.* Amsterdam: Rodopi.

Poncini, G. (2004). *Discursive strategies in multicultural business meetings.* Bern: Peter Lang.

Reeves, N., & Wright, C. (1996). *Linguistic auditing: A guide to identifying foreign language communication needs in corporations.* Clevedon: Multilingual Matters Ltd.

Richards, K. (2006). *Language and professional identity: Aspects of collaborative interaction.* Basingstoke: Palgrave Macmillan.

Schnurr, S. (2012). *Exploring professional communication: Language in action.* London & New York: Routledge.

Willing, K. (1992). *Talking it through: Clarification and problem solving in professional work.* Sydney: National Centre for English Language Teaching & Research, Macquarie University.

Yamada, H. (1992). *American and Japanese discourse: A comparison of interactional styles.* Norwood: Ablex.

Yotsukura, L. A. (2003) *Negotiating moves: Problem presentation and resolution in Japanese business discourse.* Burlington: Elsevier.

Edited collections

Angouri, J., & Marra, M. (Eds.) (2011). *Constructing identities at work.* Basingstoke: Palgrave Macmillan.

Aritz, J., & Walker, R. C. (Eds.) (2012). *Discourse perspectives in organizational communication.* Lanham, MD: Fairleigh Dickinson University Press.

Bargiela-Chiappini, F., & Gotti, M. (Eds.) (2005). *Asian business discourse(s).* Bern: Peter Lang.

Bargiela-Chiappini, F., & Harris, S. (Eds.) (1997). *The languages of business: An international perspective.* Edinburgh: Edinburgh University Press.

Bargiela-Chiappini, F., & Nickerson, C. (Eds.) (1999). *Writing business: Genres, media and discourses.* Harlow: Longman.

Belcher, D. (Ed.) (2009). *English for specific purposes in theory and practice.* Ann Arbor: University of Michigan Press/ESL.

Belcher, D., Johns, A., & Paltridge, B. (Eds.) (2011). *New directions in English for Specific Purposes research.* Ann Arbor: University of Michigan Press.

Bhatia, V., & Bremner, S. (Eds.) (2013). *The Routledge handbook of professional communication*. London & New York: Routledge.

Bhatia, V. K. & Gotti, M. (Eds.) (2006). *Explorations in specialized genres*. Bern: Peter Lang.

Candlin, C. N and Crichton, J. (Eds.) (2012). *Discourses of trust*. Basingstoke. Palgrave Macmillan.

Candlin, C. N., & Gotti, M. (Eds.) (2004). *Intercultural aspects of specialized communication*. Bern: Peter Lang.

Cheng, W. and Kong, K. C. C. (Eds.) (2009). *Professional communication: Collaboration between academics and practitioners*. Hong Kong: Hong Kong University Press.

Drew, P., & Heritage, J. (Eds.) (1992). *Talk at work: Interaction in institutional settings*. Cambridge: Cambridge University Press.

Ehlich, K., & Wagner, J. (Eds.) (1995). *The discourse of international negotiations*. Berlin: Mouton de Gruyter.

Facchinetti, R., Crystal D., & B. Seidlhofer (Eds.) (2010). *From international to local English – and back again*. Frankfurt: Peter Lang.

Firth, A. (Ed.) (1995). *Negotiations in the workplace: Discourse and interactional perspectives*. Berlin: Mouton de Gruyter.

Garzone, G., & Ilie, C. (Eds.) (2006). *The role of English in institutional and business settings: An intercultural perspective*. Bern: Peter Lang.

Garzone, G., & Sarangi, S. (Eds.) (2006). *Ideology and ethics in specialized communication: A discourse perspective*. Bern: Peter Lang.

Garzone, G., & Sarangi, S. (Eds.) (2007). *Discourse, ideology and specialized communication*. New York: Peter Lang.

Gillaerts, P., & Gotti, M. (Eds.) (2005). *Genre variation in business letters*. Bern: Peter Lang.

Gillaerts, P., de Groot, E., Dieltjens, S., Heynderickx, P., & Jacobs, G. (Eds) (2012). *Researching discourse in business genres: Cases and corpora (Linguistic Insights 152)*. Bern: Peter Lang.

Gouveia, C., Silvestre, C., & Azuaga, L. (Eds.) (2004). *Discourse, communication and the enterprise*. Lisbon: CEAUL, University of Lisbon.

Gunnarsson, B-L., Linell, P., & Nordberg, B. (Eds.) (1997). *The construction of professional discourse*. London: Longman.

Hewings, M., & Nickerson, C. (Eds.) (1999). *Business English: Research into practice*. London and New York: Longman.

Heynderickx, P., Dieltjens, S., Jacobs, G., Gillaerts, P., de Groot, E. (Eds.) (2012). *The language factor in international business: New perspectives on research, teaching and practice (Linguistic Insights 151)*. Bern: Peter Lang.

Marschan-Piekkari, R., & Welch, C. (Eds.) (2004). *Handbook of qualitative research methods for international business*. Cheltenham: Edward Elgar.

Orr, T. (Ed.), (2002) *English for specific purposes: Case studies in TESOL*. Alexandria, VA: TESOL, Inc.

Ruiz-Garrido, M. F., Palmer-Silveria, J. C. & Fortanet-Gómez, I. (Eds.) (2010). *English for professional and academic purposes*. Amsterdam: Rodopi.

Salvi, R., & Tanaka, H. (2011). *Intercultural interactions in business and management (Linguistic Insights 146)*. Bern: Peter Lang.

Sarangi S., & Roberts C. (Eds.) (1999). *Talk, work and institutional order: discourse in medical, mediation and management settings*. Berlin: Mouton de Gruyter.

Spilka, R. (Ed.) (1993). *Writing in the workplace: New research perspectives*. Carbondale and Edwardsville, IL: Southern Illinois University Press.

Recent journal special issues (from 2002)

Asmuß, B., & Svennevig, J. (Eds.) (2009). Special Issue on discourse analysis. *Journal of Business Communication, 46*(1), 3–170.

Babcock, B., & Bhatia, V. K. (Eds.) (2013). Special issue on business and professional communication in Asia. *Journal of Business and Technical Communication.*

Bargiela-Chiappini, F. (Ed.) (2004). Special issue on organizational discourse. *International Journal of the Sociology of Language, 166,* 1–128.

Bargiela-Chiappini, F. (Ed.) (2005). Special issue on Asian business discourse(s) Part 1. *Journal of Asian Pacific Communication, 15*(2), 207–320.

Bargiela-Chiappini, F. (Ed.) (2006). Special issue on Asian business discourse(s) Part 2. *Journal of Asian Pacific Communication, 16*(1), 1–158.

Bargiela-Chiappini, F., & Nickerson, C. (Eds.) (2002). Special issue on business discourse. *International Review of Applied Linguistics in Language Teaching, 40*(4), 237–381.

Bargiela-Chiappini, F., & Nickerson, C. (Eds.) (2003). Special issue on intercultural business communication. *Journal of Intercultural Studies, 24*(1), 1–79.

Louhiala-Salminen, L., & Rogerson-Revell, P. (Eds.) (2010). Special issue on language matters (part one). *Journal of Business Communication, 47*(2), 91–228.

Nickerson, C. (Ed.) (2005). Special issue on English as a lingua franca in business contexts. *English for Specific Purposes Journal, 24*(4), 367–452.

Orr, T. (Ed.) (2006). Special issue on insights from corpus linguistics for professional communication, *IEEE Transactions on Professional Communication, 49,* (3).

Penrose, J. (Ed.) (2008). Special issue on the business communication of corporate reporting. *Journal of Business Communication, 45*(2), 91–222.

Piekkari, R., & Tietze, S. (Eds.) (2011). Special Issue on languages, *Journal of World Business, 46*(3).

Piekkari, R., & Zander, L. (Eds.) (2005). Special issue on language and communication in international management. *International Studies of Management and Organization, 35*(1), 1–103.

Rogers, P. S. (Ed.) (2006). Special issue on communication challenges from new technology. *Journal of Business and Technical Communication, 20*(3), 246–379.

Rogerson-Revell, P., & Louhiala-Salminen, L. (Eds.) (2010). Special issue on language matters (part two). *Journal of Business Communication, 47*(4), 375–531.

Svennevig, J. (Ed.) (2012). Special Issue on Interaction in workplace meetings, *Discourse Studies, 14* (1), 1–127.

9.2 Journals

This section lists the main journals related to business discourse and business communication research, together with a number of other journals that also publish relevant articles. Details of the publishers' websites are also included.

Business and corporate communication journals

Business Communication Quarterly (Sage)

BCQ is an interdisciplinary journal that focuses on the teaching of business communication. It aims to present the field from an international perspective and includes contributions from researchers and practitioners working around the world. It is published by Sage on behalf of the Association for Business Communication. http://bcq.sagepub.com

Corporate Communications: An International Journal (Emerald)

Corporate Communications addresses the issues arising from the increased awareness that an organization's communications are part of the whole organization, and that the relationship an organization has with its external public requires careful management. The responsibility for communications is increasingly being seen as part of every employee's role and not simply the function of the marketing/PR departments. The journal illustrates why communications are important and how best to implement a strategic communications plan. http://www.emeraldinsight.com/journals.htm?issn=1356-3289

Journal of Business Communication (Sage)

JBC is the scholarly journal published by Sage on behalf of the Association for Business Communication. It includes articles on all areas of business communication, such as business composition/technical writing, information systems, international business communication, management communication, and organizational and corporate communication. Like *BCQ* it includes contributions from researchers from around the world.
http://job.sagepub.com

Journal of Business and Technical Communication (Sage)

JBTC includes contributions on a range of topics of relevance to business communication, including managerial communication, collaborative writing, ethics of business communication, technical writing pedagogy, business-communication education, gender differences in writing, international communication, graphic design, ethnography and corporate culture.
http://jbt.sagepub.com

Information Design Journal (John Benjamins)

IDJ is a platform for discussing and improving the design, usability, and overall effectiveness of 'content put into form' – of verbal and visual messages shaped to meet the needs of particular audiences. *IDJ* offers a forum for sharing ideas about the verbal, visual and typographic design of print and online documents, multimedia presentations, illustrations, signage, interfaces, maps, quantitative displays, websites, and new media and brings together ways of thinking about creating effective communications for use in contexts such as workplaces, hospitals, airports, banks, schools, or government agencies.
http://benjamins.com/#catalog/journals/idj/main

IEEE Transactions on Professional Communication (The Institute of Electrical and Electronics Engineers, IEEE)

IEEE-TPC is sponsored by the Professional Communication Society of the Institute of Electrical and Electronics Engineers. Its audience includes engineers, scientists, writers, information designers and managers, as well as educators and other practitioners, and the scholarly accounts it publishes also consider the practical implications of the work presented.
http://ieeexplore.ieee.org/xpl/RecentIssue.jsp?punumber=47

Management Communication Quarterly (Sage)

MCQ is an interdisciplinary journal that includes scholarly accounts and the implications that these have for practitioners. The publications within *MCQ* represent a variety of theories and methodological approaches, and the authors draw on a number of different disciplines, such as language studies, sociology, management, psychology, communication and organizational behaviour.
http://mcq.sagepub.com

Journal of Business Anthropology

The *JBA* is an Open Access journal which publishes the results of anthropological and related research in business organizations and business situations of all kinds.
http://rauli.cbs.dk/index.php/jba

Other relevant journals which publish papers on Business Discourse and its sub-fields

Journals with an emphasis on language, discourse and communication

Discourse Studies. An Interdisciplinary Journal for the Study of Text and Talk (Sage)
http://dis.sagepub.com

Discourse & Society. An International Journal for the Study of Discourse and Communication in their Social, Political and Cultural Contexts (Sage)
http://das.sagepub.com

English Today. The International Review of the English Language (Cambridge University Press)
http://journals.cambridge.org/action/displayJournal?jid=ENG

English World-Wide. A Journal of Varieties of English (John Benjamins)
http://benjamins.com/#catalog/journals/eww

English for Specific Purposes (Elsevier)
http://www.journals.elsevier.com/english-for-specific-purposes

World Englishes (Blackwell Publishing)
http://www.blackwellpublishing.com/journal.asp?ref=0883–2919

Annual Review of Applied Linguistics (ARAL) (Cambridge University Press)
http://journals.cambridge.org/action/displayJournal?jid=APL

Journal of Applied Linguistics (JAL) (Equinox)
http://www.equinoxpub.com/JAL

Journal of Applied Linguistics and Professional Practice (JALPP) (Equinox)
http://www.equinoxpub.com/jalpp

Journal of Asian Pacific Communication (John Benjamins)
http://benjamins.com/#catalog/journals/japc

Journal of Pragmatics (Elsevier)
http://www.journals.elsevier.com/journal-of-pragmatics

International Journal of the Sociology of Language (IJSL) (Walter de Gruyter)
www.degruyter.com/loi/ijsl

Intercultural Pragmatics (Walter de Gruyter)
www.degruyter.com/view/j/iprg

International Review of Applied Linguistics in Language Teaching (Walter de Gruyter)
www.degruyter.com/view/j/iral

The Journal for Language & Intercultural Communication (Multilingua Matters)
http://www.ialic.arts.gla.ac.uk/journal.html

Multilingua (Walter de Gruyter)
www.degruyter.com/view/j/mult

TEXT & TALK. An Interdisciplinary Journal of Language, Discourse & Communication Studies
(Walter de Gruyter)
www.degruyter.com/view/j/text

Journals in management studies and organization studies

Administrative Science Quarterly (ASQ) (Cornell University)
http://www.johnson.cornell.edu/publications/asq

British Journal of Management (BJM) (Blackwell)
http://www.blackwellpublishing.com/journal.asp?ref=1045–3172

International Journal of Cross Cultural Management (IJCCM) (Sage)
ccm.sagepub.com

Organization Studies (OS) (Sage)
oss.sagepub.com

Qualitative Research in Organizations and Management: An International Journal
(QROM) (Emerald)
www.emeraldinsight.com/products/journals/journals.htm?id=QROM

Journal of Technical Writing and Communication (Baywood)
http://www.baywood.com/journals/PreviewJournals.asp?Id=0047-2816

Technical Communication Quarterly (TCQ) (Taylor & Francis) Lawrence Erlbaum Associates)
www.tandfonline.com/toc/htcq20/current

Other useful journals

College Composition and Communication (National Council of Teachers of English)
http://www.ncte.org/ccc

Gender & Society (Sage)
gas.sagepub.com

Human Relations (Sage)
hum.sagepub.com

Journal of Business Ethics (Springer)
http://www.springer.com/social+sciences/applied+ethics/journal/10551

Journal of Cross-Cultural Psychology (Sage)
jcc.sagepub.com

Journal of Intercultural Studies (Taylor & Francis)
www.tandfonline.com/toc/cjis20/current

9.3   Professional associations

Specially devoted to business discourse

Association of Business Communication (ABC)
businesscommunication.org

Asia-Pacific LSP and Professional Communication Association
http://www.engl.polyu.edu.hk/aplspca

International Centre for Research in Organizational Discourse, Strategy and Change (ICRODS)
www.management.unimelb.edu.au/icrodsc

With an interest in business discourse and business-related language teaching

American Association of Applied Linguistics (AAAL)
www.aaal.org

Association Internationale de Linguïstique Appliquée (International Association of Applied Linguistics) AILA
www.aila.info

British Association of Applied Linguistics (BAAL)
www.baal.org.uk

European Network for Communication Development in Business and Education (ENCoDe)
www.uia.be/s/or/en/1100014974

International Association for Teaching English as a Foreign Language (IATEFL)
www.iatefl.org

International Pragmatics Association (IPrA)
ipra.ua.ac.be

Teachers of English as a Second or Other Language (TESOL)
www.tesol.org

With an interest in culture, communication and management in international business

International Communication Association
www.icahdq.org

DIA: Delta Intercultural Association
http://www.dialogin.com

SIETAR: Society for Intercultural Education, Training and Research
www.sietar.org.uk

9.4   Principal conferences and workshops

Association for Business Communication (ABC)

The ABC holds annual international and regional conventions. The annual convention is general held in the US and there are other regional conventions such as *ABC Southwestern US, ABC Europe Annual Convention* and *ABC Asia and Pacific Rim.*
www.businesscommunication.org/conventions

Association Internationale de Linguïstique Appliquée (AILA) World Congress

Every three years, AILA holds its international World Congress. This is the biggest applied linguistics conference which is attended by more than 2000 researchers and practitioners over the course of five days.
www.aila.info/congresses
The AILA calendar lists conferences, seminars, and other events of interest to linguists and language teachers. Entries of potential interest to applied linguists are marked with an asterisk (*).
http://www.solki.jyu.fi/yhteinen/kongress/start.htm

Other relevant conferences and workshops

American Association of Applied Linguistics (AAAL) annual conference
www.aaal.org

Asia-Pacific LSP and Professional Communication Association
http://www.engl.polyu.edu.hk/aplspca

DiO Workshops (Discourse in Organizations)
http://www.ua.ac.be/main.aspx?c=*IBCDIO

International Conference of Discourse Communication and the Enterprise (DICOEN). Aims to promote interaction and discussion among researchers interested in interplay of discourse and communication and organizational practice.

European Society for the Study of English (ESSE)
www.essenglish.org

European Symposium on Languages for Special Purposes
http://lsp2013.univie.ac.at/home

Ethnographic Praxis in Industry and Commerce (EPIC)
http://epiconference.com

International Pragmatics Association (IprA) biannual international conference
ipra.ua.ac.be

Sociolinguistics Symposium
www.sociolinguistics-symposium-2012.de

9.5   Email lists and bulletin boards

BAALPG
http://www.jiscmail.ac.uk/lists/BAALPG.html

BUSINESS DISCOURSE NET
http://www.jiscmail.ac.uk/archives/businessdiscoursenet.html

CRITICAL-MANAGEMENT
http://www.jiscmail.ac.uk/lists/CRITICAL-MANAGEMENT.html

E-BUSINESS
http://www.jiscmail.ac.uk/lists/E-BUSINESS.html

ECON-BUSINESS-EDUCATORS
http://www.jiscmail.ac.uk/lists/ECON-BUSINESS-EDUCATORS.html

EDINEB
http://www.jiscmail.ac.uk/lists/EDINEB.html

THE LINGUIST LIST
http://www.linguistlist.org

9.6   Databases and abstracting journals

Arts and Humanities Citation Index
ip-science.thomsonreuters.com/cgi-bin/jrnlst/jloptions.cgi?PC=H

ASSIA (Applied Social Sciences Index and Abstracts)
www.csa.com/factsheets/assia-set-c.php

Business Source Premier
www.ebscohost.com/public/business-source-premier

Emerald
www.emeraldinsight.com

Google Scholar
scholar.google.com

Index to Theses
www.theses.com

Ingenta Connect
www.ingentaconnect.com

IBSS (International Bibliography of the Social Sciences)
www.proquest.co.uk/en-UK/catalogs/databases/.../ibss-set-c.shtml

Linguistics Abstracts Online
www.linguisticsabstracts.com

MLA International Bibliography
www.mla.org/bibliography

Science Direct
www.sciencedirect.com

Scopus
www.scopus.com

Social Science Citation Index
http://thomsonreuters.com/products_services/science/science_products/a-z/social_
sciences_citation_index/ Sociological Abstracts
http://www.csa.com/factsheets/socioabs-set-c.php

Studies on Women and Gender Abstracts
www.routledge-swa.com

ZETO (research database)
zetoc.mimas.ac.uk

9.7   Corpora

British National Corpus (BNC)
www.natcorp.ox.ac.uk

Cambridge and Nottingham Business English Corpus (CANBEC)
www.cambridge.org.br/for-teachers/cambridge-international-corpus

The Hong Kong Corpus of Spoken English (HKCSE)
rcpce.engl.polyu.edu.hk/HKCSE

International Corpus of English (ICE)
ice-corpora.net/ice/index.htm

The Macmillan World English Corpus
www.macmillandictionary.com/corpus.html

Vienna-Oxford International Corpus of English
http://www.univie.ac.at/voice

9.8   Postgraduate courses at Masters and PhD level

The following are examples of institutions that offer postgraduate degree programmes
related to business discourse research:.
Aalto University School of Business, Helsinki, Finland
http://communication.aalto.fi/en

Aarhus University, Denmark
http://bcom.au.dk/profile

http://www.asb.dk/en/aboutus/departments/departmentofbusinesscommunication/
research/phdprogrammes

Baruch College, The City University of New York, New York, USA
http://www.baruch.cuny.edu/wsas/academics/corporatecommunication.htm

City University Hong Kong, Hong Kong
http://www.english.cityu.edu.hk/en/programmes/maesp

Copenhagen Business School, Copenhagen, Denmark
http://www.cbs.dk/en/Research/Departments-Centres/Institutter/IBC

Hong Kong Polytechnic University, Hong Kong
http://www.engl.polyu.edu.hk/RCPCE/supervision.html

Radboud University, Nijmegen, The Netherlands
http://www.ru.nl/english/education/programmes/@682164/communication_and
http://www.ru.nl/masters/programme/business-economics/international

Singapore Management University, Singapore
http://www.business.smu.edu.sg/disciplines/corporate_communication/index.asp

University of Warwick, UK Centre for Applied Linguistics
http://www2.warwick.ac.uk/fac/soc/al/degrees/msc

References

Aaker, J. L. (2000). Accessibility or diagnosticity? Disentangling the influence of culture on persuasion processes and attitudes. *Journal of Consumer Research, 26*, 340–57.

Acuña-Ferreira, V., & Àlvarez-López, S. (2003). An interdisciplinary perspective on language and gender. *Estudios de Sociolingüística, 4*(2), i–xvi.

Akar, D. (2002). The macro contextual factors shaping business discourse: The Turkish case. *International Review of Applied Linguistics in Language Teaching, 40*, 305–22.

Akar, D., & Louhiala-Salminen, L. (1999). Towards a new genre: A comparative study of business faxes. In F. Bargiela-Chiappini & C. Nickerson (Eds.), *Writing business: Genres, media and discourses* (pp. 227–54). Harlow: Longman.

Al-Ali, M. N. (2004). How to get yourself on the door of a job: A cross-cultural contrastive study of Arabic and English job application letters. *Journal of Multilingual and Multicultural Development, 25*(1), 1–23.

Allwright, J., & Allwright, R. (1977). An approach to the teaching of medical English. In S. Holden (Ed.). *English for Specific Purposes* (pp. 58–62). Oxford: Modern English Publications.

Almagro Esteban, A., & Pérez Cañado, M. L. (2004). Making the case method work in teaching Business English: A case study. *English for Specific Purposes, 23*, 137–61.

Alvesson, M., & Kärreman, D. (2011). Decolonializing discourse: Critical reflections on organizational discourse analysis. *Human Relations, 64*(9), 1121–46.

Andrews, D. (2002). *Technical communication in the global community*. Upper Saddle River, NJ: Prentice Hall.

Angelmar, R., & Stern, L. (1978). Development of a content analytic system for analysis of bargaining communication in marketing. *Journal of Marketing Research, 15*, 93–102.

Angouri, J., & Bargiela-Chiappini, F. (2011). 'So what problems bother you and you are not speeding up your work?' Problem solving talk at work. *Discourse & Communication, 5*(3), 209–29.

Angouri, J. & Marra, M. (Eds.) (2011). *Constructing identities at work*. Basingstoke: Palgrave Macmillan.

Antaki, C. (Ed.) (2011). *Applied conversation analysis: Intervention and change in institutional talk*. Basingstoke: Palgrave Macmillan.

Archer, Aijman, & Wichmann (2012). *Pragmatics: An advanced resource book for students*. Abingdon: Routledge.

Argenti, P. A. (2012). *Corporate communication* (2nd edn). New York: McGraw-Hill Education.

Argenti, P. A., & Forman, J. (2002). *The power of corporate communication. Crafting the voice and image of your business*. New York: McGraw-Hill Higher Education.

Aritz, J. (2012). Review of G. Fairhurst (2010). The power of framing: Creating the language of leadership. San Francisco, CA: Jossey-Bass. *Journal of Business Communication, 49*(1), 95–100.

Aritz, J., & Walker, R. C. (Eds.) (2011) *Discourse perspectives on organizational communication*. Lanham, MD: Fairleigh Dickinson University Press.

Arnfalk, P., & Kogg, B. (2003). Service transformation: managing a shift from business travel to virtual meetings. *Journal of Cleaner Production, 11*(8), 859–72.

Ashcraft, K. L., & Mumby, D. K. (2003). *Reworking gender: A feminist communicology of organization*. Beverly Hills: Sage.

Askehave, I., & Nielsen, A. E. (2005). What are the characteristics of digital genres? Genre theory from a multimodal perspective. *Proceedings of the 38th Hawaii International Conference on System Sciences*. Retrieved 24 April 2006 from: http://csdl2.computer.org/comp/proceedings/hicss/2005/2268/04/22680098a.pdf.

Atkinson, J. M., & Heritage, J. (1984). Preference organization. In J. M. Atkinson & J. Heritage (Eds.), *Structures of social action: Studies in conversation analysis* (pp. 53–6). Cambridge: Cambridge University Press.

Austin, J. L. (1975). *How to do things with words*. Cambridge, MA: Harvard University Press.

Azuma, S., & Sambongi, R. (2001). *Business Japanese*. Georgetown: Georgetown University Press.

Baba, M. L. (2012). Anthropology and business: Influences and interests. *Journal of Business Anthropology, 1*(1), 20: 71.

Bäck, B. (2004). *Code choice im österreichischen Export in die Romania. Ein Modell und drei Fallstudien*. Unpublished PhD Dissertation, Wirtschaftsuniversität Wien, Vienna.

Baker, P. (2006) *Using Corpora in Discourse Analysis*. London: Continuum.

Baker, P. (2010) *Sociolinguistics and Corpus Linguistics*. Edinburgh: Edinburgh University Press.

Baldry, A., & Thibault, P. J. (2006). *Multimodal transcription and text analysis*. London: Equinox.

Barbara, L. M., Celani, A. A., Collins, H., & Scott, M. (1996). A survey of communication patterns in the Brazilian business context. *English for Specific Purposes, 15*(1), 57–71.

Barclay, L. A. (2010). Review of A. J. Zaremba (2010). Crisis communication. Armonk, NY: M. E. Sharpe. *Business Communication Quarterly, 73*(4), 473–7.

Bargiela-Chiappini, F. (2004a). Language at work: The first ten years. *ESP Across Cultures, 1*, 22–34.

Bargiela-Chiappini, F. (2004b). Intercultural business discourse. In C. N. Candlin & M. Gotti (Eds.), *Intercultural aspects of specialized communication* (pp. 29–52). Bern: Peter Lang.

Bargiela-Chiappini, F. (Ed.) (2004c). Special issue on organizational discourse. *International Journal of the Sociology of Language, 166*, 1–128.

Bargiela-Chiappini, F. (2005a). Asian business discourse(s). Special issue of the *Journal of Asian Pacific Communication*, Part 1, *15*(2).

Bargiela-Chiappini, F. (2005b). In memory of the business letter: Multimedia, genres and social action in a banking website. In P. Gillaerts & M. Gotti (Eds.), *Genre variation in business letters* (pp. 99–122). Bern: Peter Lang.

Bargiela-Chiappini, F. (2006). Asian business discourse(s). Special issue of the *Journal of Asian Pacific Communication*, Part 2, *16*(1).

Bargiela-Chiappini, F. (Ed.) (2009) *Handbook of business discourse*. Edinburgh: Edinburgh University Press.

Bargiela-Chiappini, F. (2011a) Discourse(s), social construction and language practices: in conversation with Alvesson and Kärreman. *Human Relations, 64*(9), 1177–92.

Bargiela-Chiappini, F. (2011b) Asian Business Discourse(s). In J. Aritz, & R. C. Walker (Eds.), *Discourse perspectives on organizational communication*. Lanham, MD: Fairleigh Dickinson University Press, pp. 59–80.

Bargiela-Chiappini, F. (2013) Embodied discursivity: Introducing sensory pragmatics. *Journal of Pragmatics*, forthcoming.

Bargiela-Chiappini, F., Bülow-Møller, A. M., Nickerson, C., Poncini G., & Zhu, Y. (2003). Five perspectives on intercultural business communication. *Business Communication Quarterly, 66*(3), 73–96.

Bargiela-Chiappini, F., & Gotti, M. (Eds.) (2005). *Asian business discourse(s)*. Bern: Peter Lang.

Bargiela-Chiappini, F., & Harris, S. (1997a). *Managing language: The discourse of corporate meetings*. Amsterdam & Philadelphia: John Benjamins.

Bargiela-Chiappini, F., & Harris, S. (Eds.) (1997b). *The languages of business: An international perspective*. Edinburgh: Edinburgh University Press.

Bargiela-Chiappini, F., & Haugh, M. (Eds.) (2010). *Face, Communication and Social Interaction*. London: Equinox Publishing Ltd.

Bargiela-Chiappini, F., & Nickerson, C. (Eds.) (1999). *Writing business: Genres, media and discourses*. Harlow: Longman.

Bargiela-Chiappini, F., & Nickerson, C. (2002). Business discourse: Old debates, new horizons. *International Review of Applied Linguistics in Language Teaching (IRAL)*, *40*(4), 273–381.

Bargiela-Chiappini, F., & Nickerson, C. (Eds.) (2003). Special issue on intercultural business communication. *Journal of Intercultural Studies*, *24*(1), 1–79.

Bargiela-Chiappini, F., & Nickerson, C. (2001). Partnership research: A response to Priscilla Rogers. *Journal of Business Communication*, *38*(3), 248–51.

Bargiela-Chiappini, F., & Tanaka, H. (2012) The mutual gaze: Japan, the West and management training. In S. Nair-Venugopal (Ed.), *The gaze of the West and framings of the East* pp. 139–55. Basingstoke: Palgrave Macmillan.

Bargiela-Chiappini, F., & Zhang, Z. (2012) Business English. In B. Paltridge & S. Starfield (Eds.), *The handbook of English for Specific Purposes*, pp. 193–212. Malden, MA: Wiley Blackwell.

Basturkmen, H. (2005). *Ideas and options in English for specific purposes*. Hillsdale, NJ: Lawrence Erlbaum Associates.

Bateman, J. A. (2008). *Multimodality and genre: A foundation for the systematic analysis of multimodal documents*. Basingstoke: Palgrave Macmillan.

Baxter, J. (Ed.) (2006) *Speaking out: The female voice in public contexts*. Basingstoke: Palgrave: Macmillan.

Baxter, J. (2010). *The Language of female leadership*. Basingstoke: Palgrave Macmillan.

Baxter, J. (2011). Survival or success?: A critical exploration of the use of 'double-voiced discourse' by women business leaders in the UK. *Discourse and Communication*, *5*, 231–45.

Baxter, J. (2012). Women of the corporation: a sociolinguistic perspective of senior women's leadership language in the UK. *Journal of Sociolinguistics*, *16*(1), 81–107.

Baxter, J. & Wallace, K. (2009). 'I'm not going to talk to whatever her name is': Constructing professional identities through male solidarity and female exclusion in builders' discourse. *Discourse & Society*, *20*(4), 411–29.

Baxter, R., Boswood, T., & Peirson-Smith, A. (2002). An ESP program for management in the horse-racing business. In T. Orr (Ed.), *English for specific purposes* (pp. 117–46). Alexandria, VA: TESOL, Inc.

Bazerman, M. H., Lewicki, R. J., & Sheppard, B. H. (Eds.) (1991). *Research on negotiation in organization: Handbook of negotiation research* (Vol. 3). Greenwich, CT: JAI Press.

Bazerman, M. H., & Neale, M. A. (1992). Negotiator rationality and negotiator cognition: The interactive roles of prescriptive and descriptive research. In P. H. Young (Ed.), *Negotation analysis* (pp. 109–29). Ann Arbor, MI: University of Michigan Press.

Beamer, L., & Varner, I. (2010). *Intercultural communication in the global workplace*. Boston: Irwin.

Beattie, V. & Jones, M. J. (2001). A six-country comparison of the use of graphs in annual reports. *Int. J. Account. 36*(2), 195–222.

Bednarek, M., & Martin, J. R. (Eds.) (2010). *New discourse on language: Functional perspectives on multimodality, identity, and affiliation*. London: Continuum.

Becker, H. S. (1993). How I learned what a crock was. *Journal of Contemporary Ethnography 22*(1), 28–35.

Beer, David. (2008). Social network(ing) sites . . . revisiting the story so far: A response to danah *boyd* & Nicole Ellison. *Journal of Computer-mediated Communication, 13*, 516–29.

Belcher, D. (Ed.) (2009). *English for specific purposes in theory and practice*. Ann Arbor: University of Michigan Press/ESL.

Berry, D. M. (2004). The contestation of code. A preliminary investigation into the discourse of the free/libre and open source movements. *Critical Discourse Studies, 1*(1), 65–89.

Berry, J. W. (1989). Imposed etics-emics-derived etics: The operationalization of a compelling idea. *International Journal of Psychology, 24*, 742–35.

Bhatia, T. K. (1992). Discourse functions and pragmatics of mixing: advertising across cultures. *World Englishes, 11* (2/ 3), 195–215.

Bhatia, V. K. (1993). *Analysing genre: Language in professional settings*. London: Longman.

Bhatia, V. K. (2004). *Worlds of written discourse: A genre-based view*. London: Continuum.

Bhatia, V. K. & Bremner, S. (2012). English for business communication. *Language Teaching, 45*(4), 410–45.

Bhatia, V. K., & Candlin, C. N. (Eds.) (2001). *Teaching English to meet the needs of business education in Hong Kong*. Hong Kong: City University of Hong Kong.

Bhatia, V. K. & Gotti, M. (Eds.) (2006). *Explorations in specialized genres*. Bern: Peter Lang.

Bilbow, G. (1995). Requesting strategies in the cross-cultural business meeting. *Pragmatics, 5*(1), 45–55.

Bilbow, G. (1997). Spoken discourse in the multicultural workplace in Hong Kong: Applying a model of discourse as 'impression management'. In F. Bargiela-Chiappini & S. Harris (Eds.), *The languages of business: An international perspective* (pp. 21–48). Edinburgh: Edinburgh University Press.

Bilbow, G. (2002). Commissive speech act use in intercultural business meetings. *International Review of Applied Linguistics in Language Teaching, 40*(4), 287–303.

Björge, A. (2010). Conflict or cooperation: The use of backchannelling in ELF negotiations. *English for Specific Purposes 29*, 191–203

Black, T. (1999). *Doing quantitative research in the Social Sciences: An integrated approach to research design, measurement and statistics*. Thousand Oaks, CA: Sage.

Blalock, M. (2002). Review of D. Andrews (2002). Technical communication in the global community. Upper Saddle River, NJ: Prentice Hall. *Business Communication Quarterly, 65*(4), 134–6.

Blicq, R. (1993). *Technically – write! Communicating in a technological era* (4th edn). Engelwood Cliffs, NJ: Prentice Hall.

Blommaert, J. & co-authors, (2004). Guidelines for the use of language analysis in relation to questions of national origin in refugee cases. *The International Journal of Speech, Language and the Law: Forensic Linguistics, 11*(2), 261–66.

Blommaert, J. (2009). Language, asylum and the national order. *Current Anthropology 50*(4), 415–41.

Blum-Kulka, S., House, J., & Kasper, G. (Eds.) (1989). *Cross-cultural pragmatics: Requests and apologies*. Norwood, NJ: Ablex.

Bock, G. (1994). Unappreciated writers: a survey of technical writers in Germany. In M. Steehouder, C. Janssen, P. Poort, P. van der, Poort, & R. Verheijen (Eds.), *Quality of technical communication.* (pp. 249–57). Amsterdam: Rodopi.

Boden, D. (1994). *The business of talk: Organizations in action*. London: Polity Press.

Boswood, T. (2002). Review of S. Donna (2000). Teach business English. Cambridge: Cambridge University Press. *English for Specific Purposes, 21*(1), 102–04.

Bremner, S. (2010). Collaborative writing: Bridging the gap between the textbook and the workplace. *English for Specific Purposes, 29*, 121–32.

Brett, P. (2000). Integrating multimedia into the Business English curriculum: a case study. *English for Specific Purposes, 19*, 269–90.

Briguglio, C. (2005a). Developing an understanding of English as a global language for business settings. In F. Bargiela-Chiappini & M. Gotti (Eds.), *Asian business discourse* (pp. 313–44). Bern: Peter Lang.

Briguglio, C. (2005b). *The use of English in multinational settings and the implication for business education*. Unpublished PhD thesis, Perth: University of Western Australia.

Brislin, R. W. (1980). Translation and content analysis of oral and written materials. In H. Triandis & J. W. Berry (Eds.), *Handbook of cross-cultural psychology* (pp. 389–444). Boston: Allyn and Bacon.

Brown, B. (1977). Face saving and face restoration in negotiation. In D. Druckman (Ed.), *Negotiations: Social-psychological perspectives*. Beverly Hills, CA: Sage.

Brown, P., & Levinson, S. (1987). *Politeness*. Cambridge: Cambridge University Press.

Brown, T. P., & Lewis, M. (2002). An ESP project: Analysis of an authentic workplace conversation. *English for Specific Purposes, 22*(1), 93–8.

Buchanan, D. & Dawson, P. (2007). Discourse and audience: Organizational change as multi-story process. *Journal of Management Studies 44*(5), 669–86.

Bueno Lajusticia, M. R. (2003). *Lenguas para fines específicos en España a través de sus publicaciones (1985–2002)* [Editorial]. Madrid: Universitas.

Brummas, B. H. J. M., Cooren, F., & Chaput, M. (2009). Discourse, communication and organizational ontology. In F. Bargiela-Chiappini (Ed.), The *Handbook of business discourse*, pp. 53–65. Edinburgh: Edinburgh University Press.

Byrne, D. (1971). *The Attraction Paradigm*. New York: Academic Press.

Cameron, D. (2000a). Styling the worker: Gender and the commodification of language in the globalized service economy. *Journal of Sociolinguistics, 4*(3), 323–47.

Cameron, D. (2000b). *Good to talk? Living and working in a communication culture*. London: Sage.

Cameron, D. (2001). *Working with spoken discourse*. London: Sage.

Cameron, D. (2007). *The myth of Mars and Venus: Do men and women speak the same language?* Oxford: Oxford University Press.

Cameron, A., & Webster, J. (2005). Unintended consequences of emerging communication technologies: Instant messaging in the workplace. *Computers in Human Behavior, 21*(1), 85–103.

Candia, R. (2001). The business letter in Spanish: A cultural perspective. *Global Business Languages* (pp. 134–9). Purdue University: Department of Foreign Languages and Literatures.

Candlin, C. (1990). What happens when applied linguistics goes critical? In M. A. K. Halliday, J. Gibbons, & H. Nicholas (Eds.), *Learning, keeping and using language* (pp. 461–86). Amsterdam: John Benjamins.

Candlin, C. N. (1997). General Editor's preface. In B.-L. Gunnarsson, P. Linell & B. Nordberg (Eds.), *The construction of professional discourse* (pp. viii–xiv). London: Longman.

Candlin, C. (2002). *Speculating on futures, drawing on current accounts*. Plenary address given at the ABC European Convention. Aarhus, Denmark: Aarhus School of Business (23 May 2002).

Candlin, C. N. (2006). Accounting for interdiscursivity: Challenges to professional expertise. In M. Gotti & D. Giannone (Eds.), *New trends in specialized discourse analysis* (pp. 21–45). Bern: Peter Lang.

Candlin, C. N & J. Crichton (2011a). Emergent themes and research challenges: Reconceptualising LSP. In M. Pedersen & J. Engberg (Eds.), *Current trends in LSP research* pp. 277–316. Bern: Peter Lang Verlag.

Candlin, C. N. & Crichton, J. (2011b). Introduction. In C. N. Candlin & J. Crichton (Eds.), *Discourses of deficit* (pp. 1–22). Basingstoke: Palgrave Macmillan.

Candlin, C. N., & Crichton, J. (Eds.) (2012) *Discourses of Trust*. Basingstoke: Palgrave Macmillan.

Candlin C. N. & Crichton, J. (2012) From ontology to methodology: exploring the discursive landscape of trust. In C.N. Candlin & J. Crichton (Eds.) *Discourses of trust*. Basingstoke: Palgrave Macmillan.

Candlin C. N. & Crichton, J. (2013) Putting our trust in the learner. In J. Arnold and T. Murphey (Eds.) *Meaningful action: Earl Stevick's influence on language teaching*. Cambridge. Cambridge University Press

Candlin, C. N., & Gotti, M. (Eds.) (2004). *Intercultural aspects of specialized communication*. Bern: Peter Lang.

Candlin, C. N., Maley, Y., & Sutch, H. (1999). Industrial instability and the discourse of enterprise bargaining. In S. Sarangi & C. Roberts (Eds.), *Talk, work and institutional order* (pp. 323–50). Berlin: Mouton de Gruyter.

Candlin, C. N., & Sarangi, S. (2004). Making applied linguistics matter [Editorial]. *Journal of Applied Linguistics, 1*(1), 1–8.

Candlin, C. N. & S. Sarangi (Eds.) (2011) *Handbook of communication in organizations and professions*. Berlin: Mouton de Gruyter.

Cardel Gertsen, M., & Søderberg, A. (2010). Expatriate stories about cultural encounters: A narrative approach to cultural learning processes in multinational companies. *Scandinavian Journal of Management 26*, 248–57.

Cardel Gertsen, M., & Søderberg, A. (2011). Intercultural communication stories: On narrative inquiry and analysis as tools for research in international business. *Journal of International Business Studies 42*, 787–804.

Carter, R., & McCarthy, M. (1997). *Exploring spoken English*. Cambridge: Cambridge University Press.

Cassady, M., & Wasson, L. (1994). Written communication skills of international business persons. *ACBA Bulletin, December*, 36–40.

Castor, T., & Cooren, F. (2006). Organizations as hybrid forms of life: The implications of the selection of human and non-human agents in problem- formulation. *Management Communication Quarterly, 19*(4), 570–600.

Catenaccio, P. (2007). New(s) genres and discursive identity: the changing face of press releases in the age of the Internet. In G. Garzone, G. Poncini and P. Catenaccio (Eds.), *Multimodality in Corporate Communication: Web Genres and Discursive Identity*. pp. 55–71. Milan: Franco Angeli.

Cefkin, M. (2012) Close encounters: Anthropologists in the corporate arena. *Journal of Business Anthropology, 1*(1), 91–117.

Cesiri, D. (2011). Intercultural communication in business promotion through corporate websites: the case *of Kraft Foods* and *Nestlé*. In R. Salvi & H. Tanaka (Eds.), *Intercultural Interactions in Business and Management*. pp. 91–118. Bern: Peter Lang.

Chaney, L. & Martin, J. (2010). *Intercultural business communication*. Upper Saddle River, NJ: Prentice Hall.

Charles, M. (1995). Organizational power in business negotiations. In K. Ehlich & J. Wagner (Eds.), *The discourse of international negotiations* (pp. 151–74). Berlin: Mouton de Gruyter.

Charles, M. (1996). Business negotiations: Interdependence between discourse and the business relationship. *English for Specific Purposes, 15*(1), 19–36.

Charles, M. (2009). Future horizons: Europe. In F. Bargiela-Chiappini (Ed.), *The handbook of business discourse* pp. 454–64. Edinburgh: Edinburgh University Press.

Charles, M., & Marschan-Piekkari, R. (2002). Language training for enhanced horizontal communication: A challenge for MNCs. *Business Communication Quarterly, 65*(2), 9–29.

Charteris-Black, J., & Ennis, T. (2001). A comparative study of metaphor in Spanish and English financial reporting. *English for Specific Purposes, 20*(3), 249–66.

Cheng, A. (2011). Review of M. Ruiz-Garrido, J. Palmer-Silveira & I. Fortanet-Gómez (Eds.) (2010). English for professional and academic purposes. Rodopi, Amsterdam. *English for Specific Purposes, 30* (4), 310–12.

Cheng, W. (2009). Future horizons: Asia. In Bargiela-Chiappini, F. (Ed.) (2009). *Handbook of business discourse* pp. 481–95 Edinburgh: Edinburgh University Press.

Cheng, W., & Kong, K. C. C. (2009). *Professional communication: Collaboration between academics and practitioner.* Hong Kong: Hong Kong University Press.

Cheng, W., & Mok, E. (2006). Cultural preferences for rhetorical patterns in business writing. *Hong Kong Linguist, 26,* 69–80.

Cheng, W. & Mok, E. (2008). Discourse processes and products: Land surveyors in Hong Kong, *English for Specific Purposes 27,* 57–73.

Cheng, W., & Warren, M. (2005) // well I have a Different // THINking you know //: A corpus-driven study of disagreement in Hong Kong business discourse. In F. Bargiela-Chiappini & M. Gotti (Eds.), *Asian Business Discourse(s)* pp. 241–70. Bern: Peter Lang.

Cheng, W. & M. Warren (2006) I would say be very careful of . . . : Opine markers in an intercultural business corpus of spoken English. In J. Bamford and M. Bondi (Eds). *Intercultural and interdiscoursal perspectives* pp. 46–58. Rome: Officina Edizioni.

Chew, G. C. L. (2005). The function of 'du'oc' in business communication in Vietnam. Asian business discourse(s). Special Issue of the *Journal of Asian Pacific Communication,* Part 1, *15*(2), 229–56.

Chew, S. K. (2005). An investigation of the English language skills used by new entrants in banks in Hong Kong. *English for Specific Purposes, 24*(4), 423–35.

Cho, S., & Huh, J. (2010) Content analysis of corporate blogs as a relationship management tool. *Corporate Communications: an International Journal, 15,* 30–48.

Christian, P. (1998). French and American business professionals: A discourse analysis study of cultural differences. *Intercultural Communication Studies, 8*(2), 1–18.

Christie, H., Hagen, S., Sheikh, H., Kenny, B., Chapman, I., Staden, M. van, Jorgensen, L., & Lindquist, P. (2001). *Elise survey overview of European findings: European language and international strategy development in SMEs* [online source]. Accessed 28 April 2006, at: http://www.stb.tno.nl/uploads/ELISEOverview Report.pdf

Cicourel, A.V. (1992). The interpenetration of communicative contexts: examples from medical encounters. In A. Duranti, & C. Goodwin, (Eds.). *Rethinking Context* (pp. 291–310). Cambridge: Cambridge University Press.

Cicourel, A.V. (2007). A personal, retrospective view of ecological validity. *Text & Talk 27*(5), 735–52.

Clampitt, P. (2000). *Communicating for managerial effectiveness* (2nd edn). London: Sage Publications.

Clifton, J. (2010). Review of G. Garzone & S. Sarangi, (Eds.) (2007). *Discourse, ideology and specialized communication.* New York: Peter Lang. *Journal of Business Communication, 47*(1), 79–82.

Clifton, J. (2012). Conversation analysis in dialogue with Stocks of Interactional Knowledge: Facework and appraisal interviews. *Journal of Business Communication 49*(4), 283–311.

Clyne, M. (1994). *Inter-cultural communication at work.* Cambridge: Cambridge University Press.

Clyne, M. (2003). *Dynamics of language contact: English and immigrant languages.* Cambridge: Cambridge University Press.

Collins COBUILD (2004). *Business vocabulary in practice.* London: Collins Publishers.

Collot, M., & Belmore, N. (1996). Electronic Language: A new variety of English. In S. C. Herring (Ed.), *Computer-mediated communication: Linguistic, social, and cross-cultural perspectives* (pp. 13–28). Amsterdam: John Benjamins.

Comfort, J. (1998). *Effective negotiating*. Oxford: Oxford University Press.

Conaway, R. N., & Wardrope, W. J. (2004). Communication in Latin America: An analysis of Guatemalan business letters. *Business Communication Quarterly, 67*(4), 465–74.

Connor, M., Rogers, P. S., & Wong I. (2005). Reinventing ourselves: Collaborative research initiatives between Singapore & US Business Schools. *English for Specific Business Purposes, 24*, 437–46.

Connor, U. (1999). 'How like you our fish?' Accommodation in international business communication. In M. Hewings & C. Nickerson (Eds.), *Business English: Research into practice* (pp. 115–28). Harlow: Pearson Education.

Connor, U., Davis, K., & De Rycker, T. (1995). Correctness and clarity in applying for overseas jobs: A cross-cultural analysis of U.S. and Flemish applications. *Text, 15*(4), 457–76.

Connor, U., Davis, K., De Rycker, T., Phillips, E. M., & Verkens, J. P. (1997). An international course in international business writing: Belgium, Finland, the United States. *Business Communication Quarterly, 60*(4), 63–74.

Connor, U., & Upton, T. (2004). *Discourse in the professions: Perspectives from corpus linguistics*. Amsterdam: John Benjamins.

Cooren, F., & Bencherki, N. (2010). How things do things with words : Ventriloquism, passion and technology. *Encyclopedia: Journal of Phenomenology and Education, XIV*, 35–61.

Cornelissen, J. (2011). *Corporate communication: A guide to theory and practice*. London & New York: Sage.

Cortes Gago, P., & Bittencourt Silveira, S. (2009). The co-construction of the transition relevance place in a Brazilian consumers' product safety commission meeting: Some structural properties of institutional interaction in a conflict situation, In F. Ramallo, L. M. Anxo, X. P. Rodriguez-Yáñez, & P. Cap (Eds.). *New approaches to discourse and business communication* pp. 171–89. Basingstoke: Palgrave Macmillan.

Coupland, J. (Ed.). (2000). *Small talk*. London: Longman.

Courtis, J., & Hassan, S. (2002). Reading ease of bilingual annual reports. *Journal of Business Communication, 39*(4), 394–413.

Covarrubias, P. & Hymes, D. (2005). *Culture, communication and cooperation: Interpersonal relations and pronominal address in a Mexican organization*. Lanham, M.D: Rowman & Littlefield Publishers.

Cowling, J. (2007). Needs analysis: Planning a syllabus for a series of intensive workplace courses at a leading Japanese company. *English for Specific Purposes 26*, 426–42.

Cox, J. L., Martinez, E. R., & Quinlan, K. B. (2008). Blog and the corporation: managing the risk, reaping the benefits. *Journal of Business Strategy 29*(3), 4–12.

Crawford Camiciottoli, B. (2009a). 'Just wondering if you could comment on that': Indirect requests for information in corporate earnings calls. *Text & Talk, 29*(6), 661–81.

Crawford Camiciottoli, B., (2009b). The teaching style of the business educator: A corpus-based investigation of the relationship between language and identity. *International Journal of Business & Economics, 9*, 117–36.

Crawford Camiciottoli, B., (2009c). Collective and individual identities in business studies lectures. In M. Gotti (Ed.) *Commonality and Individuality in Academic Discourse* pp. 141–160. Bern: Peter Lang.

Crawford Camiciottoli, B. (2010). Earnings calls: Exploring an emerging financial reporting genre. *Discourse & Communication, 4*(4), 343–59.

Crichton, J. (2003). Issues of interdiscursivity in the commercialisation of professional practice: The case of English language teaching. Unpublished doctoral thesis. Sydney: Macquarie University.

Crichton, J. (2010). *The discourse of commercialization*. Basingstoke: Palgrave Macmillan.

Crichton, J. (2010). Why a multi-perspectived approach to discourse? In J. Chrichton, (Ed.), *The Discourse of Commercialization* (pp. 20–48). Basingstoke: Palgrave Macmillan.

Crismore, A. (1989). *Talking with readers: Metadiscourse as rhetorical act.* New York: Lang.

Crismore, A., Markkanen, R., & Steffensen, M. (1993). Metadiscourse in persuasive writing: A study of texts written by American and Finnish university students. *Written Communication, 10*(1), 39–71.

Cross, G. A. (2000). Collective form: An exploration of large-group writing [1998 Outstanding researcher lecture.] *Journal of Business Communication, 37,* 77–100.

Cross, G. A. (2001). *Forming the collective mind: A contextual exploration of large-scale collaborative writing in industry.* Cresskill, NJ: Hampton Press.

Cross, G. A. (2010). *Envisioning collaboration: Group verbal-visual composing in a system of creativity.* Amityville, NY: Baywood Publishing Company.

Crystal, D. (1997). *English as a global language.* Cambridge: Cambridge University Press.

Cui, S. (2004). *Business Chinese: An advanced reader.* Hong Kong: Chinese University Press.

Cyr, D., Bonanni, C., Bowes, J., & Ilsever, J. (2005). Beyond trust: Website design preferences across cultures. *Journal of Global Information Management, 13*(4), 24–52.

Czarniawska-Joerges, B. (1998). *Narrative approach in organization studies.* Thousand Oaks, CA: Sage.

Czarniawska, B. (2012). Organization theory meets anthropology: A story of an encounter. *Journal of Business Anthropology, 1*(1) 118–40.

Daft, R. L., & Lengel, R. H. (1984). Information richness: A new approach to managerial behavior and organizational design. In L. L. Cummings & B. M. Staw (Eds.), *Research in Organizational Behavior* (pp. 191–233). Homewood, IL: JAI Press.

Daublebsky, S. (2000). *La langue française dans le monde du travail. Étude sur les diplômés des années quatre-vingts de l'Université de Sciences Économiques de Vienne.* Master's thesis, Wirtschaftsuniversität Wien, Vienna.

de Groot, E. (2012). Personal preference or policy? Language choice in a European-based international organization. *Corporate Communications: An International Journal 17*(3), 266–71.

de Groot, E. B. (2008). *English annual reports in Europe: a study on the identification and reception of genre characteristics in multimodal annual reports originating in the Netherlands and in the United Kingdom.* Published PhD thesis. Nijmegen/Utrecht: Radboud University Nijmegen/LOT.

de Groot, E. B., Korzilius, H. P. L. M., Gerritsen, M. & Nickerson, C. (2011). There's no place like home: UK-based financial analysts' response to Dutch-English and British-English annual reports texts. *IEEE Transactions on Professional Communication, 54*(1), 1–17.

de Groot, E., Korzilius, H., Nickerson C. & Gerritsen, M. (2006). A corpus analysis of text themes and photographic themes in managerial forewords of Dutch-English and British annual general reports. *IEEE Transactions on Professional Communication, 49*(3), 217–35.

de Jong, M., & Schellens, P. (1997). Reader-focused text evaluation: An overview of goals and methods. *Journal of Business and Technical Communication, 11*(4), 402–32.

Delin, J. (2005). Brand tone of voice. *Applied Linguistics, 2*(1), 1–44.

Delin, J. (2012/3). Trusting the high street bank: understanding consumer trust in a major financial institution. In C. Candlin and J. Crichton (Eds.), *Discourses of trust* (pp. 183–202). Basingstoke: Palgrave Macmillan.

Delin, J. and Bateman, J. (2002). Describing and critiquing multimodal documents. *Document Design, 3*(2), 140–55.

de Melo Resende, V. (2010). Between the European legacy and critical daring: Epistemological reflections for critical discourse analysis, *Journal of Multicultural Discourses, 5*(3), 193–212.

de Mooij, M. (2004). *Consumer behavior and culture consequences for global marketing and advertising*. Thousand Oaks, London, New Delhi: Sage.

de Moraes Garcez, P. (1993). Point-making styles in cross-cultural business negotiation: A microethnographic study. *English for Specific Purposes, 12*(2), 103–20.

Deneire, M. (2008). English in the French workplace: realism and anxieties. *World Englishes, 27*(2), 181–95.

Dennett, J. T. (1988). 'Not to say is better than to say': How rhetorical structure reflects cultural context in Japanese-English technical writing. *IEEE Transactions on Professional Communication, 31*, 116–19.

Deresky, H., & Christopher, E. (2012). *International management: Managing cultural diversity*. 2nd edition. Sydney: Pearson.

Dhanania, K., & Gopakumaran, S. (2005). Marwari business discourse: An analysis. Asian business discourse(s). Special Issue of the *Journal of Asian Pacific Communication*, Part 1, *15*(2), 287–312.

Dhir, K. & Savage, T. (2002). The value of a working language. *International Journal of the Sociology of Language 158*, 1–35.

Ditlevsen, Marianne Grove (2012). Revealing corporate identities in annual reports. *Corporate Communications: An International Journal, 17*(3), 379–403.

do Carmo Leite de Oliveira, M., & Gomes da Silva, J. R. (2009) The composition of a participative view for the management of organizational communications. In F. Ramallo, M. L. Anxo, X. P. Rodriguez-Yáñez, & P. Cap (Eds.), *New approaches to discourse and business communication*. pp. 190–211. Basingstoke: Palgrave Macmillan.

Donna, S. (2000). *Teach business English*. Cambridge: Cambridge University Press.

Donohue, W. A., & Diez, M. E. (1985). Directive use in negotiation interaction. *Communication Monographs, 52*, 305–18.

dos Santos Pinto, V. B. M. (2002). Genre analysis of business letters of negotiation. *English for Specific Purposes, 21*(2), 167–99.

Douglas, D. (2000). *Assessing languages for specific purposes*. Cambridge: Cambridge University Press.

Dressen-Hammouda, D. (2010). Review of V. K. Bhatia, & M. Gotti (Eds.) (2006). *Explorations in specialized genres*. Bern: Peter Lang. *English for Specific Purposes, 29*(4), 299–301.

Drew, P., & Heritage, J. (Eds.) (1992). *Talk at work*. Cambridge: Cambridge University Press.

Du-Babcock, B. (2002). Review of S. Niemeier, C. P. Campbell, & R. Dirven (Eds.) (1998). *The cultural context in business communication*. Amsterdam: John Benjamins. *English for Specific Purposes, 21*(4), 410–13.

Du-Babcock, B. & Tanaka, H. (2010). Turn-taking behavior and topic management strategies of Chinese and Japanese business professionals: A comparison of intercultural group communication. 2010 Annual Convention Proceedings: The Association of Business Communication (ABC) (http://businesscommunication.org/conventions/abc-convention-proceedings/2010-annual-convention-proceedings/).

Earley P. C. & Ang, S. (2003). *Cultural intelligence: Individual interactions across cultures*. Standford, CA: Stanford Business Books.

Ehlich, K., & Wagner, J. (Eds.) (1995). *The discourse of international negotiations*. Berlin: Mouton de Gruyter.

Ehrenreich, S. (2010). English as a business lingua franca in a German multinational corporation: Meeting the challenge. *Journal of Business Communication, 47*(4), 408–31.

ELAN (2006). *Effects on the European Economy of Shortages of Foreign Language Skills in Enterprise*. A Report prepared by CILT, the National Centre for Languages, for the European Commission. Principal Investigator: Stephen Hagen. Retrieved 15 September 2009, from: http://ec.europa.eu/education/policies/lang/doc/elan_final_report_en.pdf

ELISE (2001). *European Language & International Strategy Development in SMEs. (co-funded by the Leonardo da Vinci Programme).* Retrieved 10 September 2009, from: http://www.interactint.com/projects.htm).

ELISE Project, http://www.interesourcegroup.com/elise/

Ellis, R. J. (2003). *Interdisciplinarity.* The Higher Education Academy (HEA).

ELUCIDATE Survey (1999). *Business Communication Across Borders: A Study of Language use and practice in European companies.* S. Hagen, (Ed.). London: CILT.

Emmett, K. (2003). Persuasion strategies in Japanese business meetings. *Journal of Intercultural Studies, 24*(1), 65–79.

EPIDASA Project, http//www.epidasa.org

Epstein, M. H. (1999). Teaching field-specific writing: Results of UAC survey. *Business Communication Quarterly, 62*(1), 29–41.

Erling, E. & Walton, A. (2007). English at work in Berlin: A report on a survey of seven multinational companies in Germany. *English Today, 23,* 32–40.

Evans, S. (2010). Business as usual: The use of English in the professional world in Hong Kong. *English for Specific Purposes, 29*(3), 153–67.

Evans, S. (2012). Designing email talks for the Business English classroom: Implications from a study of Hong Kong's key industries. *English for Specific Purposes, 31*(3), 202–12.

Facchinetti, R., Crystal D. & Seidlhofer, B. (Eds.) (2010). *From international to local English – and back again.* Frankfurt: Peter Lang.

Fairclough, N. (1993). Critical discourse analysis and the marketisation of public discourse: The universities. *Discourse & Society, 4,* 133–68.

Fairclough, N. (2003). *Analyzing discourse: Textual analysis for social research.* London & New York: Routledge.

Fairhurst, G. (2010). *The power of framing: Creating the language of leadership.* San Francisco, CA: Jossey-Bass

Farache, F. & Perks, K. J. (2010). CSR advertisements: A legitimacy tool? *Corporate Communications 15*(3), 235–48.

Feely, A. J., & Harzing, A. W. K (2003). Language management in multinational companies. *Cross-Cultural Management, 10*(2), 37–52.

Field, A. (2009). *Discovering Statistics Using SPSS (Introducing Statistical Methods series).* Thousand Oaks, CA: Sage Publications.

Firth, A. (Ed.) (1995). *The discourse of negotiation: Studies of language in the workplace.* Oxford: Pergamon.

Fisher, W., & Ury, M. (1991). *Getting to yes.* New York: Penguin Books.

Flowerdew, A. & Wan, J. (2006). Genre analysis of tax computation letters: How and why tax accountants write the way they do. *English for Specific Purposes 25,* 133–53.

Flowerdew, L. (2012). *Corpora and language education (Research and Practice in Applied Linguistics Series).* Basingstoke: Palgrave MacMillan.

Folger, J., & Poole, M. (1984). *Working through conflict: A communication perspective.* Glenview, IL: Scott, Foresman.

Fombrun, C. & Shanley, M. (1990). What's in a name? Reputation building and corporate strategy. *Academy of Management Journal 33*(2), 233–58.

Ford, G. (2010). Review of E. H. Schein (2009). *The corporate culture survival guide.* San Francisco, CA: Jossey-Bass. *Business Communication Quarterly, 73*(2), 233–6.

Forey, G. & Lockwood, J. (2007). 'I'd love to put someone in jail for this': An initial investigation of English in the business processing outsourcing (BPO) industry. *English for Specific Purposes, 26*(3), 308–26.

Gains, J. (1999). Electronic mail: A new style of communication or just a new medium? An investigation into the text features of e-mail. *English for Specific Purposes, 18*(1), 81–101.

Gallion, L. M., & Kavan, C. B. (1994). A case study in business writing: An examination of the documents written by executives and managers. *The Bulletin of the Association for Business Communication*, December, 9–11.

Garbarino, E., & Johnson, M. (1999). The different roles of satisfaction, trust, and commitment in customer relationships. *Journal of Marketing*, 63, 70–87.

Garcez, P. (1993). Point-making styles in cross-cultural business negotiation: A microethnographic study. *English for Specific Purposes*, 12(2), 103–20.

Gardner, R. (1987). The identification and role of topic in spoken interaction. *Semiotica*, 65 (1/2), 129–41.

Garfinkel, H. (1967). *Studies in ethnomethodology*. Englewood Cliffs, NJ: Prentice Hall.

Garzone, G. (2002). Describing e-commerce communication: Which models and categories for text analysis? In P. Evengelisti & E. Ventola (Eds.), *TEXTUS (English in Academic and Professional Settings: Techniques of Description/Pedagogical Application)* pp. 279–96. XIV, 2.

Garzone, G. (2004). Annual company reports and CEO's letters: Discoursal features and cultural markedness. In C. Candlin & M. Gotti (Eds.), *Intercultural aspects of specialized communication* (pp. 311–40). Bern: Peter Lang.

Garzone, G. (2005). Letters to shareholders and chairman's statements: Textual variability and generic integrity. In P. Gillaerts & M. Gotti (Eds.), *Genre variation in business letters* (pp. 179–204). Bern: Peter Lang.

Garzone, G. (2007) Genres, multimodality and the World Wide Web: Theoretical issues. In G. Garzone, G. Poncini and P. Catenaccio (Eds.), *Multimodality in Corporate Communication: Web Genres and Discursive Identity* pp. 15–30. Milan: Franco Angeli.

Garzone, G. (2009) Multimodal analysis. In: F. Bargiela-Chiappini (Ed.), *The Handbook of Business Discourse* pp. 155–65. Edinburgh: Edinburgh University Press.

Garzone, G., & Ilie, C. (Eds.) (2006). *The role of English in institutional and business settings: An intercultural perspective*. Bern: Peter Lang.

Garzone, G., Poncini, G., & Catenaccio, P. (Eds.) (2007). *Multimodality in Corporate Communication: Web Genres and Discursive Identity*. Milan: Franco Angeli.

Garzone, G., & Sarangi, S. (Eds.) (2006). *Ideology and ethics in specialized communication: A discourse perspective*. Bern: Peter Lang.

Garzone, G. & Sarangi, S. (Eds.) (2007). *Discourse, ideology and specialized communication*. New York: Peter Lang.

Gatti, M. C. (2010). *Time-Space: An integrated cognitive-semiotic approach to organizational discourse for the web*. Unpublished Ph.D. Thesis. University of Verona: Italy.

Gatti, M. C. (2011a). The language of competence in corporate histories for company websites. *Journal of Business Communication*, Special Issue on Displaying Competence, 48(4), 482–50.

Gatti, M. C. (2011b). Re-constructing time and space to persuade: An Eastern-Europe case-study of organizational discourse. In R. Salvi, & H. Tanaka (Eds.), *Intercultural interactions in business and management* pp. 119–44. Bern: Peter Lang.

Gatti, M. C. (2012). *Understanding embedded meanings in business discourse: The role of spatiotemporality*. Milan: Arcipelago Edizione.

Gatti, M. C. (2013). The construction of companies' identities through memory: specialized metaphorical meanings for pastness on Italian companies' webpages. In R. Salvi & W. Cheng (Eds.), *The use of English in intercultural professional settings: Virtual encounters and identities. Textus*,1.

Gee, P. (2005). *Introduction to discourse analysis*. London: Routledge.

Geertz, C. (1973). *The interpretation of cultures*. New York: Basic Books.

Geertz, C. (1983). *Local knowledge*. New York: Basic Books.

Gerritsen, M., Korzilius, H., van Meurs, F, & Gijsbers, I. (2000). English in Dutch commercials: not understood and not appreciated. *Journal of Advertising Research, 40* (3), 17–31.

Gerritsen, M., Nederstigt, U., & Orlandini, F. (2006). Differences between Germany and the Netherlands in patient package leaflets for Ibuprofen 400 tablets and consequences for adequate drug use. In S. Carliner, J. Verckens & C. de Waele (Eds.), *Information and document design* (pp. 105–28). Amsterdam: John Benjamins.

Gerritsen, M., Nickerson, C., Hooft, A. P. J. V. van Meurs, W. F. J, Nederstigt, U., Starren, M. B. P. & Crijns, R. M. J. (2007). English in product advertisements in Belgium, France, Germany, the Netherlands and Spain. *World Englishes, 26*(3), 291–315.

Gerritsen, M., & Verckens, J. P. (2006). Raising students' intercultural awareness and preparing them for intercultural business (communication) by e-mail. *Business Communication Quarterly, 69*(1), 50–9.

Gherardi, S. (1995). *Gender, symbolism and organizational cultures.* London: Sage.

Giddens, A. (1984). *The construction of society: Outline of the theory of structuration.* Cambridge: Cambridge University Press.

Giddens, A. (1987). Time and social organisation. In A. Giddens (Ed.), *Social theory and modern sociology* (pp. 140–65). Cambridge: Polity Press.

Gillaerts, P., & Gotti, M. (Eds.) (2005). *Genre variation in business letters.* Bern: Peter Lang.

Gilsdorf, J., & Leonard, D. J. (2001). Big stuff, little stuff: A decennial measurement of executives' and academics' reactions to questionable usage elements. *Journal of Business Communication, 38*(4), 439–75.

Gimenez, J. (2001). Ethnographic observations in cross-cultural business negotiations between non-native speakers of English: An exploratory study. *English for Specific Purposes, 20*, 169–93.

Gimenez, J. (2002). New media and conflicting realities in multinational corporate communication: A case study. *International Review of Applied Linguistics in Language Teaching, 40*(4), 323–44.

Gimenez, J. (2005). Unpacking business emails: Message embeddedness in international business email communication. In P. Gillaerts & M. Gotti (Eds.), *Genre variation in business letters* (pp. 235–55). Bern: Peter Lang.

Gimenez, J. (2006a). Embedded business emails: Meeting new demands in international business communication. *English for Specific Purposes, 25*, 154–72.

Gimenez, J. (2006b). *Gender as a structural principle in social work and banking: A critical examination of non-interactional workplace talk.* Unpublished PhD dissertation. Queen Mary, University of London, London.

Gimenez, J. (2009), Mediated communication. In F. Bargiela-Chiappini (Ed.), *The Handbook of business discourse* pp. 132–41. Edinburgh: Edinburgh University Press.

Goffman, E. (1967). *Interaction ritual: Essays in face to face behavior.* New York: Garden City.

Goldstein, T. (1997). *Two languages at work: Bilingual life on the production floor.* Berlin: Mouton de Gruyter.

Gollin, S. (1999). Why? I thought we'd talked about it before: Collaborative writing in a professional workplace setting. In C. Candlin & K. Hyland (Eds.), *Writing: Texts, processes & practices* (pp. 267–90). Harlow: Longman.

Gollin, S., & Hall, D. R. (2006). *Language for specific purposes.* Basingstoke: Palgrave Macmillan.

Gollin-Kies, S. and Hall, D. R. (forthcoming). *Language for specific purposes.* London: Palgrave Macmillan.

Goodman, M. B. & Hirsch, P. B. (2010). *Corporate communication.* Bern: Peter Lang.

Gotti, M. (2004). Introduction. In C. N. Candlin & M. Gotti (Eds.), *Intercultural aspects of specialized communication* pp. 9–25. Bern: Peter Lang.

Gouveia, C., Silvestre, C., & Azuaga, L. (Eds.) (2004). *Discourse, communication and the enterprise.* Lisbon: CEAUL, University of Lisbon.

Graddol, D. (2006). *English next.* London: British Council, http://www.britishcouncil.org/ learning-research-englishnext.htm (27 September, 2012).

Graham, J. L. (1993). The Japanese negotiation style: Characteristics of a distinct approach. *Negotiation Journal, 9*(2), 13–40.

Graham, M. B. (2006). Disciplinary practice(s) in business communication, 1985–2004. *Journal of Business Communication, 43*(3), 268–77.

Greatbatch, D., & Clark, T. (2005). *Management speak: Why we listen to what management gurus tell us.* London & New York: Routledge.

Grindsted, A. (1995). Dyadic and polyadic sequencing patterns in Spanish and Danish negotiation interaction. In K. Ehlich & J. Wagner (Eds.), *The discourse of business negotiation* (pp. 203–21). Berlin: Mouton de Gruyter.

Grindsted, A. (1997). Joking as a strategy in Spanish and Danish negotiations. In F. Bargiela-Chiappini & S. Harris (Eds.), *The languages of business: An international perspective* (pp. 159–82). Edinburgh: Edinburgh University Press.

Guan, J., & Alkinkemer, K. (2002). Instant messaging: Chatting with your customers online and beyond. Paper presented at the Eighth Americas Conference on Information Systems, Dallas, TX.

Gudykunst, W. B., & Ting-Toomey, S. (1998). Verbal communication styles. In W. B. Gudykunst, S. Ting-Toomey, & E. Chua (Eds.), *Culture and interpersonal communication.* (pp. 99–117). Newbury Park, CA: Sage.

Guffey, M. E & Loewy, D. (2010). *Business communication: Process and product.* Nashville: South-Western College Publishing.

Guirdham, M. (2005). *Communicating across cultures at work.* Basingstoke: Palgrave Macmillan.

Gump, S. E. (2004). Review of Y. Pan, S. Wong Scollon, & R. Scollon (2002). *Professional communication in international settings.* Oxford: Blackwell. *Business Communication Quarterly, 67*(2), 250–4.

Gunnarsson, B. L. (2009). *Professional discourse.* London & New York: Continuum.

Gunnarsson, B-L., Linell, P., & Nordberg, B. (Eds.) (1997). *The construction of professional discourse.* London: Longman.

Guthrie, B. (2011). Review of D. Belcher (2009). *English for specific purposes.* Ann Arbor: University of Michigan Press. *English for Specific Purposes, 30*(4), 315–17.

Habil, H., & Rafik-Galea, S. (2005). Communicating at the workplace: Insights into Malaysian electronic business discourse. In F. Bargiela-Chiappini & M. Gotti (Eds.), *Asian business discourse(s)* pp. 121–43. Bern: Peter Lang.

Hagen, S. (n.d.). Effects on the European Economy of Shortages of Foreign Language Skills in Enterprise (ELAN). A Public Lecture on the Occasion of the Launch of the Chair of Multilingualism Linguamón – UOC. Accessed 10 September 2009, from: http://multilingualismchair.uoc.edu/opencms/export/sites/in3/webs/projectes/multiling/_resources/documents/HAGEN__Speech_for_Chair_in_Multilingualism_Barcelona_2.pdf

Hagen, S. (1993). *Languages in European business: A regional survey of small and medium-sized companies.* London: Centre for Information on Languages Teaching and Research: City Technology Colleges Trust Ltd.

Hagen, S. (Ed.). (1999). *Communication across borders. The ELUCIDATE study.* London: CILT.

Halmari, H. (1993). Intercultural business telephone conversations: A case of Finns vs. Anglo-Americans. *Applied Linguistics, 14*(4), 408–30.

Halvorsen, K. (2010). Team decision making in the workplace: A systematic review of discourse analytic studies. *Journal of Applied Linguistics and Professional Practice, 7*(3), 273–96.

Handford, M. (2010a). *The Language of business meetings.* Cambridge: Cambridge University Press.

Handford, M. (2010b). What a corpus can tell us about specialist genres. In M. McCarthy & A. O'Keeffe (Eds.), *The Routledge handbook of corpus linguistics* pp. 255–69. London: Routledge.

Handford, M. (2012). Professional communication and corpus linguistics. In K. Hyland, M. H. Chau, & M. Handford (Eds.), *Corpus applications in applied linguistics* pp. 13–29. London: Continuum.

Handford, M. & Koester, A. (2010). 'It's not rocket science': Metaphors and idioms in conflictual business meetings. *Text and Talk: 30*(1): 27–51.

Hanson, W. (1999). *Principles of internet marketing*. Stanford: South-Western College Publishing.

Harris, S., & Bargiela-Chiappini, F. (2003). Business as a site of language contact. *Annual Review of Applied Linguistics (ARAL), 23*, 155–69.

Harrison, C. (2003). Understanding how still images make meaning. *Technical Communication, 50*(1): 46–60.

Hartley, P. & Bruckmann, C. (2001). *Business communication: An introduction*. London & New York: Routledge.

Harvard Business Review (2011). *Harvard Business Review on communicating effectively*. Harvard: Harvard Business Review Press.

Have, P., ten (2007). *Doing conversation analysis (Second edition)*. London: Sage Publications.

Hay, L. (1976). *Management and design in the women's fashion industry*. Abingdon: Abingdon Press.

Hendriks, B., van Meurs, F., Korzilius, H., Le Pair, R., & Le Blanc-Damen, S. (2012). Style congruency and persuasion: a cross-cultural study into the influence of differences in style dimensions on the persuasiveness of business newsletters in Great Britain and the Netherlands. *IEEE Transactions on Professional Communication 55*(2), 122–41.

Herring, S. C., Scheidt, L. A., Bonus, S., & Wright, E. (2004). Bridging the gap: A genre analysis of weblogs. Proceedings of the 37th Hawai'i International Conference on System Sciences (HICSS-37). Los Alamitos: IEEE Computer Society Press.

Hewings, M., & Nickerson, C. (Eds.) (1999). *Business English: Research into practice*. London and New York: Longman.

Hirsch, H. (2003). *Essential communication strategies: For scientists, engineers, and technology professionals*. Hoboken, NJ: John Wiley & Sons Inc.

Hodge, R., & Kress, G. (1988). *Social semiotics*. Cambridge: Polity Press.

Hoeken, H., van Brandt, C., Crijns, R., Dominguez, N., Hendriks, B., Planken, B., & Starren, M. (2003). International advertising in Western Europe: Should differences in uncertainty avoidance be considered when advertising in Belgium, France, the Netherlands and Spain? *The Journal of Business Communication, 40*(3), 195–218.

Hofstede, G. (1984). *Culture's consequences*. Beverly Hills: Sage.

Hofstede, G. (1991). *Allemaal andersdenkenden. Omgaan met cultuurverschillen* (Translated from *Cultures and organizations. Software of the mind*) Amsterdam: Uitgeverij Contact.

Hofstede, G. (2001). *Culture's consequences* (2nd edn). Thousand Oaks, CA: Sage.

Hogarth, W., & Burnett, L. (1995). *Talking it through: Teacher's guide and classroom materials*. Macquarie University, Sydney: National Centre for English Language Teaching and Research.

Holden, N. J., & Ulijn, J. (Eds.) (1992). *Global cross-cultural communication and negotiation: Linguistic, psychological and technical aspects*. London: McGraw-Hill.

Holmes, J. (1988). Doubt and certainty in ESL textbooks. *Applied Linguistics, 9*(1), 20–44.

Holmes, J. (2000a) Victoria University's Language in the Workplace Project: An overview. *Language in the Workplace Occasional Papers 1.*

Holmes, J. (2000b). Doing collegiality and keeping control at work: Small talk in government departments. In J. Coupland (Ed.), *Small talk* (pp. 32–61). London: Longman.

Holmes, J. (2005). Leadership talk: How do leaders 'do mentoring', and is gender relevant? *Journal of Pragmatics, 37*, 1779–800.

Holmes, J. (2006). *Gendered talk at work. Constructing gender identity through workplace discourse*. Malden, MA: Blackwell Publishing.

Holmes, J., Angouri, J., Marra, M., Newton, J., Riddiford, N. & Vine, B. (2011). Applying linguistic research to real world problems: The social meaning of talk in workplace interaction. In C. N. Candlin & S. Sarangi (Eds.), *Handbook of communication in organizations and professions* pp. 533–50. Berlin: Mouton de Gruyter.

Holmes, J., & Marra, M. (2004). Relational practice in the workplace: Women's talk or gendered discourse? *Language in Society, 33*, 377–98.

Holmes, J., Marra M. & Vine, B. (2012). *Leadership, discourse and ethnicity.* Oxford: Oxford University Press.

Holmes, J., & Stubbe, M. (2003). *Power and politeness in the workplace.* Upper Saddle River, NJ: Pearson Education.

Hooghiemstra, R. (2008). East-West differences in attributions for company performance: A content analysis of Japanese and U.S. corporate annual reports. *Journal of Cross-Cultural Psychology 39*(5), 618–29.

Hornikx, J., van Meurs, F., & De Boer, A. (2010). English or a local language in advertising? The appreciation of easy and difficult English slogans in the Netherlands. *Journal of Business Communication, 47*(2), 169–88.

Hornikx, J., van Meurs, F., & Starren, M. (2007) An empirical study on readers' associations with multilingual advertising: The case of French, German, and Spanish in Dutch advertising. *Journal of Multilingual and Multicultural Development, 28*, 204–19.

Hornikx, J., & Starren, M. (2006) The relationship between the appreciation and the comprehension of French in Dutch advertisements. In R. Crijns and C. Burgers (Eds.), *Werbestrategien in Theorie und Praxis: Sprachliche Aspekte von Deutschen und Niederländischen Unternehmensoarstellungen und Werbekampagnen* (pp. 129–45). Tostedt: Attikon.

http://construction-language-learning.eu/ Retrieved 24 June 2012.

http://www.harzing.com. Retrieved 24 June 2012.

http://www.guardian.co.uk/uk/2011/jun/19/women-language-boardroom-study. Retrieved 25 June 2012.

Hu, J., Shima, K., Oehlmann, R., Zhao, J., Takemura, Y., & Matsumoto, K. (2004). An empirical study of audience impression of B2C web pages in Japan, China and the UK. *Electronic Commerce Research and Applications, 3*, 176–89.

Huffaker, D. A., & Calvert, S. L. (2005). Gender, identity, and language use in teenage blogs. *Journal of Computer-mediated Communication, 10*, available at: http://jcmc.indiana.edu/vol10/issue2/huffaker.html

Hulst, J., & Lentz, L. (2001). Public documents in a multilingual context. In D. Janssen, & R. Neutelings, (Eds.), *Reading and writing public documents* (pp. 85–103). Amsterdam: John Benjamins.

Hutchinson, T., & Waters, A. (1987). *English for specific purposes.* Cambridge: Cambridge University Press.

Hyland, K. (1996). Talking to the academy: Forms of hedging in science research articles. *Written Communication, 13*(2), 251–81.

Hyland, K. (1998). Exploring corporate rhetoric: Metadiscourse in the CEO's letter. *Journal of Business Communication, 35*(2), 224–45.

Hyland, K. (2005). *Metadiscourse: Exploring interaction in writing.* London: Continuum.

Hyland, K., Huat, M. H. & Handford, M. (Eds.) (2012). *Corpus Applications in Applied Linguistics.* London: Continuum

Hyland, K. & Tse, P. (2004). Metadiscourse in academic writing: A reappraisal. *Applied Linguistics 25*(2), 156–77.

Iedema, R. (2003). Multimodality, resemiotization: Extending the analysis of discourse as multi-semiotic practice. *Visual Communication, 2*(1), 29–57.

Iedema, R., Degeling, P., Braithwaite, J., & White, L. (2003). It's an interesting conversation I'm hearing: The doctor as manager. *Organization Studies, 25*(1), 15–34.

Jablin, F. M., & Putnam, L. L. (Eds.) (2001). *The new handbook of organizational communication: Advances in theory, research, and methods.* Thousand Oaks, CA: Sage Publications.

Jack, G., & Zhu, Y. with Barney, J., Brannen, M. Y., Prichard, G., Singh, & Whetten, D. (2012). Refining, reinforcing and reimagining universal and indigenous theory development in international management. *Journal of Management Inquiry*, 1056492612458453, 1st published 21 Sept. as doi: 1177/105649261245853.

Jackson, J. (2005). An inter-university, cross-disciplinary analysis of business education: Perceptions of business faculty in Hong Kong. *English for Specific Purposes, 24*(3), 293–306.

Jameson, D. (2007). Reconceptualizing cultural identity and its role in intercultural business communication. *Journal of Business Communication, 44*(3), 199–235.

Jansen, C., & Balijon, S. (2002). How do people use instruction guides? Confirming and disconfirming patterns of use. *Document Design, 3*, 195–204.

Jansen, C. & Janssen, I. (2010). Talk about it: Effects of cryptic billboards about HIV/AIDS in South Africa. *Communicatio, South African Journal for Communication Theory and Research, 36*(1), 130–41.

Jansen, C., & Maes, A. (1999). Document design and professional communication. *South African Journal of Linguistics, 17*, 234–55.

Jansen, C., & Steehouder, M. (1992). Forms as a source of communication problems. *Journal of Technical Writing and Communication, 22*, 179–94.

Jansen, C., & Steehouder, M. (2001). How research can lead to better government forms. In D. Janssen & R. Neutelings (Eds.), *Reading and writing government documents* (pp. 11–36). Amsterdam: Benjamins.

Janssen, D. (1991). *Schrijven aan beleidsnota's. Schrijfprocessen van beleidsambtenaren empirisch-kwalitatief onderzocht.* Groningen: Wolters-Noordhoff.

Janssen, D., & van der Mast, M. (2001). Collaborative writing for the government. In D. Janssen & R. Neutelings (Eds.), *Reading and writing public documents* (pp. 171–210). Amsterdam: John Benjamins.

James, C., Scholfield, P., & Ypsiladis, G. (1994). Cross-cultural correspondence. *World Englishes, 13*(3), 325–40.

Jaworski, A. (1994). Apologies and non-apologies: Negotiation in speech act realisation. *TEXT, 14*(2), 185–206.

Jefferson, G. (1972). Side sequences. In D. Sudnow (Ed.). *Studies in social interaction* (pp. 294–338). New York: Free Press.

Jenkins, J., Cogo, A. & Dewey, M. (2011). Review of developments in research into English as a lingua franca. *Language Teaching 44*(3), 281–315.

Jenkins, S., & Hinds, J. (1987). Business letter writing: English, French and Japanese. *TESOL Quarterly, 21*(2), 327–49.

Jensen, A. (2009). Discourse strategies in professional e-mail negotiation: a case study, *English for Specific Purposes, 28*(1), 4–18.

Jewitt, C. (Ed.) (2009). *The Routledge handbook of multimodal analysis.* London: Routledge.

Jian, G., Schmisseur, A. M., & Fairhurst, G. T. (2008). Organizational discourse and communication: The progeny of Proteus. *Discourse & Communication, 2*(3), 299–320.

Johansen, T. S. & Nielsen, A. E. (2011). Strategic stakeholder dialogues: a discursive perspective on relationship building. *Corporate Communications, 16*(3), 204–17.

Johns, A. M. (1980). Cohesion in written business discourse: Some contrasts. *The ESP Journal, 1*(1), 35–44.

Johns, A. M. (1986). The language and the professions. *Annual Review of Applied Linguistics (ARAL), 7*(3), 1–17.

Jones, A. and Sin, S. (2004a). The integration of language and content: action research based on a theory of task design. *Journal of Applied Linguistics, 1*(1), 95–100.

Jones, A., & Sin, S. (2004b). *Generic skills in accounting: Competencies for students and graduates.* Sydney: Prentice Hall/Pearson Education.

Jordan, M. (1984). *Rhetoric of everyday English texts.* London: Allen & Unwin.

Jung, Y. (2005). Power and politeness in Korean business correspondence. In F. Bargiela-Chiappini & M. Gotti (Eds.), *Asian business discourse(s)* (pp. 291–312). Bern: Peter Lang.

Kachru, Y. (1995). Contrastive rhetoric in world Englishes. *English Today, 41*(11), 21–31.

Kaewpet, C. (2009). Communication needs of Thai civil engineering students. *English for Specific Purposes 28*, 266–78.

Kameda, N. (2001). The implications of language style in business communication: Focus on English versus Japanese. *Corporate Communications: An International Journal, 6*(3), 144–9.

Kameda, N. (2005). *Managing global business communication.* Tokyo: Maruzen Co., Ltd.

Kameda, N. (2008). Business communication in the age of globalization: Ways to achieve smoother communication across nations and cultures. *Doshisha Business Review, 59,* (5–6), 311–20.

Kameda, N. (2012). New perspective required for cross-cultural e-trade: The greater the web use, the greater the need for face-to-face communication. In Proceedings of *8th e-Trade International Forum & 5th Logistics International Forum: e-Trade and e-Logistics in the Green Growth Era.* Korea e-Trade Research Institute, Korean Academy of International Commerce, and Northeast Asian Logistics & Distribution Institute, pp. 73–88.

Kankaanranta, A. (2006). 'Hej Seppo, Could you Pls Comment on This!' – internal email communication in lingua franca english in a multinational company. *Business Communication Quarterly 69*, 216–25

Kankaanranta, A., & Planken, B. (2010). BELF competence as business knowledge of internationally operating business professionals. *Journal of Business Communication 47*(4) 380–407.

Kankaanranta, A., & Louhiala-Salminen, L. (2010) 'English? – Oh, it's just work!': A study of BELF users' perceptions. *English for Specific Purposes, 29(3)*, 204–9.

Kaplan, R. (1966). Cultural thought patterns in inter-cultural education. *Language Learning, 16*(1), 1–20.

Kaul, A. (2003). Talking up: Study of upward influence strategies. *Proceedings of the 68th Annual Convention of the Association for Business Communication.* Retrieved 4 July 2006, from: http://www.businesscommunication.org/conventions/Proceedings/2003/PDF/22ABC03.pdf

Kaul, A. (2102). Man and woman talk in Indian organizations: Grammatical and syntactical similarities. *Journal of Business Communication, 49,* (3), 254–76.

Kaul, A., Ansari, M. A., & Rai, H. (2005). Gender, affect and upward influence. *IIMA Working Papers.* Retrieved 4 July 2006, from: http://www.iimahd.ernet.in/ publications/data/2005–03–06ashakaul.pdf

Kelleher, T., & Miller, B. (2006). Organizational blogs and the human voice: Relational strategies and relational outcomes. *Journal of Computer-mediated Communication, 11,* available at: http://jcmc.indiana.edu/vol11/issue2/kelleher.html

Kelley, H. (1966). A classroom study of the dilemmas in interpersonal negotiations. In K. Archibald (Ed.) *Strategic intervention and conflict* (pp. 49–73). Berkeley: Institute of International Studies.

Kelly-Holmes, H. (2005). *Advertising as multilingual communication.* New York: Palgrave Macmillan.

Keyton, J. (2004). *Communication and organizational culture: A key to understanding work experiences.* London: Sage Publications.

Ki, E. and Hon, L. (2006). 'Relationship maintenance strategies on Fortune 500 company web sites'. *Journal of Communication Management, 10*(1), 27–43.

Kjellmer, G. (1994). *A dictionary of English collocations* (3 Vols.). Oxford: Clarendon Press.

Knox, J. S. (2009a). Visual minimalism in hard news: Thumbnail faces on the *smh online* home page. *Social Semiotics, 19*(2), 165–89.

Knox, J. S. (2009b). Punctuating the home page: Image as language in an online newspaper. *Discourse and Communication, 3*(2), 145–72.

Koester, A. (2004). *The language of work.* London & New York: Routledge.

Koester, A. (2006). *Investigating workplace discourse.* London: Routledge.

Koester, A. (2012). *Workplace discourse.* London: Continuum.

Koester, A. & Handford, M. (2011). Spoken professional genres. In J. P. Gee, & M. Handford (Eds.), *The Routledge handbook of discourse analysis.* Abingdon: Routledge.

Koester, A. Pitt A., Handford, M., & Lisboa, M. (2012). *Business advantage: Theory, practice, skills (intermediate level).* Cambridge: Cambridge University Press.

Korzilius, H., van Meurs, F., & Hermans, J. (2007). The use of English in job advertisements in a Dutch national newspaper: On what factors does it depend? In R. Crijns & C. Burgers (Eds.), *Werbestrategien in Theorie und Praxis: Synchrone, Diachrone und Interkulturelle Perspektive.* Tostedt: Attikon Verlag.

Kotthoff, H., & Spencer-Oatey, H. (Eds.) (2007). *Handbook of intercultural communication* (Handbooks of Applied Linguistics Vol. 7). Berlin: Mouton de Gruyter.

Kraushaar, J. & Novak, D. (2010). Examining the affects of student multitasking with laptops during the lecture. *Journal of Information Systems Education, 21*(2), 241–51

Kress, G. (2003). *Literacy in the new media age.* New York: Routledge.

Kress, G., & van Leeuwen, T. (2013). *Reading images: The grammar of visual design.* London and New York: Routledge, 3rd edn.

Kress, G., & van Leeuwen, T. (2006). *Reading images: The grammar of visual design.* London and New York: Routledge, 2nd edn.

Kress, G., & van Leeuwen, T. (1996). *Reading images: The grammar of visual design.* London & New York: Routledge.

Kress, G., & van Leeuwen, T. (2001. *Multimodal discourse: The modes and media of contemporary communication.* London: Arnold.

Kress, G., & Ogborn, J. (1998). *Modes of representation and local epistemologies: The presentation of science in education. Subjectivity in the school curriculum.* London: University of London.

Krider, D. S., & Ross, P. G. (1997). The experiences of women in a public relations firm: A phenomenological explication. *Journal of Business Communication, 34*(4), 437–55.

Krippendorff, K. (1980). *Content analysis: An introduction to its methodology.* Beverly Hills, CA: Sage Publications.

Kubista-Nugent, A. (1996). *La lingua italiana nelle imprese austriache. Un indagine sul fabbisogno della lingua italiana condotta nella zona di Vienna.* Master's thesis, Wirtschaftsuniversität Wien, Vienna.

LaFasto, F., & Larson, C. (2001). *When teams work best: 6,000 team members and leaders tell what it takes to excel.* London: Sage.

Lagerwerf, L., & Bossers, E. (2002). Assessing business proposals: Genre conventions and audience response in document design. *Journal of Business Communication, 39*(4), 437–60.

Lampi, M. (1986). *Linguistic components of strategy in business negotiations.* Helsinki School of Economics, Studies B-85, Helsinki: Helsinki School of Economics.

Lampi, M. (1990). *Business negotiations: Linguistic strategies and the company agenda.* ERIC Document Reproduction Services No. ED 338016 [Microfiche]. Washington DC: Center for Applied Linguistics.

Lappin, S., & Leass, H. J. (1994). An algorithm for pronominal anaphora resolution. *Computational Linguistics, 20*(4), 535–61.

Larson, B. (1990). Present-day influence of English on Swedish as found in Swedish job advertisements. *World Englishes, 9*(3), 367–9.

Lavric, E. (1991). Welche Sprachen für Europa? Fremdsprachliche Lernerbedürfnisse in Österreich im Kontext der EG-Annäherung. In S. Griller, E. Lavric & R. Neck (Eds.), *Europäische Integration aus österreichischer Sicht: Wirtschafts-, sozial- und rechtswissenschaftliche Aspekte (Schriftenreihe des Forschungsinstituts für Europafragen 3)* (pp. 357–88). Vienna: Orac.

Lavric, E. (Ed.) (2009). *Sprachwahl in Unternehmen: Tiroler Fallstudien. Ergebnisse eines Projektseminars an der Leopold-Franzens-Universität Innsbruck.* Innsbruck: Innsbruck University Press

Lechner, C. (2010). *Vouloir c'est pouvoir. Les choix linguistiques et les stratégies linguistiques dans une PME autrichienne.* Master's Thesis, University of Innsbruck.

Lee, C. M. & Gudykunst, W. B. (2001). Attraction in initial interethnic interactions. *Int. J. Intercult. Rel. 25*(4), 373–87.

Lee, S. M., Hwang, T., and Lee, H. H. (2006). Corporate blogging strategies of the Fortune 500 companies. *Management Decision 44*(3), 316–34.

Lee, S. Brett J., and Park, J. H. (2012). East Asians' social heterogeneity: Differences in norms among Chinese, Japanese, and Korean negotiators. *Journal of Negotiation, 24*(4), 529–52.

Lemke, J. L. (2002). Travels in hypermodality. *Visual Communication, 1*(3), 299–325.

Levine, T. R., Park, H. S., & Kim, R. K. (2007). Some conceptual and theoretical challenges for cross-cultural communication research in the 21st century. *Journal of Intercultural Communication Research, 36*, 205–21.

Levinson, S. (1983*). Pragmatics.* Cambridge: Cambridge University Press..

Li, X. (1999). *Chinese–Dutch business negotiations: Insights from discourse.* Amsterdam & Atlanta, GA: Rodopi.

Li So-mui, F., & Mead, K. (2000). An analysis of English in the workplace: The communication needs of textile and clothing merchandisers. *English for Specific Purposes, 19*, 351–68.

Lipovsky, C. (2006). Candidates' negotiation of their expertise in job interviews. *Journal of Pragmatics 38*(8), 1147–74. Electronic version (corrected proof) accessed on 28 April 2006, at http://www.sciencedirect.com/science

Livesey, S. (1999). McDonald's and the environmental defense fund: A case of a green alliance. *Journal of Business Communication, 36*, 5–39.

Livesey, S. (2001). Eco-identity as discursive struggle: Royal Dutch Shell, Brent Spar, and Nigeria. *Journal of Business Communication, 38*, 58–91.

Livesey, S. (2002a). The discourse of the middle ground: Citizen Shell commits to sustainable development. *Management Communication Quarterly, 15*, 313–49.

Livesey, S. (2002b). Interpretative acts: New vistas in qualitative research in business communication: A guest editorial. *Journal of Business Communication, 39*(1), 6–12.

Livesey, S. (2002c). Global warming wars: Rhetorical and discourse analytic approaches to ExxonMobil's corporate public discourse. *Journal of Business Communication, 39*(1), 117–48.

Livesey, S. M., & Graham, J. (2007). Greening of corporations? Eco-talk and the emerging social imaginary of sustainable development. In S. K. May, G. Cheney, & J. Roper (Eds.), *The debate over corporate social responsibility.* Oxford: Oxford University Press.

Livesey, S. M., Hartman, C. L., Stafford, E. R., & Shearer, M. (2009). Performing sustainable development through eco-collaboration. *Journal of Business Communication, 46*(4), 423–54.

Locker, K. & Kaczmarek, S. (2010). *Business communication: Building critical skills.* Upper Saddle River, NJ: McGraw-Hill.

Lockwood, J. (2002). Review of F. Bargiela-Chiappini & C. Nickerson (Eds.) (1999). *Writing business: Genres, media and discourses.* Harlow: Longman. *English for Specific Purposes, 21*(4), 413–16.

Lockwood, J. (2012). Developing an English for specific purpose curriculum for Asian call centres: How theory can inform practice. *English for Specific Purposes, 31*(1), 14–24.

Lockwood, J., & Forey, G. (Eds.) (2012). *Globalization, communication and the workplace: Talking across the world.* London & New York: Continuum.

Lockwood, J., & McCarthy, H. (2010). *Contact US.* Cambridge: Cambridge University Press.

Lopez, K. A., & Willis, D. G. (2004). Descriptive versus interpretative phenomenology: Their contributions to nursing knowledge. *Qualitative Health Research, 14*(5), 726–35.

Louhiala-Salminen, L. (1995). *'Drop me a fax, will you?': A study of written business communication.* Jyväskylä: University of Jyväskylä.

Louhiala-Salminen, L. (1996). The business communication classroom vs reality: What should we teach today? *English for Specific Purposes, 15*(1), 37–51.

Louhiala-Salminen, L. (1997). Investigating the genre of a business fax: A Finnish case study. *The Journal of Business Communication, 34*(3), 316–33.

Louhiala-Salminen, L. (1999). 'Was there life before them?' Fax and email in business communication. *The Journal of Language for International Business, 10*(1), 24–42.

Louhiala-Salminen, L. (2002). The fly's perspective: Discourse in the daily routine of a business manager. *English for Specific Purposes, 21,* 211–31.

Louhiala-Salminen, L. (2009). Business communication. In F. Bargiela-Chiappini (Ed.), *The handbook of business discourse* (pp. 305–16), Edinburgh: Edinburgh University Press.

Louhiala-Salminen, L., Charles, M., & Kankaanranta, A. (2005). English as a lingua franca in Nordic corporate mergers: Two case companies. *English for Specific Purposes, 24*(4), 401–21.

Louhiala-Salminen, L., & Kankaanranta, A. (2005). 'Hello Monica, kindly change your arrangements': Business genres in a state of flux. In P. Gillaerts & M. Gotti (Eds.), *Genre variation in business letters* (pp. 55–84). Bern: Peter Lang.

Lovitt, C. R., & Goswami, D. (Eds.) (1999). *Exploring the rhetoric of international professional communication.* Amityville, NY: Haywood.

Löwstedt, M., & Räisänen, C. (2012). 'Playing back-spin balls': narrating organizational change in construction. *Construction Management and Economics 30,* 795–806.

Lubinga, E. & Jansen, C. (2011). 'No 'til we know' fela ba a tseba naa? On using African languages to communicate HIV and AIDS to young South Africans. *Communicatio: South African Journal for Communication Theory and Research, 37*(3), 466–81.

Lubinga, E., Schulze, M., Jansen, C., & Maes, A. (2010). HIV/AIDS messages as a spur for conversation among young South Africans? *African Journal of AIDS Research, 9*(2), 175–85.

Lucas, U., & Tan, P. (2011). Developing a capacity to engage in critical reflection: students' 'ways of knowing' within an undergraduate business and accounting programme, *Studies in Higher Education, 38*(1), 1–20, DOI: 10.1080/03075079.2011.569706.

LWP Project http://www.victoria.ac.nz/lals/lwp

Machin, D. (2007). *Introduction to multimodal analysis.* London: Hodder Arnold.

MacKenzie, M. B. & Lutz, R. J. (1989). An empirical examination of the structural antecedents of attitude toward the ad in an advertising pretesting context. *Journal of Marketing 53*(2), 48–65.

Maier, P. (1992). Politeness strategies in business letters by native and non-native English speakers. *English for Specific Purposes, 11,* 189–205.

Markus, M. L. (1994). Electronic mail as the medium of managerial choice. *Organization Science, 5,* 502–27.

Marriott, H. (1995). Discourse in international seller–buyer negotiations. In K. Ehlich & J. Wagner (Eds.), *The discourse of business negotiation* (pp. 103–26). Berlin: Mouton de Gruyter.

Marriott, H. (1997). Australian–Japanese business interaction: Some features of language and cultural contact. In F. Bargiela-Chiappini & S. Harris (Eds.), *The languages of business. An international perspective* (pp. 49–71). Edinburgh: Edinburgh University Press.

Marschan, R., Welch, D., & Welch, L. (1996). Control in less-hierarchical multinationals: The role of personal networks and informal communication. *International Business Review, 5*, 137–50.

Marschan, R., Welch, D., & Welch, L. (1997). Language: The forgotten factor in multinational management? *European Management Journal, 15*, 591–8.

Marschan-Piekkari, R., & Welch, C. (Eds.) (2004). *Handbook of qualitative research methods for international business*. Cheltenham: Edward Elgar.

Marschan-Piekkari, R., Welch, D., & Welch, L. (1999). In the shadow: The impact of language on structure, power and communication in the multinational. *International Business Review, 8*, 421–40.

Mascull, B. (2004). *Advanced business vocabulary in use*. Cambridge: Cambridge University Press.

Matsumoto, D., & Yoo, S. H. (2006). Toward a new generation of cross-cultural research. *Perspectives on Psychological Science, 1*, 234–50.

May, S. K., & Zorn, T. E., Jr. (2001). Gurus' views and business news: Forum introduction. *Management Communication Quarterly, 14*(3), 471–5.

McCarthy, M. & Handford, M. (2004). 'Invisible to Us': A preliminary study of a corpus of business meetings. In U. Connor and T. Upton (Eds.), *Discourse in the professions: Perspectives in corpus linguistics* pp. 167–201. Amsterdam: Benjamins.

Mead, R. (2004). *International management*. Oxford: Blackwell.

Mead, R. & Andrews, T. G. (2009). *International management*. Oxford: Wiley-Blackwell.

Melton, J. (2003). Review of F. LaFasto, & C. Larson (2001). *When teams work best: 6,000 team members and leaders tell what it takes to excel*. London: Sage Publications Ltd. *Business Communication Quarterly, 66*(3), 133–8.

Miike, Y. (2006) Non-western theory in western research? An Asiacentric agenda for Asian communication studies. *The Review of Communication, 6*(1/2), 4–31.

Miike, Y. (2010) Culture as text and culture as theory. Asiancentricity and its *raison d'être* in intercultural communication research. In T. K. Nakayama and R. T. Hulualani (Eds.), *The handbook of critical intercultural communication*. pp. 190–215. Wiley-Blackwell.

Miike, Y. (2011) De-westernizing communication theory and research: an Asiacentric bibliography. *China Media Research, 7*(3), 111–21.

Miller, L. (1994). Japanese and American indirectness. *Journal of Asian Pacific Communication, 5*(1–2), 1–19.

Miller, L. (2000). Negative assessments in Japanese–American workplace interaction. In H. Spencer-Oatey (Ed.), *Culturally speaking: Managing rapport through talk across cultures* (pp. 240–54). London: Continuum.

Mills, S. (1993). *Michel Foucault*. London: Routledge.

Mondada, L. (2011a). Understanding as an embodied, situated and sequential achievement in interaction. *Journal of Pragmatics, 43*, 542–52.

Mondada, L. (2011b). The interactional production of multiple spatialities within a participatory democracy meeting. *Social Semiotics, 21*(2), 283–308.

Mondada, L. (2012). Video analysis and the temporality of inscriptions within social interaction: the case of architects at work. *Qualitative Research, 12*(3), 304–33.

Moore, N. (2002). Review of D. Douglas (2000). *Assessing languages for specific purposes*. Cambridge: Cambridge University Press. *English for Specifc Purposes, 21*(3), 294–7.

Mrázová, Ž. (2005). Le choix des langues dans une équipe de vente multinationale en France. Communication externe avec les clients, et interne au sein de l'entreprise. Master's Thesis, Wirtschaftsuniversität Wien.

Mulholland, J. (1991). *The language of negotiation: A handbook of practical strategies for improving communication*. New York: Routledge.

Mulholland, J. (1999). E-mail: Uses, issues and problems in an institutional setting. In F. Bargiela-Chiappini & C. Nickerson (Eds.), *Writing business: Genres, media and discourses* (pp. 57–84). Harlow: Longman.

Mullany, J. L. (2003). Identity and role construction: A sociolinguistic study of gender and discourse in management. Unpublished PhD thesis, Nottingham Trent University, Nottingham, UK.

Mullany, J. L. (2007). *Gendered discourse in professional communication*. Basingstoke: Palgrave Macmillan.

Munter, M., & Netzley, M. (2002). *Guide to meetings*. Upper Saddle River, NJ: Prentice Hall

Nair-Venugopal, S. (2000). *Language choice and communication in Malaysian business*. Bangi: Penerbit Universit Kabangsaan Malaysia.

Nair-Venugopal, S. (2001). The sociolinguistics of choice in Malaysian business settings. *International Journal of the Sociology of Language, 152*, 21–52.

Nair-Venugopal, S. (Ed.) (2012) *The Gaze of the West and Framings of the East*. Basingstoke: Palagrave Macmillan.

Nardi, B., Whittaker, S., & Bradner, E. (2000). Interaction and Outeraction: Instant Messaging in Action. Paper presented at the computer supported cooperative work conference, Philadelphia, PA.

Nelson, M. (2000). *The Business English lexis site*. Retrieved 8 April 2006, from: http://users.utu.fi/micnel/business_english_lexis_site.htm

Nelson, M. (2006). Semantic associations in Business English: A corpus-based analysis. *English for Specific Purposes Journal, 25*(2), 217–34.

Neu, J. (1985). *A multivariate sociolinguistic analysis of the speech event negotiation*. Unpublished PhD thesis, The Graduate School, University of Southern California, Los Angeles, USA.

Neu, J., & Graham, J. (1995). An analysis of language in negotiations: The role of context and content. In K. Ehlich & J. Wagner (Eds.), *The discourse of business negotiations* (pp. 243–72). New York: Mouton de Gruyter.

Neumann, I. (1991). How to get a word in edgeways. 2nd ENCoDE Seminar on Language, Culture and Management in Tomorrow's Europe, Paris.

Neumann, I. (1994). *Realisation of requests in intercultural negotiations: On pragmatic method*. Halden, Norway: Østfold College.

Neumann, I. (1997). Requests in German–Norwegian business discourse: Differences in directness. In F. Bargiela-Chiappini & S. Harris (Eds.), *The languages of business: An international perspective* (pp. 72–3). Edinburgh: Edinburgh University Press.

Nickerson, C. (1998). Corporate culture and the use of written English within British subsidiaries in the Netherlands. *English for Specific Purposes, 17*, 281–94.

Nickerson, C. (1999). The use of English in electronic mail in a multinational corporation. In F. Bargiela-Chiappini & C. Nickerson (Eds.), *Writing business: Genres, media and discourses* (pp. 35–56). Harlow: Longman.

Nickerson, C. (2000). *Playing the corporate language game: An investigation of the genres and discourse strategies in English used by Dutch writers working in multinational corporations*. Amsterdam & Atlanta: Rodopi.

Nickerson, C. (2005). English as a lingua franca in international business contexts. *English for Specific Purposes, 24* (4), 367–80.

Nickerson, C. (2011). Review of M. Handford (2010). *The language of business meetings*. Cambridge: Cambridge University Press. *English for Specific Purposes, 30*(4), 313–4.

Nickerson, C. (2012a). English for specific purposes and English as a lingua franca. In B. Paltridge & S. Starfield (Eds.), *The handbook of English for specific purposes* (pp. 445–60), Oxford: Wiley-Blackwell.

Nickerson, C. (2012b). Unity in diversity: The view from the (UAE) classroom. *Language Teaching,* DOI: http://dx.doi.org/10.1017/S0261444812000237.

Nickerson, C. (2014). Business communication. In S. Bremner & V. K. Bhatia, (Eds.), *The handbook of professional communication,* London: Routledge.

Nickerson, C., Gerritsen, M., & van Meurs, F. (2005). Raising student awareness of the use of English for specific business purposes in the European context: A staff–student project. *English for Specific Purposes, 24*(3), 333–46.

Nickerson, C., & de Groot, E. (2005). Dear shareholder, dear stockholder, dear stakeholder: The business letter genre in the annual general report. In M. Gotti & P. Gillaerts (Eds.), *Genre variation in business letters* (pp. 325–46). Bern: Peter Lang.

Nickerson, C. & Planken, B. (2009). Europe: the state of the field. In: F. Bargiela-Chiappini (Ed.), *The Handbook of Business Discourse* (pp. 18–29). Edinburgh: Edinburgh University Press.

Niemeier, S., Campbell, C. P., & Dirven, R. (1998). *The cultural context in business communication.* Amsterdam: John Benjamins Publishing Company.

Norris, S., & Jones, R. (Eds.) (2005). *Discourse in action: Introducing mediated discourse analysis.* London: Routledge.

Odell, L., & Goswami, D. (1985). *Writing in non-academic settings.* New York: Guildford.

O'Halloran, K. L. (2005). *Mathematical discourse: Language, symbolism and visual images.* London and New York: Continuum.

O'Halloran, K. L. (Ed.) (2004). *Multimodal discourse analysis: Systemic functional perspectives.* London and New York: Continuum.

Oliveira, M. do Carmo Leite, Vilhena, J., & Vilhena Novaes, J. (2012). Lack of trust in the organizational context: A study of accounts in a privatized company. In C. N. Candlin & J. Crichton (Eds.), *From ontology to methodology: Exploring the discursive landscape of trust* (pp. 300–14). Basingstoke. Palgrave Macmillan.

Oppenheim, A. N. (2000). *Questionnaire design, interviewing and attitude measurement.* Amsterdam: Continuum International Publishing Group – Academi.

Orlikowski, W., & Yates, J. (1994). Genre repertoire: The structuring of communicative practices in organizations. *Administrative Science Quarterly, 39,* 541–74.

Orr, T. (Ed.) (2002). *English for specific purposes: Case studies in TESOL.* Alexandria, VA: TESOL, Inc.

Orr, T. (Ed.) (2006). Special issue on insights from corpus linguistics for professional communication, *IEEE Transactions on Professional Communication, 49.*

Ostendorf, A. M. (2012). Review of L. Chaney, & J. Martin (2010). *Intercultural business communication.* Upper Saddle River, NJ: Prentice Hall. *Business Communication Quarterly, 75*(2), 221–24.

Pacheco de Oliveira, L. (2009) Brazil. In F. Bargiela-Chiappini (Ed.), *Handbook of business discourse* pp. 400–11. Edinburgh: Edinburgh University Press.

Pal, M. & Buzzanell, P. (2008). The Indian call centre experience: A case study in changing discourses of identity, identification, and career in a global context. *Journal of Business Commuication, 45*(1), 31–60.

Paltridge, B. (1995). Working with genre: A pragmatic perspective. *Journal of Pragmatics, 24,* 393–406.

Paltridge, B, and Phakiti, A. (Eds.), (2010). *Companion to research methods in applied linguistics.* London: Continuum.

Paltridge, B., & Starfield, S. (Eds.) (2012). *The Handbook of English for Specific Purposes.* Oxford: Wiley-Blackwell.

Pan, Y. (1994). *Politeness strategies in Chinese verbal interaction: A sociolinguistic analysis of spoken data in official, business and family settings.* Washington, DC: Georgetown University.

Pan, Y., Wong Scollon, S., & Scollon, R. (2002). *Professional communication in international settings.* Oxford: Blackwell.

Paramasivam, S. (2007). A discourse-oriented model for analysing power and politeness in negotiation interaction: A cross-linguistic perspective. *Journal of Universal Language, 8,* 91–127.

Pardo, L. (2010) Latin-American discourse studies: State of the art and new perspectives. *Journal of Multicultural Discourses, 5*(3), 183–92.

Pauleen, D. J., & Yoong, P. (2001). Facilitating virtual team relationships via Internet and conventional communication channels. *Internet Research: Electronic Networking Applications and Policy, 11*(3), 190–202.

Peck, J. J. (2000). The cost of corporate culture: Linguistic obstacles to gender equity in Australian business. In J. Holmes (Ed.), *Gendered speech in social context: Perspectives from gown and town* (pp. 211–30). Auckland: Victoria University Press.

Peck, J. J. (2005). Negotiating the gendered workplace: Linguistic strategies for a hierarchical structure. In M. Barrett & M. J. Davidson (Eds.), *Gender and communication issues at work* (pp. 50–66). Aldershot: Ashgate.

Pennycook, A. (2004). Critical applied linguistics. In A. Davies & C. Elder (Eds.), *Handbook of applied linguistics* (pp. 784–807). Oxford: Blackwell.

Peräkylä, A., & Vehviläinen, S. (2003). Conversation analysis and professional stocks of interactional knowledge. *Discourse & Society, 14,* 727–50.

Pereira das Graças Dias, M. (2004). Constructing identities and searching for partnerships in a meeting of Portuguese and Brazilian businessmen. In C. Gouveia, C. Silvestre & L. Azuga (Eds.), *Discourse, communication and the enterprise* (pp. 169–94). Lisbon: ULICES, University of Lisbon.

Piekkari, R., Vaara, E., Tienari, J., & Säntti, R. (2005). Integration or disintegration? Human resource implications of the common corporate language decision in a cross-border merger. *International Journal of Human Resource Management, 16*(3), 333–47.

Piekkari, R., & Zander, L. (Eds.) (2005). Special issue on language and communication in international management. *International Studies of Management and Organization, 35*(1), 1–103.

Pike, K. L. [1954, 1955, 1960] (1967). *Language in relation to a unified theory of the structure of human behavior* (2nd edn). The Hague: Mouton.

Piller, I. (2003). Advertising as a site of language contact. *Annual Review of Applied Linguistics, 23,* 170–83.

Planken, B. (2002). *Face and identity management in negotiation.* Nijmegen: Nijmegen University Press.

Planken, B. (2005). Managing rapport in lingua franca sales negotiations: A comparison of professional and aspiring negotiators. *English for Specific Purposes, 24*(4), 381–400.

Planken, B. (2012). The changing landscape of business communication: Developments and directions in research. In P. Heynderickx, S. Dieltjens, G. Jacobs, P. Gillaerts & E. de Groot, (Eds.), *The language factor in international business: New perspectives on research, teaching and practice* (pp. 17–40). Bern: Peter Lang.

Planken, B., van Hooft, A., & Korzilius, H. (2004). Promoting intercultural communicative competence through foreign language courses. *Business Communication Quarterly, 67,* 308–15.

Planken, B. C., van Meurs, W.F.J., & Radlinska, A. (2010). The effects of the use of English in Polish product advertisements: Implications for English for business purposes. *English for Specific Purposes, 29*(4), 225–42.

Pogner, K. (1999). *Schreiben im Beruf als Handeln im Fach (Forum für Fremdsprachenforschung 46).* Tübingen: Narr.

Polanyi, M. (1966), *The tacit dimension.* London: Routledge & Kegan Paul.

Poncini, G. (2004). *Discursive strategies in multicultural business meetings.* Bern: Peter Lang.

Poncini, G. (2007). Corporate podcasts and blogs: Exploring the voices of emerging genre. In G. Garzone, G. Poncini & P. Catenaccio (Eds.), *Multimodality in Corporate Communication: Web Genres and Discursive Identity* pp. 148–67. Milan: FrancoAngeli.

Prasad, A., & Mir, R. (2002). Digging deep for meaning: A critical hermeneutic analysis of CEO letters to shareholders in the oil industry. *Journal of Business Communication, 39*(1), 92–116.

Putnam, L. L., & Jones, G. M. (1982). The role of communication in bargaining. *Human Communication Research, 8*(3), 262–80.

Putnam, L. L., & Krone, K. J. (Eds.) (2006). *Organizational communication* (5 volumes). London: Sage Publications. Sage Major Works Volumes.

Putnam, L. L., & Pacanowski, M. E. (Eds.) (1983). *Communication and organizations: An interpretative approach.* Beverly Hills: Sage.

Putnam, L. L., & Roloff, M. E. (Eds.) (1992). *Communication and negotiation.* Newbury Park, CA: Sage.

Raiffa, H. (1985). *The art and science of negotiation.* Cambridge, MA: Belknap Press of Harvard University Press.

Räisänen, C., & Gunnarson, S. (2007). Learning to know and knowing to learn: discursive practices as knowledge enabler, *Proceedings of CME 25 'Construction Management and Economics: Past. Present and Future'*, 16–18 July. Reading: Taylor and Francis.

Ramallo, F., Anxo, M. L., Rodriguez-Yáñez, X-.P, & Cap, P. (Eds.) (2009). *New approaches to discourse and business communication.* Basingstoke: Palgrave Macmillan.

Randall, M. & Samimi, M. A (2010). The status of English in Dubai. *English Today 101, 26*(1), 43–50.

Reeves, N., & Wright, C. (1996). *Linguistic auditing: A guide to identifying foreign language communication needs in corporations.* Clevedon: Multilingual Matters Ltd.

Reflect Project, www.Reflectproject.com

REFLECT (2002). *Review of Foreign Language and Cultural Training Needs: Comparative Overview of Survey Results.* London: InterAct.

Renkema, J. (2009). Improving the quality of governmental documents. In W. Cheng & K. C. C. Kong (Eds.), *Professional communication: Collaboration between academics and practitioners* (pp. 173–90). Hong Kong: Hong Kong University Press.

Renkema, J., Vallen, E., & Hoeken, H. (2001). Tuinapparatuur of garden equipment? Verschillen in betekenisnuance tussen Nederlandse en Engelse termen. *Onze taal, 10*(70), 257–9.

Rheindt, S. (1997). *La importancia de la lengua española en las empresas autríacas.* Master's thesis, Wirtschaftsuniversität Wien, Vienna.

Richards, K. (2009). *Language and professional identity: Aspects of collaborative interaction.* Basingstoke: Palgrave Macmillan

Roberts, C. (2010). Language, migration and the gatekeepers, *Language Issues, 2*(21), 4–18.

Roberts, C. (2011). Gatekeeping discourse in employment interviews, In C. N. Candlin, & S. Sarangi (Eds.), *Handbook of communication in organizations and professions* (pp. 407–32). Berlin: Mouton de Gruyter.

Roberts, C. & Sarangi, S. (2003). Uptake of discourse research in interprofessional settings: Reporting from medical consultancy. *Applied Linguistics 24*(3), 338–59

Rogers, P. (2000). CEO presentations in conjunction with earnings announcements: Extending the construct of organizational genre through competing values profiling and user-needs analysis. *Management Communication Quarterly, 13*(3), 426–85.

Rogers, P. (2001). Convergence and commonality challenge business communication research (Outstanding Researcher Lecture). *Journal of Business Communication, 38*(1), 79–129.

Rogers, P. S. (Ed.) (2006). Special issue on communication challenges from new technology. *Journal of Business and Technical Communication, 20*(3), 246–377.

Rogers, P. S., Gunesekera, M. & Yang, M. L. (2011). Language options for managing: Dana Corporation's Philosophy and Policy Document, *Journal of Business Communication*, *48*(3), 256–99.

Rogers, P., & Swales, J. M. (1990). 'We the people?' An analysis of the Dana Corporation policies document. *Journal of Business Communication, 27*(3), 293–314.

Rogerson-Revell, P. (1998). Interactive style and power at work: An analysis of discourse in intercultural business meetings. Unpublished PhD Thesis, University of Birmingham, Birmingham, UK.

Rogerson-Revell, P. (2007) Using English for International business: a European case study. *English for Specific Purposes 26*(1), 103–120.

Rogerson-Revell, P. (2008). Participation and performance in international business meetings. *English for Specific Purposes 27*, 338–60.

Rogerson-Revell, P. (2010). Can you spell that for us non-native speakers?: Accommodation strategies in international business meetings, *Journal of Business Communication, 47*(2), 432–54.

Rubin, J., & Brown, B. (1975). *The social psychology of bargaining and negotiation*. New York: Academic Press.

Ruiz-Garrido, M. F., Palmer-Silveria, J. C. & Fortanet-Gómez, I. (Eds.) (2010). *English for professional and academic purposes*. Amstedam: Rodopi.

Saal, E. (2009). *The persuasive effect of teenager slang in printbased HIV messages*. Unpublished PhD thesis, Nijmegen: Radboud Universiteit Nijmegen.

Sacks, H. (1963). Sociological description. *Berkeley Journal of Sociology, 8*, 1–16.

Salvi R. & Tanaka, H. (Eds.) (2011). *Intercultural interactions in business and management*. Bern: Peter Lang.

Sarangi, S. (2002). Discourse practitioners as a community of interprofessional practice: Some insights from health communication research. In C. N. Candlin (Ed.), *Research and practice in professional discourse* (pp. 95–135). Hong Kong: City University Press..

Sarangi, S. (2005). The conditions and consequences of professional discourse studies. *Journal of Applied Linguistics, 2*(3), 371–39.

Sarangi, S. & Candlin, C. N. (2001). Motivational relevancies: Some methodological reflections on social theoretical and socio-linguistic practice. In N. Coupland, S. Sarangi and C. N. Candlin (Eds.), Socio-linguistics and Social Theory (pp. 350–88). London: Pearson.

Sarangi, S., & Candlin, C. N. (2003). Editorial. Trading between reflexivity and relevance: new challenges for applied linguistics. *Applied Linguistics 24*(3), 271–85.

Sarangi, S. & Candlin, C. N. (2010). Applied linguistics and professional practice: Mapping a future agenda. *Journal of Applied Linguistics and Professional Practice, 7*(1), 1–9.

Sarangi, S. & Candlin, C. N. (2011). Professional and organisationl practice: A discourse/communication perspective. In C. N. Candlin, & S. Sarangi (Eds.), *Handbook of communication in organizations and professions* pp. 3–58. Berlin: Mouton de Gruyter.

Sarangi, S., & Roberts, C. (Eds.) (1999). *Talk, work and institutional order: Discourse in medical, mediation and management settings*. Berlin: Mouton de Gruyter.

Schegloff, E. (2003). Response. In C. L. Prevignano & P. J. Thibault (Eds.), *Discussing conversation analysis: The work of Emanuel A. Schegloff* (pp. 157–64). Amsterdam: John Benjamins.

Schegloff, E., & Sacks, H. (1973). Opening up closings. *Semiotica, VIII*(4), 290–327.

Schein, E. H. (2009). *The corporate culture survival guide*. San Francisco, CA: Jossey-Bass.

Scheuer, J. (2001). Recontextualisation and communicative styles in job interviews. *Discourse Studies, 3*(2), 223–48.

Schmeltz, L. (2012). Consumer oriented CSR communication: Focusing on ability or morality? *Corporate Communications, 17*(1), 29–49.

Schnurr, S. (2012). *Exploring professional communication: Language in action.* London & New York: Routledge.

Schriver, K. (1989). Evaluating text quality: The continuum from text-focused to reader-focused methods. *IEEE Transactions on Professional Communication, 32*(4), 237–55.

Schriver, K. (1997). *Dynamics in document design.* New York: John Wiley & Sons.

Schwartz, S. H. (1992). Universals in the content and structure of values: Theoretical advances and empirical tests in 20 countries. In M. Zanna (Ed.), *Advances in experimental social psychology* (Vol. 24, pp. 1–65). Orlando, FL: Academic Press.

Scott, M. (1999, 2004, 2012). *WordSmith Tools.* Retrieved 7 October 2012, from: http://www.lexically.net/wordsmith/

Sealy, A., & Carter, B. (2001). Social categories and sociolinguistics: Applying a realist approach. *International Journal of the Sociology of Language, 152,* 1–19.

Seeböck, M. (1999). La lingua italiana nel mondo del lavoro. Indagine sui laureati degli anni Ottanta dell'Università di economia e commercio di Vienna. Master's thesis, Wirtschaftsuniversität Wien, Vienna.

Seidlhofer, B. (2002). The shape of things to come? Some basic questions. In K. Knapp & C. Meierkord (Eds.), *Lingua franca communication* (pp. 269–302). Frankfurt am Main: Peter Lang.

Seidlhofer, B. (2004). Research perspectives on teaching English as a lingua franca. *Annual Review of Applied Linguistics, 24,* 209–39.

Seidlhofer, B. (2010). Lingua franca English: The European context. In A. Kirkpatrick (Ed.), *The Routledge handbook of world Englishes* (pp. 355–71). Oxford: Routledge.

Seshadri, S., & Theye, L. (2000). Professionals and professors: Substance or style? *Business Communication Quarterly, 63*(3), 9–23.

Shelby, A. N. (1998). Communication quality revisited: Exploring the link with persuasive effects. *Journal of Business Communication, 35,* 387–404.

Shwom, B. G. & Gueldenzoph Snyder, L. (2011). *Business communication: Polishing your professional presence.* Upper Saddle River, NJ: Prentice Hall.

Sifianou, M. (1989). On the telephone again! Differences in telephone behavior: England versus Greece. *Language in Society, 18,* 527–44.

Sifry, D. (2004). Sifry's Alerts: October 2004 State of the Blogosphere. Retrieved March 30, 2005, from http://www.sifry.com/alerts/archives/000390.html

Silverman, D. (2001). *Interpreting qualitative data: Methods for analyzing talk, text and interaction.* Thousand Oaks, CA: Sage Publications.

Silvestre, M. C. (2003). *Continuities and changes in gender relations in the entrepreneurial discourse: From representations to leadership practice – A critical discourse analysis.* (Permanencias e mudanças nas relações de genero no discurso empresarial: Das representações as praticas de chiefía. Um estudo de analise critica do discurso). Unpublished PhD thesis, University of Lisbon, Lisbon, Portugal.

Silvestre, M. C. (2004). Top positions in Portuguese entrepreneurial context: A place of male and female asymmetries. In C. Gouveia, C. Silvestre & L. Azuga (Eds.), *Discourse, communication and the enterprise* (pp. 283–304). Lisbon: ULICES, University of Lisbon.

Sin, S., Jones, A., and Petocz, P. (2007). Evaluating a method of integrating generic skills with accounting content based on a functional theory of meaning. *Accounting and Finance, 47,* 143–63.

Sin, S., Reid, A., and Jones, A. (2012). An exploration of students' conceptions of accounting work. *Accounting Education: An International Journal, 21*(4), 323–40.

Sinkovics, R. R., Penz, E., & Ghauri, P. N. (2008). Enhancing the trustworthiness of qualitative research in international business. *Management International Review, 48,* 689–714.

Skapinker, M. (2012). Choose the English that helps you win. *Financial Times,* 23 May 2012. http://www.ft.com/intl/cms/s/0/10c8a320-9f3b-11e1-a455-00144feabdc0.html#axzz1yQxFk5nt.

Sless, D. (1999). The mass production of unique letters. In F. Bargiela-Chiappini, & C. Nickerson (Eds.), *Writing business: Genres, media and discourses* (pp. 85–98). Harlow: Longman.

Smakman, D., Korzilius, H., van Meurs, F., & van Neerven, E. (2009). English words and phrases in radio commercials in the Netherlands: Their use and effects. *ESP Across Cultures, 6*, 107–28.

Smart, G. (1998). Mapping conceptual worlds: Using interpretive ethnography to explore knowledge-making in a professional community. *Journal of Business Communication, 35*, 111–27.

Smith, G. N., Nolan, R. F., & Dai, Y. (1996). Job-refusal letters: Readers' affective responses to direct and indirect organizational plans. *Business Communication Quarterly, 59*(1), 67–73.

Smith, R. E. (1993). Integrating information from advertising and trial: Processes and effects on consumer response to product information. *Journal of Marketing Research 30*(2), 204–19.

Smudde, P. M. (2005), Blogging, ethics and public relations: A proactive and dialogic approach. *Public Relations Quarterly, 50* (3), 34–8.

Spencer-Oatey, H. (Ed.) (2000a). *Culturally speaking: Managing rapport through talk across cultures*. London: Continuum.

Spencer-Oatey, H. (2000b). Rapport management: A framework for analysis. In H. Spencer-Oatey (Ed.), *Culturally speaking: Managing rapport through talk across cultures* (pp. 11–46). London: Continuum.

Spencer-Oatey, H. and Franklin, P. (2009) *Intercultural interaction: A multidisciplinary approach to intercultural communication*. Basingstoke: Palgrave Macmillan.

Spencer-Oatey, H., & Jiang, W. (2003). Explaining cross-cultural pragmatic findings: Moving from politeness norms to sociopragmatic interactional principles (SIPs). *Journal of Pragmatics, 35*(10), 1633–50.

Spencer-Oatey, H., & Xing, J. (2003). Managing rapport in intercultural business interactions: A comparison of two Chinese–British welcome meetings. *Journal of Intercultural Studies, 24*(1), 33–46.

Spencer-Oatey, H., & Xing, J. (2005). Managing talk and non-talk in intercultural interactions: Insights from two Chinese–British business meetings. *Multilingua, 24*(1–2), 55–74.

Spilka, R. (Ed.) (1993). *Writing in the workplace: New research perspectives*. Carbondale and Edwardsville, IL: Southern Illinois University Press.

Sproull, L., & Kiesler, S. (1991). *Connections: New ways of working in the networked organization*. Cambridge: MIT Press.

St John, M. J. (1996). Business is booming: Business English in the 1990s. *English for Specific Purposes, 15*(1), 3–18.

Stafford, L. & Canary, D. J. (1991). Maintenance strategies and romantic relationship type, gender, and relational characteristics. *Journal of Social and Personal Relationships, 8*, 217–42.

Stalpers, J. (1995). The expression of disagreement. In K. Ehlich & J. Wagner (Eds.), *The discourse of business negotiations* (pp. 275–90). New York: Mouton de Gruyter.

Steehouder, M., & Jansen, C. (1992). Optimizing the quality of forms. In H. Pander Maat & M. Steehouder (Eds.), *Studies of functional text quality. Utrecht Studies in language and communication, nr. 1.* (pp. 159–72). Amsterdam/Atlanta: Rodopi.

Steiner, J. (2009/2011). *Il plurilinguismo nel calcio. L'analisi delle situazioni e delle strategie comunicative attorno a squadre multilingui*. Master's Thesis, University of Innsbruck, Autriche (2009), Innsbruck University Press.

Stubbe, M. (2001). From office to production line: Collecting data for the Wellington Language in the Workplace Project. *Language in the Workplace Occasional Papers, 2*.

Stubbe, M., & Brown, P. (2002). *Talk that works: Communication in successful factory teams: A training resource kit.* Wellington: School of Linguistics and Applied Language Studies, Victoria University of Wellington.

Stubbe, M., Lane, C., Hilder, J., Vine, E., Vine, B., & Marra, M. (2003). Multiple discourse analyses of workplace interaction. *Discourse Studies, 5*, 351–88.

Subbiondo, J. L. (2005). Benjamin Lee Whorf's theory of language, culture, and consciousness: A critique of western science. *Language & Communication, 25*, 149–59.

Suh, K. S. (1999). Impact of communication medium on task performance and satisfaction: An examination of media-richness theory. *Information & Management, 35*, 295–312.

Swales, J. M. (1990a). *English in academic and research settings: Genre analysis and its applications.* Cambridge: Cambridge University Press.

Swales, J. (1990b). *Other floors, other voices: A textography of a small university building.* London: Lawrence Erlbaum Associates.

Swales, J. M. (2000). Languages for specific purposes. *Annual Review of Applied Linguistics, 20*, 59–76.

Swales, J. M., & Rogers, P. S. (1995). Discourse and the projection of corporate culture: The mission statement. *Discourse and Society, 6*(2), 223–42.

Swanepoel, P. and Hoeken, H. (Eds.) (2008). *Adapting health communication to cultural needs: Optimizing documents in South African health communication on HIV and AIDS.* Amsterdam: Benjamin.

Tanaka, H. (2011). East-West business communication from an East Asian perspective. In R. Salvi & H. Tanaka (Eds.), *Intercultural interactions in business and management* pp. 211–13. Bern: Peter Lang.

Tanaka, H. (2014). Lying in intra-Asian business discourse in an ELF setting. *Journal of Business Communication, 51*(1).

Tannen, D. (1995). *Talking from 9 to 5: Men and women at work.* New York: Harper Paperbacks.

Tardy, C. M. (2009). *Building genre knowledge.* West Lafayette, IN: Parlor Press.

Taylor, J. R. & Van Every, E. J. (2010). *The situated organization: Case studies in the pragmatics of communication research.* London: Routledge.

Tebeaux, E. (1999). Designing written business communication along the shifting cultural continuum: The new face of Mexico. *Journal of Business and Technical Communication, 13*, 49–85.

Thatcher, B. L. (1999). Cultural and rhetorical adaptations for South American audiences. *Technical Communication: Global Issues, Local Concerns, 46*(2), 177–95.

Thatcher, B. L. (2000a). Adapting to South American communication patterns: Odyssey's proposal to remedy inconsistent car sales. In D. Bosley (Ed.), *Global documentation: Case studies in international technical communication* (pp. 81–95). Boston: Allyn & Bacon.

Thatcher, B. L. (2000b). Writing policies and procedures in a U.S. and South American Context. *Technical Communication Quarterly, 94*, 365–400.

Thatcher, B. L. (2000c). L2 professional writing in a U.S. and South American context. *Journal of Second Language Writing, 9*(1), 41–69.

Thomas, D. (2008). *Cross-cultural management: Essential concepts.* 2nd edition. London: Sage.

Thomas, J. (1983). Cross-cultural pragmatic failure. *Applied Linguistics, 4*(2), 91–112.

Thomas, J. (1997). Discourse in the marketplace: The making of meaning in annual general reports. *Journal of Business Communication, 34*(1), 47–66.

Tietze, S., Cohen, L., & Musson, G. (2003). *Understanding organizations through language.* London: Sage.

Trompenaars, F. (1993). *Riding the waves of culture.* London: Nicholas Brealey.

Trosborg, A. (1995). A special issue on intercultural negotiation. *Hermes,* Aarhus (Denmark): Aarhus Business School.

Trosborg, A., & Flyvhom Jørgensen, P. E. (Eds.), (2005). *Business discourse: Texts and contexts*. Bern: Peter Lang.

Tsoukas, H. & Chia, R. (2002). On organizational becoming: rethinking organizational change. *Organization Science, 13*(5), 567–82.

Turnbull, J. (2011). How 'glocal' is corporate discourse? A case study of a multinational's website. In R. Salvi & H. Tanaka (Eds.), *Intercultural interactions in business and management* pp. 73–90. Bern: Peter Lang.

Turner, T., Qvarfordt, P., Biehl, J., Golovinchky, G., & Back, M. (2010). Exploring the workplace communication ecology. *Proceedings of CHI 2010*, April 10–15, Atlanta, Georgia.

Turner, J. W., & Reinsch, L. N. (2007). The business communicator as presence allocator: Multicommunicating, equivocality, and status at work. *Journal of Business Communication, 44*(1), 36–58.

Turner, J. W. & Reinsch, L. N. (2010). Successful and unsuccessful multicommunication episodes: Engaging in dialogue or juggling messages? *Information Systems Frontiers 12*(3), 277–85

Tyler, L. (2004). Review of P. Argenti & J. Forman (2002). *The power of corporate communication: Crafting the voice and image of your business.* New York: McGraw-Hill Higher Education. *Journal of Business Communication, 14*(1), 100–04.

Ulijn, J. M., & Li, M. (1995). Is interruption impolite? *TEXT, 15*(4), 589–627.

Ulijn, J. M., & Verweij, M. J. (2000). Questioning behaviour in monocultural and intercultural technical business negotiations: The Dutch–Spanish connection. *Discourse Studies, 2*(2), 217–48.

Unsworth, L. (Ed.) (2008). *Multimodal semiotics: Functional analysis in contexts of education.* London: Continuum.

Upton, T. A., & Connor, U. (2001). Using computerized analysis to investigate the text linguistic discourse moves of a genre. *English for Specific Purposes, 20*, 313–29.

Ury, W. (1993). *Getting past no: Negotiating your way from confrontation to cooperation.* New York: Bantam.

Vandermeeren, S. (1998). *Fremdsprachen in Europäischen Unternehmen. Untersuchungen zu Bestand und Bedarf im Geschäftsalltag mit Empfehlungen für Sprachenpolitik und Sprachunterricht.* Waldsteinberg: Heidrun Popp Verlag.

Vandermeeren, S. (1999). English as a lingua franca in written corporate communication: Findings from a European survey. In F. Bargiela-Chiappini & C. Nickerson (Eds.), *Writing business: Genres, media and discourses* (pp. 273–92). Harlow: Longman.

van de Kopple, W. (1985). Some exploratory discourse on metadiscourse. *College Composition and Communication, 36*, 82–93.

van den Hooff, B. (2004). Electronic coordination and collective action: use and effects of electronic calendaring and scheduling. *Information & Management, 42*, 103–14.

van der Mast, N., & Janssen, D. (2001). Strategic revision of public documents: How policy writers revise documents in order to reach consensus. In D. Janssen & R. Neutelings (Eds.), *Reading and writing public documents* (pp. 211–32). Amsterdam: John Benjamins.

van der Wijst, P. (1996). *Politeness in requests and negotiations.* Dordrecht: ICG Printing B.V.

van der Wijst, P., & Ulijn, J. (1995). Politeness in French/Dutch negotiations. In K. Ehlich & J. Wagner (Eds.), *The discourse of business negotiations* (pp. 313–48). New York: Mouton de Gruyter.

van Hest, E., & Oud-de Glas, M. (1991). *A survey of the techniques used in the diagnosis and analysis of foreign language needs in trade and industry.* Office for Official Publications of the European Communities.

van Leeuwen, T. (1999). *Speech, music and sound.* Basingstoke: Palgrave Macmillan.

van Leeuwen, T. (2005). *Introducing social semiotics.* London: Routledge.

van Meurs, F., Korzilius, H., & Hermans, J. (2004). The influence of the use of English in Dutch job advertisements: An experimental study into the effects on text evaluation, on attitudes towards the organisation and the job, and on comprehension. *ESP Across Cultures, 1*, 93–110.

van Meurs, W. F. J., Korzilius, H. P. L. M. & den Hollander, A. I. (2007). The use of English in job advertisments on the Dutch job site Monsterboard.nl and factors on which it depends. *ESP Across Cultures, 3*, 103–23.

van Meurs, W. F. J., Korzilius, H. P. L. M., Planken, B. C., & Fairley, S. (2007). The effect of English job titles in job advertisements on Dutch respondents. *World Englishes, 26*(2), 189–205.

van Mulken, M., & van der Meer, W. (2005). Are you being served? A genre analysis of American and Dutch company replies to customer enquiries. *English for Specific Purposes, 24*, 93–109.

van Nus, M. (1999). 'Can we count on your bookings of potatoes to Madeira?' Corporate context and discourse practices in direct sales letters. In F. Bargiela-Chiappini & C. Nickerson (Eds.), *Writing business: Genres, media and discourses* (pp. 181–206). Harlow: Longman.

van Riel, C. B. M. (1995). *The principles of corporate communication.* Upper Saddle River, NJ: Prentice Hall.

Valdez, P. N. (2011). Review of B. L. Gunnarsson (2009). *Professional communication.* London & New York: Continuum. *English for Specific Purposes, 30*(3), 241–3.

Varner, I. (2000). The theoretical foundation of intercultural business communication: A conceptual model. *Journal of Business Communication, 37*(1), 39–57.

Vaughan, A., & Voss, J. (2011). Review of H. Basturkmen (2005). *Ideas and options in English for specific purposes.* London & New York: Routledge. *English for Specific Purposes, 30*(1), 78–80.

Ventola, E., & Moya Guijjaro, A. J. (Eds.) (2009). *The world told and the world shown: Multisemiotic issues.* Palgrave Macmillan.

Verckens, J. P., De Rycker, T., & Davis, K. (1998). The experience of sameness in differences: A course in international business writing. In S. Niemeier, C. P. Campbell & R. Dirven (Eds.), *The cultural context in business communication* (pp. 247–61). Amsterdam: John Benjamins.

Victor D. A. (2012). Global advances in business communication from multiple perspectives: A panel discussion from experts in the field. *Global Advances in Business Communication, 1*(2), 1–26.

Villemoes, A. (1995). Culturally determined facework priorities in Danish and Spanish business negotiation. In K. Ehlich & J. Wagner (Eds.), *The discourse of business negotiation* (pp. 291–312). New York: Mouton de Gruyter.

Villemoes, A. (2003). How do southern Spaniards create the conditions necessary to initiate negotiations with strangers? *Hermes, 31*, 119–34.

Vine, B. (2004). *Getting things done at work: The discourse of power in workplace interaction.* Amsterdam: John Benjamins.

Vine, B. (2009). Directives at work: Exploring the contextual complexity of workplace directives. *Journal of Pragmatics 41*, 1395–405

Vuorela, T. (2005). Laughing matters: A case study of humour in multicultural business negotiations. *Negotiation Journal, 21*, 105–30.

Waldvogel, J. (2001). Email and workplace communication: A literature review. *Language in the Workplace Occasional Papers 3.*

Waner, K. K. (1995). Business communication competencies needed by employees as perceived by business faculty and business professionals. *Business Communication Quarterly, 58*(1), 51–6.

Warfield Rawls, A., (2008). Harold Garfinkel: Ethnomethodology and workplace studies. *Organization Studies 29*(5), 701–32.

Wasson, C. (2003). The Janus-faced power of language in organizations. In A. P. Müller & A. Kieser (Eds.), *Communication in organizations: Structures and practices* (pp. 21–46). Frankfurt am Main: Peter Lang.

Wegner, D. (2004). The collaborative construction of a management report in a municipal community of practice: Text and context, genre and learning. *Journal of Business and Technical Communication, 18*(4), 411–51.

Wei, L., Hua, Z., & Yue, L. (2001). Interpersonal harmony and textual coherence in Chinese business interaction. *Multilingua, 20*(3), 285–311.

Weick, K. E. (1996). *Sensemaking in organizations*. Thousand Oaks: Sage.

Williams, M. (1988). Language taught for meetings and language used in meetings: Is there anything in common? *Applied Linguistics, 9*(1), 45–58.

Willing, K. (1992). *Talking it through: Clarification and problem-solving in professional work.* Sydney: National Centre for English Language Teaching and Research.

Wodak, R. & Kryzanowski, M. (2008). *Qualitative discourse analysis in the social sciences.* Basingstoke: Palgrave MacMillan.

Wodak, R. Kwon, W. & Clarke, I. (2011) 'Getting people on board': discursive leadership for consensus building in team meetings , *Discourse & Society, 22*(5), 592–644.

Wodak, R., & Meyer, M. (2001). *Methods of critical discourse analysis (Introducing qualitative methods series)*. Thousand Oaks: Sage Publications.

Wooffitt, R. (2005). *Conversation analysis and discourse analysis: A comparative and critical introduction*. Thousand Oaks: Sage Publications.

Wong, Z., & Aiken, M. (2003). Automated facilitation of electronic meetings. *Information & Management, 41*, 125–34.

Wozniak, S. (2010). Language needs analysis from a perspective of international professional mobility: The case of French mountain guides. *English for Specific Purposes, 29*(4), 243–52.

Wright P. (2012) Using graphics effectively in text. In C. Abraham & M. Kools (Eds.), *Writing educational and persuasive text: An evidence-based guide for health professionals* (pp. 63–82). London: Sage.

Wright, P., Soroka, A. J., Belt, S., Pham, D., Dimov, S., DeRoure, D., & Petrie, H. (2008). Modality preference and performance when seniors consult online information. *Gerontechnology, 7*, 293–304.

Wright P., Soroka, A. J., Belt, S., Pham, D., Dimov, S., DeRoure, D., & Petrie, H. (2010). Using audio to support animated route information in a hospital touch-screen kiosk. *Computers in Human Behavior, 26*, 753–59.

Yamada, H. (1990). Topic management and turn distribution in business meetings: American versus Japanese strategies. *TEXT, 10*(3), 271–95.

Yamada, H. (1992). *American and Japanese business discourse: A comparison of interactional styles*. Norwood, NJ: Ablex.

Yamada, H. (1997; 2002). *Different games, different rules: Why Americans and Japanese misunderstand each other*. Oxford: Oxford University Press.

Yates, J., & Orlikowski, W. (1992). Genres and organizational communication: A structurational approach to studying communication and media. *Academy of Management Review, 17*(2), 299–326.

Yates, J., & Orlikowski, W. (2002). Genre systems: Structuring interaction through communicative norms. *Journal of Business Communication, 39*(1), 13–35.

Yates, J., Orlikowski, W., & Okamura, K. (1999). Explicit and implicit structuring of genres in electronic communication: Reinforcement and change of social interaction. *Organization Science, 10*(1), 83–103.

Yeung, L. (1997). Confrontation or resolution management: Discourse strategies for dealing with conflict in participative decision-making. *Journal of Applied Management Studies, 6*(1), 63–75.

Yeung, L. (1998). Linguistic forms of consultative management discourse. *Discourse and Society, 9*(1), 81–101.

Yeung, L. (2000). The question of Chinese indirectness: A comparison of Chinese and English participative decision-making discourse. *Multilingua, 19*(3), 221–64.

Yeung, L. (2003). Management discourse in Australian banking contexts: In search of an Australian model of participation as compared with that of Hong Kong Chinese. *Journal of Intercultural Studies, 24*(1), 47–63.

Yeung, L. (2004a). The paradox of control in participative decision-making: Gatekeeping discourse in banks. *International Journal of the Sociology of Language, 166*, 83–104.

Yeung, L. (2004b). The paradox of control in participative decision-making: Facilitative discourse in banks. *Text, 24*(1), 113–46.

Yigitoglu, N. (2011). Review of C. Tardy (2009). *Building genre knowledge*. West Lafayette, IN: Parlor Press. *English for Specific Purposes, 30*(1), 73–5.

Yli-Jokipii, H. (1994). Requests in professional discourse: A cross-cultural study of British, American and Finnish business writing. *Annales Academiae Scientiarum Finnicae Dissertationes Humnarum Litterarum*, 71. Helsinki: Suomalainen tiedeadatemia.

Yotsukura, L. A. (2003) *Negotiating moves: Problem presentation and resolution in Japanese business discourse*. Burlington: Elsevier.

Yüce, P., & Highhouse, S. (1998). The effects of attribute set-size and pay ambiguity on reactions to 'help wanted' advertisements. *Journal of Organizational Behavior, 19*, 337–52.

Yugo, J. E. (2012). Review of E. H. Schein (2009). *The corporate culture survival guide*. San Francisco, CA: Jossey-Bass. *Business Communication Quarterly, 75*(2), 228–31.

Zander, L., Mockaitis, A., Harzing, A. W. et al. (2011). Standardization and contextualization: A study of language and leadership across 17 countries. *Journal of World Business, 46*(3), pp. 296–304.

Zaremba, A. J. (2010). *Crisis communication*. Armonk, NY: M.E. Sharpe.

Zemke, R., & Connellan, T. (2001). *E-Service: 24 ways to keep your customers – when the competition is just a click away*. New York: AMACOM.

Zhang, Y., & Gelb, B. D. (1996). Matching advertising appeals to culture: The influence of products' use conditions. *Journal of Advertising, 25* (3), 29–46.

Zhu, Y. (2000). Rhetorical moves in Chinese sales genres, 1949 to the present. *Journal of Business Communication, 37*, 156–72.

Zhu, Y. (2005). *Written communication across cultures: A sociocognitive perspective on business genres*. Amsterdam: John Benjamins.

Zhu, Y. (2009). Managing business relationships in New Zealand and China: A semantic perspective. *Management International Review, 49*, 225–48.

Zhu, Y., & Bargiela-Chiappini, F. (2013). Balancing emic and etic: Situated learning and ethnography of communication in cross-cultural management education. *Academy of Management Learning and Education*. Special issue on 'Cross-cultural management learning & education: Exploring multiple aims, approaches and impacts', *12*(4).

Zilles, S. (2004). Offers in German and Irish English business negotiations: A cross-cultural empirical analysis of micropragmatic and macropragmatic aspects. Paper delivered at the ABC European Conference, Milan, 22 May.

Index

application letter, 13, 20, 105, 117ff
applied linguistics, 4, 5, 6, 9, 29–30, 45,
    46, 34, 74, 77, 78, 83, 93, 124, 166,
    205, 242
    critical applied linguistics, 29–30
Asian intercultural communication, 47

back translation method, 255
BELF (Business English as a Lingua
    Franca), 10, 22, 109, 110, 215–16
British National Corpus, 103
business communication, 9, 19–21, 31–2,
    39, 44, 52, 69, 87, 92, 110, 160, 175
    and business discourse, 4, 5
    in the US, 5, 18, 33
    in Europe, 36, 112
    in Japan, 21
Business English
    BEC (Business English Corpus), 103
    CANBEC (Cambridge Nottingham
        Business English Corpus), 23
    corpus based research, 158
    development of teaching materials, 155,
        169, 259, 263
    ESBP (English for Specific Business
        Purposes), 156, 158
    in Mainland China, 102
    in Malaysia, 116
business writing, 14, 18, 21, 92ff, 109,
    117, 121, 158, 200, 213, 217
    business letter, 12–13, 58, 120, 163,
        212, 219–20, 245
    CIBW (Corpus of International Business
        Writing) 109, 121ff
    collaborative writing, 77, 144–5, 234–5,
        240

code choice 19, 204–5, 268
    model, 130
computer-mediated communication
    (CMC), 211
corporate communication, 34, 74, 147,
    157ff, 166, 175, 276, 279, 290–1
    annual report, 64, 95, 103, 182, 204,
        221, 226, 234, 272, 279, 284–5

English as a corporate language, 135, 137
    horizontal, 131, 153
    linguistic audit of, 134–5, 153
    mission statement, 32, 73–4, 186ff
    social media, 208, 210, 290–1, 296
    social responsibility, 147, 166, 182, 288
corpus-based research, 14, 17ff, 41, 53, 73,
    91, 95, 111, 117, 123, 141, 144, 158,
    168, 172, 181, 191, 268, 272, 274
    BNC (Business National Corpus), 103
    Business English, 102
    Business English Corpus (BEC), 103
    CANBEC (Cambridge Nottingham
        Business English Corpus), 103
    IBLC (Indianapolis Business Learner
        Corpus), 91, 117ff
    LBM (Language of Business Meetings)
        corpus, 23
    PMC (Published Materials Corpus), 103,
        111
    VOICE (Vienna-Oxford International
        Corpus of English) Project, 109
    Wordsmith Tools, 103ff, 120, 182
critical approaches, 27, 28
crosscultural management, 48
    emic and etic, 48

decision-making, 23, 25, 43, 137, 216
DIRECT project, 176
document design
    applications of, 147, 152
    definition of, 202
    EPIDASA project, 130
    HACALARA project, 150
    as an innovative development, 130
    investigating forms in, 147ff

ELISE project, 129, 201
ELUCIDATE project, 129–30, 201, 212
English
    and Arabic, 20
    dominance of, 14, 19, 20, 34, 46, 129
    research in languages other than, 19–20
    for Specific Purposes (ESP), 5, 6, 12,
        98–100, 143, 205

English as a Lingua Franca (ELF)
  Centre for Global Englishes, 110
  recent developments in, 109
experimental study, 190, 197, 206
explicit knowledge, 22

face, 65ff, 70, 71, 153, 244–6, 266
  facework, 68, 248–9

genre analysis, 6, 18, 20, 58, 92, 102, 117,
    245, 267
  early work on, 12–13
  social media, 219–20

Hong Kong
  banking sector in, 99
  Cantonese use in, 96
  English for Business Education project,
    96ff
  English use in, 96, 116
  Jockey Club project, 143 ff
  Putonghua use in, 96
hypermodality, 59, 62

IBLC (Indianapolis Business Learner
    Corpus) research initiative, 83, 101,
    103
ICT and new media
  studies of, 208–12
impression management, 161, 230
inter-Asian discourse(s), 39
Intercultural communication, 24, 25, 28,
    160
  Afro-American critique, 56
  Asiacentricity, 57
  intercultural business discourse, 247,
    252
  Latin American critique, 56–7
intercultural communicative competence,
    112–16
interculturality, 41, 46
inter-rater reliability, 280
interviews, 13, 18, 26, 50, 52, 70, 73, 91,
    95, 127, 132, 133, 136, 204–7, 260–1
ITES (Information Technology Industry)
  call centres, 36, 136–7, 171

Japanese business communication, 21, 39

language and leadership, 42
  impact of different languages in, 137
  influence of gender in, 142

Likert scale, 93
lingua franca, 110, 129, 133, 201
  BELF, 109, 215, 265
  study of English as, 20, 22, 39
  use of English as a, 46, 52, 55, 72, 109,
    178, 180, 213, 221, 225, 264
linguistic audits, 135
LWP (Language in the Workplace project),
    138ff
  small talk in, 140

media richness theory, 33, 209, 211, 212,
    156, 166, 172
meetings, 8, 10ff, 18, 23, 31, 34ff, 72, 95,
    103, 116, 131, 139, 182, 225, 229,
    239, 269–70
  CA approach to, 11
  Chinese-British, 50–1
  and gender, 21, 72
  Japanese v. American, 10
  Language of Business Meetings (LBM)
    corpus, 23
metadiscourse, 95, 215, 269, 272ff
moves analysis, 20, 119–20, 182, 218,
    235
multicommunication, 210ff, 296
multidisciplinarity, 18, 69, 70, 77
multidisciplinary studies, 69ff, 76–8
multi-layered analysis, 207
multi-method approach, 34, 86, 89, 111,
    157, 202, 225, 241, 251, 267
multimodality, 45, 58ff, 65, 283
  definition of, 59
  hypermodality, 59, 62
multiperspective approach, 207–8

narrative accounts
  as a method, 299–301
needs analysis surveys, 98
  in the European Union, 131
  at the Hong Kong Jockey Club, 144
  at Kone Elevators, 131–4
  as a linguistic audit, 135
  REFLECT (Review of Language and
    Cultural Training Needs) project,
    127–9
negotiations, 8, 12, 31, 46, 49, 52, 55,
    114, 166, 215, 224ff
new media, 41, 58, 62, 175, 208,
    219
Nijmegen business language projects,
    112ff

organizational discourse, 4, 9, 44, 75, 85, 263, 297

partnership research, 52, 69, 79, 87, 146
politeness, 13, 32, 39, 47, 49, 75, 105, 111, 117ff, 229–30, 233
popular management writing, 157, 161
power, 4, 24–5, 36, 39, 43, 49, 57, 82, 129, 212, 215, 222, 225–6, 233, 240, 253
practice-based research, 175–6, 191, 198, 258
pragmatics, 37, 41, 47, 49, 82, 141, 227
   definition of, 228
   sensory pragmatics, 76
problem-solving, 8, 23, 111, 169, 241
pronouns (personal), 52, 54–5, 72, 305

qualitative research, 37, 76, 86, 199, 204ff
   action research, 76
   case-studies, 72, 95, 128, 130, 160ff, 207, 214, 226
   content analysis, 51, 226, 290–1, 296
   critical hermeneutics, 76
   ethnographic methods, 185–6, 239
   Foucauldian discourse analysis, 29, 77
   phenomenology, 76
quantitative research, 198–9, 202–3, 264

rapport management, 45ff, 233
reader response, 91, 241–2
REFLECT (Review of Language and Cultural Training Needs) project, 217ff

respondent surveys, 92–3, 128, 148, 179, 201, 209, 213, 253, 260ff
   Likert scale, 93, 256, 287
   scales, 62, 93, 151, 194, 256, 287, 305

SIPs (Sociopragmatic Interactional Principles), 47
social semiotics, 61–2, 217
speech act theory, 24, 141, 221, 227–8
   speech acts, 49, 221, 227ff, 233
standardization and adaptation, 129, 132, 137, 303
survey research, 94–5, 129, 176

tacit knowledge, 22, 206
Talking it Through project, 141
teaching materials, 12, 32, 55, 97, 102
   accounts of teaching projects, 124
   data-driven, 166–71
   practice-driven, 160–1
   survey of BC teaching materials, 156–7
   survey of ESBP teaching materials, 156, 158
   survey of LSBP teaching materials, 156
   teaching accountancy discourse, 12
   theory driven, 164–5
   use of case studies in, 161–3
text analysis, 182, 214, 235–6
   text evaluation, 151, 194, 234, 237
   text production, study of, 234, 239, 241
   text quality, study of, 234, 237–8, 241

Wordsmith Tools, 104–5, 120, 126, 182

Printed and bound by CPI Group (UK) Ltd, Croydon, CR0 4YY